Grief and Loss Across the Lifespan

A Biopsychosocial Perspective

Carolyn Ambler Walter, PhD, LCSW, is a professor at the Center for Social Work Education at Widener University, Chester, PA. Dr. Walter received her MSS and her PhD from Bryn Mawr College, Graduate School of Social Work and Social Research, and her BA from Juniata College. Dr. Walter has 40 years of experience in the field of social work, as a practitioner, teacher, and author. She has had professional interests in grief, loss, and bereavement for over 20 years. At Widener, Dr. Walter was elected as a member of The Honor Society of Phi Kappa Phi, was awarded the Faculty Award for Excellence in Teaching, College of Arts and Sciences (1992–1993), and the Service Award for Contributions in Shaping the Center for Social Work Education (1997).

In addition to teaching, Dr. Walter maintains a private clinical social work practice, specializing in grief and loss issues and women's health issues. Dr. Walter is the author of *The Loss of a Life Partner: Narratives of the Bereaved* (2003). She is the co-author of *Breast Cancer in the Life Course: Women's Experiences* (1991, Springer Publishing Company) and is the author of *The Timing of Motherhood* (1986). Dr. Walter has published many articles in professional journals on topics such as women's issues, grief, and social work education. Dr. Walter has served as an invited speaker at state and regional hospice conferences throughout the United States. She has also presented at international and national conferences, including ADEC (Association for Death Education and Counseling), NASW (National Association of Social Workers), and CSWE (Council on Social Work Education). Comments can be addressed to the co-author at drcwalter@comcast.net or at her Web site—www.drcarolynwalter.com.

Judith L. M. McCoyd, PhD, LCSW, QCSW, is Assistant Professor at Rutgers University, School of Social Work. She graduated from Albright College with a Bachelor's of Science (Individualized Study) in Biology–Social Welfare–Psychology in 1983. She graduated from Columbia University Graduate School of Social Work in 1985 (Health/Mental Health) and went on to work in obstetrical and oncological health care settings. She has been an active member of both the National Association of Perinatal Social Workers and the Perinatal Social Work Network in Philadelphia. She was certified by the Pennsylvania Society for Clinical Social Work Institute after their 3-year post-Master's training in psychodynamic psychotherapy.

In 2003, she earned her doctorate from Bryn Mawr College, Graduate School of Social Work and Social Research, and has taught research and practice courses there. Her research interests include bereavement, perinatal health care, and the ways medical technology affects decision making and grief. Her dissertation research was supported by an American Dissertation Grant from the American Association of University Women and explored the bereavement process of women who terminated desired pregnancies after the discovery of a fetal anomaly. She has presented extensively on issues of reproductive health and bereavement (as well as qualitative research), both nationally and internationally. At Rutgers University, School of Social Work, she developed a class to explore loss over the course of the lifespan in addition to the typical death-and-dying focus, supported by the (then) new Dean of Social Work, Richard Edwards. Dr. McCoyd also maintains a private practice.

Grief and Loss Across the Lifespan

A Biopsychosocial Perspective

CAROLYN AMBLER WALTER, PhD, LCSW

JUDITH L. M. McCOYD, PhD, LCSW, QCSW

SPRINGER PUBLISHING COMPANY
New York

Springer Publishing Company, LLC
11 West 42nd Street
New York, NY 10036
www.springerpub.com

Acquisitions Editor: Sheri W. Sussman
Production Editor: Pamela Lankas
Cover design: David Levy
Composition: International Graphic Services
Ebook ISBN: 978-0-8261-2758-7

11 12 13 / 5 4 3 2

Library of Congress Cataloging-in-Publication Data

Walter, Carolyn Ambler.
  Grief and loss across the lifespan : a biopsychosocial perspective / Carolyn
Ambler Walter, Judith L.M. McCoyd.
     p. cm.
  Includes bibliographical references and index.
  ISBN 978-0-8261-2757-0 (alk. paper)
  1. Bereavement—Psychological aspects. 2. Death—Psychological aspects.
3. Loss (Psychology). 4. Grief. I. McCoyd, Judith L. M. II. Title.
  BF575.G7W3434 2009
  155.9'3—dc22
                          2009001211

Printed in the United States of America by Bang Printing

This text is dedicated to:

The family of Carolyn Walter: Bruce Bryen, Carolyn's husband, who has supported her in all of her efforts to complete this work; Carolyn's children, Kim Remley and Brian Walter; and her grandchildren, Matthew and Connor, who have brought incredible joy to her during midlife.

Deceased loved ones of Judie McCoyd: Miriam Mentzer, Judith L. Achuff, Mary and Walter McCoyd, Eunice and Ben Maurer, and Doug Moyer.

Contents

Preface   xv
Acknowledgments   xvii

1   Introduction   1

Text Structure   2
Introduction to Grief Theory   3
   Classical Grief Theory: Task-Based Theories   4
   Classical Grief Theory: Stage-Based Theories   7
The Transition to Postmodern Grief Theory   13
   Meaning-Making and Grief   14
   Dual Process Theory   16
   Continuing Bonds and Grief   17
   Disenfranchised Grief   18
   Ambiguous Loss   19
Biological Effects of Grief   20
Issues of Intervention   23
A Final Word About Grief Work   25

2   Perinatal Attachment and Loss   27

Developmental Aspects of Pregnancy   28
   Biological Developmental Context of Pregnancy   29
   Psychological Aspects of Pregnancy   30
   Social Aspects of Pregnancy   33
Summary of Development in the Prenatal Period   35
Loss as Experienced by a Fetus   36
Loss of a Fetus as Experienced by Significant Others   37
   Infertility   37
   Reproductive Health Conditions   38
   Biological Changes Associated With Intrauterine Fetal Death   39

Psychological Aspects of IUFD 41

Social Aspects of IUFD 46

Readings

Hyperemesis Gravidarum: A Medical Complication of Pregnancy 49

Shari Munch

Heartbreaking Choices and Losses of Potential 58

Anonymous

Summary 66

3   Infancy and Toddlerhood 69

Developmental Stage: Trust Versus Mistrust and Autonomy Versus Shame 70

Biological Development 71

Psychological Development 72

Social Development 74

Losses Experienced in Infancy and Early Childhood 75

Loss of Caregiving 75

Death of a Caregiver 78

Loss of a Child's Own Health 80

Parental Loss of an Individual at This Age 80

Death of an Infant or Toddler 80

Loss of the Idealized Child 81

Maturational and Other Losses Experienced at This Age 82

Birth and Gradual Loss of Complete Care 82

Readings

Starting With Abandonment and Loss 84

Virginia McIntosh

Baby James 89

Carolyn Faust Piro

Nina's Travels Through the Foster Care System 94

Tara Sinclair

Summary 100

4   Elementary-School-Age Children 103

Developmental Stage: Initiative Versus Guilt and Industry Versus Inferiority 104

Biological Development 105

Psychological Development 107

Social Development 109

Loss Experienced by an Individual During the Elementary School Years   110
  Age Differences in Perceptions of Loss   110
  Loss of a Pet   111
  Losses Resulting From Sexual Abuse   112
  Loss Caused by Parental Divorce   112
  Loss and the Military   113
Intervention Issues With Elementary School Children   114
Loss of an Individual of That Age as Experienced by Others   116
  Parents' Loss of a Child   116
Readings
  The Challenged Child   119
  Carolyn Faust Piro
  Loss of a Pet in Childhood: The Loss of a Companion   121
  Toni Griffith
Summary   126

5   Tweens and Teens   129

Development: Identity Development Versus Identity Diffusion   130
  Biological Development   130
  Psychosocial Development   133
Losses of Adolescents   137
  Teens' Experience of Death (Others' or Their Own)   138
  Death of a Sibling   140
Response to the Death of a Teen   142
  Parents' Loss of a Tween or Teen   142
Other Losses Experienced by Teens   143
  Maturational Losses   143
Readings
  Childhood Chronic Health Conditions and Sibling Loss: Celebrating Strengths and Acknowledging Difficulty   147
  Melissa H. Bellin
  Teenagers and Traumatic Grief: Tina's Story   152
  Celeste M. Johnson
  Loss of Love for an Adolescent: Carolyn's Public and Private Loss   162
  B. Frankie Lamborne
Summary   168

6 Young Adulthood 171

Developmental Crisis: Intimacy Versus Isolation 172
    Social Development 172
    Psychological Development 173
Losses Experienced by Young Adults 174
    Chronic Illness 174
    Death of a Parent 177
Maturational Losses in Early Adulthood 178
    Delaying Decisions About Childbearing 178
    Infertility 178
    Losses Connected With the Transition to Parenthood 179
    Loss of Romantic Relationships 180
    Addictions 181
Loss of a Young Adult as Experienced by Others 181
    Mental Health Problems and Loss Related to the War in Iraq 181
    Death of a Spouse 182
    Death of a Nonmarried Opposite-Sex Partner 185
    Death of a Gay Partner 185
    Death of a Lesbian Partner 186
Readings
    The Case of a Young Adult Who Has Lost a Parent 187
    Julianne S. Oktay
    The Losses of Infertility 194
    Barbara Gilin
    Case of a Young Adult Struggling With Addictions 204
    Theresa M. Agostinelli
Summary 208

7 Middle Adulthood 211

Developmental Crisis: Generativity Versus Stagnation 212
    Psychological Aspects of Development 212
    Biological Aspects of Development 214
    Social Aspects of Development 214
Loss Experienced by Midlife Adults 215
    Transformation of Identity and "Letting Go of Past Dreams" 215
    Immigration as an Example of Transformation of Identity 216
    Facing a Chronic or Life-Threatening Illness 217
    Death of Parents 219
    Death of a Sibling in Adulthood 221

The Loss of the Midlife Adult as Experienced by Others   222
    Death of a Spouse   222
    Death of a Nonmarried Opposite-Sex Partner   223
    Death of a Lesbian Partner   224
    Death of a Gay Partner   225
Maturational Losses of Midlife Adults   226
    Loss/Transition of Employment   226
    *Loss Experienced by Parents When Adult Children Are
    Leaving Home*   228
    The Loss of the Family Home   229
    Off-Time Issues of Parenthood—Fertility Issues Arise Again   230
Readings
    *Illness Doesn't Discriminate: One Story From the Gay
    and Lesbian Community*   231
    Rev. Susan Vollmer
    Losses of Professional Identity and Career Aspirations   241
    Corey S. Shdaimah
    Kudu's Story: Changing Lives   246
    Chawezi Mwantembe
Summary   250

8 Retirement and Reinvention   253

The Transition to the Third Quarter of Life:
Retirement or Reinvention?   254
Losses Experienced by Adults During Retirement
and Reinvention   257
    Loss and Transformation of Identity   257
    Loss of Routine: Search for Balance   260
    Loss of or Change in Relationships   261
    Changes Within the Marital/Partner Relationship   262
    Changes in Relationships With Friends   264
    Loss of Financial Resources   265
    *Loss of or Change in One's Belief System:
    The Importance of Spiritual Growth*   266
    Changes in Relationship to One's Community   266
    The Process of Change: Coping With the Transition Process   267
Loss of Adult as Experienced by Others   268

Adult Children   268
Parents   269
Readings
Case Study on Midlife Career/Life Transition   270
Susan M. Larson
Early Retirement Among Baby Boom Women:
Some Losses and Some Gains   273
Fontaine H. Fulghum
Summary   280

9   Older Adults   281

Developmental Crisis: Integrity Versus Despair   282
Social Changes   283
Psychological Changes   284
Biological Changes   284
Losses Experienced by Older Adults   285
Resilience   285
Developing a Point of View About Death   287
Coping With Chronic/Life-Threatening Illness   289
Death of a Spouse   291
Death of a Nonmarried Opposite-Sex Partner   295
Death of an Adult Child   297
Death of Friends   298
Maturational Losses   299
Loss of Home/Relocation   299
Grandparent Caregivers   300
Hospice as a Resource for Patients and Their Families   302
Readings
The Story of Rachael and Hal   302
Carol Lovett
Marital Bereavement in Later Adulthood   309
Virginia Richardson
Olivia's Journey   315
Michelle Brooks
Summary   320

10   Conclusions   323

Maturational Losses as Examples of Disenfranchised Losses   324
Importance of the Dual Process Model of Coping With Bereavement   327
Importance of Continuing Bonds   329
Meaning-Making as a Process of Growth   331
Interventions   334

References   337

Index   367

Preface

The idea for this book grew from our work together as consultants for an urban hospital serving children and adolescents as well as from our belief as educators that there was a need for a text that examined the issues of loss across the lifespan. Each of us has been teaching courses about grief and loss across the lifespan for several years at their respective universities and longed for a text that we might use with our students. We are committed to our belief that loss is at the heart of growth. We recognize that many forms of loss are not about death, yet we also recognize the importance of the continuation of bonds with the deceased or lost object when death occurs. Further, we value the process of meaning-making in the healing process and hope to help practitioners understand the importance of validating dual-process shifts during the meaning-making process.

We were approached by Sheri Sussman from Springer at an Association of Death Education and Counseling (ADEC) conference 2¹/₂ years ago to consider producing an outline for such a text. As excited as we were about the prospect of a text that would meet our pedagogical needs, we were also thrilled to have another opportunity to collaborate. The complementarities of JLMM's interest in prenatal issues through adolescence and CAW's interest in adulthood and chronic illness made for a perfect "marriage." Although we both contributed to the book equally, we adopted a nonconventional listing of the authors' names because of an anticipatory loss—CAW's impending retirement from full-time teaching (and time for reinvention!).

Current available texts for Death and Dying courses in social work, nursing, counseling psychology, and medicine have traditionally focused on topics such as the experience of going through the dying process, the delivery of health care during the end of life, and the experience of mourning the loss after it has occurred. Many texts include death rituals in Western and other cultures as well. Classics such as Rando's (1993) *Treatment of Complicated Mourning* and Worden's (2008) *Grief Counseling and Grief Therapy,* now in its 4th edition, are frequently used because they address a broader perspective of loss than just death at the end of a long life, and because they further address aspects of intervention that budding (and seasoned) practitioners must understand.

This text is different in that it is informed by a biopsychosocial perspective on the person-in-environment and addresses death experiences across the lifespan, along with identification and intervention strategies for normative and maturational (disenfranchised or not) losses. As social workers with expertise in medical areas of loss and bereavement, we are uniquely suited to develop this text, which covers the topic of loss from a more complex set of perspectives than is customary.

Carolyn Ambler Walter
Judith L. M. McCoyd

Acknowledgments

We have many to acknowledge and thank for their help in our work with this text. First, we would like to thank all of those experts in various fields who contributed the wonderful and very powerful readings that appear at the end of each of the chapters of this text. The readings provide beautiful examples of work with clients and nonclients who have endured painful losses throughout the life cycle. Without their contributions this text could not have been written. We also want to thank our own clients and research participants who have shared their loss experiences and meaning-making, thereby teaching each of us about the subtleties and nuances of multiple types of loss. Another group of people to whom we owe a debt are the people who, by their own deaths, taught us about loss experientially. JLMM remembers and thanks Judy Achuff, who was a "best friend" during the tumultuous junior and senior high school years. Her death at the hands of a drunk driver when both were 21 years old was a formative experience that taught much about the amputation of death, the challenges of coping, the value of continuing bonds, and the ways that grief can be disenfranchised. The death of JLMM's grandmother Eunice Maurer during JLMM's doctoral work and the death of her only sibling, Doug Moyer, during the final stages of manuscript preparation for this text, brought further personal lessons about coping with loss. Likewise, CAW's life has been framed by loss with the death of her father, Joseph Penrose Ambler, when CAW was 16, and the early death of her first husband, John Walter; these losses taught CAW many important lessons in grief, recovery, and meaning-making. Both of these individuals were incredibly sensitive, caring men who loved their families deeply. They have guided CAW in her journey in life and in her work with loss and grief, both as a teacher and as an author.

We are immensely grateful to our families and friends, who have supported us in this endeavor. CAW thanks Janet Neer, who read several chapters of the manuscript and provided feedback. JLMM likewise thanks Corey Shdaimah, who read the entire first half of the book and provided feedback in her customary "tenacious critic/supportive friend" manner. Her assistance and companionship in balancing the pulls of academic and family life are also much appreciated. Further, although dedicating the book to lost loved ones, JLMM's "boys" are the heart of her life—husband Patrick, and sons Ryan and Ian, make life worth living.

Thanks to Widener University for granting CAW two Faculty Development Options Awards to help with the completion of the manuscript. Provost Jo Allen, Dean Wilhite, and Associate Dean Paula Silver were all helpful in the pursuit and granting of time releases from teaching to work on this book. A special thank you to the graduate assistants at Widener's Center for Social Work Education for providing much needed research assistance. Thanks also to Rutgers University and School of Social Work Dean Richard Edwards for a "junior sabbatical." Without such, JLMM's work toward tenure and writing half of this text would have been mutually exclusive. The support of other Rutgers faculty, Jean Mahoney (administrative assistant), and Carolyn Curran (research assistant), has provided a positive work environment.

Finally, we wish to thank Sheri W. Sussman at Springer for helping us bring this book to publication.

1 | Introduction

Loss is at the heart of life and growth. This seems a bit paradoxical, but the reality is that new life, change, and forward movement only come as a result of losing (changing) a prior lifestyle, behavior pattern, or other functioning of the status quo. As practitioners who strive to assist clients in their growth, we must be aware that change and maturation, even toward a more positive state of functioning, also involve losses that are often unrecognized, but felt nonetheless. We offer this text to reflective practitioners of all levels of experience as well as to educators searching for a text on loss that explicates developmental differences. We believe the unique focus on loss as a normative, though destabilizing, experience (and process) will enhance clinical practice by synthesizing the most recent understandings of loss and grief theory, developmental aspects of grief from a biopsychosocial perspective, research on specific responses to loss situations, and discussion of intervention strategies that are supported by both practice wisdom and empirically based research. Normal maturational changes are recognized not only as growth, but also as a unique form of loss in which one is expected to delight in the growth and ignore the loss aspect of the change, a perspective we challenge. The normative, destabilizing force of loss also promotes self-reflection and growth, particularly when the mourner's experience is validated and supported.

The normative approach is quite deliberate. This is not just an identification of various losses that come as normative developmental stages, though we certainly include these. Even more important, however, is our perspective that loss itself, and the grief individuals go through as a result of that loss, is itself normative. That is to say, we believe loss and grief, though uncomfortable, are part of human existence, not a pathological state. We believe these loss states can produce growth and insight, with or without professional help, though we also believe that most people process losses more easily when they talk with someone. Although complicated grief reactions exist, we are also aware that people have experienced losses since the beginning of humankind, but grief therapy has only existed for a little over a century. We write from the perspective of clinicians who fully believe in the power of most human beings to manage their grief responses, while also believing in our ability to be present with people as they make this journey in ways that are beneficial and promote the most growth and insight.

Often, clinicians themselves experience the parallel process of feeling overwhelmed by client losses and moving into a passive role of hopelessness. We hope this text allows practitioners to understand the ways that individuals experience grief as it is influenced by biological responses to stress, by psychological responses to loss in the face of previous attachments, and by social norms and support networks. We further hope that this understanding allows practitioners to conceptualize the work with individuals in ways that allow the mourner to make meaning of the loss and process it in his or her unique way. We envision a practitioner who may *seem* passive in not "pushing" one grief model, but who actively helps the mourner explore her or his new identity in the face of the loss, learning more about himself or herself and his or her "fit" in the world as a result of the work together.

TEXT STRUCTURE

This text is arranged using a developmental framework so that each level of development from infancy through aging will be addressed in four ways. Each chapter will open with a vignette about an individual who is experiencing losses characteristic of a specific age group. That will be followed by a review of normal developmental issues for that age, particularly the abilities and challenges that are specific to it. The next section will describe how an individual of that age tends to cope with a serious loss, including how s/he may personally experience life-threatening illness. The third section will address how significant others tend to react and mourn in the face of the death of someone in that age range. The fourth section of each chapter will identify the normative losses someone of that age is likely to experience and address protective and risky ways of coping with those losses.

Normative losses are defined by us as losses that are relatively common in each age group (though not necessarily experienced by every particular individual of that age), but that often are met with little support precisely for the reason that they are either considered "fairly normal" or are stigmatized. Some of these losses are a result of normal development, as when a toddler loses unconditional positive regard and is no longer viewed as "cute" for misbehavior, but is held accountable for that behavior; these we will refer to as maturational losses. Other losses such as pet loss are normative in that they are likely to occur typically at a specific age. Crucially, these types of losses require theorization and clear explanations about interventions for assisting people in various developmental stages on managing the varied losses. Experts in various types of loss have written short readings to share ideas about the uniqueness of the varied losses, while also providing intervention suggestions from practice wisdom and empirically supported research perspectives.

INTRODUCTION TO GRIEF THEORY

This section will meet several objectives:

- Review classical grief theory and the implications of task-based and stage-oriented grief theory.
- Describe current topics in grief, including continuing bonds, meaning-making, ambiguous loss, disenfranchised loss, and the need to incorporate spiritual understandings of loss.
- Use the perspective that loss is a normal and necessary part of life. Although challenging, it also has the potential to create growth. Maturational losses, normative losses, and other less rec-

ognized losses create challenges that are often not recognized and supported, but still provide opportunities for growth when individuals are able to manage them reflectively, with or without professional assistance.

Classical Grief Theory: Task-Based Theories

> Mourning is regularly the reaction to the loss of a loved person, or to the loss of some abstraction which has taken the place of one, such as one's country, liberty, an ideal, and so on. (Freud, 1917/1957, p. 243)

Grief was not a subject of scholarly attention until relatively recently. Although assumed to be experienced since the beginnings of human attachment and separations, Freud was one of the first to address grief, melancholia, and mourning in a scholarly manner. He contributed the understanding that mourning can occur for things/values and statuses and does not only occur in response to a death. He also assures that grief and mourning are "not pathological" but goes on to say:

> This demand (to de-cathect libidinal drive) arouses understandable opposition—it is a matter of general observation that people never willingly abandon a libidinal position, not even, indeed, when a substitution is already beckoning to them. This opposition can be so intense that a turning away from reality takes place. (Freud, 1917/1957, p. 244)

Freud allowed for the possibility of psychotic (turning away from reality) thoughts, feelings, and behaviors as an understandable (and normal) reaction to loss. He theorized this in ways that may seem quite odd to grief-work practitioners today. In many ways, his was a "task-based theory," predicated on the idea that the mourner must de-cathect from the lost entity. Freud's theory of behavior states that the psyche "cathects" people and loved entities with libidinal energy that must be withdrawn for a mourner to heal after loss. He believed people experiencing melancholia (what we might now refer to as dysthymia or depression) had not successfully withdrawn the libidinal energy (cathexis) and needed help to do this. In Freud's understanding, the next task was to transfer cathexis to a new love object. He asserted (Freud, 1917/1957) that mourning is only completed when the ego becomes free by virtue of de-cathecting libido from the lost love object. He suggested a year as the customary amount of time necessary for this process to occur. As a person of Jewish heritage, despite his skepticism of religious belief and practice, he may have internalized the traditional year of mourning accepted and ritualized in the Jewish faith.

Freud's was the primary theoretical paradigm for early grief-work efforts. Usually couched in the language of "letting go," counselors have long held to the idea that a mourner must separate from his or her attachment to the lost entity, even if s/he or he did not necessarily view this through Freud's paradigm of de-cathexis. Though simplistic, this task-based model for grief work has periodically reemerged as a template for grief work in other forms. Indeed, the task of de-cathexis or separation continues to be a theme running through practitioners' practice wisdom, despite the development of new theoretical under-standings of loss and grief. Freud himself set the context for some of the modern reinterpretations of grief work. Freud wrote to a friend who experienced the death of a child (as Freud himself had):

> Although we know that after such a loss the acute state of mourning will subside, we also know we shall remain inconsolable and will never find a substitute. No matter what may fill the gap, even if it be filled completely, it nevertheless remains something else. It is the only way of perpetuating that love which we do not want to relinquish. (E. L. Freud, 1961)

He implies that de-cathexis may occur, but that re-cathexis is not likely to fill the gap, that it "remains something else" as a way of not relin-quishing the loved one. This is something to which we will return as we address the theories of meaning making (Neimeyer, 2001) and continuing bonds (Klass, Silverman, & Nickman, 1996).

Some of the first empirical work to explore the grieving process was done by Erich Lindemann (1944). Lindemann studied the responses of people following the Cocoanut Grove nightclub fire in Boston in November 1942, thereby precluding anticipatory grief as a factor that might change mourners' responses. Trauma theory had not yet devel-oped and was not incorporated into his theory about grieving and loss. He theorized that grief normally includes somatic distress, preoccupa-tion with the deceased, guilt, and sometimes hostile reactions. He as-serted that eight to ten sessions with a psychiatrist over the course of a month and a half were sufficient to manage grief work (1944). As an assertion based on research rather than theoretical speculation, this met with widespread acceptance. He believed that tasks of grief must be accomplished, but moved beyond Freud's two tasks of de-cathexis and re-cathexis. He postulated the following tasks:

1. emancipation from bondage to the deceased
2. readjustment to the environment in which the deceased is missing
3. formulation of new relationships

In some ways, step one mirrored de-cathexis and step three mirrored re-cathexis, but Lindemann contributed the idea that this was not a totally interior, psychological process. He acknowledged through step two that bereft individuals live in a social world and that they must adjust to a world that no longer has their loved one living in it. Yet he allowed 4 to 6 weeks as the time frame to accomplish these tasks as a norm. The unfortunate consequence of his time frame was that mourners who wanted to be perceived as healthy would avoid grief expression after 4 to 6 weeks and grief-work practitioners began to view grief that lasted much longer as pathological in some way.

Bertha Simos, a social worker who recognized the limitations of task- and stage-centered grief theories, said, "Anyone who took longer than the prescribed number of weeks to get over a loss was considered maladjusted and treated as emotionally disturbed. Thus the helping professionals themselves became deterrents to the proper working through of grief" (1979, p. 41). Lindemann contributed the understanding that symptoms experienced by bereaved people are quite customary and expected and that the social world has an impact on grief. He did little, however, to normalize and validate the grief experience of the majority of people who experience grief and mourning long after 2 to 3 months postloss.

Most recently, William Worden (2008) has become known for his task-based grief theory and intervention framework, developed as a response to some of the stage- and phase-based models of the late 1960s through the early 1990s. Worden's model includes the following steps:

1. Accept the reality of the loss.
2. Experience the pain of the grief.
3. Adjust to a world without the deceased.

4. Find an enduring connection with the deceased while embarking on a new life.

Worden adds the experience of emotional ventilation, something that has recently become known as the grief-work hypothesis. Many embraced Worden's and others' implication that emotional ventilation (crying, mourning, anger) needed to be expressed before one could begin to heal from a significant loss. Further, the implication was that if this type of ventilation did not occur and the person was seemingly healthy, the attachment to the lost one must not have been that strong. This has been found to be inaccurate in multiple studies (Carr, Nesse, & Wortman, 2006; Stroebe & Stroebe, 1991; Wortman & Silver, 1989, 2001), which reveal that a significant group of bereaved people actually become worse if emotional ventilation is pushed on them; this subgroup can do quite well without any professional intervention. Yet Worden's tasks allow for recognition that a relationship with the decreased does continue in a modified manner—this is a major step forward in grief work and grief theory.

Freud de-pathologized grief, and the other task-based theorists helped to explicate what tasks the bereaved needed to accomplish to heal. Yet the tasks were invariant, oversimplified, and implied that work on each of these tasks would lead to a completion of the grief and mourning in a "cookie-cutter" type of intervention. The same critique of an invariant and oversimpled model is often also applied to stage-based theories.

Classical Grief Theory: Stage-Based Theories

Elisabeth Kübler-Ross (1969) was, like Lindemann (1944), more interested in empirical data than theorizing. She is known as a leader in the field of death and dying, yet her classic stages have been applied to a population that was different from the population she researched. She was interested in people who were dying. She lived through the societal transition from when people died at home surrounded by family to when people died in hospitals, often with little information about the true status of their prognosis. As part of a seminar on death and dying at Chicago Theological Seminary, she and her students began interviewing dying people about their beliefs and experiences. Her book *On Death and Dying: What the Dying Have to Teach Doctors, Nurses, Clergy and*

Their Own Families (1969) was the source of the now widely accepted and reified stages of Denial and Isolation, Anger, Bargaining, Depression, and Acceptance. It is notable that following these stage-based chapters in her book is a chapter entitled "Hope," a characteristic that she identifies as crucial:

> No matter what we call it, we found that all our patients maintained a little bit of it and were nourished by it in especially difficult times. They showed the greatest confidence in the doctors who allowed for such hope— realistic or not—and appreciated it when hope was offered in spite of bad news. This does not mean that the doctors have to tell them a lie; it merely means that we share with them the hope that something unforeseen may happen that they may have a remission, that they will live longer than is expected. If a patient stops expressing hope, it is usually a sign of imminent death. (Kübler-Ross, 1969, pp. 139–140)

Her stages of adjustment to a terminal diagnosis are now widely applied to all types of losses, despite their development from an anticipated loss of self after critical illness.

The stage of denial is particularly misunderstood. Kübler-Ross originally conceptualized it as a stage during which the diagnosed would "shop around" to ensure an accurate diagnosis and/or express hopes that the testing results and terminal diagnosis were incorrect. She viewed this as a "healthy way of dealing with the uncomfortable and painful situation with which these patients have to live for a long time" (1969, p. 39). It is unfortunate that this stage has been widely misinterpreted and misapplied in grief counseling. It has often been viewed as a stage to be "broken through" or confronted, with counselors often applying Draconian methods to ensure that denial is not maintained in connection with a death loss. Indeed, Vamik Volkan (1985) developed regrief therapy as an intervention for those viewed as pathologically bereaved. His useful concept of a linking object, an object that reminds the mourner of the lost one, is used within a therapy designed to cut through any denial that may remain:

> Throughout treatment, patients experience a variety of emotions as they gain insight into their inability to let the dead person die...The use of the linking object brings about special emotional storms that are not curative without interpretation that engages the close scrutiny of the patient's observing ego. (Volkan, 1985, pp. 289–290)

This assertive confrontation of denial has become one of the suspect interventions associated with early grief-work counseling. The fact that denial is viewed as a stage to get through, rather than as the protective adjustment time that Kübler-Ross described, reveals one of the difficulties of stage theories more generally. Individuals, both the bereaved and less reflective practitioners as well, can view these models as a recipe, an intervention plan to be broadly applied. This assumes a one-size-fits-all quality to mourning. It also implies that knowledge of the stages or phases can allow one to move more quickly through them—a fallacy with major implications.

Kübler-Ross's (1969) model of moving from this protective denial to a state of anger and irritation (in her study, often directed at caregivers) is usually viewed as a one-way journey. It is portrayed as if an individual, once in touch with the reality of his or her loss, will now become angry (either at the lost loved one or at others), and will then move into a bargaining stage. Clinical work with bereaved individuals shows that anger and irritation often accompany many phases of the bereavement experience. Further, the bargaining that was so intuitive with the terminally ill patients Kübler-Ross interviewed (e.g., if I make amends to everyone I have wronged, I will get well/improve), seems less so when applied to the bereaved. Once aware of the loss, particularly a death loss, there is little that the bereaved has to bargain *for* as the loved one is, according to the resolution of the denial stage, aware that the loved one cannot return from death. Yet grief-work counselors can fall prey to believing that expressions of bargaining are necessary before a client can move into the depressive states so characteristic of grief. Once a bereaved individual moves into expressions of sadness, tearfulness, and depressed activity, social networks and professionals often recognize this stage as classic grief and mourning. Although this is true, the bereaved individual can fluctuate among the various stages and acceptance comes gradually (most often) as opposed to in one delineated event. The stages imply a progressive movement through the stages rather than the back-and-forth movement seen most commonly among the bereaved. It is notable that acceptance for Kübler-Ross's population has a very different quality than that of the acceptance of a loss by a bereaved person. For Kübler-Ross:

> Acceptance should not be mistaken for a happy stage. It is almost void of feelings. It is as if the pain had gone, the struggle is over, and there

comes a time for "the final rest before the long journey" as one patient phrased it. This is also the time during which the family needs usually more help, understanding, and support than the patient himself. While the dying patient has found some peace and acceptance, his circle of interest diminishes. He wishes to be left alone or at least not stirred up by news and problems of the outside world. (1969, p. 113)

This is quite different from acceptance in the bereaved, from whom we expect *more* breadth of emotional expression (including happiness occasionally), *more* involvement with prior interests and *more* engagement with the greater world. These differences are seldom acknowledged in the simplified formats often provided as the stage theories for loss. Kübler-Ross herself was quite clear that these were stages developed from empirical data about individuals who were dying, which may not apply to other populations. She also cautions against believing stages will occur in exact sequences. Her cautions are seldom incorporated when people learn the stages she postulated.

A second classic stage theory grows from the empirical data of John Bowlby (1980/1998), who followed the children of World War II as they were separated from their parents in war-torn countries and cared for in safer areas. He later studied widows (and a few widowers) and believed that this population confirmed his findings in the children's study. He postulated stages of:

- **Numbness**—defined as being shocked and stunned, not as denial; Bowlby identified the protective nature of this stage.
- **Separation Anxiety** (yearning/searching)—defined as an alternating state of despair and denial, with anger folded in, much like that found in children separated from parents. He claims that pathological grief is characterized by being stuck in one of these modes—either yearning, or angry and detached.

Thus anger is seen as an intelligible constituent of the urgent though fruitless effort a bereaved person is making to restore the bond that has been severed. So long as anger continues, it seems, loss is not being accepted as permanent and hope is still lingering on. (Bowlby, 1980, p. 91)

- **Despair and Disorganization**—As the loss sinks in, there is an attempt to recognize the loss and develop a "new normal." It is a time of lost objects (keys, etc.) as well as lost thoughts and lost time.

■ **Acquisition of New Roles/Reorganization**—When the bereaved relinquishes attempts at preparing for the deceased's return (gets rid of clothes, etc.) and moves into new aspects of life and relationships with others, the bereaved is viewed as moving through reorganization.

Bowlby's (1980/1981) stages are reminiscent of what he recognized in children—they yearn and pine for their parent(s) when separated. He theorized that the attachment style that the child exhibited (secure, anxious, avoidant) would influence the impact of the loss and that children who were less secure in their attachments would be more likely to exhibit anxious or detached feelings when experiencing a loss. He and others have speculated that these influences carry on into adulthood, with adults playing out their reactions to loss via one of the attachment styles. This is an important conceptualization, though it does not incorporate the reality that children (and newly bereaved adults) experience a sense of uncertainty about what the future holds, a legitimate uncertainty as many of the plans for the future have been abruptly changed through loss and separation. This uncertainty itself may provoke anxious behavior and attempts to defend against attachments that may leave the individual open for more emotional distress if circumstances change once again.

Maciejewski, Zhang, Block, and Prigerson (2007) recently explored the stage theories of Kübler-Ross (1969) and Bowlby (1980) and found support for the stages they theorized. They studied 233 bereaved individuals over the course of 2 years and concluded that stages of disbelief, yearning, anger, and depression all had discrete peaks over time and that acceptance ran as a concurrent trend in a linear positive fashion. Almost immediately, their findings were questioned. Roy-Byrne and Shear (2007) asserted that the authors had "overstated their findings" and that they "drew oversimplified conclusions that reinforce formulaic, unhelpful ways of thinking about bereavement." Concerns about stage theories and their susceptibility for being approached as a recipe for grief, with the implication that they are applicable to all, remain.

A recent classic comes from the work of Therese Rando (1993). Although framed as processes the bereaved go through rather than stages, Rando continues the paradigm that individuals move through similar phases (whether stages or processes) that are fairly universal. She identifies these as the Six "R" processes—a blend of stage- (phase in her language) and task-centered models that she asserts are the outcome of a healthy grieving process. Her model (1993, p. 45), is listed below and consists of phases and tasks for the mourner to accomplish in each of the processes. It is prescriptive in that it describes a process the bereaved must participate in if s/he is to proceed toward healing:

Avoidance Phase*
1. Recognize the loss. The bereaved must acknowledge and understand the reality of the death.

Confrontation Phase
2. React to the separation. The bereaved must experience the pain of the loss, give it expression, and mourn secondary losses.
3. Recollect and reexperience the deceased and the relationship. The bereaved is to review and remember the relationship realistically and also review and reexperience the feelings he or she has as a result of that relationship.
4. Relinquish the old attachments to the deceased and the old assumptive world. The bereaved is to let go of previous bonds and beliefs and develop a "new normal" with new relationships and attachments.

Accommodation Phase
5. Readjust to move adaptively into the new world without forgetting the old. The bereaved is to revise his or her assumptive world, develop a new relationship with the deceased, adopt new ways of being in the world, and form a new identity.
6. Reinvest. This is a time to invest in new relationships and roles and indicates a resolution to active grieving.

Although Rando (1993) provides a model with more room for individualized tailoring of the treatment process, it remains an accepted assumption that complicated grief is common and requires treatment when grief is deemed to be too extended, too brief (or absent), or when it

---

*Note that the terminology for the phases is Rando's (1993), with descriptive sentences from this author.

does not follow the typical trajectory as outlined in these various stage and process models. Despite Rando's obvious compassion and concern for bereaved people, she is subject to some of the same criticisms as the other early grief-work theorists: These models are viewed as normative in a way that means that any deviation from the models is viewed as pathological.

THE TRANSITION TO POSTMODERN GRIEF THEORY

Some theorists in the Foucauldian tradition critique Rando (1993) and others for the "disciplining of grief" (Foote & Frank, 1999). This is viewed as a means of pathologizing grief in ways that allow therapeutic intervention as a form of diffuse power, which produces conformity to societal norms. This is not overt coercion, but a form of self-care and self-improvement (something Foucault [1988] calls "technologies of the self") that functions to contain grief within a therapeutic context. Foote and Frank also note that Kübler-Ross's (1969) focus on psychological processes means less (or no) focus on the actuality of the physical and social changes that occur concurrently, allowing people to avoid the discomfort of confronting these very real aspects of dying and death. They comment:

> Grief, like death itself, is undisciplined, risky, wild. That society seeks to discipline grief, as part of its policing of the border between life and death, is predictable, and it is equally predictable that modern society would medicalize grief as the means of policing. (Foote & Frank, 1999, p. 170)

T. Walter (1999, 2000) too has recognized how policing grief can be destructive. He traces the evolution of policing grief from an enforcement of contained, formalized, and time-limited grieving during the Victorian era to a current expectation of more expressive grief with a tendency toward medicalization of the grief process. He asserts that mutual help/self-help support groups have evolved as a form of resistance to policing and medicalization, while themselves evolving norms that contain an expectation of grieving similarly to other group members (2000). He notes:

> In postmodern times, both old and new maps are challenged by those who claim no maps can be made of a land that is entirely subjective and

individual (Stroebe, Gergen, Gergen, & Stroebe, 1992)....Yet the evidence presented in this article also suggests that the desire (of both mourners and their comforters) for security, for a map, for fellow travelers, for rules that must be policed, is sufficiently strong that most mourners will never be allowed to be entirely free spirits. (2000, pp. 111–112)

Postmodern theories of grief grow from a social constructionist understanding of the world (Berger & Luckmann, 1967), which asserts that humans construct their understanding of the world in ways that they then see as self-evident and believe to be true. This "true-ness" is part of the construction because others will construct their own truths in different ways. This leads to the postmodern understanding that there are many truths, each created within the context of that particular individual's social and historical milieu, his or her individual and family experiences, and his or her capacity for reflection and insight. The narrative tradition of therapy (White & Epston, 1990) grew from these social constructionist and postmodern understandings and is predicated on each individual developing his or her own story with the help of the therapist as someone to help construct, edit, and frame the story. Making meaning of the deceased's life, death, and relationships becomes critical to the bereaved processing his or her grief (Neimeyer, 2001).

Along with the evolution of this meaning-making approach to grief work, grief theorists and practitioners began to question classic models and templates for grief. The implications of social constructionism and postmodernism include the idea that no individual's grief must follow a certain preset path; further, decathexis, resolution and/or acceptance were no longer envisioned as unitary end states for all. This allowed Klass, Silverman, and Nickman (1996) to theorize about what many mourners had been saying all along, that the end of active grieving does not have to entail a separation from the deceased. Indeed, most often, it actually entails continuing bonds that change in quality. Foote and Frank (1999) assert that postmodern meaning-making narrative approaches provide more promise for resistance to disciplining of grief, at least until they too are institutionalized and become a form of policing grief.

Meaning-Making and Grief

Although Vicktor Frankl is most associated with *Man's Search for Meaning* (1946/1984) and White and Epston (1990) are most associated with the application of meaning-making and storytelling via narrative therapies, Robert Neimeyer is perhaps the best known for application of these concepts to grief theory and intervention. He traces this back to:

> ...Kant (1787/1965) who emphasized that the mind actively structures experience according to its own principles and procedures. One contemporary extension of the argument is that narrative—the distinctly human penchant for storytelling—represents one such ordering scheme (Bruner, 1986)....Significant loss—whether of cherished persons, places, projects, or possessions—presents a challenge to one's sense of narrative coherence as well as to the sense of identity for which they were an important source of validation....Bereaved people often seek safe contexts in which they can tell (and retell) their stories of loss, hoping that therapists can bear to hear what others cannot, validating their pain as real without resorting to simple reassurance. Ultimately, they search for ways of assimilating the multiple meanings of loss into the overarching story of their lives, an effort that professionals can support through careful listening, guided reflection, and a variety of narrative means for fostering fresh perspectives on their losses for themselves and others (Neimeyer, 1998). (Neimeyer, 2001, pp. 263–264)

This is quoted at length because Neimeyer's (2001) explanation fits with our own perspectives—that understanding grief and working with people in grief therapy is a mutual project, not one of diagnosis and therapeutic intervention. Grief therapy is a respectful project and process of hearing and witnessing the stories people tell of their lives and their losses, questioning them in ways that allow them to open other perspectives while also leaving room for them to reject those possibilities. At its best, grief work encourages mourners as they construct and reconstruct stories of meaning that enable them to move into their new lives and their new assumptive worlds in the physical absence of the entity who/which was lost. It is important that clinicians working with people who are grieving recognize that the stories will take multiple forms and the task of the therapist is *not* to force an adherence to a "true" or "real" one. Instead, we are to help the client create his or her own coherent story while assisting in shining new light on the possibilities of blind spots that may enable a story that fits the client's evolving and dynamic worldview in evermore useful and function-promoting ways. This is a relational project involving a willingness on the part of the therapist to truly engage with the client in an authentic and caring manner, exhibiting genuine curiosity about the way the client is unfolding her or his story. Successful grief therapists convey realistic hope that this process will enable the client to return to full engagement with her or his life and loves.

Dual Process Theory

Dual Process Theory is another evolution of grief theory built upon the ideas of Bowlby (1980/1998) and the stages of disorganization and reorganization. Although Bowlby conceptualized these as discrete stages one passes through as one heals from a loss, Stroebe and Schut (1999) envisioned an ongoing process of loss orientation and restoration orientation. These differ from the organization stages in that the bereaved person cycles between times of experiencing the grief actively and focusing on the loss, and then moving into times of restoration orientation. During the restoration orientation, the bereaved focuses on rebuilding one's new life and engaging in new relationships, activities, and other distractions that move one away from active grieving. It is imperative to understand that these are not viewed in any hierarchy of value for the bereaved; indeed it is clear that both have value and that the cycling back and forth between these two orientations allows for distraction and restoration time that allows the mourner to move into new roles and activities. Alternately, moving into a loss orientation allows a processing time for the loss. Both are necessary. Notably, children and adults seem to cycle between these stages somewhat differently, with children spending more time in restoration orientation (particularly using distraction), whereas adults may linger in loss orientation more frequently.

Another concept that is implicit within the Dual Process Theory is the revision of the assumptive world. Parkes (1988) was one of the first to write about the assumptive world as a set of assumptions (e.g., my husband will always be there to kiss me good night) that coalesce into a schema that defines how one views one's world. Parkes (1988) defines grief as a psychosocial transition necessitating a readjustment of the assumptive world:

> For a long time it is necessary to take care in everything we think, say, or do; nothing can be taken for granted any more. The familiar world suddenly seems to have become unfamiliar, habits of thought and behavior let us down, and we lose confidence in our own internal world. (Parkes, 1988, p. 57)

Parkes implies this is primarily an issue of "our own internal world," yet the assumptive world entails levels of assumptions from personal to societal, and we argue these must be understood in much the way social workers use an ecological perspective. For instance, on the micro levels, assumptions exist along the lines of "I'll predecease my child"; on the mezzo level, one may hold assumptions like "once a mother, always a mother"; but macro level assumptions can be violated too as when Hurricane Katrina devastated Mississippi and Louisiana and assumptions that "communities and the country will always take care of people when tragedy hits" were shown to be false. Whenever assumptions require revision, an individual's world feels uncertain, yet when these assumptions are dashed at multiple levels, it may be assumed that the challenges to adapting and revising the assumptive world will be greater.

Continuing Bonds and Grief

A pivotal understanding in contemporary grief theory came when Klass and colleagues (1996) each examined the data from their disparate research populations and realized that "Rather than letting go, they [the bereaved] seemed to be continuing the relationship" (1996, xviii). They challenged the notion that disengaging from the deceased or lost one is the goal and illuminated the concept that "the bereaved remain involved and connected to the deceased, and that the bereaved actively construct an inner representation of the deceased that is part of the normal grieving process" (p. 16). They later note:

> When we discuss the nature of the resolution of grief, we are at the core of the most basic questions about what it is to be human, for the meaning of the resolution of grief is tied to the meaning of our bonds with significant people in our lives, the meaning of our membership in family and community, and the meaning we ascribe to our individual lives in the face of absolute proof of our own mortality. The book challenges the idea that the purpose of grief is to sever the bonds with the deceased in order for the survivor to be free to make new attachments and to construct a new identity...the constant message of these contributions is that the resolution of grief involves continuing bonds that survivors maintain with the deceased and that these continuing bonds can be a healthy part of the survivor's on-going life. (1996, p. 22)

Again, this is quoted at length because it clearly defines a major paradigm shift in how grief theorists and therapists approach the nature and goals of grief. Aside from the implication that, like meaning-making, each individual will have a fairly unique outcome to her or his grief, this also carries a caution. Just as bereaved people were "policed" into nonexpression of their grief (or more recently into full expression even when this did not fit their needs), we must remain cognizant that some subgroup of grievers may not feel the need to have continuing bonds, whereas many others will find this comforting.

Cultural understandings are important here as well. Mexican "Day of the Dead" celebrations and Buddhist worship at shrines of deceased loved ones reflect only two of many cultures that have allowed maintenance of continued bonds, despite the fact that most U.S. culture had not recognized these ties/bonds. The individualized assessment of the client, the discussion of cultural inputs into the grief process and customs, the intuitive and respectful stance of the therapist, and the awareness of the wide range of ways people move through and process their grief are imperative for sensitive, competent grief work with bereaved people. Another imperative is to recognize that although grief is partially a psychological state, it is also socially defined in both cultural context and normative inputs and has physical effects as well. When social expectations are violated, grief and grieving are affected. The notions of disenfranchised grief and ambiguous grief are fundamentally social as well and have also been part of the evolving theorizing of grief.

Disenfranchised Grief

Doka (1989, 2000a, 2002) coined the term *disenfranchised grief* to conceptualize grief that is not recognized, validated, or supported by the social world of the mourner. Essentially, the concept of disenfranchised grief involves the grief not meeting the norms of grief in the griever's culture. Hochschild (1979, 1983) has referred to norms such as these that guide the individual in what is an "appropriate" feeling in a given situation as *feeling rules*. Disenfranchised grief comes as a result of breaking the feeling rules, or of living in a time when feeling rules are not established or are discrepant (McCoyd, 2009). This then leaves the griever uncertain if s/he is "allowed" to feel sad about a loss experience that is not recognized by social peers. Further, it may leave the griever wondering if s/he is even "allowed" to call the experience a loss. Doka now breaks the types of disenfranchised grief into five categories: (a) grief in which the relationship is not recognized, such as gay and lesbian relationships, extramarital relationships, and other relationships that lack social sanction; (b) grief in which the loss is not acknowledged by societal norms as a "legitimate" loss, as when abortion, adoption, pet loss, amputation, and other losses are not viewed as worthy of sympathy; (c) grief in which the griever is excluded as is often the case for individuals who are children, who are aged, or who are developmentally disabled and are (inaccurately) not believed to really experience grief; (d) grief in which the circumstances of death cause stigma or embarrassment, such as when a person dies of AIDS, alcoholism, crime, or in other ways that are viewed as moral failures on the part of the deceased; and (e) grief that is expressed in nonsocially sanctioned ways, as when a griever is deemed to be either too expressive, or not expressive enough—reminiscent of the policing of grief discussed previously (Doka, 2002).

The nature of disenfranchised grief means that grieving individuals do not receive the social support and sympathy from others that has been shown to be crucial to being able to process grief and move on from it in healthy ways. The very core of this experience (for most) is to actively engage the pain of grieving. Yet, many have that pain exacerbated by social isolation or rejection with little support (if any) provided. Many of the losses discussed in the following chapters fall into some of these categories, particularly losses that are not recognized as worthy of support by others. In these cases, the mere validation that it is accurate to perceive the event as a loss and normalizing the grief response can allow the griever to move through the loss response without the complications that may occur when the griever is bereft not only of the lost entity, but of validation, recognition, and normalization of his or her grief.

Ambiguous Loss

Ambiguous loss (Boss, 1999) appears to be a form of disenfranchised loss. What Boss describes as "frozen grief" is certainly difficult to process because the definition of who is lost is so uncertain. In ambiguous loss, the lost entity is

- physically present but psychologically absent—for instance, a loved one with Alzheimer's or head trauma/brain injury; or
- physically absent but psychologically present—such as when someone is kidnapped or missing in action during a war.

These types of losses are confusing because it is unclear how one is to adjust to them. Without an overt death in the first case, it seems premature and even cruel to grieve in socially sanctioned ways; in the second, to begin to grieve would remove the hope of the return of the lost one to the social milieu. Boss points to the following factors as creating difficulty for those experiencing ambiguous loss:

- Uncertainty means adjustment cannot occur because it is uncertain what one is supposed to adjust to.
- Rituals are not available and there are few social supports.
- The irrationality of life is on display. It is hard to feel that there is a rational world when nothing seems clear or rational.
- The grief is unending. The uncertainty drags out and there is little ability for resolution.

These types of losses also confuse formal and informal support people who are just as perplexed about whether to express sympathy or maintain a stolid sense of normalcy and/or hope. Disenfranchised and ambiguous losses are heightened in intensity by the lack of social support. This may be why peer support and mutual help groups seem so efficacious with grievers such as these. Theoretically, it is appropriate to create groups for those for whom social nonrecognition of the loss occurs because the group members are all in similar situations and are aware of a sense of loss. Although having similar types of losses does not ensure having similar responses to that loss, the social milieu can be discussed and strategies for coping with it addressed.

BIOLOGICAL EFFECTS OF GRIEF

The biopsychosocial approach requires an understanding of the ways that mind and body interact within a social context. The biological impact of psychosocial factors is seldom explicitly addressed in much of the therapeutic literature. That said, the link between higher mortality and bereavement has been strong, long-lasting, and significant (Bowling, 1988; Parkes, Benjamin, & Fitzgerald, 1969; Stroebe, Stroebe, Gergen, & Gergen, 1981; Young, Benjamin, & Wallis, 1963), despite findings that the rates are higher for widowers than widows (Helsing, Comstock, & Szklo, 1982; Jones, 1987; Stroebe & Stroebe, 1993) and that a few studies actually find no significantly statistically raised risk (Clayton, 1974; Niemi, 1979). Understanding the possible mechanisms for the increased mortality and morbidity risk is important.

A full understanding of the interaction of emotions and physical health is beyond the scope of this book, but having a basic understanding of how immune systems, neurological systems, and cardiovascular systems may be affected by stress and grief (and by depression and anxiety) can help practitioners to think about ways of promoting health despite bereavement, and of recognizing the impact of psychosocial factors on physical health.

The immune system is one of the most potent mediators of the interaction between mental and physical health (Cohen & Rodriguez, 1995; Herbert & Cohen, 1993; Pennebaker, Kiecolt-Glaser, & Glaser, 1988; Salovey, Rothman, Detweiler, & Steward, 2000). There is a significant body of work (well summarized in Salovey et al., 2000) that shows that negative emotions decrease secretory immunoglobulin A (S-IgA), which then causes individuals to be much more susceptible to infection from viruses such as the common cold. The natural killer cells associated with good immune system functioning are also lower in the presence of negative mood and unpleasant affective states (Knapp et al., 1992). More recent studies in nonhuman primates have worked to differentiate psychoneuroimmune functions in monkeys who are separated from their mothers (some of whom receive surrogate maternal care and some of whom do not) and found that they each experienced reduced levels of immunoglobulin M (IgM) and immunoglobulin G (IgG) along with other lymphocytic activity necessary for ideal immune system functioning (Laudenslager, Boccia, & Reite, 1993). Further studies have found that monkeys with longer term separations from their mothers experienced long-term decreased lymphocytic activation and lower natural killer cell activity into adulthood, even after reunification (Rager, Laudenslager, Held, & Boccia, 1989), which implies the potential for longer term effects than just the discrete bereavement period.

Neurotransmitters and other neurochemical interactions also play a major role in the interaction of mental and physical health. The major mediator of brain chemistry under stress is the hypothalamic–pituitary–adrenal axis (HPA), which, when activated, causes a release of cortisol, the stress hormone. Norepinephrine and adrenocorticotropic hormone (ACTH) are also released when the HPA is activated, with rises in ACTH typically providing a feedback loop with cortisol (which then rises, ideally leading to lowered ACTH production). This feedback loop seems to break down in depressed individuals, with cortisol staying elevated. These hormones promote hypervigilance; decreased food intake; reduced libido; poor sleep; and increased blood pressure, heart rate, and cardiac output (K. Kim & Jacobs, 1993). This disturbance of the ACTH–cortisol feedback loop has not been found in bereaved people, despite many of the same behavioral symptoms, though higher levels of norepinephrine were found in bereaved individuals (K. Kim & Jacobs, 1993). An important caveat to many of these studies exists: The subgroups of the bereaved (gender, age, social network availability, relationship to the deceased, coping styles) have been found by various researchers to affect neuroimmune function as well, and the individual differences may well be masked when averages hide individual differences (Kent & Hayward, 2002).

  Recent work (Gundel, O'Connor, Littrell, Fort, & Lane, 2003; Kiecolt-Glaser & Glaser, 1992; O'Connor, Gundel, McRae, & Lane, 2007) provides an intriguing link between the biological effects of grief and the reasons narrative meaning-making is a useful intervention. The researchers used functional magnetic resonance imaging (fMRI) to scan acutely bereaved individuals' brains after interviewing them about their loss. They then said words from the interview to the bereaved and watched the response on the fMRI. They discovered that the posterior cingulate cortex, the cerebellum, and the inferior temporal gyrus are all affected and each has a role in autobiographical memory and creation of the "storyline" of individual's lives. Van der Kolk, McFarlane, and Weisaeth's (1996) understandings about trauma suggest grief is affected differently when the loss is experienced as traumatic. At that point, the emotional memory of the loss is "stamped in" by the flood of neurotransmitters that occurs at the time of a trauma; further, the amygdala is activated, though often in a less than conscious manner so that similar events and thoughts may provoke the amygdala to continue to send signals of arousal even when the loss has already occurred (Van der Kolk, 1998).

The physiological effect on the cardiovascular system of hormones like cortisol and neurotransmitters like norepinephrine and epinephrine as a result of psychological factors is fairly well established (Booth-Kewley & Friedman, 1987). Cardiac arrhythmias also appear to occur more commonly during separations (Laudenslager et al., 1993). The positive connection between cardiac well-being and generalized health (or its opposite, sudden death) appears well established; therefore, factors that create stress on the cardiac system are believed to be another mechanism for interaction between mental and physical health, and particularly between bereavement and morbidity and mortality (Stroebe & Stroebe, 1993).

In light of the physical aspects of bereavement just described, it becomes important for the grief counselor to be aware of how to promote physical health. Regular exercise, a balanced diet with an increase of B vitamins and antioxidants, increased omega-three intake, and exposure to light (Zisook & Shuchter, 2001) should all be encouraged. During the bereavement period, a checkup by a physician is indicated along with the provision of self-care and a decrease in risks to one's health.

ISSUES OF INTERVENTION

As noted in the many task- and stage-related grief theories detailed earlier, there is a tendency among grief theorists to identify phases (and associated tasks) through which the mourner must move to heal. Newer theories avoid the prescriptive nature of many of the earlier theories, yet the onus remains on the bereaved to move through the process. Interestingly, when working with students and others who want to be of use in assisting those who are grieving, their question tends to be "What can I do?" not "What should the bereaved do?" This is actually a much more important question and newer theories of meaning-making, although critically important, provide little guidance on what the practitioner is to do to intervene effectively. Lloyd (2002) suggests that the practitioner is to (a) explore attitudes toward death and dying from psychological, sociological, and philosophical/religious perspectives; (b) explore and analyze the bereaved's constructions of life; and (c) explore the processes of adjustment to the world without the lost entity. Within each area for exploration, attention is to be paid to how the bereaved is redefining roles, rebuilding identities, negotiating transitions, surviving trauma, and maintaining the spirit.

Another framework for intervention was developed by McCoyd (1987) for use with perinatal loss, but has been applied by master's in social work students to multiple types of loss over the last decades. Called the Five Vs, this model provides domains for exploration as well as interventions the practitioner can use to guide the work without resorting to structured, predetermined tasks. The Five Vs are validating, valuing, verifying, ventilation, and being visionary. Validating is often one of the first steps of work with the bereaved, particularly if the loss is a disenfranchised one. Helping the bereaved to identify any areas where they may not feel they have social sanction for grieving, and helping to recognize and validate the individual's right to be a mourner, is a major aspect of the validation domain. Valuing and verifying are often subsumed within the validating domain in that recognizing that the lost entity had value to the mourner and supporting the bereaved in discussing all aspects of the way the lost entity/person had value to him or her is a major part of validating the importance of the bond that has been disrupted. Verifying is any intervention done to assist the bereaved in gathering concrete mementos and/or developing rituals that "make real" the loss. These concrete reminders may be used to help enlist the support of social networks. Ventilation is the domain with which most social workers and other grief therapists are very familiar; it has become almost stereotyped in that people are urged to "vent," to "let it all out," or in other ways to be emotionally expressive. Ventilation can be done in a variety of ways and does not always need to incorporate tears. Indeed, if the therapist falls prey to the grief-work hypothesis and insists on tears as a form of ventilation, s/he actually risks harming the mourner. The ventilation domain entails an expectation that the bereaved is able to talk about the loss with authenticity and consistent affect and content, not necessarily overt tears. Ventilation is often the domain within which meaning-making begins to occur and the bereaved is helped to explore the many ways the loss has affected the bereaved person's life. Further, this is the domain in which the grief therapist is most compelled to remain quiet and provide support but not utter platitudes or trite phrases that could interrupt the mourner's ability to ventilate her or his thoughts, feelings, and reflections freely. The final domain, being visionary, is often a part of the ending process, but is found in small amounts throughout the work (whether formal grief work in a therapeutic setting or in informal supportive friendships). This generally entails assisting the bereaved person to think through events that are likely to occur in the future and recognize their potential for intensifying grief feelings. Rando (1993) calls these STUG reactions—sudden temporary upsurges of grief. Often, they come without warning, but in being visionary, the grief therapist can share lessons learned from others about where grief is likely to be heightened. For instance, with perinatal loss, the arrival of the due date for a pregnancy that has been lost is often a time of revived feelings of grief; the bereaved will likely need to allow time for reflection and mourning. This Five Vs can provide a model for grief therapists who desire some structure for the work, yet who recognize the importance of allowing the bereaved to follow their own needs and inclinations for grief work.

C. Walter (2003), in her research with people who were adapting after the loss of a life partner, also emphasized the issue of validation, particularly for gay and lesbian couples who may have little recognition and validation of the nature of the love relationship. Mourning an often disenfranchised loss, and often denied access to the rituals of support after death that others have, these individuals benefit from having someone with whom to reflect on the ways their identity is changing and has changed. Further, C. Walter recognizes the "two incompatible urges" (p. 245) of wanting to cling to the pain of the loss, but also to move on and begin to reinvest in the new life ahead. Seldom do people have social contacts ready and able to provide the nondirective approach necessary to accompany bereaved individuals as they review these opposing urges and consider the experiences that have led them to the present. This means that grief counselors will often be called on to witness the pain and growth that comes from these types of loss.

A FINAL WORD ABOUT GRIEF WORK

In 1991, Stroebe and Stroebe asked the question, "Does 'grief work' work?" Their answer was a tepid "maybe." Findings that widowers who avoided emotional expression did seem to have worse outcomes than those who were not actively avoiding their grief showed tepid support for grief work; however, widows did not exhibit this same association. This led the authors to suggest that "the view 'Everyone needs to do grief work' is an oversimplification" (1991, p. 481). Indeed, Bonanno,

Wortman, and Nesse (2004), in a prospective study with 276 older couples, found that 46% of the older widows and widowers they interviewed were classified as "resilient," with little depression or active search for meaning-making after their spouse's death, but neither were they considered avoidant. Another 10% were called "depressed improved" and actually improved in mood and coping after the death of the spouse (these were often those who were caretakers or who had been abused). The people they classified with "common grief" typically experienced depressive symptoms intensifying to about 6 months post loss and then resolving over the course of the following year. This implies that more than half of typically bereaved mourners are capable of adapting to loss given time and a modicum of supportive social outlets. This reinforces the notion that grief is a normal part of life and something that can promote growth, even in the absence of professional assistance. Yet, another 25% or so do struggle to manage adaptation after loss and these individuals may benefit from someone with whom to reflect on their loss and its meaning in their lives.

Whether we are concerned about avoiding the policing of grief in ways that are detrimental, or whether we question the efficacy of grief work, the reflective practitioner must weigh these factors against the paralysis that can result from giving so much weight to these concerns that we neglect to provide support for those who are asking for the assistance of our presence and expertise. Remaining open and reflective about new understandings in grief theory, while also using the empirical data derived from one's actual interaction with individual clients, and how they perceive the work to be useful (or not), are requirements of ethical and sensitive practice in the world of grief support.

2 Perinatal Attachment and Loss

Maggie is a social worker who arrived in the office looking upbeat and athletic, even as she told me how depressed she was. She was starting to feel hopeless about her ability to have children after having "failed" three attempts with intrauterine insemination (IUI) and was considering an in vitro fertilization (IVF) cycle at her reproductive endocrinologist's suggestion. We worked together with her husband to identify the challenges and hopes connected with pursuing IVF, particularly her concern that she would need to expend the most physical and emotional energy, but wanted to know that he would remain supportive, even when her depletion meant she "might not be so nice and caring" as she usually is.

Over the course of 3 years, Maggie had two full fresh IVF cycles with several frozen attempts following each failed fresh cycle. She delivered a healthy baby girl after the second cycle, followed by a miscarriage, and then had another (third) IVF cycle that resulted in a second daughter and three "left over" frozen embryos. Throughout, she deeply mourned each cycle during which she saw the implanted embryos in her uterus; she also experienced the loss when the pregnancy did not "take." She and her husband had many months of tension and anger. These years of alternating despair and anger now "feel worth it" after the births of their two daughters, yet Maggie still mourns "the triplets" (the frozen embryos) and the two singleton pregnancies that she lost. She also recognizes the loss of the months of her life during which she "just lived from one medical procedure to the next." She is a very involved mother, yet has times when she "feels the depression trying to catch up with me."

DEVELOPMENTAL ASPECTS OF PREGNANCY

A major aspect of pregnancy is the development of an emotional bond between the growing fetus and the mother. Indeed, most behavioral theory focuses to some degree on the relationship between the infant and the mother or primary caregiver as the main force behind most relational behavior. Psychoanalytic theory views this relationship as secondary, with the discharge of drives and the development of the structures of ego and superego from the id as the primary driving forces of behavior (Greenberg & Mitchell, 1983). The various schools of object relations change the focus, giving the mother–infant relationship primary status for determining the infant's behavior and ability to be in relationships over the course of the lifespan. Indeed, the attachment theorists [like Bowlby (1977, 1980/1998) and Ainsworth (1969, 1982)] would claim that "all anxiety, phobic and otherwise, is related to separation from the mothering figure" (Greenberg & Mitchell, 1983, p. 185). Still other behavioral theorists focus more on the social environment (Bandura, 1977; Bronfenbrenner, 1979; Germain & Gitterman, 1980; Hochschild, 1979, 1998; Schott & Henley, 1996). They assert that "people are neither driven by inner forces nor buffeted by environmental stimuli. Rather, psychological functioning is explained in a continuous reciprocal interaction of personal and environmental determinants" (Bandura, pp. 11–12). It is assumed these would include interactions of the mother during the prenatal period, which may define her bonding to, and perception of, her fetus. Suffice it to say that virtually all credible behavioral theory considers the role of the mother–infant relationship, yet very little work has been done to understand how that bond develops prior to the baby's birth.

Here we explicate what is known about the biological, psychological, and social aspects of the formation of the bond with a fetus during pregnancy and what is lost when a pregnancy ends prior to birth. In light of the strong focus on the mother–infant bond, research efforts continue to strive to understand the nature of that bond (Klaus & Kennell, 1976; McCoyd, 2003; Stern & Bruschweiler-Stern, 1998). The mother's perspective of that bond, including the role of the mother's biopsychosocial context during pregnancy, and the ways it sets the stage for the beginning attachment once a baby is born, is seldom considered. Here, we review the literature about the nature of the mother–fetus relationship prior to birth from biological, psychological, and social perspectives.

Biological Developmental Context of Pregnancy

The beginning of a pregnancy causes radical changes in a woman's body. Instead of moving through a hormonal cycle to which she has become accustomed every 28 days or so since her adolescence, she ends up plateaued at a part of her cycle during which high levels of both estrogen and especially progesterone are secreted (Benedek, 1970). Additionally, other hormones including human chorionic gonadotropin (HCG) are secreted in ever-increasing amounts. Aside from the physical effects of breast tenderness, bloating, and nausea that accompany the presence of these hormones, emotional aspects such as irritability, labile moods, and an increased sense of vulnerability are believed to be associated with these hormones as well. The pregnant woman seems to swing between a need to be assured of connection and a need to be self-reflective.

The emotional changes in a pregnant woman may be caused by hormonal and metabolic alterations as well as psychogenic factors. She may experience changes such as nausea and mood swings even before she knows she is pregnant. Her increased fatigue in the first trimester decreases her ability to manage stress. Petty annoyances that she might have once overlooked now take on major proportions (Haber, Hoskins, Leach, & Sidelow, 1987).

Nursing texts focus on the physical aspects of emotional change for the pregnant woman. These physical changes clearly influence the woman in her emotional life, and may have implications for her attachment to the fetus. On the one hand, these changes provide concrete evidence of the fetus's presence in her body; on the other hand, these same changes may lead to feelings of losing control over one's own body and may further inspire resentment and blame of the fetus if the changes are overwhelming or unwelcome. In short, the physical changes can be either a reassuring reminder of the fetus's presence or a burden to be borne. How a mother views these physical changes will likely have a strong influence over her emotional state generally, and her attachment to the fetus specifically.

As the fetus grows, it makes its presence increasingly known, first by gentle brushings (quickening) often experienced as "butterfly wings inside," but progressing to large movements in confined spaces as the fetus moves and tries to stretch in the latter stages of pregnancy. This corresponds with the woman's body getting larger, a development often connected to one's sense of attractiveness (or lack thereof) and worth (Barry, 1980). Additionally, the new center of gravity and increased weight alter body dynamics in such a way as to increase the sense and actuality of vulnerability. A sense of being a stranger in her own body may lead to high levels of psychological discomfort, particularly for women whose self-image is highly tied to physical appearance, or for women who have high levels of need for control. These physical effects may affect the way a woman perceives her growing fetus.

Some theorize that the physical aspects of pregnancy mirror the psychological ones or may be the image that the psychological tasks are mirroring. These tasks are defined by Haber et al. (1987, pp. 1026–1027) as: (a) incorporating the fetus into the mother's consciousness and self-image (mirroring the time of conception and implantation); (b) differentiation, recognizing that the fetus, who had been accepted as a part of self, is a distinct being (mirroring the first felt movements of the fetus, which are not under the mother's control); and (c) preparation for separation as birth becomes imminent (mirroring the separation that occurs as a result of giving birth). These physical events are virtually impossible to extricate from their psychological ramifications. The use of technology to visualize the fetus affects these stages as well (Ginsburg & Rapp, 1995; Haraway, 2000; McCoyd, 2007; Morgan & Michaels, 1999).

Psychological Aspects of Pregnancy

The psychological aspects of pregnancy have been a focus of theorizing since the time of Freud. Pines (1993) comments:

> Freud, a man of his time, believed that pregnancy and birth gratified every woman's basic wish. The gift of a child would partially compensate for the unfulfillable wish for a penis. My analytic experience does not confirm this view.... I shall discuss the revival in pregnancy of infantile fantasies about herself as the intrauterine foetus in her mother's body which are

activated by her narcissistic identification with the foetus now situated inside her body. (p. 97)

Ballou, in her 1978 study of 12 pregnant women, theorizes that the primary task of pregnancy is to resolve maternal ambivalence about one's relationship with one's own mother and to develop a relationship of either identification with, or nurturing responsibility toward, the fetus. She asserts that the pregnant woman's tendency toward reconciliation with her own mother over the course of the pregnancy is primary. She claims that women benefit when they are married to men able to act as:

> the giving, approving "mother," [and] also the "Oedipal father" who admires and encourages the woman's sexuality, who protects the girl from her mother, and who helps her, through his alliance with her, both to reconcile with the mother and to differentiate from her. (Ballou, 1978, p. 30)

The psychoanalytic viewpoint posits a strong level of connection to the fetus dating early in the pregnancy. This cathexis is believed to form the bond between mother and baby and is bounded only by the intensity of the mother's drives (Bibring, 1959). The implication is that all women will experience levels of cathexis to the fetus in similar ways.

Object Relations and Attachment Theory Understandings About Pregnancy

Object relations theory posits that a person's experience of important relationships in childhood will influence subsequent relationships. Most especially, relations with the primary caregiver define the way the person will approach future relationships. Similarly, this relationship will have a strong impact on the way a mother will view her growing relationship with the fetus inside of her (Bibring, Dwyer, Huntington, & Valenstein, 1959; Turrini, 1980).

Raphael-Leff (1980) uses an object relations framework, suggesting that the pregnant mother goes through Mahler's (1975, 1985) stages of development during pregnancy as a sort of rehearsal for the raising of the child once s/he is born (Raphael-Leff, 1980, pp. 191–192). Just as infants go through a separation-individuation process once they are born (Mahler, 1975; Mahler, Pine, & Bergman, 1985), Raphael-Leff theorizes a sort of psychological birth of the mother. The pregnancy process involves a move from the normal autistic phase ["a state of 'alert inactivity' during which the woman…is involved mainly in minimizing her disorientation and achieving a state of well-being" in early pregnancy (Raphael-Leff, p. 191)], to symbiosis (during which the mother–child dual unity is felt), to individuation (during which the mother practices the separation in her mind, gathering information and fantasies about the coming child), and rapprochement (during which repetitious fantasies of delivery play a part), and finally to separation (actual delivery).

Bowlby, too, considers patterns of attachment as indicative of how an individual will form relationships in adulthood:

> Attachment behaviour, like other forms of instinctive behaviour, is mediated by behavioural systems which early in development become goal-directed.…The goal of attachment behaviour is to maintain certain degrees of proximity to, or of communication with, the discriminated attachment figure(s). (Bowlby, 1980/1998, pp. 39–40)

Ainsworth's (1982) typology identified babies as having attachment styles that were either securely attached or anxiously attached; the latter group broke down into two groups, those who were anxiously attached (ambivalent) and those who were avoidant. Attachment is viewed by Bowlby and Ainsworth as innate (instinctive) and one might interpret the goal of pregnancy completion as a way of accomplishing new degrees of proximity to, or attachment with, a new attachment figure (the baby). Indeed, the implication of Bowlby's lecture "The Making and Breaking of Affectional Bonds" (1977, 1979/2000) lead one to question the process of attachment in pregnancy. The focus is clearly on the relationship between born-child and the mother and how that relationship defines future attachment patterns of the growing child. Nevertheless, the clear implication is that mothers, driven by both species-survival forces (which Bowlby constantly alludes to but never fully defines) and their own attachment patterns, will attach to newborns fairly immediately. This implies that some process went on before the birth that primed the woman for the attachment once the baby is born. Bowlby does not address this, focusing instead on the nature of the behavior of the newborn and the way it elicits caretaking behaviors on the part of its mother. Although he ties this to other attachments in later life, it was left to others to develop this idea in regard to the beginning of the attachment from the mother's side of the relationship.

Stern and Bruschweiler-Stern (1998) developed Bowlby's (1977, 1979/2000) ideas along these lines. Although they never cite Bowlby or Ainsworth (1969, 1982), they describe an attachment process that closely mirrors Ainsworth's typology and Bowlby's theory. Written for a lay audience, they theorize the process of pregnancy as the mother having a gradual birth of her own, the birth of the mother mind-set. They believe that "mothers everywhere share a unique mindset" (p. 19). Although they acknowledge that "a new mother... will also have to deal with the peculiarities of our society and our time in history, both of which further impact development as a mother," they also assert that "most women follow one of three general patterns" (p. 41). These attachment patterns are the dismissing attachment pattern, the en-meshed attachment pattern, and the autonomous attachment pattern (Stern & Bruschweiler-Stern, 1998, pp. 42–43). The dismissing attach-ment pattern is characterized by not being totally absorbed by the pregnancy and dismissing one's own family history in terms of its relevance to how one will parent. The second, the enmeshed attachment pattern, entails a very close (enmeshed) relationship with one's own mother and an overly absorbed approach to pregnancy (constant worry) and implies that a similar relationship is likely to evolve with the baby. The third, the autonomous attachment pattern, balances the other two patterns: "[The mother] is willing to lose herself in her relationship with her infant, and also become involved with her mother in the present, but in a measured fashion" (Stern & Bruschweiler-Stern, 1998, p. 43); she is willing to reflect on those relationships.

Social Aspects of Pregnancy

Bandura (1977) theorizes that social learning processes such as model-ing, reinforcement, and expectancy learning teach individuals how to grow into roles such as "mother." Modeled events occur on the level of watching one's own mother, playing with dolls, babysitting, and observing the pregnancies of friends. Additionally, books such as *What to Expect When You're Expecting* (Eisenberg, Murkoff, & Hathaway, 1991) and media in U.S. culture provide another social context for learning how one is "supposed" to fulfill the role of pregnant mother-to-be and then mother. The prevalence of societal messages about pregnancy and the reinforcement of various behaviors during practicing modes such as childhood play and babysitting can have a strong impact on the pregnant woman's feelings and behavior regarding the pregnancy.

Glenn, Chang, and Forcey (1994) might describe this social environment "as a social, rather than a biological, construct" (p. 3). They comment that "mothering is a contested terrain in the 1990's" (p. 2). They comment indirectly on ambiguous and contrasting norms about how one is expected to behave when pregnant. Glenn et al. use differing ideologies of motherhood to consider the messages being sent to women about how they should conceptualize motherhood. They note that ideologies begin to have power from the moment one considers the possibility that one may become a mother at some time in the future. Although the aim is to identify the nature of these messages, and particularly to expose divergent, non-"White, American, middle-class" models of motherhood, they also effectively provide a way of considering how the social environment helps to construct the norms and expectations that guide behavior and thought. When messages about norms are in conflict or discrepant, this seems to make the emotions and lessons even more complex and challenge coping capacities (McCoyd, 2009).

One aspect of the social environment concerns the cultural practices with which one is reared and the societal norms about pregnancy, particularly as portrayed in the mass media. In Western (particularly mainstream U.S.) culture, new norms about the roles of women have influenced expectations about motherhood (Bassin, Honey, & Kaplan, 1994; Glenn et al., 1994). Likewise, cultural heritage and religion will influence expectations, attitudes, and practices regarding pregnancy, beliefs about the fetus, and childbirth (Schott & Henley, 1996). If the messages received are that pregnant women are to avoid any physical labor, to be coddled, and to focus inward (as in U.S. mainstream culture from the postcolonial days through the late 1950s), women are likely to follow this behavioral script/template. If the societal messages are to continue to work until the onset of labor, to give birth and to continue on with work as soon as physical recovery occurs (as in agricultural societies and recent U.S. feminist culture), then this is more likely to occur. Women who elect to step outside the norms of their given culture are likely to be ostracized on some level (Schott & Henley, 1996), providing feedback to discourage similar future behavior and providing others with vicarious learning experiences. An example of this is the relatively rapid change in U.S culture that allowed pregnant women to drink alcohol while pregnant in the 1970s but now ostracizes and criminally prosecutes women who drink alcohol while pregnant (Golden, 2000).

Cultural components play an active role. Some social environments give very clear messages that pregnancy-loss levels are high and that it is in one's interest to avoid giving much thought to one's pregnancy until very close to delivery. Other social environments (especially current U.S. culture) encourage early pregnancy testing, visualizing the fetus on ultrasound, and often even naming the fetus from the moment one is aware of its existence. Again, failure to adhere to the given norms brings sanctions from family members, friends, and pregnancy-care providers. This implies that one's attachment to pregnancy is clearly defined by the social environment in which one lives. It further suggests that attachment may be limited in cultures that do not recognize the pregnancy as something to bond with prior to birth. The earlier interpretations of attachment [per Mahler (1975), Mahler et al. (1985), and Bowlby (1977, 1980/1998)] as a psychobiological imperative would not necessarily hold. Instead, conformity to the determinants of one's culture would be the primary determinant of prenatal bonding behavior.

New technologies of high-resolution ultrasound, nuchal fold testing, chorionic villi sampling, and others are used frequently and often viewed by pregnant women as bonding tools (as opposed to fetal health testing, their true intent) (McCoyd, 2007; Morgan & Michaels, 1999). Hearing fetal heart tones, visualizing the fetus on ultrasound, and identifying the fetus's sex are now all typical experiences for pregnant women that connect them more strongly on emotional levels. This may enhance bonding in normal circumstances, but may also intensify grief if a perinatal loss is experienced.

SUMMARY OF DEVELOPMENT IN THE PRENATAL PERIOD

Pregnancy involves the development of both the fetus (from multicelled blastocyst through embryonic stages and into a fetus that is eventually capable of living independently) and of the woman (from individual through pregnant woman through mother with responsibilities toward another person). The developments as described previously are prime exemplars of a maturational loss as we are defining it. Maturational losses are viewed as both a form of growth and maturation, but entail losses as a known and comfortable stage of life is left behind for a new, unknown stage. In ideal circumstances of a planned pregnancy lovingly accepted by prepared parents (and extended families) who traverse pregnancy and delivery with no real complications, people still experience losses. The woman loses a true independence in that she must consider how her self-care and nutrition affects her pregnancy. Her partner may feel a similar loss of independence as s/he is now tied more tightly to the pregnant woman and may be relied on for economic, emotional, and other support. Although these losses are generally welcomed as a sign of maturation and movement toward a chosen goal, they are losses nonetheless. The ultimate loss is experienced by the fetus at delivery as s/he is thrust from the womb where every need has been met and, other than growing, no demands have been placed on the fetus. The moment of delivery requires the baby to breathe; do the work of swallowing to get nutrition; respond to stimuli and lose the protected, darkened calm of the uterine environment. We tend to focus only on the growth of maturation, but nearly all maturation involves these types of poorly recognized losses as well.

LOSS AS EXPERIENCED BY A FETUS

Little is known about the experience of a fetus. Developmental milestones occur from the time of conception (when egg and sperm join to become one cell) and the germinal period (the time when this single cell starts reproducing to create multicelled spheres for approximately 2 weeks). From 2 to 6 weeks postconception (8 weeks from the time of the last menstrual period), the embryo grows and primitive nervous and circulatory systems develop. At the beginning of the third lunar month, the rudiments of all of the systems are present and the entity is called a fetus. The fetus starts at about one and a half inches at this point and grows to approximately 20 inches by the end of the 40th week of gestation. The genitalia and facial features develop during the third to fourth lunar month and bones begin to harden. The fifth and sixth months are a time of rapid growth. Sensory development occurs and eye movements begin between 16 and 24 weeks, with patterning of eye movements occurring by around 36 weeks of gestation that indicate sleep patterns (Birnholz, 1981). It is believed that shades of light and dark are perceived, but with little stimuli from the external environment it is unlikely that any interpretation of these light/dark patterns can occur. Likewise, fetuses respond to auditory stimulation between 24 and 28 weeks of gestational age (Birnholz & Benacerraf, 1983), indicating the ability to begin taking in stimuli from the external world. Despite these sensory developments, most sense-making and meaning-making seem to rely on experience with the environment; the stimulus of light changes or auditory input likely makes no sense when the fetus has no context with which to interpret the sensations.

Some speculate that the mother's emotional state has more bearing on fetal experience than the sensory stimuli because of the chemical and metabolic substances that cross the placenta via the mother's blood supply and may have physical effects such as increased heart rate and so forth on the fetus (Ottinger & Simmons, 1964). Indeed, recent research shows strong associations between a mother's anxiety and depression and the neonate's birth weight and temperament, as well as other complications of pregnancy (Abrams & Curran, 2007). It is possible that the fetus experiences the physical aspects of some emotions (oxytocin leading to warm and comfortable feelings; adrenaline leading to anxious feelings); yet again, with no prior experience through which to interpret these sensations, it appears unlikely that the feelings carry great salience.

LOSS OF A FETUS AS EXPERIENCED BY SIGNIFICANT OTHERS

Infertility

Infertility is defined as a year of unprotected heterosexual intercourse that does not lead to a pregnancy (Greenfield, 1997) and is experienced as a perinatal loss (see Gilin reading in chapter 6, this volume). Although conception may never occur, women and couples who have infertility issues are pursuing a goal of pregnancy and creation of a larger family and feel deeply the loss of those hopes and dreams. The "reproductive story" (Diamond, Diamond, & Jaffe, 2001) starts for many people long before they even enter puberty as they begin to visualize the hopes they have for when they will pursue pregnancy and how they will bear children. Infertility is an assault to these expectations and involves losses, including an increased sense of vulnerability, a loss of self-esteem, and a belief that one's body is defective and/or has betrayed one (Lind, Pruitt, & Greenfield, 1990). This is a silent, disenfranchised loss that brings little support from one's social network, many of whom may not be aware of the issue at all. This network may believe myths that demean the expense, both financially and emotionally, that infertile couples experience. Although a full explication of infertility is beyond the scope of this chapter, please see the reading at the end of chapter 6 for discussion of the experience of infertility and its impact over decades of the woman's life.

Reproductive Health Conditions

Women often expect that pregnancy, once achieved, will proceed with little effect on their lives until the time of delivery. Advances in pregnancy care mean that maternal death and pregnancy complications have been minimized over the last century. Nevertheless, complications in pregnancy occur in 10% to 20% of pregnancies and range from hyperemesis gravidarum to placenta previa to premature labor to pregnancy-induced diabetes or hypertension (Rich, 1991). Conception of multiples (twins or more) has risen as a result of the increase in infertility treatment and these pregnancies are considered high risk for complications as well. All of these conditions have biological, psychological, and social aspects that are unique to the condition (see the reading by Munch at the end of this chapter), but all have several outcomes in common. Women experiencing these conditions encounter a sense of loss of control, both because of the fact that their bodies are not behaving in the ways they would choose, but also because the medical care itself entails mobility and activity limitations (Bachman & Lind, 1997). Anxiety, grief, boredom, fear, ambivalence, and guilt are also commonly found in women experiencing pregnancy complications (Bachman & Lind, 1997). Social workers and other caregivers can provide validation that these complications are frustrating and frightening; these caregivers can also help to problem solve ways of continuing to have control where it is possible.

When a pregnancy is not only affected by a complication but has also ended with the death of the fetus, there are biological, psychological, and social effects as well. This type of loss is more recognized now than in previous years, though social rituals and support are still limited. Miscarriage and stillbirth remain common (and challenging for mourning), though new types of loss such as multifetal pregnancy reduction and pregnancy termination for fetal anomaly are newer permutations of pregnancy loss that add ever-newer levels of complexity to grief.

Biological Changes Associated With Intrauterine Fetal Death

The experience of miscarriage, intrauterine fetal death (IUFD), or other pregnancy loss will lead to an abrupt change in the biological status of the woman. If labor must be induced, the experience of laboring to produce a dead fetus/baby is grueling on physical and emotional levels. Hormone levels will drop dramatically; "there is an abrupt alteration in the endocrinological milieu brought about by the many physiological changes that occur with parturition" (Filer, 1992, p. 153). These changes fall into three broad areas: (a) the delivery of the placenta and fetus precipitously remove a large source of hormone production (especially steroids, progesterone, estrogen, and androgens); (b) the drop in estrogen at the time of delivery lowers serum-binding proteins; and (c) prolactin is secreted as a result of delivery, leading to milk production and inhibition of the estrogen/progesterone hormonal cycle (Filer, 1992). This prolactin release will signal oxytocin release and the woman will have to cope with breast enlargement and milk production until bound and unused breasts quit secreting milk. Some studies have suggested that endorphin levels are high during late pregnancy and delivery (Browning, cited in Filer, 1992) and these also drop off dramatically after delivery. These hormonal and other metabolic changes happen regardless of whether the fetus is born alive or not. It is assumed by most obstetricians and perinatal observers that these changes promote feelings of depression, ranging from "baby blues" to postpartum depression. To date, it appears that no one has written about how these changes play a role in depression and/or grieving after a perinatal loss. Nevertheless, it must be assumed that the drop in hormone levels creates a propensity toward depressive moods that a pregnancy loss will exacerbate.

A sense of the failure of one's body to accomplish the task of pregnancy is common among mothers who experience pregnancy loss, and body image is likely to be affected (Grubb-Phillips, 1988; Mahan & Calica, 1997). Barry explains that "[b]ecause the pregnant body is the first 'nest' for the child, positive feelings toward her body may contribute to the woman's beliefs concerning her ability to develop and provide a future home" (1980, p. 229). This implies that the inability to provide a "safe nest" may be interpreted by the woman as a failure of her body, and brings into question her future ability to sustain a pregnancy. This implication is borne out in clinical experience as women frequently comment on a mistrust of their body's ability to sustain pregnancy. They often globalize this mistrust into mistrusting their bodies in a variety of ways, including questioning their ability to have a successful future pregnancy. Maggie, from, p. 27, often spoke about questions of whether she could trust her body to become pregnant or to sustain a pregnancy if it occurred. This was true even after her first successful pregnancy. Certainly the language of perinatal loss—"failed" IVF cycles, "mis" carriage, "incompetent" cervix, and "elderly" primagravida (older first-time mothers) all carry implications of character fault and/or failure on the part of the mother.

Although not totally consistent, most studies have found higher levels of grief associated with fetal death or stillbirth [defined as death after 20 weeks estimated age of gestation (EGA)] as compared to those experiencing miscarriage (prior to 20 weeks EGA) (Cole, 1995; Theut, Zaslow, Rabinovich, Bartko, & Morihisa, 1990). This result will be discussed at more length under the psychological aspects of IUFD. However, there is a biological interpretation as well. The hormonal drops may be less precipitous earlier in pregnancy (as it is known that levels continue to rise for the duration of a pregnancy) and a smaller drop may lead to less intense mourning from a biological standpoint. The medical literature is silent on this subject.

A phenomenon frequently mentioned in the lay support literature (Borg & Lasker, 1981; D. L. Davis, 1996; Layne, 2003; Panuthos & Romeo, 1984) is the physical sensation of aching arms, a feeling of an abdominal void, and occasionally hearing baby cries when no babies are around. These sensations have provoked little interest from the medical community; however, many peer counselors (parents who have had previous perinatal loss) believe that these are biological phenomena. They explain that the mother's body was primed to respond by holding the baby, with the weight of the baby supported by the mother's arms and belly/lap, and that one's body is in mourning for these sensations.

Some even speculate that hearing baby cries results from a heightened awareness (with the implication that this is also biologically primed) that either allows one to hear at great distance or that interprets other sounds as the sounds one was expecting to hear.

It is worth noting that a study by Jessner, Weigert, and Foy (1970) concluded that "All women were haunted at times by the fear of producing a monster or a dead infant" (p. 222). Additionally, they comment that in the antenatal period, "there comes a saddening awareness that the child will—and should—move further away from her" (p. 224). These two quotes are juxtaposed to show the antenatal stage as the precursor to pregnancy loss. When pregnancy loss occurs, the mother's fear of producing a monster and/or dead child comes true. Additionally, the natural process of separating and distancing from the fetus via its continued development is interrupted and abbreviated, which complicates not only differentiation/separation (as will be discussed in the section on psychological ramifications), but also complicates grieving. The mere physical fact of delivering a dead and/or deformed fetus resonates on both the level of a dream (nightmare) come true and the level of one's body bringing forth a monstrosity. These show a degree of magical thinking and body image that have psychological components.

Psychological Aspects of IUFD

Psychoanalytic Understandings and Their Impact on Pregnancy Loss

The loss of any cathected entity (particularly self) is understood by Freudians to inspire mourning and melancholia. According to Freud (1917/1957), to mourn any loss involves de-cathecting the object, optimally by identifying with the lost object, and internalizing that introject, thereby re-cathecting self. Pines (1993) is one of the few psychoanalytically trained therapists to turn a scholarly eye on pregnancy loss. She asserts:

> analysis of women patients who have miscarried often reveals, many years after this event, their sense of loss, prolonged grief and unresolved mourning—a longstanding depression, a loss of self-esteem and a hatred of their female bodies which do not bear live children as their mothers did. Their self-representation is damaged. (p. 116)

Furman (1996) also considered perinatal loss from a psychoanalytic perspective, but with a different focus. She develops the premise that perinatal loss constitutes an injury to body ego and starts from an assumption that women's body egos are more flexible to accommodate sharing one's body with a fetus during pregnancy. She interprets the crisis of perinatal loss to involve "the process of transferring her cathexis of the inside baby to the outside baby [to] provide some opportunity for object cathexis" (p. 433). This, she says, is a customary process for any mother giving birth, but is hastened and made much more complex by virtue of perinatal loss. Instead of delivering a live baby to whom object cathexis can occur, the dead baby does not allow transition of the cathexis of the inner baby to an exterior living object. She provides theoretical support for interventions that have been carried out for the last 3 decades. These interventions, originally suggested by Klaus and Kennell (1976), are based on what the perinatally bereaved said they wanted after a fetal death. The bereaved had asked for opportunities to see and hold their babies and many wished to have funeral services or other rituals of closure, a request that physicians and hospitals had long resisted. Furman encouraged parents' active roles in planning funerals and so on for the purpose of allowing the development of an exterior object attachment in lieu of the internal one.

Furman (1996) explains the phenomena of aching arms and abdominal voids as well. She intervenes to verbalize the integral role the fetus had to the mother's own body and that the "lack of restitution by being unavailable on the outside" (p. 432) led to these bodily sensations as a result of violated body ego integrity. She views the flexible body ego boundaries as too quickly stretched with no time to transition: the change from allowing another (the fetus) within oneself to a return to just oneself within one's skin happens rapidly. This quick return to a nonpregnant state, with no subsequent close physical contact with a dependent baby, leads to a sense of violated body ego that requires time for readjustment. She notes that therapeutic interventions designed to acknowledge the loss of the mother's bodily integrity (as with an amputation) and designed to promote a sense of the baby's external existence (something the lay literature refers to as memory-building) are beneficial to this readjustment.

Ballou's (1978) study included one woman who experienced miscarriage. Because her findings supported the belief that there is a growing attachment to the fetus as the pregnancy progresses and as the pregnant woman reconciles to her mother, Ballou theorizes a direct connection between the chronological length of the pregnancy (gestational age) and the amount of grief experienced by the woman. This would be an understandable prediction in light of psychoanalytic theory as well as of object relations theory. Actual results of studies done to explore this question have been mixed, with the majority finding that gestational age is a factor in increased expressions of grief (Goldbach, Dunn, Toedter, & Lasker, 1991; Theut et al., 1990), particularly for men (Johnson & Puddifoot, 1996). However, other studies point to the possibility that there is no direct connection. Indeed, the developers of the scale most commonly used to assess perinatal grief (the Perinatal Grief Scale) have found that complicated, chronic, and delayed grief responses are found most commonly in those who experienced early-pregnancy loss (Goldbach et al., 1991; Lasker & Toedter, 1991). They suggest that social support (or lack thereof) is a suspected factor in persons having more difficulty with grieving. Object relations theorists, particularly attachment theorists, might suggest a different reason why some have complicated, delayed, or chronic grief reactions.

Object Relations/Attachment Theory Understandings of Loss

Psychoanalytic theory focuses on the investment of libido through cathexis. Object relations and Attachment theories focus instead on the quality of the evolving bond between a child and her or his primary caregiver. Any disruption of valued bonds inspires anxiety. Bowlby notes:

> many of the most intense emotions arise during the formation, the maintenance, the disruption and the renewal of attachment relationships.... Similarly, a threat of loss arouses anxiety and actual loss gives rise to sorrow, while each of these situations is likely to arouse anger. (1980/1998, p.40)

He further theorizes that the person is then strongly motivated to maintain the affectional bond and "all the most powerful forms of attachment behaviour become activated" (p. 42). It is easy to see these behaviors and attempts to recapture pregnancy in the denial experienced by women when told that their fetus has died *in utero*. Bowlby focuses on the biological function of attachment more than most other behavioral theorists. He emphasizes the survival value of attachment (Bowlby, 1977, 1980/1998). Bowlby theorizes that attachment styles may influence one's response to death, and one might assume these responses would apply to the loss of a pregnancy/fetus as well. He says:

> In the case of the anxiously attached, mourning is likely to be characterized by unusually intense anger and/or self reproach, with depression, and to persist for much longer than normal. In the case of the compulsively self-reliant [the avoidant], mourning may be delayed for months or years. (1977, pp. 139–140)

This provides a different interpretation for why some women experience chronic, complicated, or delayed grief reactions (an interpretation that has nothing to do with gestational age). One might assume that the securely attached would grieve in a healthy manner, whereas women who have anxious attachment patterns may grieve in an extended, or alternatively delayed, manner.

Bowlby (1980/1998) differentiates pathological from healthy mourning. He proposes several criteria for healthy mourning. He asserted that the bereaved must: (a) withdraw emotional investment in the lost person and prepare to make a new relationship (p. 25); (b) accept that pain is inevitable (p. 26); (c) acknowledge that feelings swing between poles of anxiety and despair until grief is resolved (p. 27); (d) experience an urge to recover the lost person, including yearning for the lost person and searching for him or her (p. 28); (e) express anger toward the deceased or the one believed to be responsible for the death (p. 29). Bowlby also believed: (f) there is no strong need to identify with the lost person—a deviation from Freudian psychoanalytic theory (p. 30); (g) there is likely to be hatred toward the lost person at varying points in the process—again, a break with Freudian theory (p. 30); and (h) the ability of children (younger than adolescence) to grieve in a healthy manner is limited without additional support (p. 31). Furman (1974) supports this last assertion after fairly extensive study of bereaved children; however, her study group of children were in large part selected from a group that had already been involved in psychotherapy (Bowlby, 1980/1998).

Klaus and Kennell (1976) were seemingly the first to empirically study perinatal loss. They were pediatricians who were influenced by Bowlby's theoretical conceptualizations about maternal–infant bonding.

They compared perinatal loss to the loss of a spouse. In 1976, this was a major step forward, because the prevalent approach at the time was to view pregnancy loss as something to be forgotten as quickly as possible. In fact, most women were told to go home and get pregnant again as quickly as physically possible. Hospitals disposed of the fetal remains, with women assured that they should not concern themselves about what happened to the remains. Women found little support for their sense of loss and felt stifled in any attempts to express their grief (multiple personal communications with women bereaved in the 1950–1960s). Klaus and Kennell supported the development of hospital protocols that allowed contact with the infant and avoidance of tranquilizing medications (noting that they interfere with grief work), and they introduced the idea of "group discussions," noting that the mothers benefit from reading other bereaved mothers' diaries (pp. 235–239).

It is interesting that, although it was a step forward to compare perinatal grief to being widowed, this conceptualization does not recognize the unique aspects of perinatal grief. Bowlby (1977, 1980/1998), Peppers and Knapp (1980), and Furman (1996) allude to these unique characteristics. One difference is that grieving a perinatal loss involves losing a part of oneself (the pregnancy), which differs from mourning an object separate from the self (a spouse). Further, social norms about the care and responsibility parents owe to children are unique to the parent–child bond, adding levels of guilt that are qualitatively different from those found among spouses. Parents are expected to protect children from all harm, yet the loss belies this expectation.

Bowlby (1980/1998) accepts Klaus and Kennell's (1976) assertion that mourning a stillbirth is like the mourning of the widowed. Bowlby acknowledged that perinatal bereavement includes "[n]umbing, followed by somatic distress, yearning, anger, and subsequent irritability and depression... [as] are preoccupations with the image of the dead baby and dreams about him" (1980/1998, p. 122). He supports changed hospital protocols allowing women to hold their dead babies and to encourage naming them and conducting simple funerals. He seems to recognize women's need to acknowledge the baby's existence as a separate entity to effectively mourn it. He quotes Lewis's saying "this loss becomes a non-event with no one to mourn" (1976, p.123). Bowlby acknowledges the need to attach to the deceased baby to be able to mourn.

The phenomenon of "replacement pregnancy" may exist when fetal loss occurs and the mother is unable to work through the task of separation from the expected child. Klaus and Kennell (1976) identified this in a brief section directed to other physicians about how to manage communications with bereaved parents. They say:

> we strongly encourage the parents to refrain from having a replacement infant until they have completed their mourning reaction. We explain that it is difficult to take on a new baby at the same time one is giving up the baby who has died. (p. 237)

They suggest a waiting period of at least 6 months. This is not well developed in terms of a theoretical base for such a prescription. It is likely that it is based in Bowlby's (1980/1998) ideas that grief work is necessary to resolve loss and an implicit understanding that attachment to others will be disrupted until this grief work is accomplished. More recently, the replacement-child concept has been called a myth (Grout & Romanoff, 2000), yet it is clear that meaning-making (Neimeyer, 2001) is part of what makes the difference. When attachment has been strong, the loss is a challenge to both a sense of coherence (meaning) and processing of the trauma of the loss of the assumptive world (Uren & Wastell, 2002). Both of these psychological factors are responses to the social context and availability of social support, which can allow meaning to be made and validated in conjunction with caregivers and informal social supports.

Social Aspects of IUFD

Thankfully, pregnancy loss is not an extremely common occurrence, though it occurs more frequently than most people believe. Statistics show that 15% to 20% of all recognized pregnancies result in miscarriage or fetal death (Cole, 1995), and the numbers for miscarriage prior to knowledge of pregnancy are likely much higher. Nevertheless, social recognition of this kind of grief is quite limited and, in the past, even the medical providers tended to dismiss the intensity of this loss (Ilse & Furrh, 1988) instead of recognizing and validating the bereavement and mourning. Frequently, family and peers offer little comment, assuming that the woman (and they) can move on as if nothing has occurred. The general lack of rituals for closure in this type of loss differs drastically from other types of loss in which funerals, memorial services, and social support are common following a death. This lack of ritual has consequences as the mother and her supporters try (mostly in vain) to either move on without acknowledgment (difficult because the mother is feeling loss) or to find new ways of observing the loss and providing closure rituals and social support.

Although Bowlby (1980/1998) is identified with attachment theory in an object relations tradition, he is very aware of the influence of culture on mourning, in terms of its rituals and social supports, and in terms of what occurs regardless of culture. In his chapter on "Mourning in Other Cultures," he cites Firth's (1961) observations that funerals have three functions: (a) "bringing home that the loss has occurred" (p.127) by virtue of allowing public expression of grief and inducting the bereaved into new roles; (b) allowing the community to say farewell and thereby reconstitute itself as a changed community; and (c) the interchange of goods and services occurs, which allows expression of reciprocal altruism. Bowlby (1980/1998) adds three observations of his own: (a) a funeral allows the opportunity for the living to express gratitude to the deceased and to take action to honor the deceased; (b) anger may be given a socially acceptable expression (as in groups who direct anger at neighboring tribes or at the deceased during the ritual); and, (c) a funeral usually provides some acceptable period of mourning.

It is important to recognize that the perinatally bereaved frequently receive none of this support because funerals are rarely held (particularly for those who terminate as a result of fetal anomaly). This has immense social implications for these bereaved parents, as they have no community to validate their loss through a ritual, no recognition by the community that it has experienced a change, and little exchange of goods and services that might enable a woman or couple to feel supported. Additionally, expressions of gratitude or caring toward the baby who has never really had a role within the social community are virtually impossible and expressions of anger toward a baby are socially proscribed. All of the above, combined with little definition of appropriate grieving periods, even in customary types of deaths, leave the woman with little social structure for grieving. Indeed, the implicit message is that the baby did not have standing in the community and that mourning should be done quickly and out of sight. In light of our knowledge that grieving rituals and social support enable more effective resolution of grief, it is not surprising that this set of circumstances would impact negatively on the mourning process of bereaved parents.

Social recognition of loss is complicated even further when the mother is diagnosed as having an anomalous fetus that is subsequently aborted. Women desire these pregnancies but elect to end the pregnancy when a fetal anomaly or genetic condition is diagnosed. This makes emotional and social ramifications even more complicated (McCoyd, 2003, 2007, 2008b, 2009; Rapp, 1999; Rose, 1995; Van Putte, 1988). If miscarriage and stillbirth are silent disenfranchised losses, the termination of a pregnancy affected by fetal anomaly is actively hidden because of the stigma associated with abortion in U.S. culture (McCoyd, 2008a). Although women may acknowledge the pregnancy loss to their social network, the fact that they have not provided the full story often leaves them feeling that any support they receive is deceptively gotten and they have difficulty using the support effectively (McCoyd, 2003, 2007).

Even with newer hospital protocols that have developed to encourage viewing the dead baby and/or to have funerals or other rituals, this is often done in a one-size-fits-all manner (Leon, 1992) that may or may not truly be helpful when applied across the spectrum of bereaved women (Hughes, Turton, Hopper, & Evans, 2002). Schott and Henley (1996) caution against this approach. They describe cultural beliefs within some communities whereby the fluids associated with birth are considered polluted; therefore handling newly born babies, dead or alive, becomes polluting to the handler. Handling a baby's body immediately after its birth is anathema for these women. Aside from strong cultural prohibitions like this, Hughes et al. (2002) certainly give pause to the practice-wisdom belief that women should see and hold their babies after death, indicating that this may raise anxiety. That said, there are concerns that the study design used comparison groups that were not valid in that they had not experienced a loss. In any case, it appears that sensitive clinical assessment and support is required for perinatally bereaved women as they decide whether to view and/or hold their deceased baby.

Additionally, the common practice of cutting a lock of hair to provide the bereaved parents with a concrete memento (and proof of the object-status of the baby's exterior existence) would also be prohibited in some cultures. Schott and Henley's (1996) constant refrain is to "listen to the woman" about how social norms define the ways that the particular woman needs to deliver and mourn. This becomes important to conceptualizing the role of the social environment in perinatal bereavement. It is clear that some of these social norms supercede cathexis, attachment styles, and seeming biological imperatives. For instance, some cultures (including the United States prior to 1970) actively discouraged prenatal attachment and encouraged a dismissing type of emotional response to perinatal death. Although there were definitely many exceptions, most women accepted this social message and actively avoided expressions of grief. If the grief was solely biologically or psychically determined, these adjustments to fit social realities would not have been possible. It is clear that perinatal bereavement is multifactorial in the way it is experienced, as well as in the way it is expressed. This supports the notion that a full biopsychosocial assessment must occur to allow "best practices" support of perinatally bereaved women and families.

READINGS

HYPEREMESIS GRAVIDARUM: A MEDICAL COMPLICATION OF PREGNANCY

Shari Munch, PhD, LCSW

Shari Munch is associate professor at the School of Social Work, Rutgers University, New Jersey, USA. She teaches courses in advanced direct practice and human behavior in the social environment (HBSE). Her clinical and research interests include health care, perinatal health care, and clinical social work (e.g., medically complicated pregnancy, patient–provider relationship, gender-bias in women's health care, compassion fatigue). She has 25 years of direct practice social work experience and maintains a psychotherapy practice. Her research has been published in *Social Work; Health & Social Work; Social Work in Health Care; Social Science & Medicine; Journal of the American Medical Association; Journal of Psychosomatic Obstetrics & Gynecology; Journal of Perinatology; and Women & Health.*

> I thought I was going to die. I felt unlike I had ever felt before in pregnancy. I was convinced that I was going to die. Come to find out, I had no

potassium left in my body; and it was making me kind of wigged out.... It was to the point of where my fingertips were flaking off, my lips were flaking off, my hair was falling out in bunches. I couldn't stand up; to vomit I would just lean over and vomit into a bucket because there was no way I could get up and go to the bathroom....You know, I was a gray, pasty mess.

Hyperemesis gravidarum (HG), extreme nausea and vomiting of pregnancy (NVP), is a debilitating pregnancy complication that warrants serious attention because of its potentially severe effects both to the mother and to her baby (ACOG, 2004). Approximately 0.5% to 2% of pregnancies involve HG and it is the most common indication for hospital admission during early pregnancy (compared to other pregnancy complications for sustained pregnancies). It is second only to preterm labor as the most common reason for hospitalization during pregnancy (Adams, Harlass, Sarno, Read, & Rawlings, 1994; Gazmararian et al., 2002). Cross-nationally, the incidence reported for Chinese women is within the range reported for U.S. and European countries (Chin, Lao, & Kong, 1987). Prior to the use of intravenous (IV) fluids, HG was a significant factor leading to neurologic disturbance and even maternal death (Cowan, 1996; J. Williams, 1923). With advancements in IV fluid therapy, the risk of these outcomes is greatly reduced. The typical illness course includes a gradual recovery, frequent relapses, multiple episodes of inpatient management, and/or the use of home health care services, such as intravenous hydration (Naef et al., 1995). There is some evidence to suggest that infants born of women who had HG are more likely to experience decreased gestational age (premature delivery) and increased length of hospital stay (Pauww, Bierling, Cook, & Davis, 2003). Moreover, HG and its less severe counterpart NVP, are expensive health problems that are also responsible for an estimated 8.5 million working days lost per year in the United Kingdom (Gadsby, 1994). Still, there is a lack of research conducted in the area of pregnancy nausea and vomiting (Swallow, Lindow, Masson, & Hay, 2002) and, although the literature supports that HG is a multifactorial disease (Philip, 2003), there remains no known cause or cure (Goodwin, 2004).

Medical professionals tend to characterize HG as a psychogenic disorder despite scientific evidence (Munch, 2002a). This may have impeded progress in searching for the proper etiology (Bogen, 1994) and to understand the illness experience of patients (B. O'Brien & Naber, 1992). The *Practice Bulletin of the American College of Obstetricians and Gynecologists* (ACOG, 2004) reports that there are no studies to date that support the psychogenic hypothesis, which may help to mitigate this tendency and associated ramifications. Nevertheless, recent studies report that women with HG encounter physicians and other health care professionals (HCP) who either doubt, ignore, or trivialize their symptoms (Munch, 2002b; B. O'Brien, Evans, & White-McDonald, 2002). Moreover, there is some evidence to suggest that delayed diagnosis and treatment of HG occurs (Munch, 2000), thereby affecting patient satisfaction with their physicians and possibly maternal and infant health outcomes.

Losses Associated With HG

Losses abound for women as a result of this pregnancy complication. The *biological* losses are especially complex because two beings are involved—mother and her fetus. Women with HG can experience significant physical limitations during pregnancy. The extensive nausea and vomiting causes dramatic weight loss and exhaustion, resulting in hospitalization, bedrest, and a whole host of medications and invasive medical interventions such as IV hydration and total parenteral nutrition therapies. In addition to the short-term loss of physical health during pregnancy, some women experience long-term medical complications postpartum (e.g., gastrointestinal, esophageal, and dental problems). Though modern medicine can usually save women, women can and do die from HG. Moreover, concerns regarding the health of the fetus are apparent, and some women have noted developmental delays of their older children (MacGibbon, personal communication, 2005). Ultimately, worst-case scenarios are the pregnancies that end in miscarriage or stillbirth, and termination of wanted pregnancies (therapeutic abortion) because the mother's life is in critical danger.

The *psychological* impact of experiencing a pregnancy complication is immense. Of primary import is the loss of security in the face of physical danger for self and unborn baby. The severity and chronicity of the nausea and vomiting associated with HG create emotional responses such as fear and worry about the health of oneself and the unborn baby, sadness and depression, and guilt regarding the effect on partner and children (Munch, 2002b). Pregnancy is often associated with a happy time for women. Thus, another significant loss is the loss of the wished-for pregnancy—women grieve the fact that they are so sick that they are unable to enjoy the pregnancy. Mirroring chemotherapy patients, HG women look physically ill—dehydration and starvation bring some women close to death—and their appearance lacks the healthy glow of pregnant women that one sees on television commercials. Ambivalence about a desired pregnancy can become pronounced as a woman desperately tries to cope with the debilitating illness, contributing to feelings of guilt and shame. The loss of self-esteem can be even more insidious as some women begin to feel like less than a woman, blame themselves for their illness, and experience self-doubt ("Why am I so sick? Why can't I handle pregnancy? Maybe I am not trying hard enough. Maybe I am overreacting.") (Munch, 2002b).

In addition to the physical and psychological toll, the *social* impact of HG is significant. HG interferes with, and negatively affects, women's daily lives (Munch, 2002b). Examples include lost wages and lost jobs, inability to perform self-care and/or household responsibilities, children being shuffled among many caregivers, and learning to operate complex home care equipment. These stressors are only compounded when the validity of symptoms is challenged by family, friends, and caregivers (B. O'Brien & Naber, 1992).

CASE PRESENTATION

The quotes throughout this narrative are excerpts of true stories as told by women with HG. Following are comments specifically related to incidents of stressful interactions with health care professionals, family/friends, employers, and others in society. Unfortunately, these examples are the types of comments common to pregnant women who are diagnosed with HG.

Health Care Professionals

> When I was released home from the hospital, my doctor told me to drink broth. We made up some with bouillon and I got sick on it. He put me on the phone with him and he said, "Do you want to be hospitalized

again? You've got to stop doing this." And that, to me, was a slap in the face, like I had a choice to be sick. I think he thought it was just all in my head. But, I thought, "I'm sick because I'm sick, not because I want to be sick."

My nurse forced me to empty my own vomit basin.

I was irritated with the social worker because the questions she asked sounded like she thought that HG could be prevented if I did this or that...I don't know what she was looking for, but the questions did irritate my husband and me.

Family

His family caused the most stress because my housework suffered and I wasn't taking care of my husband...and his family was having a hard time with that, that it [HG] was a problem. They didn't understand why I couldn't do those things. And we didn't get any help from them.

Employer

A lot of other women said that I was making it up, that I couldn't possibly be this sick. In fact, my office called because I couldn't come to work for a couple of weeks and told me that if I wanted my job I better get back to the office. I came in the next day, and I spent almost all day in the bathroom; and they finally understood that I was not lying.

Society

As far as other women in the public and other people, they think it's all in your head, and they don't understand why you're so sick. Because they weren't sick, they think you're just weak.

Enough people tell you it is all in your head, you almost start to believe it yourself, and that makes it even worse because you don't choose to throw up 25 times a day. You don't choose not to have a social life, to get up and share in regular things like going outside and smelling fresh air. You don't choose to be on your back for that long.

Unexpected Loss:
Diminished Trust in Helping Professionals

Still another less apparent loss is the *deterioration of the patient–provider relationship* (in social work terms, the therapeutic relationship or therapeutic alliance). When HG patients perceive that their account of their symptoms is belittled or not taken seriously, and they are being blamed for causing or prolonging their illness (e.g., attributed by health care providers [HCPs] to psychological problems, poor coping skills, marital discord, and so on, in the face of no evidence to support such a claim), they can experience a loss of trust in their HCP. This is truly an unanticipated "complication" that women do not expect to experience. HG patients expect that their HCPs will respect their integrity (i.e., that one is neither fabricating symptoms nor overreacting about minor symptoms) (Munch, 2000). The literature suggests that in addition to expecting expert medical care, generally patients prefer doctors who take their symptoms seriously, listen, and ask questions about their symptoms (Arborelius & Bremberg, 1992). Certainly diminished trust can result from interaction with professionals whom the patient perceives as technically incompetent. Yet, the focus here is on the fractured relationship that results from being treated in a less than humane manner.

Background: Gender-Biased Diagnosing
of Female Medical Conditions

The biopsychosocial well-being of women patients and their families throughout the perinatal period, which includes pregnancy, birth, and the neonatal (newborn) phase, is rife with yet-untested myths and folklore concerning the health of the mother. Medical practice and research in the area of maternal–child health are hindered by a long history of bias against women (Munch, 2004). Women's somatic complaints are more likely to be labeled by physicians and other health care professionals as nonserious and/or psychologically based, especially when the condition has an obscure etiology. Under conditions of medical uncertainty, psychogenic explanations for illness are often made, to the exclusion of possible biologic considerations. For example, women presenting with symptoms characteristic of interstitial cystitis are frequently labeled with the psychiatric diagnosis of somatization disorder, which results in subsequent mistreatment of the disease (Webster, 1993). Persons (mostly women) with fibromyalgia and chronic fatigue syndrome (CFS) find that their symptoms are often belittled or ignored (Clarke, 2000; Hart & Grace, 2000); and the conditions are viewed as psychogenic in nature (Richman, Jason, Taylor, & Jahn, 2000). This phenomenon is described as psychologization in which "female illness is socially constructed as erroneously or disproportionately embracing psychiatric or sociocultural contributors" (Blaxter, 1983; Richman et al., 2000, p. 178). Women with reproductive disorders (e.g., premenstrual symptoms, dysmenorrhea, pelvic pain with unknown etiology), in particular, experience the impact of gender stereotypes and attitudes, especially when medical professionals are unable to uncover the specific etiology of the condition (Laurence & Weinhouse, 1997; Stellman, 1990).

Hyperemesis gravidarum (HG) is another example of such a problem. Understanding and treating HG are further compounded by the tendency of HCPs to negatively label women suffering from this complication. Unfortunately, HCPs (e.g., nurses, psychiatrists, psychologists, social workers) often view the condition as something of a nuisance. Some contend that patients with HG "garner little attention and engender little sympathy from their physicians" (Abell & Riely, 1992, p. 835).

Contemporary research refutes the theory of psychogenesis (Simpson et al., 2001) and provides new conceptualizations suggesting that sociocultural factors (outdated theories of female psychology; medical folklore) rather than scientific evidence have shaped the overarching and predominant illness paradigm of psychogenesis (Munch, 2002a). Despite reports of positive physician relationships (Munch & Schmitz, 2006), far too many women still encounter negative attitudes of HCPs based on erroneous assumptions about the cause of and remedy for HG.

The Patient–Health Care Professional Relationship: Loss of Trust

In research on high-risk obstetric patients, Wohlreich (1986) identified that it is not uncommon for HCPs to become alarmed at a woman's expression of ambivalence about her pregnancy; they may respond in nonproductive ways by becoming annoyed, withdrawing from the patient, or labeling the patient "crazy." It is quite common for pregnant women to experience ambivalence during early pregnancy; even more usual for HG patients, in particular, as a result of the severity and duration of their symptoms. Katz (1984) posited that some physicians psychologically abandon their patients by withdrawing "behind a curtain of silence or evasion" (p. 206); this unintentional, psychological abandonment may affect a patient's physiological and psychological health as well as her willingness to comply with medical recommendations.

The unique nature of high-risk pregnancy as a stressful life event is well documented (Yali & Lobel, 1999), yet HCPs can inadvertently *add to* a woman's distress. HG patients often feel that they must "prove" to others that they are "really" sick (Munch, 2000). Overt or covert messages that imply the patient's symptoms are "all in your head" or that she "isn't trying hard enough" can lead to diminished hope, diminished trust, self-doubt, and despair (Munch 2000), thereby contributing to therapeutic ruptures and impasses (Safran & Muran, 2000). Similarly, Swedish scholars conceptualize "abuse in health care" to include the notion of feeling "nullified"—that is, patients who feel powerless, feel ignored, experience carelessness, and experience nonempathy. "Being nullified" is a state of lost dignity, frustration, and anxiety that increases the patient's feelings of vulnerability and makes the patient feel worthless, creating personal suffering (Swahnberg, Suruchi, & Bertero, 2007).

Intervention

HG is nausea and vomiting of pregnancy in its most extreme and complicated form and goes beyond "normalcy" and requires validation and subsequent medical intervention. Social work, medicine, and the nursing profession desperately need education not only about the physical and psychosocial aspects of women's health and illness, but also the impact of sociocultural, historical, and epistemological (e.g., flawed research) factors that shape social constructions of HG (Munch, 2002a). In addition to providing psychosocial counseling interventions, social workers serve as mediators between the health care system and consumers (Browne, 2006) and thus can facilitate improved health care policies and practices for HG women and their families.

Furthermore, the supportive nature of a patient–provider relationship is particularly salient for this population. Women experiencing pregnancy complications may be especially vulnerable, both physically and emotionally (Kemp & Hatmaker, 1989; MacMullen, Dulski, & Pappalardo, 1992; Merkatz, 1978), and may, thereby, place a greater emphasis on the importance of the relationship with their physicians and other health care providers. Clinical assessment of both physical and psychosocial events should occur in most cases of any medical illness. The danger occurs when female patients with certain disease/illness entities are singled out based on stereotypical assumptions and attitudes. HCPs should be mindful to seek current information about HG, examine their own attitudes and stereotypes, and listen to patients' accounts of their illness experience.

A reevaluation of the ways in which a health care professional's interaction with HG patients may, in and of itself, be a psychosocial stressor that contributes to exacerbating symptoms and impeding recovery is invaluable for promoting better patient care (Munch, 2000). Patient satisfaction is associated with women's perceptions that physicians believed their accounts of their symptoms (i.e., that the woman is neither fabricating symptoms nor overreacting) (Munch, 2000). Moreover, the perception of being believed by doctors (and other HCPs) was shown to be imperative to women seeking and receiving medical care; perceived delays in diagnosing and/or instituting treatment were viewed as contributing to unnecessary exacerbations of the illness, hospitalizations, and psychological distress. Being believed empowers patients and can enhance women's self-confidence and ability to stand up against the skepticism of others. The remarks from one HG woman:

> If you feel comfortable knowing that your doctor believes in you, and tries to understand what you're going through, that is going to relax you a little more. You are going to relax and put yourself more in their hands and let them treat you. I think that's a stress reliever right there. If you think someone's not quite buying what you're saying, you know, you get a little up in arms.

Proper therapeutic communication (Wachtel, 1993) and interpersonal relational skills are paramount to the helping relationship; social workers can learn how to avoid and/or address common mistakes in relating with clients (Dillon, 2003). Humane qualities (e.g., compassion, understanding, respect) are key (Munch, 2000) indicating that in addition to expecting expert medical [and by extension, social work] care, patients tend to be more satisfied with physicians who demonstrate positive interpersonal interactions and humane characteristics (Kenny, 1995). In addition to medical treatment, the natural course of the disease process and the spontaneous recovery from illness, the interpersonal interaction of the patient–physician encounter can be characterized as having a placebo effect that contributes to the healing process and should be regarded as a primary therapeutic tool (Brody, 1992). Physicians (and other health professionals, such as social workers) are not only prescribers of therapy, but can be therapeutic themselves (Epstein, Campbell, Cohen-Cole, McWhinney, & Smilkstein, 1993).

HEARTBREAKING CHOICES AND LOSSES OF POTENTIAL

The following was written by a bereaved mother who participated in a research study. We attempted to contact her to ask whether she would like to be credited as the source, but were unable to do so. Her consent to participate in interviews and her wholehearted participation in sharing her story (with an expressed hope that it would be shared with others) was deemed supportive of the use of her story here. Her words are precisely as she wrote them as part of an e-mail interview (McCoyd & Kerson, 2006), so they are written as if she were speaking. The convention "sic" will not be used, nor were brief comments changed to make them full sentences. We have kept her identity and potentially identifying information confidential to respect her privacy, as promised. Her story, in her own words, is shared here, as it is both compelling and typical of the experiences of women who decide to end a pregnancy affected by fetal anomaly. We thank her for her willingness to participate in the research from which this is excerpted (McCoyd, 2003) and express gratitude for the ways she can continue to teach others about this experience.

Beginnings and Attachment

I found out at age 35 through testing, that I had very limited viable egg quantity left. An ultrasound showed that I probably could not have another child without fertility intervention. I had not used birth control in years and had not become pregnant. And then my periods became erratic. My mother and grandmother had complete menopause at age 40. The consensus of my doctors was that I would too. So for over a decade I used no birth control and learned to adjust to periods that were missed for months on end. And that is how all of this began.

In October, I did not get my period. I did not worry since this was common. I was starting a new position at work and I was working very long days. My office building was under reconstruction and so I attributed the nausea and tiredness to stress and the environment. In early February I started feeling a flutter sensation. My pants and skirts were getting tight. I began worrying that maybe I had some sort of tumor. I consider myself intelligent, but honestly the idea of being pregnant seemed too remote of a concept to me. I worried secretly all of February. One afternoon I was sitting in a very dull meeting and I felt a kick. I almost jumped out of my seat. That is seriously the first time I thought oh my God, I am pregnant. I went home and told my husband. He thought I was exaggerating the kick. He asked me when the last time I had my period was, and I told him the previous September. He then suggested if it would make me feel better I should buy a pregnancy test and regardless I should call my gynecologist for an exam. So on a night in February, I bought a test and took it. In less than ten seconds the test turned colors. I could not breathe. I felt the room swirl. I truly thought it would not change. But it did. Wow. I called my husband into the bathroom. He looked shocked. He told me to breathe and calm down. That sometimes those tests are wrong. I told him they give a false negative not a false positive usually. He did not believe me. That night I was in bed rubbing my stomach. Wondering why and how and what; What would happen? I was happy. But scared to death as well. Scared that at 43 I was too old for a healthy child. Scared that my career would be in turmoil now. Scared I could not keep up with a toddler anymore....I was, I guess, a little in shock. At 22 weeks I knew (or thought I knew) that all possibilities of a termination were over. Besides I wanted the baby. Had always wanted another child. My husband and I began making plans.

On the day of the perinatal visit I was a little scared. I tried to convince myself we were just going to see how far along I was and maybe see if it was a boy or a girl. When I entered the ultrasound room I started to feel tense. The technician did not smile. In fact she looked rather gloomy. She was all business. After getting me settled on the table she left the room. Her coldness frightened me. When she left the room I burst into tears. I felt absolute terror. My husband tried to soothe me. When she returned, though it was obvious I was upset, she ignored it. She set about doing the ultrasound, in silence. I looked at the screen. I saw no nuchal fold. I was relieved. The baby looked ok to me. Nothing jumped out at me at least, and so I started calming down a bit. But still this woman said not one word. Nothing. Her sour expression kept me in fear. Finally she took a picture with the baby's little hand kind of waving and gave it to us. She told me to take my time sitting up and then to have a seat outside the door. The counselor would talk to us. Counselor? What counselor? I had no idea who or what she meant. Now I was certainly worried. I cried some more.

Then on Tuesday evening about 7 P.M. the phone rang and it was [the genetic counselor]. She said the "fish" test had come back. I took a deep breath. She said that they had tested 12 cells. Eleven were completely normal and one did show T21. I asked what that could mean. She said that sometimes cells overlap in a "fish" test. That it might be a fluke. But that the fact there were normal cells was what was a good sign. And she told me the baby was a boy.

We were thrilled. So happy. Normal cells and a boy!! Wow. I put that one cell out of my mind. I chose to ignore it. We then told the whole world it was a boy and it was alright. We started talking about changing over the other bedroom for a baby. Moving furniture around. My mom sent me a huge box of new boy baby clothes and some baby furniture. She must have ordered it the second I hung up the phone.

Diagnosis and Endings

Then Saturday morning came. At 8 A.M. the phone rang and it was Dr. [perinatologist] himself. Panic time. I remember thinking why is he calling me this early? He asked how I was feeling since the amnio. I started to calm a little thinking he was just doing a follow-up call. But then he told me why he had called. He said he had just personally finished reviewing the amnio. He had run some other tests. Our baby had T21. I was in shock. My heart literally felt like it had stopped beating. He sounded so sorry in his voice. I was trembling. I asked him how that was possible with the "fish" test having been so positive. He said he did not know. That the "fish" test was wrong. He was positive of it now. I thought my husband had gone to the store but then I heard someone downstairs. I screamed for him to come upstairs. My husband heard the news. He started screaming at Dr. [perinatologist]. Yelling at him about the fish test. Finally I took back the phone. Dr. [perinatologist] said if yelling would change the results he would not mind if my husband yelled at him all day. But these results were correct. He then said we should take time and think. That he would help us to terminate if we wanted. He knew where we could go. He also told me that he would want to send me to other specialists to have more thorough ultrasounds done. He said he would call us on Monday, but to call him in the meantime if we had any questions before then.

So there I sat on the end of the bed holding my tummy in a state of shock. My husband was in a rage. I quietly told my husband about the someone who could end the pregnancy and the someones who would do further tests. My husband was insisting that we could not have a baby with T21. We had to choose termination. I just kept crying saying no no no. My husband argued with me while I just sat and sobbed saying no.

As I said I was told by [Obstetrician] about [Dr. who could terminate pregnancy (wctp)]. Putting Dr. [wctp]'s name into the computer brought up anything but positive results. Instead I was brought to a website of pro-life politics, bashing Dr. [wctp] who I had never heard of before. But luckily the bashing included a link to Dr. [wctp]'s own website. So I did find it that morning. I read it over and over. I realized I was not alone in this decision, and I felt a flood of relief.

[She found an online support group and began connecting with women there.]

Let me side track here and say that being what we all call a T21 Mom is hard. We know our children would most likely have survived well into adulthood. Physical and many medical problems yes. But they would have survived. In cases of T18 or T13 or all the various trisomies out there they know that their child will not make it in the end. Somewhere down the line the child will die if it even survives the first days of life. But to be a T21 Mom requires more rationalizations. We all have many reasons for our choices but in the end they sometimes fall a little flat. So belonging to this [Internet support] group from the start helped me feel not so much isolation. Not so evil.

All of my family called in tears and support. I felt hopeful that we would make it. I did call my best friend. She told me she was sorry for me. But though she is not opposed to abortion I did not receive from her the kind of support I needed. Not then and not since. For her it was never a child of mine. It was like telling a stranger. You get sympathy but no great emotional response. She was wound up in her own troubles. I wanted to say to her look, your wanting out of your marriage is not as bad as me losing a child. You have a choice, I do not. You can leave your husband. I will have to live with a T21 child all my life or the guilt at terminating.

When we found out that Luke had T21, my hub called his sister and asked her to come over. I had already told my family via the phone. His sister gets on my nerves, but she is a nice person and would never say a bad word about anyone. She came over and we told her about the T21. Though she does not approve of abortion she said she understood how we felt. So she was with us and not against us. But she thought we should never tell my mother-in-law. Let her think I miscarried. Well, how could we do that part? Besides my hub wanted her support. Something he has gone all of his life without for the most part. She usually only really is nice to him when she needs money. Otherwise she ignores us. But for some reason he wanted her to act like his mother and support him in all of this. So against my sister-in-law's wishes he went and saw his Mom. She made him cry. She could not condone our actions. Although she herself had 2 abortions while drinking heavily, she could not see how we could go through with all of this. We should have Luke and raise him. She said she would not help us raise him because "retarded" children make her too upset. But still we should do it anyway. Did that make sense? So she was against us. She put an anti-abortion sticker on her car. She started wearing that dumb rose pin. She has made no pretense at support for any of our pain. Her view is that abortion is supposed to cripple the person who chooses it, and that unless we go to confession and then take a Right To Life stance we are not to be forgiven.

The Procedure

As far as the clinic goes, I did find the staff very warm. Caring and kind. It was not easy for me. I was not a good candidate to begin with.

I only have one other child who was delivered by C-section. I was older than most of the women. I have severe anemia. I was a big risk. But I made it.

The eerie part is not remembering any of it. Being in such horrible pain and then seeing the one nurse I loved slipping a needle in my hand. Hearing like a distant echo someone telling me that I should leave the clip alone on my finger. That it told them my vitals. Wiggling my finger. Remembering wiggling my finger back and forth. And then hearing someone tell me to lift my butt up a little bit. Getting ready to say but I can't lift it cause the labor pains are too strong, and yet being able to lift it right up because it was all over. I was in another room. Another bed. It was all over.

Physically I only suffered pain for about 4 hours. Chills were the worst. Shaking so uncontrollably. For the first 2 days of laminaria insertion I was not uncomfortable at all. Worried and scared. But not in pain. Unable to sleep at the hotel. I had fever-like symptoms off and on but nothing too horrible. The third day I started having chills and labor like pain. It hurt to sit, breathe, stand, lay... you name it. But I was also taking pain pills that made time and space seem unreal.

As for the group counseling I think it was great. My hub and I became friends with two other couples. There were six couples altogether. But two of them and us became kind of buddies. One was from [Midwest]. Their baby girl had T18 and so many physical problems it was a wonder she was alive at all. The other couple was from [Canada], and their baby girl had a rare heart defect that had been misdiagnosed until [the woman] was 32 weeks along. I (we) would not have made it without these friends. We all kept each other sane. Talking helped us. We had someone else to lean on. All the husbands kept each other strong. I am glad I met them.

When Luke was born, I saw he had a club foot. I wonder whether that was the tip of the iceberg as far as physical deformities go. I will never know. But I did understand the problems I might have faced. Problems of loneliness for him. Isolation. Mental retardation of course and possible mental illness too. Heart problems. Vision and hearing problems. All of those things. Unlike the commercials where the kids are all sweet smiling little ones, that is not reality to me. I saw them each day [she worked with special education]. And though I loved some of them and liked working with them, I wonder today if they are still alive and where they are now. The ones who were institutionalized worry me most. Where did they go?

The Aftermath of Loss

I got a call from the insurance company through which I have disability insurance. I remember the woman asking in a smart voice why was I on disability if I was just pregnant? After all she said I was "only 26 weeks" along. I remember answering her in a very flat tone like this: "Pay me, don't pay me, the baby is dead. He died. I delivered his little dead body last week. Is that a good enough reason not to be at work?" It kind of summed up the whole thing for me. Needless to say I got disability. My full paycheck. In fact I had a hard time stopping it. They kept sending me checks even after I went back to work.

All I guess I felt then and feel now is that I lost my baby in a way that I would not wish on my enemies. It was my choice. But it was not my wish.

It is the anniversary of Luke's death. I can never bring myself to use the word "termination." Sounds too cold. That is one thing I think any parent of an unborn child needs to realize. They did not terminate something. Sounds too much like they had ants in their kitchen and they called and had them exterminated. Ending a pregnancy by choice is not a clinical event even for those who lead their lives as though it is clinical. It is emotional, and because it is a part of our emotions, it should be viewed as true death. No, I could never ever tell any parent who is facing such a choice that they must think of it as death. Too hard to deal with at that time. But if afterwards they never see it as a death of a child, then I do not know if they can ever truly go forward. Death regardless of how it came about requires grieving. To not grieve puts too much strain on a relationship, a life, a family, a job, all of it.

And I feel most sorry for those who have no one at all to grieve along with and share the sorrow. I think that is why social workers and nurses and doctors and counselors need to push, and forcefully push if need be, a family towards support. Whether they get it from a church group, or a loss group or even the Internet group I found. Until you can freely feel the loss with people who have felt the same type of loss, I do not think that you can really move forward. Covering it up is the best that can be done.

Advice and Interventions

OK, advice for women facing this kind of decision. Look at where you are in life. Try and see the future and what it will hold for you and your family based on the decisions made. Can you handle a sick child for the rest of your life? Is there enough help for that burden to be shared? If not, then do not feel as though this is your cross to bear. Believe in God if you have such beliefs. Be angry and know that you are allowed to be angry. Be sad and share that sorrow with those you love. Go through the grief process as if that child had been alive and known to everyone. For in your heart the child is a child. Not tissue, not a fetus, not cells. A child. And grieving a death is so much healthier and wiser than pretending you have no right to grieve.

For all professionals who handle such cases. Take off the clinical mask and see the person as a person. That could be hard. A person can only take on so much of anyone else's pain. But it hurts no one to touch a shoulder or talk in gentle tones. It hurts no one to show yourself as a kind person rather than a professional. No one should get into this type of field if they are not kind.

As for spouses. Well I am not sure that men ever understand women. Hormonally we are so different. Emotionally women let the water run ever so much more deeply. But men grieve too. And they always want to make it all better. That is a man's role in society. To make it all better. But I feel for the man who cannot touch his own heart and see he too has rights at grief. And it may be helpful to let a woman going through this with a spouse know that she is not alone suffering even if her husband is full of strength. He is just doing his job. But inside he needs the same love and compassion as we women. Men rarely seek help for grief. It is a shame. But maybe some can be guided toward it from a professional angle by just letting them know that it is understood that they are hurting too.

One more thought. If a parent is facing a second or third trimester ending I think they need to be told of options. Options to see the baby afterwards if it is going to be an intact delivery. Options for burial, cremation, or some service. We were told to feel free to make a death notice in a newspaper if it would make us feel better. I did not. People honor their pets in obituaries. Why should we feel we cannot honor a child we wanted and loved and had such great hopes toward. Our doctor said to let those around us pamper us in the ways that people help for any family death. Send us flowers. Bake us cookies. Allow the world to express itself and help us. For some it may make the road easier. Friends from work sent me a gift certificate for a facial and massage at a local salon. They put in the card that they wanted me to know that they knew I needed some pampering. It was very kind. And most important, give the baby a name.

SUMMARY

As this chapter shows, there is no single theoretical framework that can effectively explain prenatal bonding and no single framework that can adequately explain grieving following a perinatal loss. This has larger implications for both maternal–infant attachment and for grief theory. Both topic areas require further refinements that incorporate broader theoretical bases—including biological, psychological, and social understandings.

It is imperative that we begin to equalize the weight given to biological, psychological, and social assessments. These assessments must remain theory-based if they are to be of use in determining effective interventions. We must identify areas in which empirical research can be used to expand theoretical understandings that truly incorporate a biopsychosocial approach. By exploring the nature of prenatal attachment and perinatal bereavement, one can begin to expand on the biological, psychological, and social understandings in each area, furthering the theory base of maternal–infant attachment and grief.

The beginning of a pregnancy is a time of anticipation, uncertainty, and hopes for new beginnings. Even in the best of circumstances, maturational gains also entail losses of accustomed self-image, independence, and madcap ways. When experiences of pregnancy complication and/or pregnancy loss occur, the first loss is the loss of innocence that accompanies these types of losses. In a society in which pregnancy complications and death are hidden, expectations are that everything will go well. The loss of the innocence that allows these expectations is quickly followed by the losses involved with managing fear, uncertainty, medical treatment, and concern for the health of oneself and one's future child. There are no easy answers in these situations. Weighing the attachment to the potential baby against the possibilities of harm that could keep them from living a healthy, full life, as well as against the capabilities the mother, her partner and family, and society provide, means that each situation will have a very unique calculus. When there is a fetal demise, the parents lose the potential child and the growing attachment they had, but they also lose all of the hopes, dreams, and fantasies that they had experienced as they anticipated the birth of a new family member. Despite the fact that these losses are hidden from view and seldom acknowledged, losses at this time are some of the most potent as they occur before the bereaved have the chance to formulate memories to enable grieving rituals and active mourning. Interventions need to be developed that acknowledge and validate the loss/es while also supporting the healthy formation of families during this foundational stage.

3   Infancy and Toddlerhood

Jordan was 3¹/₂ years old when his little brother was born. He had had a relatively charmed life, born at term and developing normally—sleeping through the night at 3 months, sitting at 5 months, walking at a year and using some words to make his wishes known. By the time he was 3, he was beginning to toilet train and was able to speak in short sentences. He was very affectionate with both of his parents, but particularly liked his "cuddle time" with his mother several times a day. Jordan's parents had talked with Jordan about having a new brother and he was excited by the prospect. When Jordan's mom went into labor, his grandmother came to stay with him and they went to the hospital to see his mom and meet their new baby the next day. His parents helped Jordan "hold" his new brother and gave Jordan extra attention and praise for being such a good big brother. Things seemed great.

The following week, Jordan quit using the toilet and had several "accidents" despite his being toilet trained. He was irritable and rejected his mother's advances for cuddle time, though he accepted them at night when she came to his room to read him a bedtime story. Eventually, Jordan told his mother that he changed his mind; he didn't want a little brother anymore.

Jordan had experienced a loss. Though it was normative and matu-rational, he was no longer the sole focus of his mother's attention. He began acting out to gain her attention when his mother was busy caring for his brother. Jordan was also losing his role as "the cute little baby" now that he was an older toddler. Things that adults used to smile and laugh about now inspired reprimands and even spurred his father to say "Jordan, grow up!" when he played with his food. Jordan felt bereft of his mother's attention but had little emotional vocabulary for expressing this—a dynamic that occasionally led to him venting his frustration by hitting his brother with his favorite stuffed dog. Eventu-ally, Jordan found more positive ways to express his feelings and his parents worked hard to give him attention by himself on a regular basis. Jordan resolved his loss by learning about new "big boy" ways of interacting with his parents and new brother.

DEVELOPMENTAL STAGE: TRUST VERSUS MISTRUST AND AUTONOMY VERSUS SHAME

Infancy and toddlerhood are a time of tremendous change physically, psychologically, and socially. Infants are born at around 7 pounds, with little facility for caring for themselves (other than to send dependency signals and hope that their caregivers provide that care in an attuned manner). During infancy, Erikson (1959/1980) theorizes, individuals set a template for whether they believe they will be cared for in an adequate and loving manner. This development of trust if care is trust-worthy, or mistrust if they are not well-cared for, is believed to set the foundation for all future relationships.

By the time the child enters preschool and/or kindergarten, s/he typically weighs around 40 pounds and can walk, run, talk, and articu-late requests for care. The child has moved through Erikson's stage of Autonomy versus Shame (1959/1980) during which s/he has learned to control bodily wastes and has begun the process of gaining control over him or herself and his or her behavior. The child can make friends and play and begin to form attachments that are important in his or her current life, as well as develop the template for relationship styles over a lifetime (Ainsworth, 1969, 1982). The child has not yet entered the broader world of school, and of adults who judge the child, but instead, in ideal circumstances, has parents and relatives who love him or her unconditionally and help promote development. Even under ideal circumstances, infants and toddlers are undergoing rapid changes that exemplify the normative and maturational losses involved with growth.

Biological Development

Newborns are dependent on others for the care they need (nutrition, cleaning and hygiene, and stimulation to promote growth); they are also born with a surprising number of reflexes that help them to survive (Willemsen, 1979). The Moro reflex involves throwing one's arms out and opening one's mouth and is an early reflex movement that occurs when a newborn's head is abruptly moved. It may help the infant send a signal that such abrupt head movements are not welcome as well as help the baby to feel for a stable position. The Babkin reflex of turning toward a soft stimulus on the cheek is an active adaptation to turn and grab a nipple and gain sustenance. The tight grasp a newborn exhibits when anything is placed in his/her grip is the endearing reflex that helps the infant hold on to something solid. These are all reflexes that support survival and promote care from others (Willemsen, 1979).

Infants also differ from older humans in the amount of sleep they require. They spend around 16 hours per day sleeping, with the majority of that time spent in REM (rapid eye movement) sleep, which is believed to promote brain and coordination development. By the time the child enters school at approximately age 5, sleep time has dropped to approximately 10 hours with only about 20% of that time spent in REM sleep (Roffwarg, Muzio, & Dement, 1966).

Newborns are born with all of their sensory abilities, but some require more development and coordination than others. Vision, particularly, is limited by newborns' inability to focus much beyond 7 to 11 inches, hence promoting the stares of interest when held by a caregiver whose face is precisely at the best point of focus. Other senses appear to be relatively intact even at birth, but require experience with the world for the infant to begin to have a context in which to make sense of the stimuli. By the time they can manipulate objects in front of themselves (called midline behavior) they begin to learn and have more control over their own stimulation; this generally occurs between 3 to 5 months of age.

By the age of 4 to 5 years, most healthy children master control of most, if not all, of their bodily functions. They can run, skip, manipulate objects, and use words to express their desires. The proportions of their body and its mass distribution have changed, allowing a gait and motor coordination that was not possible before (Getchell & Robertson, 1989). They have learned to bathe themselves, feed themselves, and generally are at a stage where they can provide self-care, constituting a sense of autonomy (Erikson, 1959/1980). Individual differences of "handedness" and interest in being more sedentary or more active are revealed more fully by this age. Locomotor and brain maturation development from infancy through early school age transforms the individual from a totally dependent being to a being who can assert his or her own wishes and can physically meet his or her own needs (given exterior resources) and self-care.

Psychological Development

The physical movement from dependent being to more independent being has tremendous influence on the psychology of the individual. The infant's experience of being cared for and nurtured in a secure and trustworthy environment sets the stage for an ability to feel safe in beginning to explore the world (Fraiberg, 1959; Mahler, Pine, & Bergman, 1985; Winnicott, 1953, 1953/1965). Indeed, Winnicott (1953/ 1965) was one of the first to articulate the concept of the "good-enough mother" who adapts completely to the infant's needs, but allows "optimum frustration." She is not "perfect" and does not meet every infant or toddler desire. She allows the child to develop the ability to self-soothe and learn, within that child's capacity, to develop new skills for meeting his or her own needs.

This was a critical transition from the classical Freudian theory that held that the mother was the one responsible for any disturbances of the child's psychological growth, with an implication that the mother must be perfectly attuned and informed about the optimal ways to help the growing infant discharge drives. Winnicott (1953, 1953/1965) adapted this concept to allow mothers to "fail" to be perfectly attuned occasionally and asserted that "good-enough" parenting would allow for positive mental health. He further articulated the concept of transitional objects as a strategy toddlers could use as they grew to maintain the presence of the mother without having her actual presence. Transitional objects (such as a special blanket) allow the child to develop a sense of self separate from the mother, while still experiencing the secure base of sensing the mother's presence (via the transitional object associated with the mother) (Winnicott, 1953). Davar (2001) posits an existential object—one that not only replaces the mother when she is not available, but adds the additional quality of an "alive mother" (p.17) that confirms a sense of self by actively seeing and feeling—for the child. She theorizes that infants and toddlers who do not experience an attuned mother/caregiver are in need of an object that allows them to feel seen and cared for rather than invisible. Unlike the inanimate transitional object of Winnicott, Davar's existential object must provide interaction and validation (generally in human form).

Children's attachments and ability to trust early caregivers create a template or schema that directs their attachments later in life. Ainsworth (1969), and later she and her colleagues (Ainsworth, Blehar, Waters, & Wall, 1978), asserted that patterns of ability to tolerate separation from primary caregivers set the template for attachments in the future. These patterns were defined as secure, insecure (with subtypes of anxious avoidant and anxious resistant), and disorganized. These attachment styles are said to develop as a result of the mother's attunement and adequate caregiving; neglectful or abusive parents form patterns for their children that create future interactions and attachments that are insecure, anxious, and/or disorganized (Bacon & Richardson, 2001). Children from infancy to age 4 to 5 are seen as particularly vulnerable to the detrimental consequences of neglect and abuse because these attachment styles have been developed and, without intervention to provide a sense of safety in attachments, will carry into adulthood, creating one unsatisfactory relationship after another (Applegate & Shapiro, 2005; Zilberstein, 2006).

Temperament is a further characteristic that emerges and evolves during the period from infancy to early childhood. Thomas, Chess, and Birch (1970) documented a set of infant temperaments. They saw them as inborn and based on nine characteristics (activity level, rhythmicity, distractibility, approach/withdrawal, adaptability, attention span, intensity, responsiveness, and quality of mood) which, when rated as high or low, fall into three categories of temperament: easy, slow to warm up, and difficult. These temperaments are noticed in the newborn nursery and seem to provide a behavioral template for the infant's behavior stretching through early childhood. It is believed that they can only be moderated in later childhood and adulthood with overt effort.

These temperaments likely have a biological base, but are modified in the interaction with caregivers. For instance, a difficult and fussy infant will push away from the caregiver, will reject new foods, and will seldom allow a full night's sleep. An adult who is also of a difficult temperament will have a challenging time adjusting to this infant style and may have great difficulty providing attuned care, thus amplifying the child's difficult temperament and setting the stage for poor attachment. In contrast, a patient, secure caregiver could help the infant feel safe, help contain him or her when distressed by swaddling, and gently but persistently provide gradated new experiences, without becoming angry and loud with the child. This allows the child to desensitize and learn to accept help in self-soothing and development of strategies to cope with transitions.

Social Development

Another major accomplishment during the time from birth to entry into school is the development of the ability to communicate via language. This opens other capacities such as imagination, play, memory, empathy, and the beginnings of symbolic thought. Babbling and vocalization with affective tones occurs by the age of 6 months (Dale, 1976) and infants seem inclined to do this more and in evolving ways when they receive the feedback of others in their social environment (Tomlinson-Keasey, 1972; Wiegernick, Harris, Simeonson, & Pearson, 1974). Advances in neuroscience have suggested that infants begin to process the language they are hearing long before they can speak and that this lays down the pattern for beginning exploration of use of language (Dehaene-Lambertz, Hertz-Pannier, & Dubois, 2006). The vital need for language to allow social interactions is further confirmed in the assertion that deaf infants must be exposed to sign language in early infancy to promote easy acquisition and ability to be socially involved to be able to learn (Magnuson, 2000). The primacy of language (signed or vocal) is clearly a major factor in ability to interact socially.

From infancy through early childhood, the family (however constituted in that child's environment) ideally creates the social interaction that both promotes the infant's development and allows him or her to have a sense of his or her own self-efficacy (Leach, 1984, 1986; Shapiro, Shapiro, & Paret, 2001; Spock, 1976; Willemsen, 1979). Even when socialization into customary social norms has not been successful, interventions to repair the quality of the parent–child relationship appear to improve the child's ability to interact acceptably, as when aggressive children become less so after improved parenting (Granic, O'Hara, Pepler, & Lewis, 2007). Further, the quality of the maternal attachment early in life is theorized to have a strong impact on the child's adaptation to the school environment, particularly in the form of managed (or not) anxiety (Dallaire & Weinraub, 2007). It is intuitive that children who have high anxiety in first grade are less likely to have a positive experience and this can set the stage for social and learning difficulties in the future.

Further, when parents were less emotionally available in early childhood (e.g., because of alcoholism, emotional distancing, or substance use), children exhibited less ability to emotionally self-regulate and exhibited more externalizing behaviors upon entrance to school (Eiden, Edwards, & Leonard, 2007). The converse is true as well; when children received attuned caregiving, they exhibited more empathy, eagerness to perform well, and prosocial behavior (Kochanska, Forman, & Coy, 1999). This ability to fit within the school environment is critical to children's social development. Aside from the formal learning of skills and knowledge that occurs in schools, the development of peer relationships, the ability to accept and adapt to constructive feedback, and other social skill development are part of the implicit curriculum of schools as they promote higher levels of cognition and social development (Case, 1985; Fischer, 1980).

LOSSES EXPERIENCED IN INFANCY AND EARLY CHILDHOOD

Loss of Caregiving

Literature on the development of infants and toddlers very quickly emphasizes how important the primary caregiver (generally the mother) is for the individual's healthy development. During this stage, the infant or toddler's whole life is bound by the care and stimulation s/he receives from caregivers; therefore, the most traumatic loss endured at this stage is the death of a primary caregiver and/or parent. Although death of the parent at this stage is less common, the infant/toddler is likely to experience the loss of the caregiver in both normal developmental ways as well as more dramatic ways. Certainly, the use of optimal frustration, as Winnicott (1953/1965) discussed it, is a mild form of losing the caregiver; the felt need/desire of the infant/toddler is not met immediately and s/he feels abandoned. Because infants have not yet grasped the idea of object constancy (the idea that people continue to exist even if the baby does not see them), when the mother is gone the baby feels as if the mother is lost forever. The same phenomenon that does not allow the infant to know that his or her mother continues to exist also allows him/her to adapt to the surroundings of the present moment with great joy when mother does return. These are normal, maturational losses that contribute to the development of the child. As s/he begins to recognize that his or her mother is sometimes absent, but returns and generally provides attuned care, the concepts of object constancy grow and a sense of security develops. These types of maturational loss occur within a secure and trustworthy relationship and promote development.

Another maturational loss that deserves mention is the more abrupt loss an older infant or toddler experiences at the time of a sibling's birth. The child (one hopes) has been the "apple of the parent's eye" to that point and has received attention and care without needing to share the parents' attention. At the birth of a sibling, the infant or toddler is abruptly moved to the side while family members and friends come to visit the new baby, bring gifts to the new baby, and generally give attention and care to the new baby. The young child may have even been looking forward to having a new brother or sister, only to experience a wish that the new baby would disappear. Like Jordan in the opening vignette, reactions to this type of loss range from dysfunctional attempts to get parental attention with poor behavior, to developmental regressions resulting from grief, to overt aggression toward the new baby and others. Providing reassurance of care and nurture is critical to the child processing the grief of losing the parents' sole attention and finding new ways of accepting the existence of the new baby (Faber & Mazlish, 1987/1998).

In contrast, children born to mothers who are experiencing major depressive disorder and/or postpartum depression do not have these experiences of finely tuned optimal frustration geared to the baby's ability to tolerate the separation and delay in meeting the infant's desires. Indeed, children born to mothers who had prenatal onset of depression or onset right at the time of delivery may never experience the sense of total care and attunement that infants ideally receive to allow them to develop attachments and a sense of trust in the world. It is ideal if the father or other surrogate caregiver meet the needs of the infant at this point. Often, other adults believe that the mother's mere physical presence is enough to keep herself and her baby safe and she is deemed capable of managing her own and the baby's care. Without appropriate supports in place, this can lead to tragic outcomes when postpartum depression occasionally evolves into postpartum psychosis (Abrams & Curran, 2007; Field, Diego, & Hernandez-Reif, 2006).

Parental depression has ramifications beyond infancy and toddlerhood; women who have early-onset depression have children who have dysregulated emotional patterns at age 4, decreased perceived competence ratings at age 5, and decreased social acceptance when entering school (Maughan, Cicchetti, Toth, & Rogosch, 2007). It seems that women's depressive symptoms include an externalized locus of control and more difficulty managing parenting stress. These symptoms may act as mediators to either lax or overreactive parenting, which in turn places children at risk for poor attachment, a sense of mistrust, and a defensive detachment as attachment needs and attunement are sporadically and inconsistently met (Gerdes et al., 2007). There is strong and consistent evidence that the caregiver's attunement and emotional care provision assist the infant in the development of the neurobiological substrate that enables the infant to develop attachments and the ability to begin to learn self-soothing (Applegate & Shapiro, 2005). This is a circular process that builds on itself as the attached infant begins learning self-soothing behaviors from the caregiver and ultimately begins to develop mastery of his/her own affect regulation (Applegate & Shapiro, 2005). When care is unavailable because of separations from the caregiver resulting from maternal depression or other reasons such as foster care or extended hospitalizations, these neurobiological substrates in the brain have less opportunity to develop; they negatively influence the infant's ability to engage fully in other attachments and in developing affect regulation (Shapiro, Shapiro, & Paret, 2001).

Loss of the infant's or toddler's caregivers because of depression, removal from parental care, or early hospitalizations are losses that we do not view as normal maturational developmental losses. They are losses that occur as a result of life circumstances and are often not recognized as losses that may benefit from remediation. When not recognized as losses, the tendency is to assure that the infant is receiving care for basic needs such as nutrition, shelter, and hygiene, yet less attention is often paid to the infant's need for an attuned and consistent caregiver. In highlighting the ramifications of these types of losses, we hope to enfranchise the loss so that support and attempts to remediate the loss can occur.

Death of a Caregiver

Certainly the most detrimental loss is the actual death of the primary caregiver. When the attachment has formed, but the caregiver falls ill and/or dies abruptly, the infant has no language with which to process this loss and it appears unlikely that the infant has any concept of death that can assist in understanding his or her feelings of loss. There is general consensus that children under age 2 to 3 are not able to understand death, particularly its finality, though they do experience separation anxiety and exhibit the reactions of protest and despair first theorized by Bowlby (1977, 1980/1998) to attach to maternal separations and loss of any duration (American Academy of Pediatrics, 2000; Black, 1998; Willis, 2002). Parental death has classically been associated with higher levels of psychopathology in later years (Birtchnell, 1970, 1980; Brown, Harris, & Copeland, 1971) though more recent scholarship indicates that the responsiveness of the child's remaining caregiver and that person's ability to provide safe and consistent care is a better predictor of resilience or psychopathology than the mere event of a parental death (Christ, 2000; Hope & Hodge, 2006; Silverman & Worden, 1993/2006).

It remains somewhat unclear whether a child from birth to 2 or 3 processes death as anything other than separation anxiety that is not remedied by crying for the return of the caregiver. Reponses tend to take the form of bodily symptoms and regressions to earlier states of functioning. Therefore, the recommendations for care of children who experience a significant loss to death at this young age include assuring that there is a caregiver who can provide attuned, nurturing, and consistent care (despite the possibility of the caregiver's own grief), keeping the infant/toddler's routine as predictable and consistent as possible, and allowing for regression such as bedwetting, refusal to feed oneself, and other self-care that may have developed prior to the loss (American Academy of Pediatrics, 2000; Hames, 2003; Hope & Hodge, 2006; Willis, 2002). Despite the belief that children under 2 or 3 do not have the ability to conceptualize death, it should be clear that they are grieving in a manner different from adults, but no less intensely. Crenshaw (2002) clearly identifies the tendency to disenfranchise children's grief in detrimental ways by ignoring, minimizing, or otherwise not recognizing this different form of expressing grief as true grief and mourning. This is particularly a danger for infants and young toddlers; as we noted previously, though their grief is expressed quite differently, reassurance and nurture are necessary for these youngsters to move through their response and to continue to thrive. McIntosh's reading at the end of this chapter shows the long-term effects of parental loss on a very young child and the ways that loss can affect adult life.

As the toddler moves toward early school age, concepts of death evolve (Christ, 2000). Children who are 4 to 5 begin to have a basic understanding that death involves a separation from living people and a cessation of breathing and heartbeat on the part of the deceased. Yet, they have little sense of the permanence and finality of death (American Academy of Pediatrics, 2000). One study of children 3 to 5 years old found that the struggle to understand the irreversibility of death led to "befuddlement" (Christ, 2000, p. 75), intensified reactions to other separations, and repetitious questions about the location and condition of the deceased. Further, a sense of interchangeability or a sense that the lost one just needs to be replaced with another sibling/mother/father/grandparent adds to the challenge of the surviving parent's need to support, nurture, and respond to the child while s/he asks disturbing questions (Christ, 2000).

Magical thinking is also often in evidence at this stage of development and children may believe their angry thoughts caused the death of the deceased (American Academy of Pediatrics, 2000). Clear explanations grounded in concrete realities provide important ways for children to begin to understand the death and what it means. Attendance at funerals to see the body and understand the concrete nature of death is often a positive strategy as long as the child can be protected from uncontrolled outbursts of emotion, which they may find more disturbing than the death itself (Willis, 2002). Preparing the child, answering questions, and providing for the child to be with a trusted adult who is not personally severely affected by the death are all useful plans for assisting 3- to 5-year-olds through the process of mourning a significant caregiver.

Loss of a Child's Own Health

A final type of loss that young children may experience is the loss of their own health and potential death. Because of their difficulty in understanding death, children who are sick with life-threatening illnesses often have such intense medical care experiences that they and their families are caught in the moment-to-moment experiences of treatment. Hospitals that provide care for infants soon after birth and in toddlerhood are now much more attuned to the needs of children this age to maintain and continue to develop attachment relationships with their caregivers. They have embraced family-centered care models that encourage parents to be at the baby's bedside. Nevertheless, babies in institutional care or in foster care are experiencing a separation from their primary caregivers and it is important for social workers and others to acknowledge these losses and work to promote attachments to consistent and available caregivers (see Sinclair reading, p. 94).

Families often want to avoid discussion of possible death (something young children may not understand on the level of finality) and children themselves are more focused on the experience of pain, separation from family, and/or reactions to their perceptions of their caregivers' stress. Acute lymphoblastic leukemia is one of the more common life-threatening illnesses in this age group and survivors tend to experience educational delays, memory deficits, and poorer self-concept with depression, despite teacher's rating them as better behaved within the classroom (Coniglio & Blackman, 1995). Few studies delineate the experience of children coping with life-threatening illness at this young age (Felder-Puig et al., 1998; Lansky, List, & Ritter-Sterr, 1986; Schwartz & Drotar, 2006).

PARENTAL LOSS OF AN INDIVIDUAL AT THIS AGE

Death of an Infant or Toddler

The death of a child is always experienced as a life-changing event and usually as a trauma (Klass, 1996; Rando, 1993). Children from infancy through early childhood are often seen as the most vulnerable humans, inspiring a high degree of responsibility toward the well-being of the child on the part of the parent/s, possibly as part of the continuum of attachment based in ethological theories (Bowlby, 1980/1998). These early deaths are complicated by the fact that few outside the family knew the child yet, particularly when a child dies in infancy. The ability of memory to sustain and comfort is more limited because of the limited time the child lived, yet this also leaves parents open to having more hopes and dreams about who the child may have turned out to be.

Klass (1996) describes the importance of the social world sharing in the parents' grief and acknowledging the parents' loss, yet this is precisely what is often limited, particularly when the infant is quite young; this limitation also extends into toddlerhood. This lack of recognition by society seems to mirror a myth that the connection a parent feels is dependent on the length of the child's life. This myth may comfort those who remain uninformed and distant from the bereaved parents, but the reality is that parents grieve deeply and intensely regardless of the age of the child (Rando, 1993). Klass followed bereaved parents and found that they moved through stages he called "into their grief," "well along in their grief," and "resolved as much as it will be." This final stage is a comfort to most parents as an outcome because it does not imply (as words like "closure" and "acceptance" do) that the parent is to move on and forget or willingly accept what has happened, neither of which is possible. Often, the grieving itself is a comfort for parents as it aids their continued connection to their deceased child. Like a parent Klass quotes, other parents wonder "Will you forgive me if I go on?" The phenomenon of trying to find ways of memorializing one's child, whether through participation in groups like Compassionate Friends or by creating legislation related to the child's death (e.g., Megan's law for Megan Kanka) or by maintaining a charity in the child's name [Alex's Lemonade Stand for Alexandra (Alex) Scott], is also a way in which parents continue the bonds with their children (Klass, 1996). Parents have a strong tendency to find multiple ways of continuing their bonds with a deceased child.

Loss of the Idealized Child

Another loss parents experience in regard to their infants and occasionally toddlers is much less dramatic, but a loss nonetheless. The bond with a baby starts long before that baby is delivered and parents develop dreams about how they believe their baby will look, act, and progress (Diamond, Diamond, & Jaffe, 2001). The loss of the idealized child is part of nearly every parent's experience as s/he adapts to the child who has been born in contrast to the one envisioned prior to birth. Although this is seldom a loss that is recognized, it becomes even more poignant and pointed when the new baby (or toddler) is diagnosed with a developmental delay, congenital condition, or other anomaly.

For parents who receive the news that their child has some degree of impairment that will create challenges for his or her growth, the parent must mourn the dream child while also mourning the loss of the typical child. Carolyn Faust Piro describes this experience in her reading at the end of this chapter. Aside from the necessity of making medical appointments to discover diagnoses and provide treatments, parents must also cope with the social ramifications as family and acquaintances learn about the child's condition/s. Further, the self-image of the parent, particularly the mother, is often affected as she wonders why she "failed" to bring a healthy child to birth and wonders if there was some reason for the occurrence of the disability. The stigma of disability (Goffman, 1963) is not socially just, but it exists nonetheless and the woman and her family often experience some of the same stigma (Ladd-Taylor & Umansky, 1998; Phillips, 1999). Adjustment to these circumstances and bonding with the child she has, rather than the envisioned one, requires a small degree of mourning for the idealized infant, but this becomes even greater when the discrepancies between what was expected and what the reality is become clear.

MATURATIONAL AND OTHER LOSSES EXPERIENCED AT THIS AGE

Birth and Gradual Loss of Complete Care

One of the most common (probably universal) normative maturational losses at this age is poignantly described by Viorst (1986, p. 9):

> We begin life with loss. We are cast from the womb without an apartment, a charge plate, a job or a car. We are sucking, sobbing, clinging, helpless babies. Our mother interposes herself between us and the world, protecting

us from overwhelming anxiety. We shall have no greater need than this need for our mother.

Aside from this initial loss at birth, infancy and toddlerhood are defined by the optimal frustration experienced as the mother gently pulls away and allows the infant or toddler to develop his or her own self-soothing and self-entertainment skills. This necessarily involves losing the company and total security provided to that point. Even as the toddler moves into early childhood, there are often losses experienced normatively and maturationally, as behaviors that were once deemed cute (putting food in one's hair or suddenly sitting down and refusing to move) are no longer viewed as cute and can actually inspire anger in the adults.

In more drastic cases, the mother or caregiver is totally unable to provide safety and a secure base. As described earlier, children of depressed caregivers experience losses that negatively affect their development. Even more problematic, some children are abused or neglected by their parents and, although this damage is significant, it often pales in comparison to the possibility that a child-welfare decision may be made to remove the child from his or her home. Once this occurs, a cycle of trauma, acting out, and removal to a new home is often set in motion having detrimental effects on children's abilities to develop and maintain attachments (Shapiro, Shapiro, & Paret, 2001). Even when the child is adopted, s/he may "provoke rejection not only to test the commitment of the new caregivers but also to experience an intense relationship with the 'other' " (Shapiro et al., 2001, p. 39). Testing tends to occur repeatedly, leading to many losses of both caregivers and peer relationships, exhibiting the unfortunate dynamic of how one loss can start a pattern of repeated losses.

Transitions of caregiving environments are particularly problematic at this stage. Memory and anticipation are not well developed. As Leach describes "Because he can not think ahead, the toddler typically cannot defer gratification for a minute, nor calmly accept its being deferred by anyone else. What he wants, he wants now" (1986, p. 293). This is just one aspect of how toddlers then experience a sense of loss in multiple ways on a daily basis as their desires are deferred for practical or other reasons. Only consistent, attuned, and predictable care provides the support the toddler needs as s/he experiences the loss of being the total center of attention and learns to rely on him or her self and to trust the structure and routine, even as s/he is not quite ready to let go of external sources of structure more generally. When caregiving environments are changing, this routine and structure are not predictable and the child feels destabilized and lost. These losses too can create long-lasting effects as the toddler adopts a mistrustful attitude toward caregivers and, as Erikson would predict, possibly delays moving into an autonomous stage (Erikson, 1959/1980).

READINGS

Following are readings by Virginia McIntosh, Carolyn Faust Piro, and Tara Sinclair. McIntosh describes some of the long-term effects of losing a parent early in life, although, in reality, her client loses both parents, one to death and one to depression. Faust Piro describes loss from the other side as she describes one family's experience of having a child diagnosed with Down syndrome. Tara Sinclair's reading provides a bridge to elementary school as she addresses how the multiple losses entailed in foster care affect a child who was removed from her mother during toddlerhood and continued in various alternate care homes as she moved toward school age.

STARTING WITH ABANDONMENT AND LOSS

Virginia McIntosh, LCSW, BCD

Virginia (Ginny) McIntosh has had a private practice outside Philadelphia for 30 years and enjoys doing individual and couple therapy with adolescents and adults. Previously, she did clinical social work with inpatients, outpatients, and people with chronic schizophrenia at the Eastern PA Psychiatric Institute and group and family therapy at The Institute of PA Hospital. More recently, she has enjoyed teaching at Widner University School of Social Work and Bryn Mawr Graduate School of Social Work and Social Research in their master degree programs. She is currently on the faculty at the Gestalt Institute of Philadelphia. As past-president of the PA Society for Clinical Social Work, she helped usher in the Clinical Social Work License. In 2007, she received a Leadership Award from her alma mater, the University of Pennsylvania

School of Social Policy and Practice. She was inducted into the National Academies of Practice in the same year.

Adult Whose Father Has Died

A 30-year-old Italian woman, Lucia, came to me for therapy because she learned in her current marital therapy that she is "always running" and experiencing constant stress. Her husband and marital therapist don't understand why she is so driven to earn money as when she was a young child she inherited a few hundred thousand dollars from her father at the time of his death. The money has multiplied many times over since then. Now she is working a full-time professional job and taking care of four children and her home. She is suffering from physical symptoms of stress: chest pain, back problems, and gynecological symptoms. She said, "I'm killing myself while having bag lady fantasies."

When I inquired about her history, she revealed that she grew up in a mid-Atlantic state as an only child. Her father was a craftsman who died suddenly. Although provided for financially, her mother was in shock and depressed after his death and was somewhat distant from Lucia. She left her child with relatives while she tried to deal with her shock. So my client's sense of abandonment was profound. This sense of abandonment prevailed throughout her life.

When her father died, she was a child who had yet to attain a sense of object constancy, usually attained at about the age of 3. Although she had a growing attachment to father, she was not able to mentally hold the good father and bad father in mind at the same time. Separation and individuation was yet to happen. This leaves us with the question of how such a young child can absorb such a shock, loss, and abandonment? Death is also an impossible concept for a 2-year-old to grasp. She wouldn't even have language for such loss and abandonment, only hurt and anger. Susan Anderson (Anderson, 2000) speaks of withdrawal as the second stage of the abandonment process.

The withdrawal stage is like being in withdrawal from an addiction. During the worst of it, you can't get away from your conviction that without your lost loved one your life is over. This belief comes from the child within you. The child keeps telling you that you must get your loved one to come back at all costs or you'll die.

A primary relationship is a matter of survival for a child; no infant can exist without its nurturer.

My client evidenced internalization of these feelings in the form of primitive rage and hurt. We now know that her emotional brain's amygdala and hippocampus stored such loss and shock in her memory before the cerebral cortex was able to absorb it. Since the amygdala receives input about perceived threats directly from the sensory organs (i.e., eyes and ears, etc.), without processing it through the cerebral cortex first, the reactions are pure emotion and stored in one's emotional memory bank, available to be called up in the future. The logical mind processes such events in the cerebral cortex at a slower rate and does not receive the cues until after the amygdala does.

This left Lucia with a sensitivity to being rejected. Susan Anderson calls this the third stage of abandonment rejection. Internalizing means incorporating an emotional experience, making it a part of yourself, and letting it change your deepest beliefs. It is an insidious process. You don't realize how much it affects you.

Internalizing the rejection is how your body incorporates the wound of abandonment. You have taken it to heart. By internalizing rejection, you injure yourself. During the internalizing stage, the self searches desperately for its lost love, then turns its rage and frustration against itself. The wound becomes a self-contained system where self-doubt incubates and fear becomes ingrown.

Although Lucia did internalize a sensitivity to being rejected and left out, she developed good defenses so her school years had a lot of accomplishments and acknowledgments. One defense against the strong feelings of abandonment is the determination to be self-sufficient and not need to depend on anyone. Lucia used these defenses all her life. Both sides of her family have professional grandparents, aunts and uncles, so inherent expectations were high to carry on the family legacy both professionally and with progeny. But Lucia had her own inner drive to perform well since her early years of school. She excelled academically whenever possible. It is doubtful that her mother put much pressure on her to do well in school but did expect Lucia to be there for her. At the same time, Lucia could not rely on her mother to help her work out her projects or needs. She was fending for herself as a preschooler and continuously after that. So the sense of abandonment continued to the point that she had no realization that life could be any different. She consistently operated as if she had to do everything herself.

Concurrent with this was her constant vigilance against sudden shocks that came from nowhere. She had to be prepared for any possible loss or drastic change in her life, a sort of Chicken Little's "the sky is falling" phenomenon. When the best defense is a good offense, the defense is perfectionism, which feeds her drive to be self-sufficient. But now that she has children, she can't do this. Her life was turned upside down. New events from left field were happening all the time and she didn't have great models on flexibility or parenting. Her defenses weren't working and her self-doubt got stronger. Her physical symptoms became worse so she was often at the doctor's office, and often they wanted to do exploratory operations.

It was after meeting her husband that she fully realized her sense of abandonment and heretofore unrecognized need for someone in her life on whom she could rely. She had not recognized her lack of support until she met him. This was not a welcome realization, as it brought up a lot of hurt and anger and profound grief from losing her father. Although she had felt his loss at all the normative occasions when girls are expected to show up with a father and when she saw girls doing all kinds of things with their fathers, the awareness of the rage and hurt was defended against by performing at a perfect pitch. The sense of loss became ever stronger in her marital years. It was like having a man in her life was a real-life reminder of what she had missed. Watching her children relate to their father made her feel alone. The rage and hurt rose up every time things weren't going well and her somewhat elusive husband usually was the target.

Lucia felt helpless in face of these intense feelings but she couldn't grieve. She tried to put words to the feelings but the images of her father and she together were so sparse that she felt totally inadequate to the task. When I named her feeling as rage, she rose up in the chair and embraced it as, "YES, RAGE." I could almost hear the toddler in her screaming at the top of her little lungs. Then she sat down in torrents of tears. She was a little girl again. She talked about feeling this in her chest and stomach but then there were those horrible times when she felt empty. "Rage is a protest against pain. It is how we fight back, a refusal to be victimized by someone leaving us, the way we reverse the rejection….Others may not realize the scope and depth of our wound. They brush up against it with no inkling of the pain they cause. We stand guard, protector of our emerging selves."

Lucia went through this constellation of feelings several times in several sessions. She had discussed all this many times before. As I continued to validate and help her name her feelings, she was now able to cry and grieve, which naturally took a long time.

In the end, I decided to try to do eye movement desensitization reprocessing (EMDR) with her to help with the rage. Lucia chose a picture of her father in his hospital bed with everyone standing around him. She cried heavily during the EMDR and then I asked her if there were any pictures of her and her father together, because all the mementos that her mother had given Lucia were so unrelated to her. She said there was one of him holding her, so we worked with that. She visualized that picture while I continued the EMDR. Afterward, I also asked her what her father's strengths were, which she enumerated. I asked her to picture him behind her shoulder now as an adult while he invested those qualities in her and his saying that he is always with her. In subsequent weeks and months, Lucia reported feeling better and didn't complain of the emptiness. Her rage decreased and she took to talking about her intermittent but considerable anger. More important, the physical symptoms subsided to the point the doctor discharged her.

Lucia was taking more time for herself and having an easier time prioritizing her family over her career. It took more work for her to allow herself to spend money without great worry. This fear to spend money was interlocked with her fear of being left and being alone. She couldn't fathom relying on her husband because, of course, she hadn't relied on anyone before except herself. She slowly, by inches, built a trust in him, and his strengths were no longer wiped out by her perception of and anger at his weaknesses. This indicated that she was no longer thinking, believing, and feeling like a 2-year-old. She could hold his strengths and weaknesses in her mind at the same time. She still got angry and disgusted with some of his behavior but learned to lean on his strengths and listening capacity when she was concerned.

One day Lucia announced that they would be moving to a much larger house and going on an expensive family vacation. I asked her what happened to the bag lady? She said that she was still afraid but realized that her father was with her, she is capable of earning more money and her husband was coming around. Lucia continued to work on her complicated feelings about her mother and her ways of abandoning her, as well as on her defenses and her marriage. When I pursued this, it was clear that her attachment to her husband had grown and was much stronger than her fears that he'll leave her or she'll leave him. She understood that her father's money was to protect her and she now understands that it is also there to help her fulfill her dreams. This meaning of his death became a solidity within her that she had not demonstrated before. According to Neimeyer (1998, p. 90), "The attempt to reconstruct a world of meaning is the central process in the experience of grieving." It certainly seems true in this case.

BABY JAMES

Carolyn Faust Piro, BA

Carolyn Faust Piro is a graduate student in the School of Social Work at Rutgers University in Camden, New Jersey. Her interests are diverse: developmental disabilities, mental health, women's issues, and sexuality. She is a strong advocate for and fiercely loving mother of her four sons. Her goal is to open a therapeutic practice that also advocates for individuals with developmental disabilities and/or mental illness and their caregivers.

The Neonatal Intensive Care Unit (NICU) is a place of hope and of loss. The joy of parenthood can be devastatingly replaced with the diagnosis of a severe disability or the loss of a child. The social worker has little time, perhaps a few days or weeks, to connect with caregivers and support them during this fragile period. Caregiver grief can begin with many trials—loss of a child, severe illness, or diagnosis of a disability. The social worker will be called upon to assess the needs and bond with the caregiver. Some cases are simple and others can be very complex.

Case Presentation

Dave and Susan were married for almost 9 years. They now have four sons. John and Liam, their two oldest sons, have special needs. Liam has Fragile-X syndrome, an inheritable condition that causes mental retardation and severe anxiety and behavior disorders. Andrew, their third son, is typically developing. The oldest child is 6 years old. James, their fourth child, was scheduled to be delivered by cesarean section on a Tuesday. The prior weekend the mother experienced an uncomfortable feeling followed by bleeding. She was admitted Sunday night and the baby was delivered by cesarean that evening.

Susan claimed to know that something was wrong immediately by the tone of the baby's cry. James was born weighing 10 lbs, 8 oz but Susan reported "he mewed like a kitten, I expected him to howl." Because James's birth was Susan's fourth cesarean, a nurse from NICU was present. Despite the mother's concerns voiced in the delivery room, James was transferred to the newborn nursery.

The father accompanied James to the nursery, while the mother was monitored in postop. James was examined by the newborn nurses and found to be unable to maintain his body temperature and his blood sugar levels were low. He was placed under a heating lamp. When his blood oxygen levels were discovered to be low, he was transferred to the NICU. Doctors determined that James had a hole between the upper chambers of his heart, a systemic infection of unknown origin, pulmonary hypertension, and hypoglycemia. The hospital social work department was notified of the case to offer support for the family.

Dave and Susan were challenging clients. They had both experienced tremendous loss with the diagnosis of their two older children. Despite being a carrier of Fragile-X, they conceived a fourth time. Dave was very optimistic about the pregnancy. Susan, however, began therapy during the fifth month of pregnancy. She was extremely nervous about the pregnancy. Dave and Susan were experiencing loss at different phases. This case is one of those rare times when the client knows the systems of support; they had experienced loss, need, and services with their prior children. Susan was pessimistic, Dave was optimistic. Susan seemed to be skeptical of anything anyone could do for her that hadn't already been offered. Dave appeared to be joyful at the birth of their fourth son. This case presents four needs: meeting Susan on her level of grief, supporting Dave in his happiness over their child's birth, bringing Susan and Dave to some common agreement of the birth of James, and helping Susan and Dave understand the results of James's impending diagnosis and prognosis.

James was in the hospital for 10 days. He required a platelet transfusion and his blood sugar was not stabilized until he was 6 days old. Susan was discharged on day 5. She came to the hospital four times per day and pumped breast milk at night. Dave came in the evening to visit with James. Susan would stay at the hospital for up to 3 hours, holding and nursing James. When he slept, she would read in the NICU lounge.

The social work department decided to send two workers to speak with Susan while she was at the hospital to determine the primary phase of grief she was experiencing and how she was coping with James's hospitalization. Susan appeared pleasant, concerned, yet her affect was not reflecting the level of conflict that was occurring between her personal experience and that of her husband. The initial meeting was relaxed, focusing on James and how Susan was coping with caring for her children at home. Susan voiced concerns about James genetically, asking everyone who saw him if they believed there was anything genetically wrong with him, asking if they saw any physical signs. Her primary concern was not if James had a genetic disability. She wondered out loud if he could have a third condition that she would have to learn about. She already had developed expertise in autism and Fragile-X. She joked often that James had come to the right family, that he would not be getting pity but love and support. The social workers began by letting Susan talk, knowing she had extensive experiences with her other two children and that perhaps she just needed someone to listen. Here is a piece of the initial conversation after the social workers introduced themselves and asked her how she was feeling:

Susan: I knew something was wrong the minute he was born. I just don't understand. If something was going to be wrong, I wanted it to be something I already know about, not a third syndrome, that I have learn.

Social Worker1: Are you thinking that James has a syndrome?

Susan: I look at him and he is beautiful. Mary (the nurse) said his eyes may be deep set, what could that indicate?

Social Worker2: It doesn't indicate anything until the blood work comes back. How is everything at home?

Susan: Okay, the kids miss me, I miss them terribly. My parents are helping out, they've hired a baby sitter, but I don't know if she can handle the kids.

Social Worker2: You can stay at home more if you want. James is in good hands here, he has your pumped milk. You can give yourself some time to rest at home.

Susan: (chuckling) Rest doesn't happen at home. I am actually getting a break by being here.

Social Worker2: I bet. It must be really challenging to balance it all. How are your supports at home? Does your family help?

Susan: Financially. My family supports me with money. I do not get much emotional support. My parents had a very difficult time when I was pregnant. They could not understand why I was pregnant. I didn't want to be pregnant. I can't have another child with special needs, especially Fragile-X Syndrome. It's beyond challenging. And my husband is no help. He doesn't see how overwhelmed I am. I got my tubes tied during the cesarean and he's mad at me for doing that. He doesn't get it. He's in lala land.

Social Worker1: It is tough when parents are out of sync with birth-control decisions. Is there anything we can do to help?

Susan: No, thanks for coming by. I'll find you if I need you. I have a therapist that I've been seeing since I was 5 months pregnant. He specializes with families who have children with special needs. He's my biggest support right now.

Susan appeared to have no true supports other than her therapist. Without saying it exactly, Susan expressed feelings of isolation, mistrust, and anger. The social workers agreed that building a relationship with Susan would be their first priority.

The results from James's umbilical cord blood test returned on day 7 of his hospitalization. James was diagnosed with mosaic Down syndrome. The results of the Fragile-X test would not be available until he was 6 weeks old. It was possible for James to have both Fragile-X and Down syndrome since the disorders affect different genetic pairings. The doctor and the nurse practitioner decided to give Dave and Susan the diagnosis together. When Dave arrived at the NICU, he was happy. He was under the impression that the news was hopeful because it would not have been Fragile-X. Susan had a sense that it could not be good news and that it was the "third syndrome" that she had been dreading. The conversation among the doctor, nurse practitioner (PNP), and the parents went as follows:

Doctor: How are you doing today?

Dave: Good, we're good. What's the news?

Doctor: We have James's initial chromosome screening. It appears he has trisomy 21 mosaicism.

Susan: Mosaicism, I know what that is, but what's trisomy 21. I just can't think right now.

PNP: Down syndrome. I'm sorry.

Susan: Oh, my God. It's Down syndrome? He's got Down syndrome?

Dave: What? Down syndrome. But he doesn't look Downs.

Susan: It's mosaic, it's not as strong as full Down syndrome, right?

Doctor: Well, we can't really tell that now. We can arrange for a geneticist to see him. We've already ordered another test to be performed, just to make sure.

Susan: (crying) I can't believe it. Why, why does this happen? Three?

PNP: I am sorry. It's always the nice people who get the worst news.

Susan: I'm not that nice. I just can't believe it.

Dave: I want that second test performed. I want you to be sure.

Doctor: I will let you know as soon as the results come in.

Susan was devastated by the news that James had mosaic Down syndrome. She immediately went into the NICU nursery to hold James. The social work department had been notified ahead of time about when Susan and Dave would be receiving the news. The same pair that met with Susan earlier found them in the nursery with James. Susan was crying.

Susan: I guess you knew, didn't you?

Social Worker1: Yes, the doctor told us. I am so sorry.

Susan: I probably shouldn't have wished for anything. (silence) He is still a beautiful boy, isn't he?

Social Worker2: Most definitely. And you are good parents.

Susan: Yes, I guess he came to the right parents, didn't he? (she talks to James) You're out of luck kid, if you want pity. We know the deal…you're gonna get a lot of love, but no breaks.

Dave: Yes, he is beautiful. There's still a chance, though…

Susan: No, there isn't a chance. You don't get it, do you? He's got Down syndrome and now we have to wait for the Fragile-X results.

Dave did not respond. The social workers realized that this was not an area in which they could support the spouses together. It is difficult to work with a couple who are at different stages of grief. The social workers kept their focus on James and supported each parent individually. They had prepared information on mosaic Down syndrome to give to the parents. They made themselves available to the parents, but left them to continue their conversation.

James was released from the hospital when he was 10 days old. During the last 4 days of his stay, the social workers stopped in to visit Susan and Dave, mostly just to listen. They particularly focused on Susan, whose isolation was the biggest concern. With her permission the social workers contacted the county early intervention program and began the process for James to receive services. They continued to reach out to her with phone calls for 6 months after James was discharged. The social workers called to congratulate Susan when the Fragile X test was negative, using this moment to help build some optimism for Susan. Susan adjusted to the changes in her life and continued with private therapy.

This case is important, because it shows the importance of social work services even when the social worker has few concrete resources to offer a client. The fact that Susan had an extended history of loss and experience with social services was daunting to the social workers, yet they relied on the primary social work tool of support, which was to simply listen and offer to help with tasks that would ease Susan's responsibilities. Even when a family is versed in the experience of loss, diagnosis, the loss of the dream of having a typical birth and child-raising experience, and seemingly "resistant" to services, the offer of empathy and a listening ear can ease the challenges of a very difficult transition.

NINA'S TRAVELS THROUGH THE FOSTER CARE SYSTEM

Tara Sinclair, MSW, LSW

Tara Sinclair is a social worker in the Philadelphia, PA, and Camden, NJ, area who works in child protective services. Working in some of the poorest neighborhoods with some of the most disenfranchised people, she continues to advocate to keep families together where possible and to help children grow up in safe and caring environments.

Background

Foster care is an established system run by various social service agencies that can be either private or public institutions. Its purpose is to provide safe, stable, and temporary care of children who are separated from their families for various reasons. Generally these reasons pertain to parental characteristics and social conditions such as substance abuse, mental health issues, domestic violence, and chronic poverty. Abuse and neglect are also cited as reasons for removal of children from their families.

Foster care's roots spring from the child-saving movement of the nineteenth century. At that time, children who did not live with their families lived in institutions such as almshouses and asylums. Many children who were orphans and homeless were forced to live in these institutions or be on the street (Downs, Moore, McFadden, Michaud, & Costin, 2004). Foster care has been reformed and developed into common practice that includes unrelated caregivers, relatives, and group homes, and, in some cases, large treatment centers (Downs et al., 2004). Social workers and other professionals who work with children agree that children do better in home-like and family-like settings than in institutions.

Despite the benefits that foster care can provide for children, such as protecting the child from imminent risk of harm, children experience loss while in the foster care system. The types of loss are as diverse as the children themselves. Ideally all children going to foster care should be placed in homes that are "closest to home and [in the] least restrictive environment" but because there is a shortage of homes many children are forced to relocate, change schools, lose contact with friends and neighbors, and even lose their personal belongings. For many children, the separation from their family is the greatest loss; they lose the attachment to their families. They lose the most seemingly mundane material object(s) as well as their most intimate feelings such as hope and pride in who they are and to whom they "belong."

The following case study is based on several cases involving young children in foster care and serves to show the reader ways in which children experience loss in foster care.

Case Presentation

Nina is a 6-year-old girl in foster care. Nina was placed in several different homes over a period of 2 years. Since entering foster care she has lived in five different foster homes, all in different towns. She had to change schools each time she was placed and even had to adjust to several different case workers who managed her case for the social service agency that oversaw her foster care.

Nina comes from a disengaged family that has multi-generational substance abuse and dependency issues. Nina lived with her mother from the time she was born until she was 2 years old. Her mother, a single, low-income heroin addict, was constantly struggling with trying to maintain her home and care for her daughter. She had become a prostitute to feed her addiction. One day, she asked a relative to "watch" Nina and did not return for many years. The relative who cared for her quickly became overwhelmed and gave Nina to another family member. This lasted for a few months and then they located Nina's father and dropped her off at his house and left her there. Nina was only about 4 years old and had never met her father until that day. Feeling overwhelmed and unprepared he contacted his brother and gave Nina to him. Nina has three paternal half-siblings whom she never met because of the short time she had contact with her father.

Nina entered the foster care system when it was determined that she was living in her uncle's home with no utilities and no heat in the winter. A referral was received by the local child welfare agency by a concerned citizen who knew the home had no working heat. The case was opened and investigated. During the investigation it was assessed that several other issues were affecting the family. While assessing Nina's case, it came to the attention of the social worker that Nina's uncle was not caring for Nina properly. The social worker and her supervisors believed that she was not receiving the proper health, education, and mental health services she needed. The agency met with him and explained the need for these things and he agreed that she needed them but failed to follow through. The agency petitioned the court for custody and Nina was removed from his home and placed into foster care. She was placed into the home of Roberta who had agreed to keep Nina for just one night. The child being confused, scared, and exhausted began to show signs of distress as evidenced in her crying for her Mommy and her withdrawn behavior. Nina never received a full explanation about why she was moved out of her uncle's home.

Next, Nina was placed in the home of Benny; she remained in that home for about 5 months. Benny was a janitor at the preschool that Nina attended and had contacted the Child Welfare agency to offer to care for her. Benny and his wife were optimistic about Nina and they accepted her as part of their family. They were very cooperative and eager to care for Nina. Nina grew comfortable with Benny and the family. Nina bonded to the family well and things appeared to be going fine. Over time she began showing signs of problems such as stealing, cursing, and being aggressive toward the adult caregivers. Benny requested that Nina be removed from his home after Nina threatened to hurt herself and called his wife a "whore." Nina was placed in another foster home where she remains. The changes that Nina endured were beyond what most children have to deal with. For the time that Nina was moving around, she was unable to plant roots in any particular home. She struggled with feelings of anxiety, loss, fear, and uncertainty.

The Social Impact of Loss:
Attachment Theory and Its Application to Foster Care

According to John Bowlby (1977), a founder of attachment theory, it is critical to healthy childhood development that a child have attachments with his or her mother, father, or another caregiver to form the basic feeling of security. If that attachment is threatened, it can cause anxiety and stress for the child. Thus the bonding of a child and a consistent caregiver is the key to the child's development and is highly indicative of the way s/he manages relationships for life (Kaplan & Sadock, 1998). For many children, childhood is a time in their lives when their growth and development are well monitored by family, doctors, teachers, and their community. For children in foster care, the child loses the safety that comes with living in communities that are aware of the child. Nina had been cared for by a family health clinic in her aunt's town, but when she was placed into foster care, a new doctor was consulted. Her developmental milestones were based on the observations of various foster parents, doctors, and day-care providers.

The Psychological Impact of the Loss: Erikson's
Theory of Development and Its Foster Care Implications

Erik Erikson believed that there were stages in psychosocial and ego development and that the stages were based on "physical, cognitive, instinctual and sexual changes [that] combine to trigger an internal crisis whose resolution results in either psychosocial regression or growth and the development of specific virtues" (Kaplan & Sadock, 1998, p. 211). He claimed that virtues were strengths and crises were critical periods that can influence adjustment and maladjustment of the child. Nina presented to foster care during Erikson's third stage, known as *initiative versus guilt*. This stage is characterized as the period in childhood when the child seeks to master his or her environment by learning facts and actively exploring the world. This stage is rife with curiosity and a drive to compete. Children who fail during this stage experience guilt, anxiety, and inner conflict. This is a period in childhood when children can develop phobias and other issues pertaining to inhibition. For Nina, moves from her family to strangers meant that she lost her secure base and this may have compromised her development. She was changing caregivers and thus losing her trust in her surroundings. Even before her removal, it could be argued that she had a compromised sense of security with her mother and family because of a lack of stability and the abuse and neglect she experienced.

The psychological loss that many foster children face is paramount. They lose the bond between themselves and their parents. Nina experienced loss with several different foster parents and their families. The loss can be understood as an example of a fractured form of intimacy, a forced separation from one's secure relationships. Nina developed some psychological problems while in foster care. She was diagnosed with several *Diagnostic and Statistical Manual of Mental Disorders* (DSM-IV-TR; American Psychiatric Association, 2000) childhood disorders, including adjustment disorder, post traumatic stress disorder, and reactive attachment disorder. Her behavior was first noticed at preschool and led to her being evaluated by the Child Study Team, who classified Nina as Behaviorally Disabled. She frequently used profanity and exhibited biting, kicking, oppositional and defiant behavior, and overall impulsive behavior. In simple terms, she lost the ability to trust those around her and, according to Erikson, her developmental task of learning trust was compromised (Pavao, 2000).

Interventions

Interventions that appear to be effective in working with children in foster care who are coping with loss include, above all, offering as much consistency as possible. The child requires a secure relationship to rebuild the trust s/he needs to be able to develop. There must be people in the child's life who are responsible and who are willing to advocate for, and monitor, the welfare of the child. This relationship can come from the court, service providers, biological or foster family, from the educational community, or from the social worker, yet it must remain stable over time.

Keefer and Schooler (2000) found that there are strategies for foster parents that can offer help to the child, such as talking directly to the child about his or her birth family and modeling healthy behaviors for the child to learn to express his or her feelings properly. The foster parent can listen to the child and help him or her understand their situation. Just offering a chance to vent can help a child. The social worker can mitigate the loss by trying to keep the child in a stable placement and not change homes. This is especially true when the social worker locates a foster home that exceeds expectations and appears to be a good foster home. The social worker can assess the quality of the home by observing the response the foster parent has to the child's needs and the parent's frequency of advocating for the child's overall well-being. The child's experience in foster care does not have to be traumatizing, despite the experience of loss. If the child is in a home that exhibits support, love, and safety, the child can thrive as any other child would. It is placing children in homes that fail to care for the child's needs that often causes harm to the child.

A therapeutic tool that a social worker can use when working with all children in foster care is the use of the familiar object. Donald Winnicott was one of the originators and major figures in the work on transitional object theory. This theory purported that inanimate objects can help a child during a time of stress. A transitional object can be any object that is meaningful to the child, such as a blanket, soft toy, teddy bear, or even a pillow. The use of a transitional object is widely practiced among many professionals who work with children to assist a child in coping with separation and loss issues. The object can give the child a sense of security during distress. These and many other techniques can assist the child in coping with trauma while in foster care.

Discussion of Optimal Social Supports That Enable Coping With This Loss

The optimal social supports that enable coping with loss are the maintenance of relationships for the child and the opportunity to therapeutically process experiences. The social worker is in the unique position to offer support and advocacy on behalf of the child. The social worker can use his or her assessment skills to plan on behalf of the child and consider the best interests of the child; perhaps even decreasing the losses the child could incur. For example, many children have to change foster homes for superfluous reasons; an astute social worker may be able to maintain the home and thus keep the child in the same foster placement and thereby avoid another loss.

For many children, the biggest loss is the ability to trust the caregiver. The social worker offers some relief if he or she is honest with the child and explains the situation to him/her. It is true that many children internalize their move as a reflection of themselves, feeling rejected and hurt. By fully disclosing the situation to the child you are offering him or her a sense of control. This technique can be understood when considering the child who is moved as a result of difficult behaviors and the foster parents' requests that the child be removed because of the effect the foster child is having on their family. The social worker can tell the child that it is the adults who are unable to address the child's needs and that it is not a judgment on the child.

The social worker can positively affect the grieving process by offering the child a "point person" to ask questions of, in other words, a trusted adult who understands his or her circumstances. The child is otherwise supposed to function in a new and often strange environment, and to perform well. The child may not always be allowed to express his or her underlying feelings of loss, despair, anger, and fear. If the social worker is not personally equipped to therapeutically address the child's emotional needs, it is his or her duty to refer the child to the appropriate professional.

Despite the lack of training and the complexity of foster care and adoption, other systems can advocate for the support of the child, such as the school, mental health professionals, the attorney, or another professional figure who can act as the voice of the child. In addition, it is vital that the biological and foster family consider the overall welfare of the child. Often, the two parties are apprehensive about joining together and collaborating. It is a sad reality that most children who enter the foster care system experience some degree of loss; but it is the role of the social worker to minimize the loss and find a way to guide and advocate for the child so s/he can live in a home that meets his or her needs and provides appropriate care so s/he can grow happily and safely.

SUMMARY

The role of a primary caregiver is seen to be a critical component of infants' and toddlers' ability to develop in optimal ways. Although loss of total caregiving is a normal maturational loss as the caregiver provides "optimal frustration" to encourage the infant's evolving self-care, other forms of loss of the caregiver in nondevelopmentally appropriate ways (through depression, separation, or death) can have extremely detrimental effects. McIntosh shows how loss at an early age can transform itself into a vigilant hyperindependence that may actually be lauded by many, despite the fact that it is indicative of deep pain at its core. Sinclair's Nina also shows how destructive separations from parents can be, even when they occur so as to avoid even greater damage (i.e., abuse). Losses early in infancy and toddlerhood need to be reworked regularly as the child grows to allow the development of new understandings (meaning-making) appropriate to each new level of development.

When an infant is different from the parents' expectations, there is always a sense of loss, yet when this goes beyond the normal sense that the infant looks a little different or cries more than expected, the loss has even greater salience. The diagnoses of Down syndrome, Fragile X, cystic fibrosis, or other chromosomal and genetic anomalies leave a parent in mourning for the healthy child they hoped to have. These losses entail an ongoing adjustment to the new assumptive world as each new age/grade brings new reminders of the limitations and challenges their child must cope with regularly.

4   Elementary-School-Age Children

Tammy was a precocious and happy 6-year-old when she came to school for first grade. Her mother kept her at home for kindergarten, believing that she could teach Tammy her colors and shapes in ways that were more fun and engaging than in the large classes characteristic of her local public school. Tammy entered expecting to love school where she could be with other children and have a teacher because she "loved to learn new things!" Within days, Tammy's mother was worried. Tammy was sulky, withdrawn, and refused to talk about what was happening at school. When Tammy's mother made an appointment to meet with Tammy's teacher, the teacher told her that Tammy did not appear to be making any friends and that she was frequently reprimanded for getting out of her seat and talking to other children during class time. It was clear that the teacher was trying not to be harsh or single Tammy out, but that Tammy was not fitting well into her new environment.

Tammy's mother told the teacher about Tammy's love of learning and her fears that Tammy would change this characteristic if she did not start to have more positive interactions at school. Together, they worked out a way that Tammy could begin to take a leadership role in class activities and that the teacher would work to try to help Tammy *integrate into a group of girls who seemed more open and accepting of new children.*

DEVELOPMENTAL STAGE: INITIATIVE VERSUS GUILT AND INDUSTRY VERSUS INFERIORITY

Children enter school around age 5, but truly begin their academic training when they enter first grade. For some, this is their initial entry into large-group situations; for others, day care, nursery school, and kindergarten have socialized them to be able to be part of a larger group of children. Children begin to develop confidence in taking the initiative to move out into the broader world, using their language skills and imagination to engage with the greater society (Erikson, 1959/1980). In more difficult situations, some children arrive at school angry and hostile about the attention and care they have not received and can be extremely disruptive because they have not learned how to cooperate with the larger group, something Erikson would attribute to guilt. Just as the time from infancy to age 5 includes incredible development with increased body size, mobility, and skills, so too does the time from entry into school to late elementary school age when children begin early adolescence. Tammy, like any child moving into a school environment, is experiencing the developmental loss of leaving the home where she has (ideally) been nurtured and loved without many pressures to achieve. Children can experience a sense of loss of self-image as they move from the care of a loving parent to the school environment, where peers and teachers judge how well they fit the social milieu.

For others who have not received love and unconditional acceptance in their home environment, school may provide a haven where achievements can lead to positive feedback and an increased sense of self-efficacy. As children move into the higher elementary-school grades, they industriously learn and produce projects and papers and engage in creative, athletic, and other endeavors. The ability to produce in this way promotes a sense of mastery; in contrast, the child who is unable to meet this level of industry often experiences a sense of inadequacy and inferiority (Erikson, 1959/1980). Ultimately, if the child is able to meet the social and academic expectations of the school environment, s/he will be more likely to start out positively in the environment that will now occupy the vast majority of the child's waking hours.

Biological Development

On a very basic level, children nearly double their weight and height between ages 5 and 11. Weight charts show that fiftieth percentile 5-year-olds weigh 42 pounds and are about 43 inches tall. By age 11, a child in the fiftieth percentile weighs 82 pounds and is 57 inches, or nearly five feet tall. At the same time, brain development is also changing and becoming more complex. Children's brains show growth in the prefrontal cortex as well as the temporal and occipital cortices (Sowell et al., 2004). Sowell and colleagues also found changes in the relationships between gray matter and white matter in the brains of children as they age from 5 to 11. Some of these changes were highly correlated with the development of verbal skills and it is believed that the changes indicate growing connections and complexity that allow for higher level cognitive skill development.

There is some indication that these growing verbal skills occur in girls somewhat earlier, spurred on by lower levels of testosterone and socialization strategies that reinforce gender norms about cooperation and interaction (Brizendine, 2006). This is not to say that boys do not have the same growing ability to create connection. As Pollack strongly asserts, "boys' behavior is shaped more by loved ones than by nature" (1998, p. 53), which is to say that although elementary-school-age children show gender differences, these are not "hard-wired" (though there are some hormonal differences in what is bathing the brain). Rather, they are responding to differing multifactorial environmental stimuli about encouraging nurturing and cooperative behavior. Pollack makes the provocative assertion that "if we don't let our boys cry tears, they will cry bullets" (Pollack, 1999) as a way of reinforcing the importance of nurturing boys of this age to be caring (and allowing themselves to be cared for) in ways that promote human interactions.

Lenroot and Giedd (2006) have identified the prefrontal cortex as the site of developing abilities of impulse control, decision making, and integration of the brain's activities, often referred to as the executive function, also characteristic of children across this age range. Their colleague at the National Institute of Mental Health, Philip Shaw ("Inside the Brains of Smart Kids," 2006) notes that the size of a brain has little to say about the intelligence of the child who possesses it. Actually, the thickness of the prefrontal cortex increases between the ages of 6 and 11, at which time it starts to thin out again. Shaw (cited in Lenroot &

Giedd, p. 721) says, "In a way, children with the most agile minds have the most agile cortex." Research indicates that children who have experienced abuse/neglect have a 17% smaller (by area) corpus collosum (the brain structure that helps integrate both sides of the brain) than nonabused children (Teicher et al., 2004). Those who have experienced posttraumatic stress disorder as a result of maltreatment also showed smaller intracranial and cerebral volumes as well (De Bellis et al., 1999).

This brain development and ability to control impulses are critical to the ability to learn, to interact appropriately in social settings, and to develop peer relationships. When the biological substrate is not present, children in school or other settings are at a great disadvantage because the typical school environment requires an ability to remain seated, raise one's hand before speaking, and generally to think before talking or acting. At age 5, these are very difficult tasks for a large percentage of children, but by the time children move into second or third grade, these are usually skills they have mastered, likely because brain development has allowed them to develop. Yet, children who have experienced abuse and neglect have structural brain changes that may put them at a disadvantage. The 5-year-old brain is usually about 95% of its adult size, but myelination (the covering on nerves that allows them to operate well) increases and gray matter decreases with age (Giedd, 1999). Further, the corpus collosum grows by about 1.8% each year from age 3 to age 18 (Giedd, 1999). The corpus collosum is believed to be responsible for unification of the senses, attention, memory storage, and promotion of language and auditory processing (Lenroot & Giedd, 2006).

Play is another major activity of children in the 5- to 11-year-old age group. Physical play is important for developing healthy bones and muscles. This can be accomplished in the very active play of hide and seek or other active games or through involvement with sports. As a result of a proliferation of video and computer games, and fears for child safety in many neighborhoods, children may have fewer opportunities to use their large muscles and pundits have expressed concern about the development of children's bodies and the growing levels of obesity in the United States (Wallis, 2006). Others say the risk of obesity, and indeed the way the label of obesity is applied, is overstated and inaccurate (Campos, 2004; Center for Consumer Freedom, 2008). All agree, however, that children in this age group benefit from physical activity and play to maintain their health.

Certainly, if childhood obesity increases, other physical effects will occur that can limit the full development of children. Childhood obesity is highly correlated with development of Type 2 diabetes and cardiovascular disease. There are some indicators that it may affect cognitive development negatively as well (Reilly, 2007); these are generally found among the morbidly obese, in whom health has been affected, placing stress on the circulatory system and oxygenation ability. Again, fitness and activity levels seem to have greater impact than weight itself (Center for Consumer Freedom, 2008).

A very pressing concern for this age group is the effect poverty has on a myriad of characteristics. In 2000, 20% of U.S. children were being raised in poor neighborhoods and poverty has been associated with low birth weight and prematurity in infancy (making school success more difficult) as well as with poorer mental and physical health (Xue, Leventhal, Brooks-Gunn, & Earls, 2005). The concerns about obesity are even greater for minority and lower socioeconomic class children because they have been found to have higher rates of obesity and also to experience more negative health effects related to obesity (Yancey & Kumanyika, 2007). Although some people blame parents for denial of the child's obesity, most research supports the idea that parents are concerned but have many time demands that make them less available to prepare and serve healthy meals and to supervise exercise or activities; this reality is even more pronounced among poorer families (Styles, Meier, Sutherland, & Campbell, 2007). These children also may have the experience of the loss of peer approval and/or friendships, a loss that is particularly poignant during elementary school, when children are developing their social skills.

Psychological Development

As indicated by the previous discussion of brain and physical development, the elementary school years are a time of great developmental growth in academic skills as well as in brain processing and integrative cognitive skills. It is a time of tremendous learning, both of formal skills like reading, writing, and arithmetic in schools, as well as learning the skills necessary to manage in social situations. Ability to navigate these demands for learning has a great impact on children's development of a sense of self-efficacy, of a positive self-image, and of their social skill set.

Children who have learning disabilities are particularly at risk because they have difficulties at each of these developmental levels. If the
learning differences are not diagnosed early, children may grow to
believe they are incapable of success and their expectation of failure
can become a self-fulfilling prophecy (Lackaye & Margalit, 2008). Further, at a time of life when acceptance by peers is at the forefront of
the individual's sense of self, these children may experience the loss of
positive peer regard, as well as loss of esteem in the eyes of their teachers
and possibly even parents. These losses of esteem and fitting with the
social group have effects on children in ways that are disenfranchised,
both in terms of the loss itself, as well as through the myth that children
with developmental disabilities experience the loss less intensely. This
myth is aptly addressed by the Faust Piro reading at the end of this
chapter.

Erikson (1959/1980) posits that in the elementary school years,
individuals must resolve the crisis of Initiative versus Guilt followed
by Industry versus Inferiority. Given this construct, children who have
difficulty initiating success in school and peer relationships are at risk
for developing a sense of guilt and poor self-image. Between the ages
of 5 and 7, children are theorized by Piaget (1954) to move from
preoperational thought processes to concrete operations processes,
which remain with them to ages 11–12. This preoperational stage is
characterized by egocentric thinking, and (according to Piaget, though
questioned by others) an inability to put themselves in the position of
others. They tend to attribute human characteristics to inanimate objects, and magical thinking (a belief that their thoughts can influence
events) is strong. Clearly, if a loss due to death occurs, a child is at
risk if s/he believes that his/her hostile thoughts may have caused
the death.

By the concrete operations stage, children have more understanding
of causation, quantity, and symbolic action, yet they are assumed to
be unable to engage in very abstract or hypothetical thought. They can
take the role of the other and are able to play games and do role-taking
activities in ways that Piaget asserted were impossible to this point.
Language skills are developed at this stage and allow children to process
their thoughts and emotions with others in ways that were not possible before.

Social Development

Children who have not entered school generally have social relationships that are mediated by their caretakers. Seldom, outside of school
or child-care-related settings, does a child engage in unmediated relationships with peers until the child enters a school environment. Even
in these environments, much of the activity is structured and supervised
until the first "recess" at school or unsupervised play date with a peer.
This new type of interaction places demands for social skill development
on children. Learning to take turns, to engage in give-and-take conversations, to share possessions for the good of the group, and even to care
about the impressions of one's peers are all relatively new skills (Gifford-
Smith & Brownell, 2003). A strong factor in children's acceptance or
rejection by peers has to do with aggression, though not in ways that
are easily predicted. Although younger children who express aggression
physically are often rejected by the peer group (Cillessen, van Ijzendoom, van Lieshout, & Hartup, 1992), older boys (fourth grade) who
express aggression are actually more accepted over time (Sandstrom &
Coie, 1999). This is important to the understanding of loss in two ways.
If children experience a loss, they have varying developmental ways of
expressing their hurt and fear and, particularly at younger developmental stages, may act out aggressively (or alternatively withdraw) in
ways that create rejection among the peer group. This then creates a
second loss as children now lose the social support cushion that can
promote the resiliency that peer friendships may provide (Criss, Petti,
Bates, Dodge, & Lapp, 2002).

It should be noted that at later stages of elementary school, this
social network is used much more for distraction and engagement with
other activities than to verbally process feelings about loss (Christ,
2000).

The institutionalization of large bureaucratic school systems with
a focus on teaching to the test has become a newer focus in a recent
governmental era that insists on standardized testing. This seems to
have limited both the social functions of schools and the internally
driven joy of learning, losses in their own right (Gardner, 1991). Political
leaders call for accountability and have legislated for the "No Child
Left Behind" policies, yet many children live in school districts where
classes are large and educating students is secondary to keeping them

off the street and teaching only a modicum of needed mathematical and communication skills (Carlson, 2008). These conditions do not generally promote the optimal education of students and certainly leave many children in schools where help with processing losses is unlikely if not impossible.

LOSS EXPERIENCED BY AN INDIVIDUAL DURING THE ELEMENTARY SCHOOL YEARS

Age Differences in Perceptions of Loss

The developmental processes just described have great bearing on the ways that children both understand a loss as well as use the tools they have available to cope with the loss. Whereas children under 5 have few tools for processing a loss and benefit most from the security of a steady and nurturing caregiver, older children have a variety of needs for processing the loss and for gaining support. Christ's work with children who have experienced the death of a loved one is illuminating in this regard, as she describes the responses of 6- to 8-year-olds in contrast to 9- to 11-year-olds. Although she adds the caveat that there is overlap caused by differing degrees of developmental maturation, she finds that children in the 6- to 8-year-old range had a better understanding of death, particularly its finality, than younger children.

Both age groups tend to express sadness and grief in intense yet rapidly alternating spurts, showing how Dual Process Model (DPM: Stroebe & Schut, 1999) is at work somewhat differently in childhood. DPM posits the mourner's need to cycle between a disorientation (mourning) phase and a restoration phase; during restoration the mourner is distracted and focuses on events other than the loss. Children in the 6- to 8-year-old group speak about wanting to die to be with the deceased in a way that is more indicative of wishful thinking than suicidal ideation. They were more likely than other groups to enjoy talking about pleasant memories of the deceased (Christ, 2000). Children in the 6- to 8-year-old range tend to remember concrete characteristics such as hair and eye color and actions more than personality or other internal characteristics (Buchsbaum, 1996).

Children in the 9- to 11-year-old range seemed to have a stronger need for factual information and tended to avoid direct expression of emotions, preferring to compartmentalize emotion or experience it very briefly or in private. Occasionally, this led to aggression or withdrawal. On the whole, children this age seemed to benefit from attempts to help them remember happier times and memories, have a transitional object from the deceased, and affirm their tendency to move in and out of emotion about the loss (Christ, 2000). Because memory acquisition and recall are better developed by ages 9 to 11, children in this age group are more able to remember personal characteristics of the deceased and to feel a part of a relationship that went beyond just the caregiving that the deceased provided (Buchsbaum, 1996).

An important developmental concept is that when a child experiences a great loss, s/he experiences it in the developmental stage that s/he is in. Although this seems self-evident at first, it must be emphasized that as the child continues to develop, s/he must rework the loss on some level as s/he gains new developmental maturation and understanding. A child who loses a sibling or parent in toddlerhood will need to rework this loss at both earlier and later maturational stages in elementary school (as well as throughout his or her development over the lifespan— see the reading by McIntosh at the end of chapter 3).

Children are consistently found to envision deceased parents in a way that continues to create a presence in their lives (Silverman & Nickman, 1996). They tend to maintain that connection in one of five typical ways: (a) locating the deceased (e.g., in heaven), (b) experiencing the deceased (e.g., believing the deceased parent is watching them), (c) reaching out to the deceased to initiate a connection (e.g., praying to the deceased), (d) remembering (actively), and (e) keeping a belonging of the deceased. Silverman and Nickman see these strategies for maintaining the connection as part of the children's coping trajectory and found that children who could not "locate" the parent or felt a lack of ongoing connection seemed to have greater difficulty. With a colleague they developed a trajectory of the way the child perceived the connection to the deceased parent, moving from (a) seeing the parent as a visiting ghost, to (b) holding onto memories of the past, to (c) maintaining an interactive relationship, and finally (d) becoming a living legacy (Normand, Silverman, & Nickman, 1996). They hypothesize that children can move through these phases as their development progresses.

Loss of a Pet

A common loss experienced by children in this age range is the loss of a pet, often a very beloved pet who is confided in and viewed as a member of the family. Griffith's reading at the end of this chapter gives many examples of the depth of this type of loss for children in elementary school. This is often the first death they experience and may set a template for the way they process grief in the future. When this type of loss is disenfranchised through nonrecognition or outright de-meaning of the feelings of grief, the child is given the message that mourning is not acceptable. This may generalize to the experience of other losses in the future in ways that will detrimentally affect the child's ability to process grief in the future.

Losses Resulting From Sexual Abuse

A loss that seems to have lifelong impact is the experience of sexual abuse, particularly by a parent. Spiegel (2003) documents the biological, psychological, and social ramifications of sexual abuse on boys and men as does Finkelhor (1984), who focuses mostly on girls and women. Fleming and Belanger (2001) synthesize this literature with grief litera-ture to tie thanatology and traumatology together, showing how the trauma of sexual abuse in children also carries inherent losses. In particular, the child's loss of a trusting, caring relationship with the abuser entails related losses for the future when survivors have difficulty being able to trust in relationships and/or to be vulnerable within them. Further, the tendency to either hypersexualize relationships and/or withdraw from sexuality altogether represents a longer term loss as relationships are repeatedly affected in negative ways. A tendency to diminish the effects of the abuse mirrors the tendency to deny the affective impact of a loss, leading to many of the same kinds of effects as delayed grieving. Just as children bereaved in more traditional ways must rework their losses as they mature, children who experience sexual and other abuse must rework their understandings to recognize, validate, and grieve the losses involved in the betrayal of the paren-tal relationship.

Loss Caused by Parental Divorce

A more common form of loss often experienced by children of this age is the divorce of their parents. Divorce places children in several untenable positions: they often have the same kinds of beliefs of omnipo-tence and magical thinking discussed earlier and therefore believe that they themselves somehow caused the problems between their parents and/or the dissolution of the marriage. Further, children may be used as pawns between parents fighting over property, financial support, and their children's loyalty. Despite the consistent and loud expert advice to help children through their parents' divorce, children remain the forgotten mourners when parents divorce. There is more recognition of children's experience of divorce by experts who realize that children this age often need concrete examples to be able to process new events. Kroll notes that there is "the lack of a body" (2002, p.113) and yet the child has experienced a loss (certainly the loss of the parent who leaves the home and the loss of the former family constellation). The need to understand the different experiences involved, but without being put into loyalty binds, is critical for children's processing of the grief related to their parents' divorce. Developing a coherent story is part of what children need to accomplish to process the emotional loss they experience as a result of divorce (Kroll, 2002). The related losses of structure, financial well-being, and the assumptive world are just as powerful for children as for a divorcing spouse, though in different ways. Recognizing children's needs for security and stability remain key ingredients.

Loss and the Military

A new category of loss for children is the separation from parents during military deployment. Further, they can experience the death of parents during deployment and/or their return with physical and psychic injuries. Stephanie Surles remarked, "What we hear from military families is that they don't want their children treated as victims" (cited in Hardy, 2006, p. 11). Others assert that the children of military officers are accustomed to frequent moves, separations from parents, and leaving old friends. These multiple losses, and the fact that school-age children seem to tolerate them, may affect the children of military officers more than some think, but are likely to have an even greater impact on children of reservists who have not had these same toughening experiences or subculture. Further, many reservists' children are not in social situations where supports are built in because they are not living with other military families. With reports of many veterans of the Iraq and Afghanistan wars returning with brain injuries, there will be many ambiguous losses (Boss, 1999) in which the parent is physically present, but changed from the parent who left to serve in the military. The reading by Bellin (chapter 5) illuminates the experience of children and teens whose siblings have threatening illnesses. The losses of attention, support, and nurture experienced by these siblings are likely to mirror some of the dynamics that may occur for children who lose military parents, either to death or to injury.

A critical understanding of intervention derives from Bellin's (chapter 5) and Griffith's (this chapter) readings. Children in elementary school are developmentally primed to engage with peers. It is therefore not surprising that both authors describe the benefit of group intervention. Groups allow children to feel the support of others who are mourning similar losses. This reenfranchises the loss and allows children to hear from others at their developmental level about strategies for coping with their loss. Most important, it shows them that they are not alone and that others have gone through very similar losses and circumstances.

INTERVENTION ISSUES WITH ELEMENTARY SCHOOL CHILDREN

Children grieve differently, taking dual process theory (Stroebe & Schut, 1999, 2005) to the extreme: They cry one minute and play happily the next, particularly at younger ages. This has the unfortunate consequence of making it seem that they are either grieving "incorrectly" or they are perceived not to be grieving at all. These types of disenfranchised grief are detrimental (Doka, 2002) possibly even to the point where children self-disenfranchise their grief (Crenshaw, 2002). This is most often done in service of the goal of protecting the surviving parent or siblings, though it can also occur because of fears of shaming oneself with emotional flooding. Clinicians working with grieving children must show themselves as trustworthy, truly hearing and validating the grief, while also not pushing or otherwise indicating to the child that his or her emotions are anything other than what they are in the moment (Crenshaw, 2002). Questions deemed to be helpful in working with children and youth allow them to focus on the behaviors associated with grief without forcing them into internal dialogues before they are ready. For instance, Rowling (2002) suggests the following questions: "How did you react? (Not, What did you feel?); How do you experience your grief?; What did the loss mean to you?; What strategies do you use to cope that are helpful?; What kind of advice is helpful?; With whom do you share your loss?" (p. 289).

Because parents may die after an extended illness, decisions must be made about how to prepare for an impending parental death. There has been a movement toward facilitating attachments prior to a death while also acknowledging the coming loss and using time for anticipatory grieving. Saldinger and colleagues question the value of romanticizing anticipated death as allowing a "good death" (Saldinger, Cain, Porterfield, & Lohnes, 2004, p. 506), but also recognize that the facilitation of intimacy and the optimization of the remaining time with the family member may outweigh the strains of trying to both attach and detach at the same time. They studied the effect of this ambiguous position on children. They were particularly interested because Rando (1995) advocates children's involvement with dying parents so strongly. They found that children did make efforts to stay connected to dying parents, even when the parent was nonresponsive as a result of illness, or even when the dying parent acted outright "mean" (pp. 926–927). They also found that the surviving parent usually bore responsibility for mediating the relationship between the dying parent and the child to some degree. The surviving parent often is responsible for developing, or participating in, legacy projects to maintain memories and connections after the parent's death. Saldinger and colleagues also found that the unpredictability of death and the tendency of families to believe they can orchestrate a positive farewell ritual can create problems, particularly for children who are younger and may be frightened by the physical sounds and actions of individuals as they die (Saldinger et al., 2004). They conclude that a formulaic approach to fostering attachment has suspect use, but is valued when all parties are invested in pursuing it and do so with flexibility that is sensitive to the child's needs and developmental capacities.

Saldinger, Porterfield, and Cain (2004) also developed a coding scheme for child-centered parenting behaviors that includes nine criteria: providing information, communicating feelings, being aware and responsive, maintaining a stable environment, getting additional support for the child, exposing the child to the dying parent, encouraging funeral participation, facilitating relationships, and meaning-making. The extent to which the surviving parent can be child-centered in his or her approach correlated highly with the elementary-school-age child's ability to cope effectively (Bluebond-Langner, 1978). Intervention strategies within three spheres have been developed that allow professionals to support children when they have a parent or sibling in hospice care; these are the cognitive, affective, and behavioral spheres (Dunning, 2006). A professional who is not part of the family system can interact, sometimes in displaced and symbolic ways, with the children. The professional is able to convey information appropriate to the child's developmental stage, correct misconceptions caused by magical thinking and other age-related cognition, validate the child's feelings and responses, and provide support. The worker can also help interpret some of the child's behaviors to the rest of the family to minimize reactivity, misunderstanding, and/or false conclusions (Dunning, 2006).

Dunning provides many excellent examples of ways social workers can work with children on their misconceptions and fears; she emphasizes that reassurances seldom have positive impact. Children instead benefit from struggling with expressing their fears and understandings and then play can be used to help the child discover her or his own reassurances. For example, in playing nurse and mother (with the child as the mother who was the healthy parent), the child was able to state her fear that no one would be able to care for the child after the father's death. The "nurse" and "mother" then worked together to develop a list of all the people who could help the child, something that provided much reassurance for the child as she played her role of mother.

LOSS OF AN INDIVIDUAL OF THAT AGE AS EXPERIENCED BY OTHERS

Parents' Loss of a Child

When children in elementary school die, the parents and family are the ones most directly affected. The child's peers are also affected. Much like in earlier stages, parents who lose a child during elementary school are affected by a sense of responsibility for the child's well-being and therefore often have extreme levels of guilt about the death of the child. Rando (1993) asserts that loss of a child consistently correlates with complicated grief. She asserts that this is true at any age. Others (Finkbeiner, 1996) indicate that the death of a child during the ages when parents typically have a greater degree of responsibility but also less control as they move into the social world (as in elementary school) is particularly challenging. Finkbeiner (1996) reveals understandings about child death from interviews with parents after their child's death. She notes that the disorientation following a child's death is probably one of the most intense responses. The need to try and make meaning or find patterns comes to naught as nothing makes sense about the child's death. In a developed world, children's deaths are viewed as utterly preventable, either through the miracles of modern medicine or the strong focus on risk prevention and accident avoidance. Yet these views are not accurate in the Western world, just as those living in developing, under-resourced nations know; children will always be vulnerable. Still, the belief that children will outlive parents is part of the expected order of life. Death alone is disorienting, but turning the assumptive world upside down is even more disorienting. Often during this stage parents do not "so much choose to live; they just didn't choose to die" (Finkbeiner, 1996, p. 9) despite many reporting questions about whether they could continue to live when their child had died. Making a conscious decision to live usually comes later, often with some sort of "wake up" call that indicates one is barely existing, much less living. The decision to live coincides with a decision to make some sort of commemorative effort for the child. Indeed, Klass (1996, 2006) describes a grieving trajectory of parents from "newly bereaved" to "into their grief" to "well along in their grief" to "resolved as much as it will be." He observes that many bereaved parents contribute their expertise to the group Compassionate Friends because of their need to maintain the connection and commemoration of their deceased child. Maintaining the bond is critical to the parent's ability to continue to function.

A particularly challenging form of parental grief comes after a child dies of complications related to a developmental disability. As discussed earlier, all parents cope with the loss of the idealized child when a baby is born; parents whose child is ill or has a diagnosed disability feel this loss particularly. Although prior theories asserted that parents of children with disabilities had "chronic sorrow" (Olshansky, 1962), few recent studies have found this to hold true (S. E. Green, 2007; Morse, Wilson, & Penrod, 2000). Instead, the lack of formal and informal supports is what aggrieves parents with children with disabilities. Nevertheless, when a child with a developmental disability dies, there are often even fewer social supports for parents than would be optimal. In a study of mothers whose children with disabilities had died, women often felt their love for their child and their loss were not validated (Milo, 2005). Themes emerging from the study included people from the parents' social network saying things like, "Don't you think it was for the best?"—a painful dismissal of the value of their child. Further, mothers had to navigate a reworking of "Who am I now?" when so much of their identity had been involved with caring for their child. The paradox of both wishing for relief from the burdens of care but also loving their child and the gifts the child brought to their life made women struggle with the lessons gained from the experience of parenting and then losing their child with disability. Milo was able to find themes to the resolution of this struggle as well. Women often noted that the child "made me who I am today" and that they "[didn't] believe this happened for no point and no reason." Milo asserted that mothers coped better if they originally were given an accurate portrayal of the child's prognosis and were encouraged to take control where it was possible. Support groups were once again identified as the intervention of choice. When the group, or supportive professionals, helped parents recognize and accept the paradoxes of their experience, parents were better able to cope and actually be transformed positively by the loss (Milo, 2005).

Rando (1993) recognizes that the loss of a child is also the loss of the parenthood function and parental identity, along with the parts of self that are tied into each of these factors. The violation of the assumptive world leads to a heightened sense of vulnerability. The sense of parental responsibility is unique to the parent–child bond. This complicates grieving as a loss of self and sense of competence, in addition to the actual loss of the child, are all experienced simultaneously. The fact that parents may grieve differently, both because of gender differences and individual coping structures, often leave parental dyads stressed. These stresses may threaten the relationship as the mutual support between partners is lost as well; this is a particularly difficult event at a time when each may be hoping to be comforted by the other. Instead, guilt may be displaced into blame, leading to further stresses in the relationship. Yet, as Schwab shows, the belief of prevalent divorce after a child's death is inaccurate (Schwab, 1998).

Rando (1993) also notes that other children may serve as reminders of the loss and parents may actually lose a sense of competence for parenting still-living children. Yet, it is not uncommon for parents to overprotect siblings of a child who died, in the attempt to control the uncontrollable and to compensate for perceived failures in parent care for the deceased child.

READINGS

THE CHALLENGED CHILD

Carolyn Faust Piro, BA

Carolyn Faust Piro is a graduate student of Social Work at Rutgers University in Camden, New Jersey. Her diverse interests include developmental disabilities, mental health, women's issues, and sexuality. She is a strong advocate for and fiercely loving mother of her four sons. Her goal is to open a therapeutic practice that also advocates for individuals with developmental disabilities and/or mental illness and their caregivers.

Some children who are diagnosed with a disability will never be aware of their differences from typical children. For many though, the differences are obvious and painful. In the early years of education, most children with special needs are mainstreamed with peers. As a child grows older and academics become more challenging, mainstreaming or inclusion in regular education may not be possible. This awareness usually occurs during the first or second grade. Children who are considered high functioning, but not high enough to be mainstreamed, will experience grief at the realization of their differences.

Case Presentation

Philip, diagnosed with autism spectrum disorder at age 4, was the oldest of his three brothers. He did not struggle with going to school until his younger brothers began walking down the street to the bus stop for the neighborhood school. In the second grade, Philip went to a school across town that could meet his needs; he rode the "little bus," which is a universally recognized symbol. To the inexperienced and ignorant, it has been a target of ridicule and pity. To caregivers and children it is a bittersweet knowing of all the joys and woes of a life that includes the little bus.

When his younger brothers began kindergarten, they walked to a bus stop at the corner of the block that would take them to the neighborhood school. Philip never realized that there was another school in town. The first 2 weeks of that school year, Philip began to walk down to the bus stop with his brothers to get on the big bus. He would try to talk to the neighborhood children and refuse to come back to the house. The mornings were traumatic for Philip and his brothers. Philip would cry and yell. The neighborhood kids would stare at or ignore him. The realization for Philip that he did not go to school like his brothers was extremely difficult for him. He would begin crying or yell over minor incidents. He hated to get up and get ready for school. His mornings were a struggle. He could not say exactly what bothered him because of his limited expressive language skills. His parents consulted the school social worker to help him with this difficult time.

When working with kids who have limited expressive language skills, it is important to be patient when waiting for an answer and to use a variety of media to help the child express himself or herself. In the case of Philip, the social worker used pictures and stories about the situation to describe what was happening and to touch on what Philip was feeling. Philip, his parents, and the social worker all created a social story of pictures and words to describe how Philip felt, and what to do to make him feel better. A sympathetic neighbor agreed to play dates in the afternoon with her son and Philip. A reward was also set up for when Philip did not walk to the bus stop in the morning. Philip also had to learn about his diagnosis so that he could better understand why he rode a different bus.

The social worker suggested a double-sided approach to explaining Philip's diagnosis: That he is incredibly special and requires a school that can meet his needs and that the school his brothers attend cannot meet his needs. Philip seemed excited that there was a special place for him and began to adjust better to his morning routine of going a separate way from his brothers.

Despite his disability, Philip experienced aspects of grief just as a typical child would. He was angry that he could not do what his brothers and neighbors were doing. He was sad that he could not be included in the neighborhood school. He tried to make deals about his behavior so that he could ride the same bus. He denied that he was not allowed to go and insisted that he could ride the regular bus with his brothers. Finally he did achieve some acceptance. He learned about having autism. He has explained to people who do not understand him, "Be patient,

I have autism." Finally, on a brighter note, Philip, now in the eighth grade, has enjoyed his school placement, attending field trips, week-long camping experiences, and dances. Like typical children, Philip learned to make his situation work in his favor—once refusing home-work from his teacher, "I can't do that Ms. Anastasia, I have autism." With the help of his family, neighbors, and the social worker, Philip has learned to celebrate who he is and find joy in his abilities.

LOSS OF A PET IN CHILDHOOD: THE LOSS OF A COMPANION

Toni Griffith, LCSW, BCD, CT

Toni Griffith is a practicing grief therapist in New Jersey. She specializes in traumatic loss. She has facilitated pet loss support groups since 1997, starting the first one ever held by a hospice, serving both children and adults. She founded her own not-for-profit organization, Continuing Support Services, Inc., to work with students in elementary, middle, and high schools. She has worked with some 11,000 school children, families, teachers, and the community at large since 1995 using puppet presentations for loss and grief, divorce, and HIV-AIDS prevention. She has received national, state, and county awards for her innovative grief work.

The loss of a companion animal often occurs in childhood and the grief will sometimes continue long into adulthood. It can be the first loss that we face in life and it happens at a time when we are least prepared developmentally to understand the process, or the finality of death, or have the mechanisms in place to cope with the hurt.

The animal–human bond is strong. Children reciprocate the uncon-ditional love and attachment that animals show and when that animal is no longer part of their world, they grieve the loss of both the animal and the love and affection. During a group session on loss with 4th-grade children, John shared that he really missed his dog, Bailey, most of all because he could tell Bailey anything and Bailey never told anyone else. He never "ratted me out!"

Adults may not recognize the loss and the hurt that accompanies it, and often the "answer" is to replace that animal with another. With words that say, "Don't cry. Don't feel sad. It is only an animal, and we can get another," unrecognized grief becomes disenfranchised grief, unacknowledged and unacceptable, and can cause unresolved grief that is carried long into the life cycle. Ironically, the most disenfranchised pet owner who I ever met at a pet loss support group was the owner of several snakes. She seriously missed her pets but many other pet lovers had difficulty relating to her loss.

At a conference session on pet loss support, a 37-year-old woman got up and spoke of her experience of loss, which occurred when she was 7 years old. She told the audience of 60 people about her dog who had puppies, and about her father, who threatened the dog. When someone came to the house to look at the puppies, she gave them the dog. When her father came home he became enraged about what she had done, and he killed one of the puppies right in front of her. She burst into tears and told the group that she felt responsible for the puppy's death and that she had carried that guilt for all these many years. The group immediately helped her process her grief and understand that her father was the one responsible, not her. For 30 years she had denied herself the ability to have a pet as she carried the responsibility and weight of guilt. The group experience helped her to reidentify herself and recognize her father's abuse. The pet loss may have masked other abuse issues that she agreed needed to be worked through with a therapist.

Children often are told that a pet "ran away" rather than the truth that the pet died. This results in emotional turmoil because the child continues to look for the pet, care about what has happened to it, and feel abandoned and rejected wondering what s/he did "wrong" to make the pet run away.

A first-grade student returned from a weekend away to find a different hamster in the cage. Although it looked similar to the pet that had died, the child knew it was not the same animal as he tried to take it from the cage to hold it and feed it. He became angry and opened the door to let the animal go. As his father came into the room, he said, "This one can go and get Sparky back." Later, as he was finally told the truth, he began to cry about now missing both animals. The cage remained empty for several months while he was given a book about hamsters and he and his father read about better ways to keep them healthy and happy. During the grieving time the child began to look at how he could become a better pet owner and partner and thought about names that he liked and colors that were different from the original pet and what he would do to remember Sparky. This is an example of what we call meaning-making and benefit-finding in loss. Later, he and his father went to the pet store and bought two new hamsters.

During another group session with 30 4th, 5th, and 6th graders, Ron became distraught. Because this group was processing family losses, we stopped and asked Ron who he was missing. He told us that his grandmother had recently died, but that he was really missing his two guinea pigs, which had died several months ago. He began to sob uncontrollably as he told of finding them one morning dead in their cage. He had no idea that they were sick or that anything was wrong. He was allowed to have an elaborate funeral and burial for his "friends" and yet was not ready to think about getting any others. He said, "I am not ready to love anything again." As he continued to process mainly the grief about his guinea pigs during the next few weeks of group, he also told of his grandmother's illness and her death. He shared his great fear of going to her home and finding her dead. (She did not die at home.) He admitted that he missed her and was even angry not only that she died, but that (as it seemd to him) everything he loved died and went away. He chose to make a collage about the guinea pigs and not about his grandmother. At the last group session he came in with pictures of two new guinea pigs, Shadow and Ghost. Ghost was his grandmother's favorite animal color—white.

Group support for children and adults, especially among peers, is most helpful when processing pet loss. In school groups when students were asked how many have experienced the death of a pet, in any given group, usually about 80% of those present raise their hands. They talk more readily of their pet's deaths than of family member's or friend's deaths sometimes. They are often able to relate to a family member through their interactions with their pets. In pet support groups, men will often cry and get emotional when processing the death of a pet, whether it happened in childhood or in adulthood. They may be open to going back in time to the good times spent with that particular pet. Young boys also feel comfortable crying about the loss of a pet even in a group setting. One man wore the ashes of his pet cat in a silver receptacle on a chain around his neck. Another came to the pet loss group with several little wooden boxes containing the ashes of his ferrets, along with pictures of his pets. There seems to be an inherent permission to grieve and grieve emotionally the death of a pet, whereas most men are often inhibited in showing their grief for humans.

Large-animal pet loss, including horses, requires that the pet partner be allowed to fully process the depth of the relationship with the animal. Often large animals bear and carry the partner and the person holds the additional loss of a protective bond between them. Children in rural areas sometimes see animals as a food source, but often a special bond is forged with a large animal that takes additional grief processing. A teenage girl came to the pet loss support group following an accident at a riding show. Her horse stepped into a hole and stumbled. Both horse and rider came down. She was injured, her arm broken, and the horse broke its leg. Worse for her, she had to be the one who helped the veterinarian euthanize her faithful steed. She described to us the feeling of losing her protector, the one who rode like the wind with her on his back. To this day, I often think of all the young riders at the stables forming those bonds never thinking that fate may step in to break them.

Having a companion animal comes with the responsibility of caring for that animal when it becomes old and sick. Pet partners need to realize that they usually outlive their pets. Planning for the final stages of a pet's life is often difficult and leaves pet partners feeling guilty that they either "did not do enough" or "wished they had made the final decision for euthanasia sooner." Most pet partners feel a deep sense of peace knowing that they were with their pet during the pet's final moments. Using the terminology, "put the animal to sleep," or "have to put the animal down," is difficult for children to understand. More difficult for adults, but better for children is to explain the term "euthanasia" and that the decision is always made with the assistance of a veterinarian, and that it means helping the animal to die quickly and painlessly.

Children need understanding; they may not be able to tell you how they feel…sad, angry, scared, and/or confused. They need to know that it is all right, that it is normal to feel this way. They need to know that you, too, miss the pet and the good times you've had. There are many good children's books available on pet loss and remembrance that can be read to and with children as they grieve for their pets. Art work is helpful for very young children and making photo albums and collages keeps memories within easy reach when the tears need to flow.

From the ages of 3 to 7 the finality of death is not yet developed and the child might struggle with "can he come back to be with me for my birthday?" Very young children may not understand exactly what death is. A simple explanation that helps is "death is when the body stops working." Magical thinking can prolong the feeling of guilt that the child did something to cause the death. Remind the child that things don't always happen because of what s/he thinks, says or does. If guilt is a genuine factor, help the child understand that by learning to be a better, more responsible pet owner s/he can honor the pet who has died. After the age of 9 one of the most important parts of the grieving process involves the rituals of funeral and burial and remembrance. A respectful treatment of the dead animal helps children understand why we have rituals of remembrance for human beings.

There are often questions about whether animals will go to heaven. Pet partners generally believe that their pets have souls, manifested by the devotion and goodness of the pet, and are comforted by the belief that they will one day see their pet again. Several articles and books are currently available to assist pet owners with the spiritual component of their grief. One 5th-grade girl said, "I know my dog is in heaven with my grand pop. And I know how she got there—she kissed her way in."

Candles lit for the anniversary of the death, the naming of new companion animals, honoring the animal by becoming a better pet partner are all ways that pet owners use to find meaning in remembrance of their pets, as well as donations to animal shelters, and planting trees and shrubs in their animal's special places. Children also need to know that other animals in the family may be grieving for the one that died. They can develop a different identity as caregiver as well as find meaning in caring for the grieving animal. One young man whose grandfather just died, when told that the man's dog was grieving for its partner, said, "I'll take the job of caring for grand pop's dog." And from that time on, he did. He sought support 2 years later when the dog died and he grieved anew for his grandfather as well as the dog, but he acknowledged that caring for the dog had made a difference for him as he remembered his grandfather.

Children learn the lessons of grief as they find their strengths as caregivers, as animal lovers, as good stewards of this earth, and as individuals who will not willingly hurt creatures. They learn to love and care for pets even knowing that they will outlive them. Assisting children to develop their coping skills and strengths and find meaning during the grieving process for pets is one of the most important ways to ensure that they will have the ability to work through the many and ongoing losses that they will encounter as they become adults.

A note of caution: Children who abuse and hurt animals are a danger to the animal, to their families, and potentially to society. Many serial killers have been found to have abused and killed animals when they were very young children. A household of maimed and hurt animals or too many animal deaths may be a warning sign that the family in that household is in danger. Always report animal abuse—you are the voice for those who cannot speak for themselves.

SUMMARY

Children in elementary school are maturing rapidly. Much of their growth relates to moving from the family environment to the bigger world as they enter school. Normal maturational (developmental) losses occur as a result of experiencing judgments by teachers and peers instead of being unconditionally loved (ideally) in one's home. This means that the child experiences gains as s/he navigates these challenges and develops a sense of self-efficacy, or may experience a sense of failure if s/he is unable to negotiate these changes. These changes can be very challenging when a child has a disability or other difference that creates a separation from the peer group, as the story of Phillip exhibits. Helping elementary-school-age children to recognize their losses and process them, while also creating strategies of reward when they are able to cope, seems critical to surviving these types of losses.

When losses of a parent, sibling, pet, or other significant relationship occur, children in this age group have varied abilities to cope. In early elementary school, they may still not have enough verbal facility to process their feelings of loss and may withdraw or become hostile or aggressive if the loss is more than they can process. As they age through elementary school, they may be less willing to overtly express emotion, but have more ability to verbally process the loss and learn to cope by holding on to important memories and linking objects.

The role of support groups seems particularly helpful for children of this age. Although their world is much more socially connected, they seldom have networks that include others who have experienced the same loss that they have unless they are overtly welcomed into a group. The opportunity to share experiences helps the child feel less isolated and ostracized. It also provides an opportunity for validation and shared problem solving with people who are at a similar developmental level, but with the professional support to help clarify misconceptions and draw out the supportive opportunities.

NOTABLE RESOURCES

Toni Griffith

Online Resources

www.petsforum.com/deltasociety—sponsored by the Delta Society, this site has a comprehensive section on pet bereavement

www.petloss.com—a resource for pet bereavement information

www.csum.edu/pethospice—The Nikki Hospice Foundation for Pets

Children's Books for Pet Loss and Remembrance

Griffith, T. (2002). *"Good grief, it's sky blue pink!"* Cherry Hill, NJ: Pad and Publishing.
Noel, N. (1996). *All God's creatures go to heaven.* Indianapolis, IN: Noel Studio.
Rylant, C. (1995). *Dog heaven.* New York: Blue Sky Press.
Rylant, C. (1997). *Cat heaven.* New York: Blue Sky Press.
Varley, S. (1984). *Badger's parting gifts.* New York: Lothrop, Lee & Shepard.
Wilhelm, H. (1985). *I'll always love you.* New York: Crown Publishing Group.

Resources for Professionals

Anreder, P. (1995, Winter). *When the bond breaks.* Washington, DC: ASPCA Animal Watch.
Balk, D. (April 1990). *Children and the death of a pet.* Manhattan, KS: Cooperative Extension Service, Kansas State University. In conjunction with the Delta Society, Renton, WA.
Diamond, B. (1989, February). Honoring a friend. *Cat Fancy Magazine*, pp. 18–20.
Griffith, T. (1997). *When a companion animal dies...grief for the loss of a pet.* Marlton, NJ: Samaritan Hospice.
Griffith, T., & Da Rosa, J. (2000–2007). *Lunch bunch memory group for 4th, 5th, 6th grades.* Burlington City, NJ: Wilbur Watts Middle School.
Harris, E. (1996). *Pet loss, a spiritual guide.* St. Paul, MN: Llewellyn Publications.
Harris, J. (1989, March). *Children and pet loss, companion animal practice* (pp. 20–28). Santa Barbara, CA: Author.

Kelley, D. (1989, February). Coping with grief...loss of a special pet. *Cat Fancy Magazine,* pp. 15–18.

Kowalski, G. (1991). *The souls of animals.* Walpole, NH: Stillpoint Publishing.

Montgomery, H., & Montgomery, M. (1997). *Your aging pet* (pp. 24–31). Minneapolis, MN: Montgomery Press.

Montgomery, H., & Montgomery, M. (1993). *A final act of caring* (pp. 6–32). Minneapolis, MN: Montgomery Press.

Montgomery, H., & Montgomery, M. (1991). *Goodbye my friend* (pp. 6–31). Minneapolis, MN: Montgomery Press.

Ott, D. (1998). Will your pet rise again? Yes, some faiths say. *Philadelphia Inquirer.*

Stawar, T. (1999, July). Guide to surviving the loss of your dog. *Dog World Magazine,* pp. 23–25.

5 Tweens and Teens

Andrea was a high-achieving junior in high school when her boyfriend of 4 years decided they should break up. Andrea had a fairly large circle of acquaintances from multiple school activities and a handful of others she included as her close friends. Yet, she felt like her life was over. The joy she used to get from good grades and teacher's approval felt hollow. Whenever she heard music that mentioned the word "love," she broke out in tears. She wanted to retreat into her iPod, but the music disturbed her too much.

Andrea's parents had not liked her boyfriend, who had dropped out of school the year before and whom they believed was a bad influence on her. They had protested their relationship aggressively at one point when they realized that the two were sexually involved, but rapidly realized that the more they tried to stop the relationship, the more determined Andrea was to continue it. They were thrilled when he broke the relationship off, but tried not to show it. Andrea's mother kept trying to focus her toward other young men who were in Andrea's social circle at school. The more she tried to help in this way, the more Andrea withdrew into silence and isolated herself in her room.

Andrea's school work started to suffer, as did her social relationships. When Andrea was still saying things like "my life is over" 3 months after the breakup, her best friend talked to Andrea's parents and they encouraged Andrea to get counseling. Andrea recovered and returned to her customary *patterns after working with a counselor for 6 months. The counselor validated the deeply intense feelings she had for her boyfriend, while also validating her as a human being with legitimate feelings of loss. Andrea needed to process her shattered belief that she would be with her boyfriend forever; this assumption led her to decide to enter a sexual relationship with him. Without that future, she felt that she had not only lost the relationship with him, but also her planned-upon future and her self-image as a "good-girl" (who "allowed" sex because she imagined he was going to be her future husband). The counselor had to help her extricate her identity from that of being "half of the couple" she had come to believe was her future. Her self-criticism had to be tempered and she needed to have her loss valued so that she could begin to grieve and then move beyond the initial pain. Andrea's sense of self had to be rebuilt before she could reinvest in other relationships.*

DEVELOPMENT: IDENTITY DEVELOPMENT VERSUS IDENTITY DIFFUSION

Ages 11–14 are often referred to as the "tween" years, falling between the concrete operations and straightforward relationships of childhood and the abstract idealism and judgments of a true teen—a person age 14 to 18 or more. For the purposes of this chapter, "tween" and "teen" will be used to refer to individuals in those age ranges, whereas "adolescent" will be used to refer to individuals in both age groups together. These years include brain changes, consequent changes in hypothetical reasoning and abstraction abilities, growing skills for impulse control (though still not totally developed for most), and a clearer sense of self. By the latter part of the teen years, individuals begin to consolidate their own identity and often start to build intense relationships with romantic partners, as well as with close friends. Adolescents take on more adult responsibilities as they complete their own school work with little assistance from parents, take jobs, learn to drive, and even begin to vote.

Biological Development

Although there is much controversy surrounding the existence and scope of differences between teen brains and adult brains, including the ramifications of these differences on legal liability for adult crimes, there is relative consensus in the neurological literature that there are differences in function as revealed by functional magnetic resonance imaging (fMRI) in the tween, teen, and adult brain. The most obvious changes in the brain result from modifications in the activity of the prefrontal cortex, and pruning (or thinning) of "extra" neurons during adolescence. Giedd et al. (1999) have noted changes in the structures of both the prefrontal cortex and the corpus callosum, changes that are believed to gradually promote more reflective thought, impulse control, and more rational decision making.

Interestingly, some researchers take similar data and interpret it to indicate that teens actually are *too* rational (Reyna & Farley, 2007), weighing all data without running it through other known history and experience. Teens may, therefore, actually be reassured by data that would concern most adults. Reyna and Farley (2007) give the example of a teen deciding whether to risk having sex (with risk being identified as pregnancy or sexually transmitted disease) with an acquaintance; s/he may believe her/his chances of having a negative outcome to be 50-50. When given the accurate 1 in 500 statistic, the individual may actually be reassured, feeling like the risk is minimal in comparison to what s/he thought previously. These judgments are suspect and this can affect the ways adolescents perceive risks to their own health and lives, as well as the lives of ones they love (and could potentially lose).

Reyna and Farley (2007) theorize that as the brain becomes more integrated, it is more able to make use of "fuzzy trace" decision making based on getting to the "gist" of the matter and recognizing multiple factors without weighing only one or two factors out of context. Others also attribute integration and more intuitive thinking to the pruning of the dense synaptic prefrontal cortex. The pruning is necessary to allow adolescent and adult thinkers to develop a more socially competent brain that makes appropriate decisions (Blakemore, 2008)

The changes in brain structure as tweens become teens and beyond are also affected by the neurochemical state of the brain—including the hormones that bathe the brain in ways they had not before puberty. This neurochemical change is now deemed to be overrated as an explanation for the impulsive and emotionally driven decision making and behavior that often characterizes adolescence. The onset of puberty is accompanied by increased testosterone in both girls and boys and is said to swell the amygdala (Underwood, 2006). Because the amygdala is critical to emotional processing and reactions, and has a tendency to lay down traces of memory when highly stimulated (S. Johnson,

2004), it seems likely that this change contributes to the labile and intense emotions (exacerbated in grief) of adolescence, even if less than had been previously supposed.

These changes in the adolescent brain seem to set the stage for "hard-wiring" in some brain pathways that are more or less productive for the individual: for instance, use of drugs like THC (tetrahydrocannabinol), marijuana, methamphetamine, and ecstasy seem to lay down "wiring" that predisposes the individual to addictions and/or, some assert, to schizophrenia (Moore et al., 2007). Likewise, engagement in learning a language or even a video game is going to lay down traces as well, more toward a skill than toward an addiction. The "use it or lose it" brain structure aphorism is at work at this age as well (Underwood, 2006) and may have implications for adolescents who experience loss and grief at this stage of rapid brain modification.

The most obvious biological changes are connected with the onset of puberty and its accompanying bodily changes, ultimately leading to the secondary-sex-characteristic development that leaves boys looking like men and girls looking like women. Further, sexual and reproductive functions such as nocturnal emissions (male) and menses (female) develop even when the individual's experience in Western society usually has not prepared him or her for full adulthood and reproductive function. Tweens' and teens' brains may not yet have caught up with the exterior growth of their bodies (Patton & Viner, 2007). Teens both impatiently wait for, and later are embarrassed by, these dramatic bodily changes. There is growing evidence that the age of physical maturation is falling in Westernized countries (Ong, Ahmed, & Dunger, 2006; Remschmidt, 1994; Sprinkle, 2001). Lower levels of exercise and activity (Davison, Werder, Trost, Baker, & Birch, 2007), higher body mass indexes (Biro, Khoury, & Morrison, 2006), better nutrition (Gluckman & Hanson, 2006), raised socioeconomic status (Obeidallah, Brennan, Brooks-Gunn, Kindlon, & Earls, 2000), and/or exposures to chemicals and hormones (Den Hond & Schoeters, 2006; Tiwary, 1994) have all been implicated as having an influence on the lowered age of puberty, and of menarche particularly.

Aside from early onset of secondary-sex characteristics like pubic and underarm hair, breast growth in females, and genital maturation, early puberty has correlations with social outcomes such as early involvement with sexual activity (Halpern, Kaestle, & Hallfors, 2007), substance use (Ge et al., 2006; Ohannessian & Hesselbrock, 2007;

van Jaarsveld, Fidler, Simon, & Wardle, 2007), and other risk-taking behavior (Ohannessian & Hesselbrock, 2007; van Jaarsveld, Fidler, Simon, & Wardle, 2007). This engagement in "adult" types of behaviors occurs when the individual's body has only recently assumed biological maturation. Pregnancy at earlier ages is fraught with complications, substance use appears to have a greater negative impact on the brain that is still developing, and other risk-taking behavior can lead to accidents that have life-changing (or ending) consequences. In short, biological maturation, particularly when it occurs earlier than the norm, is out-of-synch with social recognition of maturation and with social roles prescribed during teen years (Gluckman & Hanson, 2006). This in itself is a loss.

Physical changes may inspire a sense of loss even when occurring at normative ages because they indicate movement away from the less responsibility-filled time of childhood. For those who mature early, the "out-of-synch" sense may also be experienced as a loss of social conformity, albeit compensated for by an attachment to more "adult" behaviors. Because change always involves a loss of the prior status quo, individuals going through the many biological changes of adolescence certainly experience maturational loss.

Psychosocial Development

Piaget (1954) identifies the hallmark of adolescence as the ability to engage in abstract thinking—ideas themselves can be manipulated and the individual is no longer reliant on seeing, hearing, or touching objects to consider their interrelationships. Erikson (1959/1980) views the psychological task of adolescence as the development of identity or the danger of identity diffusion, because the end of latency and elementary school should have yielded a resolution to the task of industry versus inferiority and the establishment of skills and abilities. During adolescence, the individual is not only thinking about who s/he is, but is thinking about how s/he appears in the eyes of others.

Along with the growing ability to see oneself through the eyes of others and to consider how and why one adopts or rejects certain social roles, Erikson (1959/1980) emphasizes the consolidation of ego identity and integration of a sense of sameness, continuity, and congruency within one's self-concept. According to Erikson, many adolescents regard differences as faults. Although they view themselves as very unique and particularly want to differentiate themselves from their family of origin, they also want to fit in with their social group of peers. Erikson notes another critical feature of adolescence, the tendency to view behavior as identity and the hazard of doing so. For instance, instead of saying that they did not get good grades one semester, adolescents tend to invoke character deficits—"I'm a moron"—that they may believe define *who* they are in a more permanent, persistent, and pervasive manner than just having a bad semester. This is crucial; Seligman (1995) has shown that attribution of situations to permanent, pervasive, and persistent character traits rather than to temporary circumstances tends to inspire a pessimistic attributional style, which places adolescents at risk for depression and anxiety. This tendency to attribute behavior to inherent personal traits is particularly true of teens who engage in risky or illicit behavior, who may then be labeled with terms such as "delinquent," "no-good" and "loser," only to have those labels become self-fulfilling prophecies. "For if diagnosed and treated correctly, seemingly psychotic and criminal incidents do not in adolescence have the same fatal significance which they have at other ages" (Erikson, 1959/1980, p. 97).

Freudian interpretations of the tasks of adolescence include the movement from the phallic stage to the genital stage, and possibly more important, the development of a superego and id mediated via the ego (Freud, 1923/1960). Neo-Freudian interpretations comment on the normative, early-adolescent development of interest in pleasure, both sexual and more generally, as a form of expression of the id. Later in adolescence, superego restraints develop and there is a growing ability of the ego to weigh the social propriety of expressing various urges and behaviors (Group for the Advancement of Psychiatry, 1968). Certainly, most parents can attest that individuals move from more impulsive behavior toward more reflective and deliberative behavior; this is a hallmark of psychosocial growth from the tween years to early adulthood.

Another feature of adolescence is the movement into ages during which mental health disorders occur in more congruence with adult psychopathology. This may relate to greater substance use in teen years. New research indicates that marijuana use is not as benign as previously reported and seems to correlate with higher incidence of psychotic and affective disorders (Moore et al., 2007). The rate of psychopathology may be related to hormone priming (Brizendine, 2006) or biological maturation occurring before full social maturation (Patton & Viner, 2007; Sprinkle, 2001). Regardless of the attribution, depression, anxiety, and other common mental health disorders of adulthood come to be diagnosed at rates on par with adults by the end of adolescence. One difficulty is that adolescents age-out of parental insurance coverage and this seems to lead to less access to mental health care just as these rates are equalizing (Pottick, Bilder, Stoep, Warner, & Alvarez, 2008).

Identity development and adaptation play particularly significant roles in the processing of loss. Sometimes the losses relate directly to the identity, for example, a teen who has lost a mother may identify herself as a motherless daughter. Teens who experience multiple losses may come to view themselves as "an angel of death," as one young client did, not able to view the confluence of loss as outside of his control, but instead seeing it as connected to his very identity. This shows the way vestiges of the magical thinking of childhood remain in adolescence and beyond. Adolescents' abstract thinking abilities are still rather new and, as such, this population may struggle more to find a way to make meaning of death.

Grace Christ and her colleagues have devoted their careers to exploring the impact of loss on children and adolescents. In a review article (Christ, Siegel, & Christ, 2002) they detail the differing needs at various developmental stages of adolescence. Specifically, early adolescents or tweens are "characterized by ambivalent expressions of dependence and independence and sometimes by angry and perplexing expressions of selfish egocentrism" (Christ et al., 2002, p. 1271). This is under normal circumstances. The additional stress of a parent's illness; requests for the tween to assist with patient or household care; and the presence of caregiving friends, family, and strangers in and out of the home all conspire to promote increased family conflict as the tweens' developmental wish for emotional distance and independence comes into conflict with family needs. By mid-adolescence, which Christ et al. define as age 15–17, individuals have developed a more accurate ability to assess situational demands and develop more empathic abilities. They have greater abilities to understand the nature of death, though they tend to maintain earlier developmental characteristics of asynchronous expressions of grief (cycling in and out in a dual process that only gradually becomes more consistent with adult tendencies to maintain longer periods of sadness and anhedonia). The psychological development of tweens and teens generally supports full disclosure of the nature of a parent's illness even when that disclosure seems to promote anger and withdrawal (Christ, 2000).

The world of the adolescent is incontestably bound by peer relationships. As indicated earlier, the tween becomes ever more aware of the world outside his or her family of origin/caregiver, and peers gain more influence. Trying on new social roles is as natural as the new body constellation individuals develop during this time. The confluence of a new body, new roles, and new friends can be confusing to adolescents as they try to adopt more adult behaviors and may receive negative sanctions for that (particularly in areas of sexuality and substance use). Yet, if they maintain more child-like roles of dependency, they are urged to "grow up already." Among their peers, individuals can gain support as they navigate these mixed messages and "try on" different identities of more or less involvement with adult roles. The typical adolescent is viewed by society as successfully navigating adolescence if s/he is able to move into young adulthood capable of committing to occupational goals (and ideally beginning to work in paid employment) and also able to commit to relationships without capriciously moving from "best" friend to best friend in a manner more characteristic of latency aged children.

Gender differences become both more defined and more blurred as individuals are urged to adopt the socialization of their gender in culture-consistent ways, but this is tempered by peer groups who expose adolescents to varied ways of expressing themselves, often in purposely androgenous ways. For boys moving from the "boy code" (Pollack, 1998) to manhood, the journey is made more difficult by competing messages about what the identity of a male adult encompasses: "The traditional image is of the man who does not express his emotions freely and favors a traditional role toward women; the 'new man' is empathic, egalitarian and sensitive" (Pollack, 1998, p. 147). Likewise, girls becoming women also negotiate socializing inputs about traditional roles of caregiving and dependency versus adoption of socially recognized occupational roles (Gilligan, 1982/1993; Pipher, 1994), yet most seem to internalize the ethic of care, something Brizendine (2006) suggests is primed by female hormones.

A loss experienced by many females across cultures is often referred to as a loss of voice, essentially adoption of silence as a safe position from which to avoid conflict (particularly with males) (Gilligan, 1982/

1993; Jack, 1991; Iglesias & Cormier, 2002). For both genders, these mixed messages about gender roles are being negotiated at the same time as mixed messages about whether they are maturing too quickly or not quickly enough. Discrepant messages add to the struggle for teens as they work to consolidate identity.

During times of loss, aside from the stress inherent in the loss more generally, adolescents have social aspects of the loss that have tremendous impact on their ability to proceed with "normal" development while also processing the loss. Loss of a same-sex parent is often particularly difficult as the role model for gender-appropriate behavior is often derived from the same-sex parent. Further, the death of any family member changes the family dynamic in ways likely to require greater involvement in family participation at the very time the adolescent is developmentally working to pull away from the family. Additionally, for adolescents who are themselves ill or dying, the developmental urge to pull away and be independent comes at a tremendous price as the need for support for illness and/or impending death can challenge coping capacities (Bluebond-Langner, 1978). Recognition of one's identity may also cause challenges, as when a teen is somewhat different from the norm and possibly is moving into socially devalued roles. The lack of support for teens who are gay, lesbian, bisexual, or transgender can be very distressing and isolating at a developmental phase when individuals need support for identity consolidation. Other losses occur frequently (e.g., loss of a love relationship, death of a pet, loss of an occupational dream or other goals, loss of self-esteem at athletic events or performance events). More detail about the experiences of loss in adolescence and how coping can be enhanced are described in the next section. It is notable, though, that many of these developmental and situational stressors cluster and make tweens and teens more susceptible to other risks such as substance use and abuse, and that even those who are not involved with substance use report high incidence of being "stressed out" (Stuart, 2006).

LOSSES OF ADOLESCENTS

When tweens and teens die, it is often due to an accident, homicide, or suicide, which by definition generally happen quickly (Matthews & Marwit, 2004; Murphy, Johnson, Wu, Fan, & Lohan, 2003). Such losses betray parents' assumptive world and often leave survivors with posttraumatic stress disorder. Following traumatic deaths, parents often require a longer time to adjust, as well as to grapple with the unfairness of life. Adolescents themselves are in a period of rapid development during which they are trying to understand their growing roles, responsibilities, and identity, but are also still affected by the vestiges of childhood whereby they may still be impulsive and have some magical thinking. They may be more susceptible to complicated grieving (Melham, Moritz, Walker, Shear, & Brent, 2007) precisely because of the many changes (and subsequent maturational losses) that are naturally a part of adolescence.

Teens' Experience of Death (Others' or Their Own)

Although accident, suicide, and drug overdoses make up the majority of deaths in this age group, with advances in medicine, more individuals affected by childhood illnesses such as leukemia, cystic fibrosis, and other conditions once fatal in childhood, now live into adolescence and beyond. The struggles of these individuals during illness and the approach of death are prolonged and poignant. Yet, surprisingly little is written about the experience of dying as a teenager; much more is available about the responses of bereaved adolescents. Much of the research reported was written prior to 1982 and it may be that research ethic boards (Institutional Review Boards) have discouraged research with adolescents who are dying. In one of the few studies of adolescents' experiences of death, Ewalt and Perkins (1979) found that many more teens (juniors and seniors in two Kansas high schools) had an experience with death than had been predicted; indeed, nearly 90% had experienced the death of a close friend or relative and 40% had experienced the death of a friend. This exposure to death is viewed by Cho, Freeman, and Patterson (1982) as a call to become more involved in educating adolescents about death and mourning and encouraging those who work with this age group to realistically and forthrightly discuss grief reactions and losses in school settings and other places where adolescents may benefit from having the opportunity to process their loss.

Typically, teens who are ill or dying struggle with the demands of differentiation and developmental maturation during a time when their health requires more dependence on the adults in their lives. Farrell and Hutter (1980) suggest several themes that emerged from their research with teens who were dying: changed perceptions of self resulting from altered appearance, lack of control over one's life and frustration about dependence on adults, isolation from peers, being a source of worry for parents, physical pain and limitations, and uncertainty and ambiguity about the future. Notably, they did not find teens expressing preoccupation with death. They recommend helping teens to continue to focus on their day-to-day lives. They encourage self-care and engagement with peers (to the extent possible), as this allows teens to continue to feel "normal" and to continue developmental tasks to the extent that they can. This focus on the teens' wishes for control and independence is often implemented in pediatric hospital settings, yet at least one scholar suggests that adolescents should not exercise independent life-and-death decision making. Instead, a shared model of decision making with parents and medical providers is prescribed because adolescents' decision-making capacity has not fully matured (Markowitz, 2007).

This contrasts with the work of Manor, Vincent, and Tyano (2004), who assert that adolescents typically use their newfound abstract thinking abilities to consider their beliefs about death and even to have wishes about death, wishes they distinguish from a desire to commit suicide. They note that adolescence is the time when an individual can begin to understand that s/he will die sometime in the future and that this starts a process predicated on thoughts about death. They posit a series of adolescent phases in response to an awareness of death. The teen begins with a phase of chaos leading to narcissistic depression and then to renewed cathexis of the object (the self) as part of customary developmental processes, resolved, with some degree of pain, in a decision to live. Adolescents who become suicidal express ideation metaphorically or literally, they may or may not actually wish to die; sometimes impulse takes over and death from accidents, suicide, and drug overdose can be the outcome (Manor et al., 2004).

As part of identity formation, religious and spiritual beliefs are also frequently part of adolescent development and these existential questions seem to become more pointed when an adolescent experiences a significant loss (Balk, 1999; Batten & Oltjenbruns, 1999). Bereavement can be viewed as a life crisis that provides an opportunity to reflect on and evoke spiritual change (Balk, 1999); adolescence can be viewed as a time of intense response to crisis and as a time of reflecting on abstract and existential questions. The intersection of bereavement and adolescence seems to be a prime developmental phase for spiritual reflection and/or growth. The response of women who lost a parent during adolescence bears this out: Women tended to reflect on religious and spiritual beliefs, though not in homogenous ways, with some embracing their faith and others rejecting or revising it (Cait, 2004). Interestingly, though, nearly all used some spiritual belief to retain connections to their deceased parent—with many struggling with the paradox of how to believe in a loving supreme being capable of allowing one's parent to die (Cait, 2004).

Death of a Sibling

Sibling bereavement provokes similar spiritual struggles, with new perspectives on self, others, the deceased sibling, life, a higher power, and death (Batten & Oltjenbruns, 1999). Although the four teens who were interviewed in this study expressed different changes in perspectives, the critical finding was that all expressed changes from their previous perspectives—none remained unchanged by the death of their sibling. This finding is consistent with earlier work on sibling loss in which grief, personal growth, and ongoing attachment were all found in research with adolescents who experienced the death of a sibling (Hogan & DeSantis, 1996). The sense of permanent change was part of the construct of grief and of personal growth, with grief also entailing an increased sense of vulnerability and desire for reunion with the sibling; the personal growth usually entailed increased resiliency in the form of optimism, maturity, and further development of a sense of self along with increased "faith consciousness" (Hogan & DeSantis, 1996, p. 244). The teens' ongoing attachment (continuing bond) with their deceased sibling included regrets, endeavors to understand the whys of the death, and attempts to "catch up" by "updating" (p. 245) the sibling on events and reaffirming the importance of the deceased sibling in the adolescent's life.

Adolescent Responses to Death Including "Double Jeopardy"

When adolescents experience the death of a loved one, the use of support is often limited to friends and family members who may have experienced the same loss. This can mean that the other people may want to talk or process their grief in ways the teens felt hindered their mourning (Rask, Kaunonen, & Paunonen-Ilmonen, 2002). This finding, from a study with 14- to 16-year-olds in Finland, is corroborated by hospice workers in the United States, who report similar experiences in their clinical caseloads wherein emotional ventilation by others inhibits the teens' private processing and meaning-making (personal communication in supervision with JLMM). Adolescents seem to rely most on helping themselves and using personal belief systems to support themselves through the active mourning stages, though Rask et al. (2002) report that about a third of their sample received significant support from friends and family (2002). Although many adolescents state their desire to use more self-help coping methods, Rask et al. also noted that participants reported fears of death, loneliness, and other inner thoughts that hindered their grief. They hesitated to tell others of these challenges to mourning and meaning-making. This implies that some interaction with adults, whether trained grief counselors or at least empathic school staff and/or attentive parents, will be beneficial for adolescents after a significant loss. A startling finding in Rask et al.'s study was the report by teens that when a friend had died, little to no support was offered by others. Disenfranchisement of grief is seemingly fairly common for both children and adolescents (Doka, 2002; Hogan & DeSantis, 1996; Rowling, 2002). The reading by Johnson at the end of this chapter, though reporting a mother who was sensitive to her daughter's grief, still includes an assertion by the teen that her mother "didn't understand how serious it was for me."

Rowling (2002) differentiates sources of disenfranchised grief as growing from both the intra- and interpersonal domains. In the former, the adolescent fears social disapproval and works very hard to remain in conformity with the peer group, something that a significant loss threatens because others are not typically experiencing deaths at that age at the same time. A 16-year-old reported that she had refrained from talking about her loss for 6½ years until a group that Rowling ran for teens yielded the impetus to share her thoughts and feelings with a close friend (Rowling, 2002, pp. 277–278).

Teens are said to experience "double jeopardy" (Oltjenbruns, 1996). They are compelled to hide the reactions to their loss, yet they are deprived of support for processing their loss because they refrain from letting others know about their thoughts and feelings. These intrapersonal strictures leading adolescents to withhold discussion of their feelings become particularly intense when they believe that expression would threaten their sense of themselves as emerging adults. The more insecure they feel, the more reluctant they are to share the vulnerabilities and distress of grief (Rowling, 2002). On the interpersonal level, parents and teachers tend not to validate the feelings of adolescents and believe that the lack of open discussion means that adolescents are not feeling the intensity of the loss in adult types of ways (Pfefferbaum et al., 1999).

RESPONSE TO THE DEATH OF A TEEN

Parents' Loss of a Tween or Teen

The most common mourners after the death of a teen are the teen's parents who are left behind. As noted earlier, teen death is often sudden, caused by accident, suicide, or overdose. It was traditionally held that violent, sudden death, particularly suicide, would raise the risk of complicated grief and posttraumatic stress disorder for survivors, especially parents (Rando, 1993). Recent empirical findings suggest that the sudden death of a child does entail more persistent and pervasive negative outcomes (as measured by death accommodation), though homicide led the way to more difficult adjustments than suicide (Murphy et al., 2003). Many researchers note the relationship tensions that occur for couples when a child dies, spurred by differences in grieving styles, the fact that both require support at the same time, and the hampering of the couple's communication (Peppers & Knapp, 1980; Rando, 1986c, 1993; Schwab, 1998; Videka-Sherman & Lieberman, 1985). Yet Klass (1986–1987) suggests that there is a paradoxical effect: Couples experience a profound bond resulting from the shared loss of a child, yet each is somewhat estranged from the other because each parent experiences his/her own singular relationship (and subsequent loss) with the deceased child. Grief affects both in ways that it does most mourners, with sadness, anhedonia, lethargy, periodic upsurges of grief, and the need to share stories of the deceased. Despite these shared experiences, the anhedonia and fatigue of grief will often lead to a decrease in support and also sexual expression for both partners, often in asynchronous ways, all of which carries the potential for added stress on the couple's relationship. In a unique longitudinal design, Murphy et al. (2003) found that marriages experienced stress after a sudden death, with marital satisfaction decreasing over time to reach a low at 5 years after the death. Despite consistent findings of lower marital satisfaction after loss, Schwab (1998) reports a lack of evidence to support the widely held myth that divorce rates increase for couples who lose children. Parents are also challenged by a sense that the world is not as benevolent as they once believed; self-worth and attempts to make meaning in the world are also negatively affected when a child dies suddenly (Matthews & Marwit, 2004).

As with the death of a child in earlier stages, the loss of the dreams parents have for children is a major part of the loss. Further, as adolescents grow, they engage on more peer-like levels with parents who may just be starting to experience the relationship as rewarding in and of itself after the normal rebellions of the tween and early teen years. It is not at all uncommon to read newspaper articles where parents are quoted as saying things like "He was just getting his life together" and "She was just at the beginning of her life" when teens die. Further, as with meaning-making in other losses, parents seem to find hope and meaning when they are able to turn a tragedy into something useful, like a memorial (Klass, 1996, 2005). Grief projects have become increasingly public since large-scale events have forced grief into the public eye. Fast (2003) suggests that mourning sudden deaths like the school shootings and deaths at Columbine High School and other events such as the bombing in Oklahoma City or the September 11, 2001, attacks have all provided an opportunity for meaning-making and social support.

OTHER LOSSES EXPERIENCED BY TEENS

Maturational Losses

Higher Expectations for
Responsibility and Independence

Teens' losses of maturation have some similarity to the losses of elementary school students in that the expectations and judgments of academic work and developing life goals are a large part of their daily lives. As children enter middle school and high school, more demands are made on their time, energy, and ability to conform to educational (as well as familial) imperatives. They begin to be viewed as responsible for their own productions of work (or lack thereof) with increasingly fewer teachers turning to parents to mediate, but holding the adolescent directly responsible. Although this is maturationally legitimate, and helpful for the individual's development, the struggle parallels toddler struggles as the teen has interest in embracing his/her growing independence, but may want to avoid the ramifications of being held responsible for his or her behavior.

Recent scholarship reveals a cynical pragmatism that has developed among many adolescents as a response to growing pressures to succeed. One example is the phenomena of "doing school" as a form of playing the game and working only as necessary to get grades and build achievements for academic success; this bypasses the more ideal motivations of self-satisfaction or work in pursuit of other life goals (Pope, 2001). These pressures can be viewed as losses of the joy of learning and gaining a sense of self-efficacy when one works toward goals and achieves them for their own sake, rather than as a means to an end. Further, aside from creating a generation of stressed out, materialistic, and miseducated students (Pope, 2001), these unrecognized losses of self-efficacy and joy may also lead to depression, as when teens express the feeling of being overwhelmed and never catching up, and the subsequent helplessness they feel (JLMM's clinical experiences).

Further, some may act on this, as evidenced in a newspaper exposé about an 18-year-old high school senior. Despite involved parents, treatment for depression, both athletic and social success (as shown by his election to the Homecoming Court), a young man still attempted suicide by jumping from a ninth-floor window and survived by a series of luck and miracles (Vitez, 2008). As noted earlier, teens, and certainly tweens, generally do not have the capacity to weigh all of the ramifications of impulsive decisions and their tendency to push parents away makes the risk even higher: The young man said, "My parents were asking me how my day was, and they would always try to get deeper in the conversation, but I just wouldn't let it happen." And at school, "I was the funny guy, always upbeat, always positive, even when I didn't feel like it on the inside" (Vitez, 2008, p. A22). A fellow student who battles depression and an eating disorder reported that she has considered suicide but had second thoughts after seeing this young man. She said, "It just made me realize you only have one life, and you could throw it away so quickly....When you're thinking about it, it doesn't seem so extreme. But when you see something like this, you understand" (Vitez, 2008, p. A21).

This reinforces the notion that teens may feel more stressors; be less able to use social support; and be more impulsive even in the seemingly positive situation of a good school system, involved parents and teachers, and success as defined by typical societal norms. Baer (1999) finds differences in deviance (using the sociological definition of out-of-the-ordinary behavior) based on gender and ethnicity even when controlled for family cohesion and parental monitoring. This implies that societal context, familial context, and developmental stage can all place teens at risk for difficulties in coping with stress, which loss certainly entails. Unrecognized losses of self-esteem and self-efficacy concomitant with pressures to achieve more may be part of the constellation that can lead to disastrous behaviors (whether toward self with suicidal behaviors or externally as with school shooters and others).

Even more commonly, tweens and especially teens must adjust to the maturational losses involved in identity formation. As noted previously, adolescence is often a time of "trying on" different identities and settling into consistency with one or more of those identities. Although this is a positive maturational step, it entails loss of the ability to continue to try out different identities and roles. Further, as self-knowledge grows, teens become aware of the discrepancies between the identity they adopt and the ones that are socially valued by society (and/or peers) at large. For some, this can be a force that brings them back into conformity with social norms, as when a teen who "experiments" with drugs and/or alcohol gets pressure to abstain from teammates within a chosen sport (these forces for conformity are more efficacious when coming from a valued peer or reference group than from parents).

Nevertheless, the same forces can encourage adoption of other behaviors and identities in negative ways as well, as when teens are urged by peers and others to engage in risky behaviors of various sorts. This desire for conformity to one's peer group (if not necessarily conformity to typical societal norms) is part of the problem experienced by the teen Gabriella in the reading by Bellin at the end of this chapter. By having a sibling who had a chronic (and noticeable) health condition, she felt herself deprived of a "normal" sibling and felt different from others, not only because of demands on her time for extra care of her sibling, but also as someone who just wanted things to be "normal" when they were not.

Another major identity issue arises as adolescents mature and they begin to have more support for relationship building. This is often a time for self-reflection and individuals may realize that their love interests revolve around same-sex relationships rather than the more common heterosexual ones. Although a positive development as one becomes more fully aware of one's self-knowledge and identity, it can also lead to secrecy and self-silencing (a form of loss) if the teen does not believe his or her identity will be supported and valued by those in his or her social milieu. Further, even if one's social group is supportive, one must make a decision about whether to share this aspect of identity because heterosexist culture makes the assumption of heterosexuality until shown otherwise (Flowers & Buston, 2001). In interviews with 20 young gay men about their experiences of recognizing their sexual identity, Flowers and Buston (2001) reported several themes: a sense of being "defined by difference," "self-reflection and inner conflict," "alienation and isolation," "living a lie," "telling others," and "wholeness and integrity," with the latter emerging as the men were able to come out to others and join in community to resist the heterosexist culture around them. The reinforcement of the notion of difference as a factor in a devalued identity seems to be a major part of the struggle as presented in the Flowers and Buston study. Kitts (2005) reports that this sense of difference and fear of ostracism can create the circumstances whereby a teen may resort to suicide to avoid the pain of stigmatization.

LaSala (2007) reveals the role of parents in not only providing support for the recognition of sexuality, but also in protection from potential harm. His research suggests that parental knowledge, involvement, and active communication about issues of sexuality can assist gay teens in using safer sex practices, suggesting implicitly that such teens also have more self-acceptance and self-care. Unrecognized losses involved in identity formation (whether issues such as sexual identification or even identification as the "band geek" or the "jock") can create the double jeopardy that adds to the risk of impulsively acting out of a fear of ostracism.

Double jeopardy, the tendency to avoid sharing feelings of loss and then being deprived of support because others are not informed (Oltjenbruns, 1996), implies that teens may also need support in dealing with these maturational and other losses. Yet they may refrain not only from talking about the losses and their ramifications, but also about the dreams and fantasies for the future that were entailed in the loss (Rowling, 2002). Even when supports are available, teens may not be forthcoming about the ways losses, such as ended love relationships, abortions, failures in school and other losses, also bring about the end of a fantasy for the future (Rowling, 2002). These then become additional aspects of disenfranchised loss about which they receive little or no support. Love relationships tend to be demeaned as "puppy love" or diminished as not worthy of the type of grief adolescents often experience once a love relationship ends (Martin, 1996). These types of unrecognized, unreported, and disenfranchised losses occur at a time when many make assumptions that adolescents are ready to handle their emotions on their own. Although this does not really apply to any age group (humans generally benefit from sharing their emotions with trusted others), for tweens and teens this may be more risky, as they believe these thoughts and feelings make them unusual. Asking adolescents to talk about their feelings directly is often unsuccessful, yet asking direct questions such as "How did you react?" and "What strategies do you use to cope with that?" are helpful (Rowling, 2002) and may allow tweens and teens to open up enough to begin to reveal the areas of pain that exist in their lives.

READINGS

CHILDHOOD CHRONIC HEALTH CONDITIONS AND SIBLING LOSS: CELEBRATING STRENGTHS AND ACKNOWLEDGING DIFFICULTY

Melissa H. Bellin, PhD, MSW, LCSW

Melissa H. Bellin is assistant professor at the University of Maryland School of Social Work, where she teaches health specialization. Dr. Bellin's research focuses on child and family adaptation to disability. Dr. Bellin has served as a member of the Centers for Disease Control Spina Bifida Transition Working Group and is currently the Principal Investigator of a multicenter prospective longitudinal study of self-management, bowel and bladder continence, quality of life, and psychological health in transition-age individuals with spina bifida.

Background

Across disciplines, a family-centered approach to research and service provision in the context of childhood chronic health conditions is gaining momentum. A hallmark of this innovative model of care is an appreciation that the impact of childhood conditions extends beyond the affected youth (B. H. Johnson, 2000). Researchers and clinicians who embrace this model recognize that the health and psychosocial functioning of the child with a chronic condition and the well-being of surrounding family members are interrelated and mutually influencing (Patterson & Hovey, 2000). Although significant inroads have been made to illuminate the parent experience, less attention has been placed on the siblings in the family unit, particularly in the context of a physical disability (Wallander & Varni, 1998). Evidence suggests, however, that some siblings are at risk for psychological and behavioral difficulty (M.S. Cohen, 1999). The following case study sheds light on some of the risk experiences that siblings may encounter in the context of a chronic health condition.

Case Presentation

Spina bifida is a congenital neural tube defect that results in a wide range of health issues, including neurological problems, bowel and bladder incontinence, neuropsychiatric deficits, and orthopedic difficulties (see Sandler, 2004, for a comprehensive review). Although the cause of this condition is unclear, it generally develops within the first several weeks of pregnancy. The defect may occur anywhere along the spinal cord, but, in general, a higher level of lesion is associated with more pronounced deficits.

Gabriella Williams is an adolescent sister of a youngster with spina bifida, Gretta. Since her birth 6 years ago, Gretta has endured numerous hospitalizations and surgeries related to her condition, including the closure of her back and placement of a shunt to protect against hydrocephalus (excess fluid in the brain) in the first days of her life. She has been hospitalized on several occasions because of shunt malfunctions and infections and has undergone three surgical revisions to her shunt. While her parents remained at Gretta's bedside, Gabriella stayed at her grandmother's home during the prolonged hospitalizations. Gabriella often feels like her parents shield her, that they do not include her in conversations about her sister's condition. This experience of "protection" has actually exacerbated her confusion and heightened her fear about the possibility of death.

Gretta has a lumbar level of lesion (midback region) that has resulted in limited sensation in her lower extremities and, consequently, altered mobility and problematic bowel and bladder functioning. Following extensive physical and occupational therapy, she is now able to ambulate with the assistance of orthopedic braces. However, Gretta tires easily and relies on a wheelchair to travel long distances. Because many public settings in the family's hometown are not accessible, the family is very limited in their social outings. Problems with bowel and bladder continence add additional complexity to Gretta's life and that of her parents and sibling. Although Gretta is learning the process of self-catheterization, her mother is primarily responsible for monitoring and managing her bowel and bladder programs. These are time-intensive activities.

The family resides in rural Ohio, where their mother, Kathy, is employed as a teacher's aide and father, John, is an owner-operator of a local grocery store. An extensive network of family and friends has helped the young family adjust and adapt to the stressors and challenges related to the chronic health condition. However, the diagnosis initially had a devastating impact on the family unit—emotionally, socially, and economically. Kathy took a leave of absence from her job to care for young Gretta. The costs associated with the surgeries, medications, rehabilitative services, and renovations to make their home more accessible significantly stressed the family's resources. Further, with her parents consumed with the caregiving needs of Gretta, Gabriella spends much of her time at friends' homes. Though she has always been anxious and concerned about the health and well-being of her younger sister, Gabriella has also struggled with intense feelings of jealousy, embarrassment, loneliness, and sadness. Furthermore, she has expressed frustration to her parents about not having a "normal" sister who can jump rope and ride bikes with her.

Dimensions of Loss

As reflected in this case, the experience of loss in the context of a childhood chronic health condition may be noted in diverse dimensions of sibling life. One aspect of sibling loss that is particularly evident in the family health literature relates to reduced or restricted time with parents. The intense and ongoing caregiving needs for youth with chronic conditions may place great demands on parents' time, energy, and emotions. Multiple visits with a range of health care professionals may create an additional layer of complexity in parents' schedules. Consequently, in some cases, parents may not be as physically or emotionally available to address and support sibling needs (Tritt & Esses, 1988). Indeed, perceived discrepancies in parental attention consistently surface as a source of frustration and resentment in research with siblings.

This loss of parental attention seems to be particularly challenging for siblings in early developmental periods. For example, the work of Bendor (1990) revealed that school-age siblings felt that they were not as valued as their brothers and sisters with the chronic condition and that their experiences of loss of parental attention spawned feelings of deprivation and anger, as well as confusion and anxiety. Adolescent participants in her work recognized that their parents were "overworked" and observed changes in the parents. Although resentment and jealousy about the reduced availability of their parents were, in general, absent from their stories, the siblings did acknowledge feeling burdened by their own sense of responsibility for the health and caregiving needs of their brothers and sisters. These reflections shed light on a different type of developmental loss experienced by siblings, namely, a change in role identity and responsibility. Whereas peers move forward in their development of individuation and pursue their own goals and aspirations, some adolescent siblings may experience conflict and guilt about separating from the family (Bendor, 1990).

Another loss described by siblings of children with chronic conditions stems from their altered relationships with their brothers and sisters. Pronounced communication deficits (Cate & Loots, 2000) or physical limitations (Bellin, Kovacs, & Sawin, 2008) may restrict their ability to engage their siblings in "typical" childhood activities. In research with siblings across diverse populations, Menke (1987) observed that siblings of youths with physical disabilities identify the limitations of their brother or sister as the most challenging aspect of the experience. Other research has similarly revealed that siblings may experience great distress because of the restricted sibling interaction (Naylor & Prescott, 2004). Although empathy and kindness are evident in sibling relationships (Kiburz, 1994), the experience of loss related to atypical interactions, particularly in socialization activities, is found in the siblings' descriptions of their lives.

Taken together, these diverse experiences of loss may threaten the psychosocial health of siblings. Indeed, research suggests that roughly half of siblings of youth with a chronic condition demonstrate adjustment difficulties (M. S. Cohen, 1999). This increased risk for maladjustment is manifested in many ways, including low self-esteem, anxiety, loneliness, depression, and social withdrawal (Cadman, Boyle, & Offord, 1988; P. D. Williams et al., 1999). Several explanatory themes accounting for the heightened risk for difficulty in siblings have been explored, including: (a) a lack of information about the chronic condition from parents and/or health care providers, (b) feelings of physical and emotional distance from parents, and (c) insufficient social support resources targeting siblings (P. D. Williams et al., 1997).

All of these explanations seem to highlight a dimension of sibling loss—whether it relates to changes in parent availability, an absence of open communication and information sharing, or a general failure to acknowledge and support the unique sibling needs. Though these risk experiences are profound and pervasive, many siblings successfully negotiate these experiences of loss and change and emerge "unharmed" if not strengthened by their exposure to adverse circumstances. Indeed, there is a continuum of sibling responses to the experience of living with a brother or sister who has a chronic health condition. Though hardships are acknowledged, siblings also describe positive aspects of their unique experiences. A review of the sibling literature found diverse personal growth opportunities emerging from the experience of having a brother or sister with a chronic health condition, including increased maturity, enhanced sensitivity, respect for diversity, and the development of leadership skills (Bellin et al., 2008).

A growing body of literature on sibling risk and resilience also suggests that there are a number of protective influences operating in their lives that may mitigate the negative effects of their risk experiences. Research with diverse sibling populations has shown that a positive attitude toward the chronic health condition, satisfaction with family interactions, warmth and closeness in the sibling relationship, and experiences of peer social support are related to positive psychosocial outcomes (Bellin & Kovacs, 2006; Fisman et al., 1996; Kaminsky & Dewey, 2002; Van Riper, 2000). Knowledge of these individual, family, and environmental influences is critical. Only through a rich under-standing of the salient risk and protective factors influencing sibling adjustment can targeted interventions be developed to support siblings as they process, and one hopes, move toward acceptance of their experiences with loss.

TEENAGERS AND TRAUMATIC GRIEF: TINA'S STORY*

Celeste M. Johnson, PhD

Celeste M. Johnson, PhD, is an Assistant Professor of Social Work at Widener University, Center for Social Work Education. She received her PhD from Bryn Mawr College, Graduate School of Social Work and Social Research. She is a licensed clinical social worker. Her scholarship interests include the impact of community violence on teens living in urban areas. Currently, she co-facilitates a community-based grief-and-loss group for at-risk adolescent teen males.

Tina's story is woven with ideas about teenage friendship, adolescent development, and traumatic grief to illuminate the unique, intense, and complex feelings that occur when teens grieve the tragic and violent death of a friend. There is a small literature about adolescent bereavement (Balk & Corr, 2009; Corr & Balk, 1996; Corr & McNeil, 1986; Raphel, 1983), a very limited literature about the death of friends during adolescence (J. M. O'Brien, Boodenow, & Espin, 1991; Oltjenbruns, 1996), and a growing literature about traumatic loss experienced by children and adolescents (J. A. Cohen, Mannarino, Greenberg, Padlo, & Shipley, 2002; Nader, 1997). Yet, given what is known about the psychosocial importance of adolescent friendships and the high incidence of tragic and violent deaths of teenagers, there is notably little literature regarding adolescent grief and loss when a friend dies a tragic and violent death (J. A. Cohen et al., 2002; B. L. Green et al., 2001). Many

*The doctoral research "When Friends Are Murdered," Bryn Mawr College Graduate School of Social Work and Social Research (C. M. Johnson, 2006) provided the information for Tina's Story and was partially funded by The Fahs-Beck Fund for Research and Experimentation (2000); SAMSHA Minority Fellowship Program (2003–2005); Christina R. & Mary F. Linback Foundation (2004). Celeste Johnson is Assistant Professor at Widener University, Center for Social Work Education.

teens have experienced the loss of friends who have died from traumatic situations. In recent years, AIDS, suicide, accidents, and homicide have been among the leading causes of death for adolescents (Barrett, 1996). With homicide, African American teens disproportionately suffer the traumatic loss of friends compared to other ethnic/racial teen populations because homicide has been a leading cause of death for African American adolescent males.

In 2003 I met Tina, a 16-year-old African American teenager, who within the 5 years prior to our meeting had lost an older sister and a close friend, Rick (age 17), in separate car accidents several years apart. However, it was her most recent loss, the murder of her friend Danté (age 21), about which Tina and I talked. Earlier that year, Danté was killed in a drive-by shooting on the streets of a large Northeastern city.

About Tina

> Other than that, I'm a normal teenager…

Tina ended her self-description with those words when I interviewed her at her high school located in a low-socioeconomic/high-crime urban neighborhood not far from where Danté was killed. She had volunteered to participate in my qualitative research study, which examined the lived experience of African American teen girls who had lost friends to murder. In a semi-structured interview, Tina spoke mostly about her bereavement experience following Danté's murder and she also talked about herself.

> [I'm] very independent, strong willed, intelligent. I can be a little aggressive but not too much. I'm kinda shy in my own way….Teachers, they say I'm college bound.

Tina was in the 11th grade. Her favorite subject was math, and she enjoyed being on her school debate team. She was a diligent student who made very good grades. As for her future, Tina "loved the law," she would say. She planned to be a prosecuting attorney. Tina lived with her mother and stepfather, both of whom worked semi-skilled jobs. Responsible, logical, and reflective, Tina said her mother called Tina her "backbone." She had a very strong Christian faith and sang in a gospel choir. Tina loved to sing. She had a boyfriend of 2 years. To make money, Tina worked at a local convenience store after school.

About Adolescent Friendship and the Significance When a Friend Dies

During adolescence, the lost presence of a friend from death has special meaning. Adolescent friendships serve key developmental functions and roles as teenagers differentiate from their families and develop their identity and sense of self. Of Tina's friendship with Danté, she said:

> We had a bond, you know. It was just real complicated.

Tina's description of her relationship with her friend Danté hinted how hard it was for her when he was murdered. Danté was not a romantic interest but a very close friend. Their families were friends and Tina often called him her "cousin":

> With Danté, that was like, my cousin, my brother, you know, he was everything.

Loss of a friend at any age is painful. Loss of a friend during adolescence is particularly difficult. Different from childhood friendships, adolescent friendships are more complex and intense. Different from adult friendships, there is a high degree of ego identification. The adolescent ego, a work in progress, is not yet as formed as in adulthood. Adolescent friendships assist in the ego's development.

In Western societies, a teenager's social world moves beyond the borders of the family; friends move to the forefront of attention. Friends serve as a relational bridge as teens are "on the way" to forming adult relationships. These relationships provide emotional support and a training ground to learn how to negotiate positive and negative interpersonal situations. Teen friendships are characterized by emotional intimacy, companionship, loyalty, and trust (Oltjenbruns, 1996). Typically, teen friends spend a significant amount of time together in person, for example, in school, at activities and events, on the phone (of all types now) and via the Internet. As confidants and buddies, teenagers share themselves, their adventures, their joys, foibles, heartbreaks, secrets, and so on. Girls tend to miss the loss of intimacy when a friend dies, boys tend to miss the loyalty and camaraderie (Walsh & McGoldrick, 2004). Tina lost a major emotional support when Danté was killed:

> At first I'm thinkin' like, "Who, who I'm goin' to turn to now?"…It was like, "Who is going to cheer me up…[when] I'm out of my mind?" With Danté, it was just like, that cousin…that relationship, that cousin is no more.

Death during adolescence is considered temporally "out of synch" with the natural order, more so when the death is violent. When teen friends mourn the death of friends, it is also considered an underacknowledged and disenfranchised loss (Doka, 1989; Sklar & Hartley, 1990; Walsh & McGoldrick, 2004). The needs of the surviving teen friends are often undervalued, misunderstood, and may go unattended (Walsh & McGoldrick, 2004).

About Adolescent Development

At age 16, Tina would be in midadolescence (Fleming & Adolph, 1986). Biopsychosocial changes begun in early adolescence continue. Physical growth and hormonal changes that produce primary- and secondary-sex characteristics signal readiness for reproduction. There is an emotionality that typically accompanies these changes. Psychologically, during midadolescence teens are developing their identity (Erikson, 1968), gaining a sense of competency, mastery, and control (Oltjenbruns, 1996). Cognitively, formal operational thinking evolves (Piaget, 1972), that is, teens are able to think in more abstract and hypothetical ways, including about consequences and about the future. Meaning-making abilities deepen and grow more complex. A mature understanding of death develops, that is, that it is universal, irreversible, and that life ceases (Noppe & Noppe, 1996). Not a child, yet not an adult, these mental capacities may be inconsistently available. In Western countries, adolescent egocentrism and a sense of invincibility are viewed as developmentally typical (Elkind, 1967). These aspects of thinking shape the teen's evolving sense of self in the world, the teen's view that "it is all about me," and that s/he is relatively invincible. However, the death of a friend puts a teenager in touch with his/her own mortality. The biological, cognitive, and psychosocial changes all contribute to a teen's unique and intense experience of his or her loss of a friend. Grieving the traumatic death of a friend during adolescence is a major stress on normal biological, cognitive, and psychosocial maturation.

Specific to adolescent bereavement, Fleming and Adolph (1986) isolated five key areas that were reflected in teens' thinking, feelings, and behavior during efforts to resolve complex feelings of grief and loss. Key areas are (a) the predictability of events, (b) self-image, (c) sense of belonging, (d) fairness/justice, and (e) mastery and control. Relevant for adolescents who experience the traumatic loss of friends, there is a loss of the assumptive world. The assumptive world includes the ideas (a) that the world is a safe place, (b) that the world is basically a predictable place, (c) that life is meaningful, and (d) that human beings are basically good (Janoff-Bulman, 1992). When a friend dies a violent and traumatic death, a teen learns that the world is not necessarily a safe place, that the world is not predictable, and that people do bad things to good people. Some teenagers have experienced a loss of the assumptive world earlier in life as a result of difficult life experiences. Today, teenagers are exposed daily to local, national, and global news broadcasts that challenge those assumptions.

There are many elements that influence the grieving process of teenagers when a friend dies a violent death. These include:

1. The level of intimacy of the friendship (Oltjenbruns, 1996)
2. The amount and quality of the time spent together (Oltjenbruns, 1996)
3. The level of ego reinforcement and ego identity served by the friendship (Podell, 1989)
4. The level of conflict and/or ambiguity in the friendship (Oltjenbruns, 1996).
5. The type and cause of the friend's death (Oltjenbruns, 1996)
6. The proximity and witness to the cause of death
7. The links and triggers to past real and perceived losses, and the nature of those losses (Podell, 1989)
8. The level of responsibility for the friend's death (Oltjenbruns, 1996)
9. The level of support from family and friends (Podell, 1989)
10. The level of coping skills of the adolescent (Podell, 1989)

Traumatic Loss, Traumatic Grief, and Tina

Ever since he died, it was just like a major effect...I went into, like, this panic state...'cause he got killed by a drive-by. So it's like, "What if I walk outside and I get shot up...and I'm an innocent bystander?"

This quote from Tina's narrative is an example of trauma-related anxiety. Trauma-related symptoms such as hyperarousal, numbing, avoidance, and traumatic memory and imagery overlap with and complicate the normal loss and restorative-oriented grief work necessary in bereavement (Stroebe & Schut, 2001). The trauma-related symptoms interfere with the bereavement process in such a way that the symptoms of one may intensify the reactions of the other and the ability to function is diminished. This is called traumatic grief (J. A. Cohen et al., 2002). There is anxiety in both traumatic grief and typical bereavement; however, the thought content, imagery, and some emotions differ and can work against each other (Raphel, 1983). The thought content and emotions of *trauma distress* (Rynearson & McCreery, 1993) involve, for example, reminders of the trauma, traumatic memories, and images. There is an effort to repel frightening and disturbing thoughts and imagery about the deceased. With normal bereavement, there is *separation distress* (Rynearson & McCreery, 1993), in which the thought content, imagery, and emotions are focused on the deceased and the loss, often with a yearning for the presence of the deceased. These processes can be cyclical and vary depending on the individual. With recovery, when the more acute trauma-related symptoms are alleviated, the more lengthy bereavement process can proceed (J. A. Cohen et al., 2002).

When a significant person in the life of children and adolescents dies a traumatic death, reminders of the trauma, reminders of the loss, and reminders of the consequent life changes complicate the grieving process (J. A. Cohen et al., 2002). Nader (1997) outlines the challenges:

1. The interplay of grief and trauma may intensify symptoms common to both.
2. Thoughts of the deceased may lead to traumatic recollections.
3. Traumatic aspects of the death may hinder or complicate issues of bereavement such as grief dream work, relationship with the deceased, and issues of identification and processing of anger and rage.
4. A sense of posttraumatic estrangement or aloneness may interfere with healing interactions. (p. 18)

Tina's thoughts and images about Danté illustrate the above challenges.

> It's like, in Danté's condition, if I constantly sit down and think about the drive-by, you know....With Danté being shot up...how did he look,

being…laying there on the ground for so long? Just imaging stuff like that, you know…especially, if you just saw that person…a week before it actually happened…just thinking about how did Danté look, you know, before all the make up? Before they did everything, what was Danté thinking about? You know, that takes you in a different mind frame, instead of thinking about the positive things.

Tina described having difficult dreams. The separation distress and the trauma distress coexisted in ways that compounded her anxiety:

After the death, it was like…after it really started hittin' me, I started having dreams about it…about him…just walking together.…It was just hard. I would wake up and say "No, you got to stop these dreams cause no matter how many dreams you have, [he's] not gonna be here no more…and then after I seen him [lying] in the casket, I had dreams about that…about him getting up out of the casket. It was real hard, you know. It was a point where I skipped school. I used to cut school just to get away from it.

Normally a source of mastery and achievement for Tina, school became a source of overwhelming anxiety of trauma reminders and loss reminders from which she had to flee.

In class.…[classmates] be like, "Oh, did you hear about Danté? He got shot up and stuff." And…it would take me back, you know, like really complicated…sometimes I just get up and move. Or, I ask the teacher, "Can I go to the bathroom?"…Just so I don't hear it, you know.

In school, seeing Danté's image on the remembrance tee shirts that she, schoolmates, and friends purchased to wear to his funeral also triggered overwhelming distress.

We all got shirts made. Sometimes I can be in the lunchroom, I see people walking about with his picture on [their] shirts and stuff…'cause he had a big funeral. Everybody was cool with [Danté]. So, it's like I see pictures, shirts walkin'…'cause everybody got shirts made for the funeral.…And I see the shirts walking around…'cause I don't wear mine. It just remind me of it…it just take me back there.

Tee shirts are a way to hold the deceased close. Tina's friends received some level of comfort in holding Danté close by wearing the tee shirts.

However, Tina had to distance herself from what served as a trigger for overwhelming discomfort. The tee shirts were a trauma-and-loss reminder. Tina was unable to join with or gain solace among her friends, a "community of mourners" identifiable by the tee shirts:

> I'm trying to eat my lunch and then [I'm] just, "Oh, I'm not hungry." My friends be like, "What's wrong with you?"...But, I just play it off, you know. "I'm not hungry no more. I'm tired,"...It was real hard.

Tina did not let her friends know what an emotionally difficult time she was having. Not letting her friends in, Tina emotionally isolated herself from her friends. At times, her friends were not able to understand Tina's behavior. This mismeeting among friends when a peer dies is known as secondary loss and incremental loss (Oltjenbruns, 1996). In this case, Tina's network of friends didn't know quite what to say to her and Tina was unable to fully use her network of friends for support, another loss.

The mix of bereavement and trauma-related symptoms were so overwhelming that Tina was truant from school for 2 weeks. She was distracted and unable to concentrate such that her grades and academic performance suffered. Catching up with school assignments, tests, and projects became an uphill battle and an additional stressor:

> I'm struggling. I'm really struggling, you know. Now I look back and just wish I never did it but it was my way of getting away, you know. I was tired of hearing my friends...talking about it. I was tired of seein' the shirts bein' worn, you know. I couldn't even focus. I'm sittin' there trying to do math and I keep thinking about him.

Intervention

Meaning-making and having someone available to empathically "bear witness" in culturally sensitive and developmentally aware ways are important elements for adolescents healing from the traumatic loss of a friend. The literature highlights individual and "trauma/grief focused" group modalities rooted in trauma and bereavement theory as treatment interventions for teens suffering from traumatic grief (J. A. Cohen et al., 2002). Layne, Saltzman, Savjak, and Pynoos (1999, cited in J. A.

Cohen et al., 2002) developed a manualized, school-based group treatment model used with war-exposed Bosnian teenagers that showed a reduction in trauma symptoms, depression, and an increase in social adjustment. This model used a psychoeducational approach with structured activities that helped the teens understand symptoms of traumatic grief, learn cognitive restructuring and stress-reducing techniques, and build problem-solving skills.

Sensitive and attuned natural supports such as family, friends, faith-based connections, and other members of a teenager's social surroundings are helpful to a teen's healing process when a friend dies a traumatic death. Expressive and reflective activities such as writing (e.g., song lyrics, raps, poetry and journal writing), music, art, filmmaking, and drama provide creative emotional outlets for teens. Social action activities with a relevant focus such as antiviolence are another outlet. Attending, participating in, and developing these programs, for example, working on school assemblies, community demonstrations, and marches are also informal avenues of emotional expression that provide a sense of community validation for teens.

Typically, for urban teens, natural supports are more immediately available to provide comfort and guidance. Tina found help in her natural supports. She talked with her mother:

> I talked to my mom 'cause she knew him, like seriously, and she knew how we were.

In the face of Tina's mother dealing with her own feelings of sadness over the loss of the son of her close friend, Tina's mother made herself available in the ways she knew how. Sometimes she did not understand the complexity of her daughter's feelings, but her sensitive presence was so important. Tina described her mother's efforts below:

> Sometimes [I'd] be sitting in my room or something with my head down on my bed...and she knew what was wrong, you know. We pray about it...or talk about it...and she try to tell me to think about the happy thoughts that we had. But it's not...it makes it harder when you think about that...'cause... 'you realize that those happy thoughts are no longer, they're just thoughts. It's not like I can call him tomorrow and say, "Let's go downtown again. Let's go to the movies. Let's," you know. It's not more of that, you know.

Tina also leaned heavily on resources from her church. She talked a lot with the youth minister of her church. When she was truant from school, she spent the days with her 19-year-old godbrother, a member of her church, who used biblical verses to try to fortify Tina:

> I was with my godbrother, you know, around the corner. And…he spent time with me reading the Bible, throwing scriptures at me…building myself up….That's where I was…but of course, my mom didn't know. Cause she'd be like, "Why you ain't in school?" [fretful] you know. But she really didn't understand how serious it was for me.

Danté's death, along with Tina's other losses, contributed to a crisis of faith out of which Tina emerged more committed to her spiritual beliefs and church community. Tina's spiritual beliefs contributed heavily to how Tina made meaning of Danté's death:

> Now…I look at it as all things happen for a reason. Maybe behind closed door Danté was miserable. God don't want his people to be miserable, you know. And that's how I look at it….Selling drugs, he [Danté] probably wasn't happy with that….But that was his way out, makin' sure his son ate…makin' sure his baby's mom was ok….So, that's how I look at it now. If it was God's…all things are for the glory of God….And He's [not] going to treat us wrong, you know….God just called him home, so. We'll never know.

Conclusion

Tina was able to reconnect with friends, catch up with her school work, graduate high school, and attend college. Constitutional factors, her meaning-making of Danté's murder, and her natural supports all contributed to her resilience. It has been found that increased psychosocial maturation can occur when a teen survives the death of a significant person in his or her life (Podell, 1989). Attention is now being given to posttraumatic growth that can result from the experience of surviving a trauma (Tedschi, Park, & Calhoun, 1998).

Tina's statements, "it's hard," "it's complicated," "it was serious," in reference to her mourning the death of Danté, may have reflected her inability to find words to convey the totality of her experience. The coexisting, colliding, and cyclical nature of the trauma and separation distress may have been indescribable. Adolescent psychosocial development and particularly psychological and cognitive development get severely taxed by the added process of negotiating the horror and sadness when a friend dies a violent death.

J. A. Cohen et al. (2002) state that symptoms will endure if children and adolescents who experience traumatic grief do not receive intervention. B. L. Green and colleagues (2001) found that sophomore college women, 4 years after the violent loss of a friend, still experienced strong feelings about the loss. A teenager's experience of life and view of the world can be forever changed when a friend dies a violent death. Tina indicated this when she said:

> With both them [Danté and Rick], it made me think that life is not a game. It's, it's much [more] serious...as what people make it seem....You know, 'cause the next second is not promised to you.

LOSS OF LOVE FOR AN ADOLESCENT: CAROLYN'S PUBLIC AND PRIVATE LOSS

B. Frankie Lamborne, MSW, LCSW

B. Frankie Lamborne is an instructor and field coordinator at the School of Social Work, Rutgers University. Professor Lamborne has worked with adolescents and their families for over 20 years as the director of School Based Youth Services in New Jersey. She has also worked extensively in her private practice with gay and lesbian individuals and families, especially in the coming-out process. The case study that follows is based on these years of experience as well as on the uniqueness of Carolyn's story. This very public outing gives a spotlighted view into what teens and their parents go through in this process. In Carolyn's case, it happened in a very nontraditional way.

Case Presentation

As I was working at home one evening, I vaguely heard a story on the news regarding a female coach from a local high school arrested on sexual misconduct charges and rape of a minor. A week later I got a call from Betty, the mother of the adolescent who was the alleged victim. Betty wanted to make an appointment for her daughter, Carolyn. She talked about Carolyn's withdrawal since the arrest of the coach and then her total shutdown since her subpoena to testify against the coach. Betty felt Carolyn needed to talk to someone because she wasn't talking to her parents and Carolyn was willing to go to therapy. I told Betty that I would see Carolyn alone but asked if she and Carolyn's father would attend future sessions if needed. Betty said she would but that Carolyn's father didn't believe in therapy so she doubted he would come.

I had intentionally avoided all further news reports concerning these events so that I could hear the story from Carolyn's perspective without a preconceived impression. A few days later a lanky, beautiful, young female athlete entered my outer office with her mother. I introduced myself and Carolyn extended her hand with a cheerful smile and said, "Hi, I'm Carolyn." When you think of the ideal American high school girl, Carolyn would fit most descriptions. She is 5'8" on the slim side of average weight with blonde hair and blue eyes. Carolyn smiles readily and appears to have more confidence than the average almost-17-year-old high school junior. She is a straight-A student, popular with peers and teachers, and has received all-county and all-state awards in two sports since her sophomore year. This very likable teen lives with her mom and dad in a rural area. She has an older married brother who lives in the next town. Everything seemed to point to a wonderful junior year for Carolyn.

My initial assessment noted an amiable, assured, mature teen who talked easily about herself, her accomplishments, her hopes for a sports scholarship, her many friends, and her close relationship with her parents, admitting "I'm really a Daddy's girl." I was beginning to wonder if her mom was seeing a problem that didn't exist. During this initial session I decided to ask, "Why do you think Mom wants you to come to therapy?" Carolyn explained that her mom was afraid that her public disclosure as a lesbian would be impossible for her, because everyone at school knew that she was the one involved with Ms. D. As we pursued this, Carolyn assured me that she had been "out" to her friends for over a year and that the school administration and staff were really handling it all very well and giving her a lot of support. She said that her problem was not the public exposure as much as the fact that the sex was consensual and she was now being compelled to testify against this woman who was her friend and lover. We spent the rest of the session talking about how the law views the relationship between a coach and a student versus how Carolyn sees it and discussed what Ms. D knew when she allowed the relationship to evolve. Carolyn could not see the validity of the imbalance in power in her relationship with the coach but gave nodding acceptance to the implications under the law. She still did not want to testify. I told her I understood but that it probably would not be a choice.

In the following sessions, we discussed their relationship. She disclosed that she really likes this woman but was not in love with her. She felt it had been a mutual attraction but that the coach had made the first move, though Carolyn said she knew exactly where it was going. Carolyn remained focused on testifying and how awful she felt about the injustice being done to the teacher. We also discussed being "out" to friends but not to family. She said she just had not figured out how to tell them in the past, but had thought she would when the time was right. "Part of me thought they knew. I never had a boyfriend. I always talk about girls and sports. I guess I was just kidding myself." I asked about her brother, with whom she seemed to have a close relationship. Carolyn said, "He's married now and it is different. We don't talk as much, but he did call after all this happened to tell me that he loved me and to just 'hang in there' and it will all turn out okay."

Most often in dealing with teens or adults coming out, I find they plan the time and manner of disclosure. They give a great deal of thought to the event and we talk about it at length. Usually someone, often a family member, is identified as a person with whom they feel safe and who is not likely to reject them. It is often a slow process and parents often present the biggest hurdle. It is hard to risk being seen as "failing" or being seen as less in our parents' eyes. This leads the gay person to silence rather than disclosure because s/he wants to remain in the comfortable place of honor he or she often holds with his or her parents. For teen girls, this is very often even more important in their relationship with their father. The subsequent loss of her relationship with her dad as a result of the sudden disclosure of her sexual identity was affecting Carolyn. She withdrew from family discussions and events, lost 12 pounds, and, although social at school, rarely talked to friends on the phone in the evening or went out on weekends. I knew we had not gotten to the core of her loss yet.

After a few less-than-productive sessions, Carolyn came in and started to cry. She began to talk about not being "Daddy's girl" anymore. She disclosed that her father did not speak to her or even look at her anymore. "I've always been so close to my dad and he was always so proud of me. Now it is like he thinks I'm not me." Carolyn had held this in for over a month and it all spilled out in sobbing gulps. For most people, the public exposure would have been devastating, even if the person was known to be gay in his or her own little circle. Carolyn seemed to navigate this part with great ease. This is what had puzzled me regarding her shutdown or withdrawal at home. When I had tried to unravel this, Carolyn insisted that that was just the way she was and that she did not know what to say. She felt that everyone was so down on the coach's behavior that she chose to say nothing at home. Now that the story was receiving less media attention, she thought her father would change his perspective; she believed that he was just upset about the publicity. The night before our session, Carolyn had asked him why he hadn't come to her practice. Her father exploded about how sick she was. He said that "being gay is disgusting." He ranted about it being unnatural, that she was too pretty to "want to do that," and on and on with accusations and humiliations. Carolyn said she couldn't even remember exactly what he had said and "probably couldn't say it out loud anyway." As we talked, I asked if her father had mentioned that she had not disclosed that she was gay. She said he had not and in fact she thought he was glad she had never told him, that he probably wished he did not know now either. Her mother, on the other hand, was very supportive and said she had always known. Carolyn said for the first time in her life she felt really close to her mom and that they were talking a lot more. Together, we decided that her mom would be included in our next session.

Betty was glad to be included in Carolyn's session. She talked freely about having an idea that Carolyn was gay since she was about 5 or 6 years old. She said she could not give specific examples but somehow she just knew. She said she was really torn now because she was happy that she and Carolyn could talk openly, but very sad that Carolyn's dad was ignoring her. By the end of the session, the three of us had decided that Carolyn would talk to her brother, Steve, about all that had happened and Betty would talk to her dad. We would meet again the following week. It did not happen the way we had planned.

A few days after our session, Carolyn came home from practice and saw her brother's car in the driveway. She had spoken with him the previous night and he had been understanding and supportive. Now she could hear loud voices as she approached the house and knew it was her dad and her brother. Carolyn went next door to her friend's house to wait until things got calmer. About an hour or so later, Steve left and her mom came home from work. Carolyn went home with much trepidation. Her father was angry, but he also had tears in his eyes. He asked if they could talk. Carolyn sat down silently in the kitchen and Betty went upstairs with a smile directed toward her daughter. Carolyn's dad ranted a little about how he felt betrayed and confused but that he wanted her to know that he still loved her and that would never change. Carolyn said she began crying and her Dad came and put his arm around her. He told her he still would not go to counseling, but that he would work to get their relationship back on track.

Betty and Carolyn returned the following week and although things had not gone as planned, which they frequently do not when teens are involved, things were improving. Carolyn's dad arranged time on Wednesday night after her practice to go get a bite to eat with her, just Dad and Carolyn. This was a plan that Carolyn, her mom, and I had set up as a possible idea if her dad was open to it. It will take time to build this relationship and trust back, but when both parties are willing, this usually results in an even closer relationship than the one that existed in the past. Betty believed that she and her daughter would be better than ever and that Carolyn knew she could come to her about anything, even her father. Carolyn agreed and was glad that she had their support because the future trial would still be hard for her.

Teens often think the situation is completed after sessions like this, so we took a break for a few weeks with the understanding she would call if she needed to talk. When she came for a session 3 weeks later, everything was going according to plan. She was still grabbing a bite to eat with her father, her brother even joined them once, and her mom was much closer to her now. She was excited that everything was so good but still had great fear about the trial and her testimony.

Experience has shown that adolescents do better in therapy when there is an urgent situation, so Carolyn and I decided we would reschedule closer to the trial. We had talked a lot about loss and grief through our previous sessions, and Carolyn was still appropriately grieving the loss of her anonymity at school and in her town as well as the temporary loss of her relationship with her dad. Summer was coming to a close and she wanted a few weeks to go to sports camp and just spend some time with friends. I agreed with the plan, predicated on the agreement that she would call if she needed to talk.

Carolyn contacted me in the fall to schedule a session to talk about going to court and her testimony. She has had no contact with the coach since the spring but is very concerned about destroying her career. This work will require that another loss be faced, that of childhood. An adolescent often cannot comprehend the distinctions made by our legal system, so Carolyn will need to use different reasoning to view the situation as an adult. She will first need to grieve the loss of childhood but will have the help of her family and many supportive friends and school officials. It is hard to watch a child be forced to grow up in the public eye, but Carolyn has the skills and help to persevere.

The following session involved a total upheaval. Carolyn and her parents arrived for the session and I was happy to see Carolyn's father (Tom) was willing to come. We briefly discussed the upcoming court case; the coach had taken a plea bargain and the family had just gotten the news that day. Each member of the family expressed satisfaction with the outcome, but the issue at hand now was redeveloping trust. Carolyn had gone to a friend's house to talk earlier in the week but had told her parents she was going out with another friend to the mall. This brought all of the issues about not knowing who their daughter is or where she is to the surface. Tom talked about his sense that he lost the respect of his employees because of all the events that occurred with Carolyn. He admits no one has said a word to him, but his company is in the same community as his daughter's school. He claims he never lied to his parents and he will not stand for her lying anymore. Carolyn's mom was quiet through most of the session. Her only input was that she wished Carolyn would feel like they could talk instead of always going to friends. This was rather quickly resolved by Carolyn agreeing to have a cup of coffee and talk with her mother once every other week as a start to building a better relationship. Carolyn's father was adamant in his assertions that he wanted Carolyn to "promise not to have sex again until college and not to hang out with any gay girls." I asked Tom, "Is this about Carolyn not being where she was supposed to be, or about being gay?" Tom adjusted himself in the chair a few times and then quietly responded he was not sure. "I just didn't want anymore attention on me or my family." He looked at Carolyn and said, "I love you but please don't do anything else to draw attention to the whole thing." Carolyn responded, "I don't care what anyone else thinks, Dad." I asked if she cared what her dad and mom thought. She said she did but also wanted to be herself.

The rest of the session was used to develop a simple trust contract. Carolyn agreed to say exactly where she was going and her mom and dad agreed to consider her request carefully before withholding permission because their daughter had earned their trust many times in the past. Building trust is a slow process and there will likely be many more sessions needed to truly begin to trust each other again, but no appointment was scheduled. This public "outing" caused a breach of trust for the parents that will involve a great deal of self-searching and honesty as they accept their daughter for who she is, with one aspect of her developing identity as a gay young woman.

Carolyn must learn to trust that her parents love her so that she can stop running from a relationship with them and instead help them to understand who she is and why she hesitated to share all of her identity struggles with them. This family has a strong bond that has been tested at its deepest levels and continues to be. If they face their collective and individual losses, they will be stronger in the future. As with other grief, processing the losses together will be important or the family may drift apart rather than go through the pain. Odd, somehow, that who someone loves can cause such grief and sense of loss.

SUMMARY

The readings that conclude this chapter bring the developmental aspects of grief and loss in adolescence into sharp relief. The unrecognized losses involved in identity formation are crucial aspects of loss at this age. Whether the struggle is to feel "normal" when a sibling has an out-of-the-ordinary persona or health condition, the loss of a trusted friend who carries part of one's acceptance of self as one is going through some of the most intense identity transformations, or the evolutions of sexual identity and growth within family roles, adolescents are challenged with a growing sense of who they are. They stand on the edge between the ability of younger children to move in and out of active grieving relatively fluidly and coping with loss as an adult, which involves more extensive periods of time in the active grieving stages of the dual process of moving in and out of active grief processing. The tendency toward "double jeopardy," and its paradox of needing more support yet being unwilling to reveal oneself, leaves adolescents particularly vulnerable at a time when depression and impulsiveness may be part of the normal developmental life cycle. For grief counselors, this requires that interventions be finely tuned to draw adolescents out of their shells without having them feel too exposed; it requires strict confidentiality and attention to trust building, while also encouraging them to make use of family, friends, and other support. In short, just as the adolescent is poised between childhood and adulthood, the practitioner must be poised between the nurturing and intervening stance one adopts with children and the more peer-related stance one may use with adults. The intensity and malleability of adolescence make it a fruitful and exciting time to help teens as they make use of the growth opportunities inherent in losses of all kinds.

6 Young Adulthood

Larry is a 29-year-old African American man who lives alone in an urban apartment and works as a counselor in an agency serving an adult population. Larry is the youngest of three, with two older sisters who have moved to other states within the United States. Larry graduated from college at 22 and found his first job through a career placement office at his alma mater. Larry lived at home with his parents in a rural setting for 3 years prior to establishing his own "bachelor pad." Although Larry did not relish the idea of living with his parents for those 3 years, he wanted to have some financial security prior to setting out on his own. It may be that Larry also needed those 3 years to work on his emotional and physical separation from his family of origin. In addition, as the youngest of three, Larry's parents may have wanted and needed Larry's presence in the household to avoid their facing the empty nest, having two older children who moved quite a distance from their family of origin. It was also during this period that Larry sought therapy to help him understand some of the transitions and sense of loss he had experienced in moving out of his parents' home and establishing his own independence, a critical task for a young adult.

When Larry did find his own apartment, his parents were pleased at his launching himself but missed having him in their home at the beginning and end of each day. Larry's job for the 3 years that he lived at home was unsatisfying to him as it involved sales in a large corporation. As Larry began

171

to own and to accept his independence, he realized that he needed a graduate degree in the human services to begin to fulfill his career dream. When he completed graduate school and found a job as a counselor, Larry was externally and internally accepting of a reduced emotional dependence on his parents. During the years that Larry lived with his parents, he continued to date a young woman whom he had met in college, but this relationship ended when Larry moved into his own apartment. Moving into the city where a few of his friends lived gave Larry the incentive to date other women and to discover more about himself.

DEVELOPMENTAL CRISIS: INTIMACY VERSUS ISOLATION

Social Development

Within this text, young adults are defined as individuals between the age of about 22 to the age of 40. However, social scientists are beginning to reconsider the span of early adulthood (Furstenberg, Kennedy, McLoyd, Rumbaut, & Settersen, 2004). Research indicates that the transition to early adulthood, usually marked by finishing school, finding a job with benefits, marriage, and parenthood will not happen for many young adults until their late 20s or even their early 30s. This society will need to "revise upward the normal age of full adulthood, and develop ways to assist young people through the ever-lengthening transition" (Furstenberg et al., 2004, p. 34).

In 2000 the U.S. Census Bureau reported that 5.5 million unmarried households existed, demonstrating an increase of more than 5.5 million such households during a 20-year period (U.S. Census Bureau, 2004). This number will increase by 2010. Because of the growing number of adults who remain unmarried but live together for an increasing number of years, having children may be delayed for some time. However, this increase has been accompanied by a growing number of children born in the context of cohabitating relationships (Newman & Newman, 2006). As a result of the growing number of adults who remain unmarried but live together in committed gay/lesbian/transgender relationships, marriage is no longer the significant marker in the transition to young adulthood.

Psychological Development

The development of intimate relationships is one of the important tasks facing young adults. Intimacy reflects "the ability to experience an open, supportive tender relationship without fear of losing one's identity in the process" and of growing close to another person (Newman & Newman, 1987, p. 446). Intimacy implies the capacity for mutual empathy and mutual regulation of needs—the capacity to give and receive pleasure. An intimate relationship encourages the disclosure of personal feelings and the sharing of plans and ideas (Newman & Newman, 2006). Intimacy allows two young people to feel meaningful and special to one another. To move toward the establishment of an intimate relationship, an adult's need for personal gratification has to be subordinated (at times) to his or her needs for mutual satisfaction. Young adults are trying out new relationships and connecting "with others in new ways while preserving their individuality" (Hooyman & Kramer, 2006, p. 192).

Erikson (1968, 1978) speaks of the crisis of intimacy versus isolation as the major thrust of young adult development. Those who resolve this crisis in favor of intimacy are able to experience love. Those adults who are unable to resolve this crisis may feel disconnected, alone, and "unable to form a significant, committed relationship" (Hooyman & Kramer, 2006, p. 192). The task of establishing intimate relationships can be inhibited when the young adult faces or is coping with a significant loss of a friend, partner, or spouse or when the young adult is faced with a chronic and/or life-threatening illness. This is so because losses and illnesses require an adult to become more self-absorbed to cope with the stress of loss. Self-absorption can make intimacy with one's partner more difficult as the young adult struggles to meet his/her own needs.

During the early phase of this developmental stage, young adults are also struggling with issues related to achieving independence from their family of origin. Often young adults want to become independent of their parents but do not want to experience the pain of separation (Oktay & Walter, 1991). This is often the first normative loss that a young adult consciously processes. Young adults can be uncertain of their ability and right to take care of themselves and because of this they can be vulnerable to staying emotionally dependent on their parents (Gould, 1978; Levinson, Darrow, Klein, Levinson, & McKee, 1978). The vignette of Larry described at the beginning of this chapter illustrates the struggle that young adults often experience when separating from their family of origin. This separation has both internal and external components. External aspects include moving out of the family's home (today, this is often delayed or young adults return to the nest after college), becoming less dependent financially, and assuming autonomous roles (Oktay & Walter, 1991). Internal aspects involve a reduced emotional dependency on parental support and authority. One task of this phase is to not end one's relationship with one's parents yet negotiate an adult-to-adult relationship.

Loss of one's parent to death, divorce, or chronic illness can seriously impact this negotiation. If one parent should die during this early phase, the other parent is often emotionally unavailable during the intense period of grieving for their spouse. The young adult is left to grieve on his or her own, but can, one hopes, engage in peer relationships for support during this period. The young adult may also have a commitment with the workplace, which potentially can offer some solace. In the reading by Oktay at the end of this chapter, Andrea is a young adult who has lost her mother to cancer. This is a devastating experience for Andrea, who has just been married and has to return from her honeymoon to juggle the demands of her mother's illness with her desire to adjust to her new marriage. Within this case we can see the struggle to become independent from her mother and establish a new marriage but at the same time she has a need to help her mother through this last phase of her life. On the flip side, when the young adult faces a chronic and/or debilitating illness and possible death, severe conflict over dependency issues can ensue as they strive hard for independence from their family of origin. This conflict is described in the next section of this chapter under the discussion of a young adult who has breast cancer.

LOSSES EXPERIENCED BY YOUNG ADULTS

Chronic Illness

When a young adult faces a chronic illness and/or life-threatening illness such as breast cancer, multiple sclerosis, or cystic fibrosis, s/he needs to become self-absorbed so as to monitor her/his physical well-being, which can make achieving intimacy more difficult. Because any serious illness involves increased self-absorption, one of the emotional risks of having a disease like breast cancer at this stage of life is that it may push a young person toward isolation, making relationships more difficult. For example, in a qualitative study done by Oktay and Walter in 1991, one young woman was 26 when she was diagnosed with breast cancer. Following a modified radical mastectomy, she discovered that she was pregnant and underwent an abortion before she began chemotherapy. In this situation, although this young woman self-reported that she went through a phase of being "mean, moody and selfish," her boyfriend accepted and understood her. However, it took the "couple longer to achieve a good sexual adjustment, because of the switch to a disruptive birth control method" (p. 67). This young woman and her boyfriend ended their long-term relationship because her boyfriend wanted her to "let go of the breast cancer" and she wanted to help other breast cancer patients with their adjustment. In the case of Ricky, described at the end of this chapter, we clearly see how a young adult who suffers from addictive behavior has great difficulty sustaining intimate relationships.

Another arena affected by chronic illness is the struggle for independence from one's family of origin at a time when the young adult who is ill might need to rely on family. In the case of the young woman with breast cancer, she relied quite heavily on her mother during the period of diagnosis and surgery, but decided to return to her own apartment after her hospital stay so that she could learn to manage the postoperative routines on her own. However, her ambivalence about this decision was revealed when she spoke of how difficult the nights were to manage on her own and how this increased her worry and concern. Farrant and Watson (2003) report that some of the effects on a young adult who copes with a chronic illness include "increased rates of depression, lack of independence from parents, poor vocational education, lower employment rates and negative body image" (p. 175).

Chronic illness in adulthood violates assumptions that many young adults have about the "just world" (Hooyman & Kramer, 2006; Oktay & Walter, 1991). Many young adults assume that "If there is pain, there is something wrong with us." Because many young adults are struggling with this issue, the wish to believe in a just world is brought into sharp focus when a young adult confronts the experience of a chronic or, in the case of breast cancer, a life-threatening illness. Young adults often attribute their illness to "something bad that was done," such as poor diets or health habits or the physician who missed a diagnosis. One young woman who was diagnosed with breast cancer in her 30s and is struggling with this just-world assumption says:

> I was always known by my friends as a health food nut. I was a very careful eater....I never ate anything like beef. I exercised....We don't have this in the family. Why couldn't it have happened to somebody older? I was just starting life. I kept thinking it wasn't fair....Nobody ever said that life was going to be fair, but I really thought it wasn't being fair. (Oktay & Walter, 1991, p. 91)

Another theme of young adulthood is finding one's place in an adult world. According to Levinson and colleagues (Levinson, Darrow, Klein, Levinson, & McKee, 1978), one of the primary tasks of the first phase of early adulthood is to "make a place for oneself in the adult world and to create a life structure that will be viable in the world and suitable to the self" (p. 72). In today's world this task probably overlaps into the 30s for many young adults because of the delay in moving out of their family home or moving back in for a while. Most young adults have a dream of the kind of life that they want to lead as adults. The dream often has "the quality of a vision, an imagined possibility that generates excitement and vitality" (Levinson et al., 1978, p. 91). Adults in their 20s tend to be goal oriented and future oriented—their sense of time is projected forward with an attitude that everything is possible (Oktay & Walter, 1991). Coping with serious illness and dying means coping with an uncertain future, which intersects with the young adult's need to find a place in the world. On the flip side, coping with a serious illness can catapult a young adult into prioritizing what is most important to him or her at a young age. It may promote the willingness to take a risk to act on a dream, which s/he may not have done if s/he had not been ill. On the other hand, obviously, dying at this phase of life can interfere with the achievement of a dream.

Research on young adults with chronic illness indicates that they "value qualities relating to personal characteristics of the provider as more important than those relating to the physical environment of the provider" (Farrant & Watson, 2003, p. 177). These young adults and their parents would like to discuss a wider range of health topics with their health care providers than they are currently receiving (Farrant & Watson, 2003). Mental health issues were topics that were least discussed with health care providers yet were those that young adults and their parents most wish to discuss. They also reported there was "limited planning with their current health provider for transition to adult health services" (Farrant & Watson, 2003, p. 177). Farrant and Watson found a major gap in planning for services that transition the older teen to adult services. As a result of the increasing survival of children with disability and chronic illness, transfer to adult services is becoming a more important part of pediatric care. Since "early initiation of transition planning is associated with increased likelihood of success" (p. 178), health care providers need to address this issue.

Death of a Parent

The death of a parent can be quite traumatic for a young adult, as s/he does not expect a parent to die during this life phase. It is also often the first time an individual consciously experiences the death of a loved one. Since this is an "off time loss" (unexpected for early adults) they often do not have peers with whom to share their feelings and reactions. The lack of social support can lead to complicated mourning for the young adult. The loss of a parent as a young adult may inhibit that adult's life with regard to working on the developmental task of intimacy with another partner because of fear of loss of a loved one. A young adult may also become more of a pseudo-adult to cope with the loss of a parent from whom the young adult is still separating. In the case study of Andrea, at the end of this chapter, the reader will see how Andrea takes over some of the roles that her mother held in the family. For a young adult this reaction either can be an impediment to further development or can enhance emotional growth and move the young adult forward in his or her life. For Andrea, at age 25, the recurrence of her mother's cancer was difficult, but the ensuing death of her mother when she was 32 collided with her transition into marriage. It is clear that the collision with tasks such as marriage for a young adult who is struggling with the death of a parent can be disruptive to ongoing developmental growth. However, in Andrea's case, despite this collision of parental death and her own marriage, in time she was able to make meaning of the loss and embrace the concept of parenthood in a way that she never believed she could.

MATURATIONAL LOSSES IN EARLY ADULTHOOD

Delaying Decisions About Childbearing

As opposed to earlier cohorts of young couples, some of whom believed that having children was the main reason for marriage, "in the 1980's and 1990's the majority of people disagreed with the idea that having children is the main reason for getting married" (Newman & Newman, 2006, p. 406). However, couples continue to embrace the value of parenting, but see it more as a choice than an obligation. Delaying parenthood until the late 20s and early to mid-30s or even the 40s has become more of a trend among young adults. "Between 1980 and 2000, the number of births per 1,000 women between the ages of 15 and 29 decreased…and the total number of births per 1,000 women between the ages of 30 and 44 increased from 35/1000 to 46/1000" (Newman & Newman, 2006, p. 406). The one normative loss that can occur with this change is that the biological limits on the age of childbearing for women are still significant. Women's fertility rates decline after age 30 and miscarriages increase by age 40 (Newman & Newman, 2006). Although reproductive technologies regarding conception have become increasingly successful, it is still difficult to conceive. In fact, natural fertilization via sexual intercourse decreases from a 40% effective rate for a woman in her 20s to less than a 10% rate for a woman in her 40s (Newman & Newman, 2006). Thus, delaying parenthood until late in one's 30s or early 40s can result in infertility.

Infertility

Fertility is also a theme of early adulthood that has often not been recognized in the literature on life-course development, which is largely based on male development as a model for human development (Oktay & Walter, 1991). Although they may not plan on having children soon (indeed young women are waiting longer and longer to have their first child), young women often take their fertility for granted. "In fact, it can be seen as an encumbrance, as a sexually active woman often bears the major responsibility for birth control. Fertility is an important component of self-esteem in both men and women" (Oktay & Walter, 1991, p. 64). Those adults who discover infertility issues experience a marked decrease in self-esteem and self-confidence. The impact of infertility on a young adult, whether in the early or later phases of early adulthood, can be devastating. The case history of Christine at the end of this chapter under the heading "The Losses of Infertility" illustrates the impact of infertility on a couple in young adulthood. Christine describes her deep sense of loss as a result of missing the developmental milestone of parenthood. However, Christine and her husband, with the help of a social worker, were able to grieve their loss of biological parenthood and make meaning from their painful loss so that they could go forward in their lives.

Losses Connected With the Transition to Parenthood

One of the maturational losses that young adults face when they become parents is a decrease in the degree of intimacy within their marriage or partnership. Society does not often recognize how much a couple has to negotiate and "give up" to assume the role of parenthood. However, there is recognition that the transition to parenthood can be stressful for marriages and parent–child relationships (A. Shapiro & Gottman, 2005). There is evidence that taking on the role of parent can decrease the quality of the marriage as well as the quality of the young adult's relationship with his/her child. The following results have been noted: (a) marital conflict increases dramatically (Belsky & Kelly, 1994); (b) marital quality decreases for 40% to 67% of couples, beginning within the first year of the baby's life (A. Shapiro, Gottman, & Carrere, 2000); (c) the quality of the marital relationship first declines for wives and later for husbands (Belsky & Pensky, 1988); (d) during the last trimester of pregnancy marital satisfaction is generally high and then declines thereafter (Cowan et al., 1985). Because one half of all divorces within the family life cycle occur within the first 7 years of marriage, these early years become a time of high risk for the marriage's survival. Especially for new mothers, depression is also more likely to occur during the transition to parenthood (A. Shapiro & Gottman, 2005).

Similarly, in the "first prospective, short-term longitudinal investigation of lesbian couples' relationship quality across the transition to parenthood," Goldberg and Sayer (2006, p. 98) found that on average "lesbians' love decreased across the transition [to parenthood], whereas conflict increased" (p. 96). In a study that focused on a White, working-class, dual-earner sample examining the effects of shift work and role overload on the transition to parenthood, both mothers and fathers reported significant increases in conflict within the marital relationship in the first year of parenthood. The results indicated that "working noonday shifts may hold some negative implications for depressive symptoms and relationship conflict for dual-earner couples" (Perry-Jenkins, Goldberg, Pierce, & Sayer, 2007, p. 136).

We as a society need to be more cognizant of ways in which we might support couples when they take on parenthood. A. Shapiro and Gottman (2005) found that 2-day psycho-communicative-educational workshops for couples making the transition to parenthood helped them to build skills in coping with conflict and the maintenance of friendship and intimacy. When considering couples from all socioeconomic levels, the workplace also needs to examine changes it can make to help young couples navigate the work/marriage/parenthood experience less stressfully. The flip side is that when a couple can manage this time together and create a changed relationship, including the children but keeping time for themselves to provide comfort and care for each other, the gains are remarkable.

Loss of Romantic Relationships

The loss of romantic relationships has become almost as frequent in adult life as in the more experimental years of adolescence (Neimeyer, 1998). More than one third of all types of partnerships (gay, lesbian, and heterosexual) dissolve within 2 years (Neimeyer, 1998). For some, the dissolution of a relationship has advantages as it contributes to the young person's personal growth, but for many others "the years of dating represent a seemingly endless series of exhilarating romantic connections, broken by disappointment and occasionally devastating disconnections" (p. 23). Some of the secondary losses are less tangible than others, such as loss of self-definition when one is no longer defined as a couple. This can have ramifications for shifting one's view of oneself, as well as how one's social world assimilates and reacts to the change. Loss of a relationship through a breakup is often not recognized as a true loss by the support networks of the young adult (family and friends), who attempt to minimize the loss by saying, "you are young and will find someone else." The mourning process for this type of loss is often privately experienced without acceptance in a public way. This type of loss may be characterized as a disenfranchised loss. Robak and

Wietzman (1994) report that the breakup of romantic relationships is frequently followed by intense grief experiences.

For young adults, the individual's support network is especially significant because personal growth and development are dominant life themes. When support systems consisting of friends and family members react to the breakup as merely a part of growing up, the meaning of the loss is minimized to the bereaved (Robak & Wietzman, 1994). One study that examined the grief reactions of nursing students to a sudden death of a classmate indicates that although core themes that emerged among these nurses included "morbid anxiety, helplessness after death, fear of disappearance and thinking of one's own future" (Jiang, Chou, & Tsai, 2006, p. 279), the students rarely shared their feelings of grief with others. Young adults may perceive that others will not be supportive of their grief over relationships that end, even in death.

Addictions

Alcoholism and drug addiction have become an increasing problem for today's youth and young adults. For those who become addicted, the loss of time in developing a commitment to work, finding a place in the adult world, and creating a life partnership (heterosexual, gay, lesbian, transgendered), is put on hold or severely delayed, depending on the intensity of the addiction and length of time one is addicted. Addicts at this stage of life lose time that they might have used developing a life—career, marriage, and family (children). Sometimes they lose jobs, health insurance, and time while in rehabilitation, even when pursuing recovery. Furthermore, when addicts are in recovery, they lose their connection to the drug of choice that helped them handle stress. The case of Ricky at the end of this chapter clearly illustrates the issues faced by young adults who are addicted but use their recovery to make meaning of their lives and move forward.

LOSS OF A YOUNG ADULT
AS EXPERIENCED BY OTHERS

Mental Health Problems and
Loss Related to the War in Iraq

Loss of a spouse or partner in early adulthood is fraught with special issues that place it apart from loss of a spouse/partner in either middle or later adulthood. There will be increasing numbers of both men and women facing such a loss as a result of the war in Iraq. As of November 2008, more than 4,000 young adults have died serving in the war (Iraq Coalition Casualty Count, 2008, retrieved November 18, 2008). One report speaks of the mental health problems that will (and have) emerge(d) as the result of this war. "US combat forces spend more time in combat without a break than those who fought in Vietnam or World War II" (Zoroya, 2007, p. A1). In other wars, combat forces were pulled off the line and then brought back in. This system is not in place for those forces in Iraq, which are in combat more consistently without a break.

Army Col. Carl Castro, a research psychologist, maintains that the stress for troops in Iraq is aggravated by "multiple hours, tours of duty, and deployments that have been extended from 12 months to 15" (Zoroya, 2007, p. A1). Army psychologists who conducted research in Iraq last year found that 30% of the troops (who spend an average of 56 hours per week experiencing high levels of combat) demonstrated signs of acute stress (28%), anxiety (13%), and depression (12%). "Outside fortified areas, three in 10 screen positive for mental health problems" (Zoroya, 2007, p. A1). This issue will intensify when young adults return from the war in Iraq and face their former lives in the workforce and cope with family issues. The returning veteran has "lost" the life s/he once knew and his/her family has been without this family member for a long period of time. Many readjustments are required at this point in their lives. PTSD will be rampant as the veterans return to the States and vividly recall traumatic experiences of wartime. Although widows and widowers (partners) of the Iraq/Afghanistan wars will have to adjust to a life after the loss of a spouse or partner, for those whose spouses (partners) return home they will likely experience the "ambiguous loss" (Boss, 1995—see chapter 1, this volume) of having the partner back physically, but without the same identity s/he had before combat.

Death of a Spouse

Here we will discuss issues that are generic to the loss of a spouse and in each following chapter will differentiate how this loss might be experienced differently by bereaved spouses in different life phases.

Holmes and Rahe (1967) claim that the loss of a spouse is the most stressful of all losses. Research on this issue points to the emotional, mental, and physical pain that is experienced by widows and widowers. This sense of loss is intensified because the grief is experienced not only over the spouse who has died, but also over the connection to the spouse, as well as the hopes, plans, and dreams for the future. Furthermore, the bereaved spouse grieves for that part of him or herself that was a part of the relationship (C. Walter, 2003). The postmodern theorists emphasize the importance of the connection with the deceased spouse. "A bereaved spouse, confronted by the reality that the dead partner is gone forever, will do whatever it takes to sustain the relationship" (C. Walter, 2003, p. 14). Conversely, evidence of the partner's existence can trigger painful feelings. This Dual Process Model (Stroebe, Schut, & Stroebe, 1998) refers to the process whereby the bereaved "accommodates to the loss by an ongoing shift back and forth between two contrasting modes of functioning" (C. Walter, 2003, p, 11). This causes the bereaved to engage in and explore all of the feelings associated with loss of the spouse, while at other times "tuning out" the feelings of acute grief to focus on the many external adjustments required by the loss. The adaptation to the loss depends on the bereaved's ability to find some means of integrating the death of the loved one and to develop a continuing form of the relationship (C. Walter, 2003). Common themes present in spousal loss include loneliness and isolation, an identity shift from "we to I," changing relationships, handling rituals and marker events, taking responsibility for self, and coping with anger (C. Walter, 2003).

The loss of a spouse at a young age places the young adult in a position that is out of sync with his or her developmental phase. Shaffer (1993) discusses various factors contributing to this position, including: (a) a lack of comfort from others of a similar age who are experiencing the same loss, (b) the lack of previous experience with the loss of a loved one, and (c) a dearth of role models to demonstrate how to cope with such a significant loss. Unlike women or men in their 50s and 60s, young adults have not been socialized as to what this experience will be like. The young adult widow has been studied much more often than the widower. Although the grief and phases of bereavement reported by young widows follow the general pattern of that observed by other researchers, the grief of young widows was characterized by "positive shifts in life perspective and by a theme of metamorphosis and rebirth" (Shaffer, 1993, p. 128).

Because the loss has been experienced at a younger age, when identity is more fluid, younger widows tend to remake their lives and "start over" in ways that might seem unrealistic to an older widow in middle or later adulthood. Several researchers note that a transition in self-concept occurs (Levinson & Levinson, 1996; DiGiulio, 1992; Shaffer, 1993). One young widow in her late 20s described both the professional and personal changes that occurred in her life following the sudden death of her 28-year-old husband. She changed her career plans from animal research to grief counseling and speaks of how she feels as though "I am a much healthier person and have much more insight into who I am...with more goals and deeper insight into the purpose of my life" (C. Walter, 2003, p. 49). Young widows demonstrated their ability to go beyond surviving of their spouses to engagement in a life that was more fulfilling than might previously have been possible (Shaffer, 1993).

The other issue that is pertinent to young adults who have been widowed and are beginning to explore their world is dating. Dating can be a conflicted and difficult issue because of the changes in social norms since these young adults last dated. Further, loyalty to one's deceased spouse may add complications. The idea of loving someone new can evoke a range of feelings, from a signal that one is healing and ready to move forward, to a perception that this is a betrayal of the marriage (C. Walter, 2003). One young widow was conflicted at first because she had known her late husband since childhood and lived in the same town as her in-laws. Her issues of loyalty to her late husband's parents were almost as weighty as those toward her deceased husband. However, she began resolving some of her conflicts when she began to emotionally relocate her late husband's "memory in a place where it is accessible to her" (C. Walter, 2003, p. 45) so that she can integrate this memory with her new relationship with a young man she dated. This ability to stay connected to the memories of the deceased while forging a new life resonates with the theoretical framework of the postmodern theorists on bereavement (Klass et al., 1996; Neimeyer, 1998; Rubin, 1999), who embrace the importance of how the continuing bonds with the deceased enhance the survivor's functioning in the present.

Death of a Nonmarried Opposite-Sex Partner

We are living in a culture in which the largest growing group of partners in both young adulthood and later adulthood are nonmarried opposite-sex partners (C. Walter, 2003). Although the presence of social support is one of the most critical factors in the healing process, those partners involved in nonmarital opposite-sex relationships "are less likely than other groups to have this support, either at the time of death or for a period of time following the death" (C. Walter, 2003, p. 87). In contrast, Alisa (one of the bereaved partners interviewed by Walter) was 23 when her fiancé, Brian, died of a sudden heart attack. Alisa received support from both her own family as well as that of Brian's family when he died. In fact, Brian's mother gave her half of the life insurance. In addition, Alisa and Brian's mother planned the funeral together, using most of Alisa's ideas. This was not true for the other opposite-sex partners who were neither engaged nor married (C. Walter, 2003). One can see the difference in the degree of social support experienced by this young bereaved partner because her relationship was sanctioned by society in that she was engaged at the time of the death of her fiancé.

Death of a Gay Partner

When a gay man loses his partner, his grief is intensified by the lack of the "mainstream culture's recognition of his relationship, his loss and his becoming a widower" (Shernoff, 1998, p. 27). Because there is little validation by our society for same-sex relationships, the bereaved gay partner may be more apt to "encounter scorn, fear or blame" (Schwartzberg, 1996) and he may suffer from disenfranchised grief. Some gay men have not experienced disenfranchised grief when they have not hidden their sexual orientation from others. When partners are "out," they are more likely to have a network of supportive friends and family who help them during bereavement (Shernoff, 1998; C. Walter, 2003).

In the case of a death caused by AIDS, the deceased partner experiences additional stresses (Richmond & Ross, 1995; C. Walter, 2003). The surviving partner may face the demands of coping with his own infection as well as the burden of losing his loved one through illness. Losing a gay partner in young adulthood flies in the face of the developmental demands placed on a young adult. Most young adults do not believe they will lose a partner. Any "off-time loss" brings with it more likelihood of complicated grieving. The issues surrounding loss of a gay partner with AIDS will be expanded on in chapter 7, with a case to illustrate the issues.

For parents and siblings, the loss of a young adult child with AIDS can be complicated by ambivalent reactions to the young adult's drug use or sexual orientation. Because death from AIDS can occur in early adulthood, this off-time loss may lead to increased guilt and secrecy about the disease for fear of stigmatization (C. Walter, 2003). Family members often worry about or actually experience isolation and the loss of social support if their network becomes aware of the diagnosis of AIDS. This can make it difficult for family members to provide necessary support to the young adult.

Death of a Lesbian Partner

Similar to the gay bereaved partner, the lesbian partner who encounters the death of her partner may suffer intense grief because of her need to lead a double life as she works "among the heterosexual majority but develop(s) hidden networks of support, activity, and resources within lesbian communities" (C. Walter, 2003, p. 30). Two qualitative studies of lesbian women who have lost partners (Deevey, 1997; C. Walter, 2003) have documented the theme of disenfranchised grief originally identified by Doka (1987). Complications of grief often occur when the death is sudden or the deceased is young. Although these supportive networks within the lesbian community are satisfying in the face of homophobia, bereavement of a partner can be very difficult (C. Walter, 2003). In Walter's (2003) study, one 32-year-old lesbian partner lost her 26-year-old partner in a tragic automobile accident. The bereaved partner reports that "we were officially living in a committed relationship for almost five years" (C. Walter, 2003, p. 162) when Jean was killed. Yet the most difficult aspect of the loss for Pauline (Jean's partner) was that it was not acknowledged. Jean was seen as a good friend, a roommate, but not a life partner. However, Pauline found that when she risked telling others outside of her lesbian network about their relationship, she received support that she never expected. It was more difficult with Jean's parents, who never mentioned her (Pauline) or her relationship with Jean in the obituary they prepared for the newspaper. This neglect as well as her own father's refusal to attend her dead partner's funeral was extremely upsetting to Pauline. In this case both women were young adults and the death was very sudden, creating a possibility for more complicated grief.

Young adults do not expect to lose their partners at this stage of life, putting the loss out of sync with adult development. However, despite her life stage and the complexity of her grief, Pauline's resilience was demonstrated by her ability to move forward both professionally and personally. She was able to make meaning from her loss by continuing her bonds with Jean through joining an organ and tissue network, which represented a way for Pauline to remain connected to Jean through one of Jean's interests. Pauline was also able to keep her memories of Jean close to her as a source of comfort while she developed a new partnership with another young woman. In the following chapter on middle adulthood, the loss of a lesbian partner will be explored in greater depth in connection with the presentation of the case of Arden in "Illness Doesn't Discriminate."

READINGS

THE CASE OF A YOUNG ADULT WHO HAS LOST A PARENT

Julianne S. Oktay, MSW, PhD*

Julianne S. Oktay received her MSW (1966) and PhD (1974) from the University of Michigan. She has been affiliated with the University of Maryland School of Social Work since 1978, where she developed and chaired the "health specialization." Her research focus has been on the psychosocial aspects of health, most specifically breast cancer. Dr. Oktay is currently a professor at the University of Maryland School of Social Work, where she has served as Director of the Doctoral Program. In 1991, she published *Breast Cancer in the Life Course: Women's Experiences* (Springer Publishing Company) with Dr. Carolyn A. Walter. This section in this book is based on Dr. Oktay's study of the experiences

---

*This entry is based on one of the cases discussed in chapter 7 "Experience of Young Adult Daughters When Mothers Die from Breast Cancer" from the book *Breast Cancer: Daughters Tell Their Stories* published in 2005 by Haworth Press. The book is based on research funded by the National Cancer Institute (#RO3 CA 70605-02).

of women whose mothers had breast cancer. This qualitative study was published in book form (*Breast Cancer: Daughters Tell Their Stories*) by Haworth Press in 2005. Her current work is on psychosocial aspects of genetic counseling and testing for breast and ovarian cancer, and studying the impact of an intervention to reduce fatigue in breast cancer survivors.

Case Presentation

Andrea was the younger of two sisters. When she was about 12, her mother was diagnosed with breast cancer, and had a mastectomy, but then returned to an active life. At 18, her parents divorced, and Andrea moved away to college and then to take a job, living independently. However, at 25, her mother's cancer returned. "I was older and I could understand and relate to it more on an adult level....It was extremely scary. At that time, I was much more aware of what cancer was and how serious it was. I remember calling her oncologist from my office cubicle, asking him to explain to me what was going on and how serious it was. He said, 'I wouldn't give her more than 2 years.' That was horrible. I remember being at my office and I was left just hysterical with the realization that her time was finite." Over the next 7 years, Andrea's mother slowly deteriorated from her cancer. In spite of this, Andrea's mother remained upbeat. "It was a fact of life, but it wasn't something that we'd belabor. She had found a way to live with it and to live an extremely fulfilled and happy life." The family followed her mother's philosophy at that point, "Taking one day at a time."

During the period between the recurrence and mother's death, Andrea, her mother, and her sister became extremely close. "We talked a lot more candidly about life, and all of our experiences, and death. The history of our family." Andrea thinks that her relationship with her mother was better because of her mother's illness. "I see some of the relationships that my friends have and they're not as open. I don't know that I would have been as forthcoming with personal details of my life, my dating life. I don't know. I was very open with her, and she was very open minded and very understanding. It was just a good relationship."

In spite of a very positive relationship, a pattern of mutual protection developed in the family. Andrea's mother continued to try to limit the involvement of her daughters, but at the same time, the daughters protected their mother from information they felt she would not want to know. "I had several conversations with her oncologist that she never knew about. I think she thought she was protecting us, but really, we had turned into adult women and were taking charge of the situation."

Because her sister was married and had two children, most of the care-giving responsibility fell onto Andrea. "I stayed with her and cooked every single meal for her. Brought it in to her, took care of her, bathed her. It was extremely difficult to be in that role. I was 32 years old and I still feel very young. It's not something that I wanted to be doing."

Six weeks before her mother's death, Andrea got married. Because of her mother's illness, Andrea returned quickly from her honeymoon and began juggling the demands of her mother's illness with her desire to adjust to her new marriage. In spite of the fact that Andrea had great difficulty with managing her mother's feeding tube and dressing change, her mother was adamantly opposed to getting home care. In the end, her mother agreed to hospice care and died peacefully at home, surrounded by family.

A hospice nurse encouraged Andrea to talk to her mother, even though she was unresponsive. "She said, 'It's good if you go in there and talk to her. She can still hear you. Tell her how much you love her.' We went in that evening and just said everything again. She was not responding, but I do think that she heard us. We said, 'It's OK now Mom. You can let go and we will be OK. We will take care of each other.' And it was that night that she died."

After her mother's death, Andrea had difficulty visiting her mother's grave. "And I go back there often. I had a lot of dreams about that. I don't really like the idea of being underground." Andrea also would go to her mother's former apartment, sit in her car in the parking lot and cry. Andrea and her sister packed up all of their mother's things several weeks after her death. "We were in such a daze when we were doing it, really. We got rid of a lot of stuff, and we ended up getting two storage units downtown. It was too hard to go through it the first time. I'd like to keep it."

Andrea's husband is not always sympathetic to her grieving. "I'll just start crying, and he won't understand. He'll say, 'What happened? What started that? You were doing so well!' It's hard for him to understand, and I'm getting tired of explaining that it's still there. It's not gonna go away. It's not like it's over. Closure. We're moving on." Andrea experiences a similar lack of understanding from other people, who expect her to be "over it."

Shortly after her mother's death, Andrea's husband got a job in a city near where her sister lives. "It's just strange how things happen. I know she [mother] would have wanted me to be closer to my sister. I'd like to think that maybe she had something to do with all that. It would have made her very happy to know my sister and I would be together."

Andrea and her sister mourned the loss of a home. Andrea explains that her mother's place "became the home. She was the one who always had holiday dinners. That's where we always gathered. That's where I would always stay....My mother was just such the connection for everything. I miss the connection." Thinking about her new home, Andrea says, "Once we get our new place, I can certainly put all of the pictures of my mother out. I'll have all of her things around me so that I'll still have her there."

Andrea thinks that having a family would be a way to keep her mother alive. "I really want to bring her alive through all my children. Since my mother's death, I have felt much more strongly that I really would love a daughter. Daughters are more interested in Grandma's things, and what Grandma was like. It's important for me for my mother to be a big part of my children's life, even though she's not here. I want her to still be a big part of them."

Andrea now feels that her mother lives within her. "I just feel sort of empowered now. I feel like I have my mother inside of me. I feel like I'm going to always carry her with me. I pull on her strength a lot when I need it." Andrea intends to continue some of her mother's roles, giving holiday dinners, and taking up tennis, which her mother so enjoyed. There is a fear behind these intentions. "I don't want to ever forget her. I can't imagine that I ever could. But I want to keep her alive. It's important to me to keep her alive."

Developmental Milestones

Andrea's mother's illness and death had the effect of pushing Andrea forward in developmental tasks. She experienced some "role reversal" during the later period of her mother's illness, communicating directly with her mother's physician, locating and arranging medical and social services, and providing direct care. During this period, Andrea also experienced difficulty balancing the need to care for her mother with other demands of young adult life. At the same time that she was providing care for her mother, and during the mourning period, she was pulled toward more age-appropriate tasks, such as starting a new marriage relationship, managing a household, and working. Most literature about the difficulty of balancing family demands and caregiving for parents comes from studies of midlife women caring for elderly parents. This literature has generated the concept of the "sandwich generation" (Brody, 1985; Dautzenberg, 2000; Horowitz, 1985). Like midlife women, young adults can find themselves sandwiched between the demands of young adult life and a parent's need for care. The major roles of the "young adulthood" phase of life are thought to be those of worker, spouse, and parent. Young adults are learning to engage in intense and meaningful relationships in marriage, with intimate part-ners, with friends and with co-workers" (Newman & Newman, 1995, p. 522). Emphasis is on the difficulties of early married life and the need for the young adult to learn to communicate, deal with conflict, develop a satisfactory sexual relationship, and manage dual careers (Newman & Newman, 1995). Rolland (1994) sees families of young adults in a centrifugal phase, in which young adults focus on their own families and do not regain closeness with families of origin until later, when parents become elderly. When a parent of a young adult becomes seriously ill, it is seen to be "out of synch" (Rossi & Rossi, 1990). Dealing with life events that are considered "untimely" is often more stressful because they are unexpected, and can be hard to explain to others (Nolen-Hoeksema & Larson, 1999). "When a disabling or life-threatening disorder occurs earlier [than expected], it is out of phase in both chronological and social time. When such events are untimely, spouse and family lack the psychosocial preparation and rehearsal that occur later, when peers are experiencing similar losses. The ill member and the family are likely to feel robbed of their expectation of a normal life span" (Rolland, 1994, p 186).

Young adults who lose their mothers also often take on family tasks that ordinarily would have been handled by their mothers. Andrea talks about how her mother's place was the "gathering place" for the family, and how her mother was the center of the family communication hub. She plans to take over these roles, in an effort to keep up the family ties.

Biological Impact

Because breast cancer can be a genetic disease, the main biological impact of her mother's death is that Andrea is aware of her own risk. Because she is "paranoid" about getting breast cancer, she tries to live a healthy lifestyle. She is also worried about her sister, who does not watch her weight or exercise. Before her mother died, Andrea's mother's doctor told her she might want to have a prophylactic mastectomy, to minimize her risk. She felt this was too radical, and could interfere with her goal of having children in the future. Nor does she want genetic testing because she would prefer not to know that she is going to get the disease, especially as there is no certain way of preventing it that is acceptable to her.

Psychological Impact

Andrea was consumed by grief following her mother's death. She cried frequently, and even passing her mother's exit on the freeway would cause her to choke up. She found comfort in visiting her mother's gravesite, and in sitting in her car in front of her mother's old apartment. One important part of the grief work for Andrea was to keep her mother's things in an attempt to keep her memories of her mother alive. Andrea described sensing the presence of her deceased mother, talking of her mother being in favor of her husband's choosing a job near the home of Andrea's sister. She says she has a sense of her mother living inside her. Another way Andrea tried to "keep mother alive" after death was to become like mother and to recreate the kind of relationship she had with her mother. One difficulty Andrea had was the discomfort of others with her ongoing grief. Andrea's husband was not comfortable with her need to grieve, and expressed concern when she continued to cry after the funeral. Her colleagues at work were also unsympathetic with expressions of grief.

Another psychological impact of her mother's death on Andrea was a shift in her priorities. She was able to reframe her loss in a constructive way by emphasizing the primary importance of the family in her life. She also has thought differently about her job. "I guess when you lose your mother, you realize that life is extremely short. It can be taken at any time. It's pointless to stay in positions that don't make you happy."

Social Impact

A mother's death is a major life loss for women. An important piece of normal life course development for women is the mother–daughter relationship, considered the most intimate of all the parent–child relationships (Rossi & Rossi, 1990). In spite of the high level of interaction, the mother–daughter relationship is highly ambivalent (Bassoff, 1987; Troll, 1987), with daughters needing to stay connected to their mothers, and at the same time needing to let go. However, if a mother is seriously ill, the more conflicted aspect of the relationship is diminished or overlooked. During the terminal period of her mother's illness, Andrea became closer to her, and they were able to communicate on an adult-to-adult level, typically not achieved between mothers and young adult daughters. After her death, mothers are often idealized, and daughters may mourn for the loss of this relationship throughout their lives. Daughters experience mother's loss over and over again as their absence is felt at events like Mother's Day, birthdays, holidays, marriages, and births. Andrea's other major relationship (her new husband) was affected by Andrea's mother's illness and death. During the courtship and wedding, Andrea was distracted by her mother's illness. During the honeymoon, she was constantly on the phone, and came back early. After her mother's death, Andrea's need to grieve and deal with her loss kept her from establishing a strong relationship with her husband.

Interventions

Interventions for the Terminal Period

Interventions, such as counseling, that are designed to increase open communication between mothers and daughters during the terminal period are essential. When patterns of mutual protection develop, this type of intervention can help both mothers and daughters to express their feelings openly. Open communication may also have helped Andrea to deal with her mother's resistance to outside help. Also, during this period, mothers can be encouraged to develop legacy materials, such as family history, stories from their own early lives, pictures, and medical information. Support groups are also helpful for the terminally ill (if they are well enough to participate) and their caregiving daughters.

Interventions During the Mourning Period

Programs that facilitate grieving are appropriate for young adults, who can take constructive steps to come to a resolution of their grief. However, one of the biggest problems this population faces is that young adults who experience losses find themselves "out of synch" with others their age. Therefore, there is a need for bereavement services that are specifically for young adults. Also, some young adult women who lost mothers have a hard time in bereavement groups where most of the other group members have lost friends or grandparents. Loss of a mother is a much different type of loss for women, and a standard bereavement group may not address some of the unique issues. One program that addresses this need is the Motherless Daughters program established by Hope Edelman. This program offers support groups for young adult daughters who have lost mothers, as well as special activities on Mother's Day—a difficult day for many daughters. Also, materials are needed that can help motherless daughters tell their children about their grand-mothers, in a way that is positive and affirming for the grandchildren, who have also suffered a loss.

THE LOSSES OF INFERTILITY

Barbara Gilin, MSW, LCSW

Barbara Gilin is an Associate Clinical Professor at the Center for Social Work Education at Widener University in Chester, Pennsylvania. She is a graduate of the Family Institute of Philadelphia and is a Clinical Member of the American Association for Marriage and Family Thera-pists. In addition to teaching full time, she maintains an active clinical practice working with individuals, couples, and families.

For people in their late 30s who have desired to become parents, the experience of infertility constitutes a major developmental crisis. The number of adults who are confronted by infertility is larger than many people realize. Specifically, "15% of all couples will experience the frustration of infertility at some point in their relationship....Of those couples who seek medical assistance, 35% to 50% still do not achieve a pregnancy" (Watkins & Baldo, 2004, pp. 394–395). "The principle causes of failure to conceive fall into four distinct groups: male infertility (32%), female infertility (32.3%), combined male and female infertility (17%), and unexplained infertility (18.7%)" (Pike & Grieve, 2006, p. 2). To help individuals who are coping with infertility, it is important to understand the multiple losses contained within this experience. The following case example will illustrate the developmental, physical, social, psychological, and emotional consequences of living through an extended period of infertility. The final section provides a summary of the knowledge and skills needed to provide appropriate and sensitive social work interventions to those who are coping with the challenges of infertility.

Case Presentation

The client, Christine, was a 39-year-old Caucasian woman who had been married for 12 years. She was a psychiatric nurse who worked in an inpatient psychiatric hospital. She and her 42-year-old husband had been trying for 4 years to conceive a child, 3 of those years with the assistance of an infertility specialist—a physician specializing in reproductive endocrinology. The client became pregnant once but suffered a very early miscarriage. Christine and her husband were close to the point where they were going to stop undergoing medical interventions, and to consider adoption as their route to becoming parents. She was finding it very difficult to discontinue the medical treatments and to let go of her hope of conceiving and giving birth to a child. Most of her friends were already the parents of young teens, and Christine described feeling "outside of the circle" of all the mothers in her life, who swapped stories about being parents. In addition, Christine has three younger siblings, all of whom have children, including one sister who has five children.

The Impact of "Missing" the Developmental Milestone of Parenthood

As stated in the case description, Christine felt a deep sense of loss as a result of not moving into "the next step" of becoming a parent, as most of her friends and family had done. "Childbearing is a normative transition, and thus being infertile thwarts a step in adult development" (Watkins & Baldo, 2004, p. 397). Because of Christine's age and marital status, people usually assumed that she had children and therefore were surprised, and sometimes judgmental, when they learned she was childless. Throughout her entire life she had expected to become a mother and therefore she expected that turning 40 would be an especially difficult time for her. "The assumption of reproductive ease is commonplace in the meaning making of many individuals" (Bridges,

2005, p.1). Many books that have been written about middle age refer to ways that women often gain a sense of freedom as their children get older, allowing these women to refocus their energy on their own lives. When Christine read those books, she felt profoundly "out of step." She was deeply sad and frustrated about missing out on the parenting experiences that she heard others discuss on a daily basis. "A diagnosis of infertility is a disruption in life course similar to the disruption caused by death or profound disability; with grief and mourning a natural outcome" (Bridges, p. 9).

Biological and Physical Losses Associated With Infertility

After 3 years of infertility treatments, Christine found it especially difficult to be in the presence of women who were pregnant or who had recently given birth. She said that it felt like "torture" at times to be sitting next to a pregnant woman or to a nursing mother. She felt acute disappointment in her own body for being unable to conceive, carry a pregnancy, give birth, or breastfeed. Her strong desire to have those experiences felt "physical" at times, and she described feeling "flawed" and "damaged" because she could not become pregnant. As it became clear to her that she would probably not have a biological child, she started to experience the accompanying loss of knowing that she and her husband would not "pass on" their genetic characteristics to a child. She knew that if she did decide to become a parent by adoption that she, her husband, and others would "miss" the experience of searching their child's face to see who s/he "looks like."

In addition, the actual medical procedures and interventions Christine was undergoing felt like an "assault" to her physical self. The most painful procedures she endured were the endometrial biopsies, and the X-rays taken after dye was injected into her ovaries and fallopian tubes (hysterosalpingogram). She was unprepared by her physician or the nurse assistant for the physical pain of each of these procedures. She longed to create a child through the pleasurable "natural" act of sexual intercourse but instead had to undergo invasive medical techniques to achieve the same end that had been reached so easily by almost everyone she knew.

During one phase of her treatment, she was required to receive injections (from her husband) of powerful drugs to stimulate ovulation.

When she asked her physician about possible side effects of the drugs, he responded that there were no known negative effects on a child born after these drugs were used. She described feeling embarrassed when she clarified that she was actually asking about the physical effects on *her*. She said that her physician seemed surprised by her question and stated that there had been no long-term studies done on the effects of these drugs on the women who received them. In order for her to continue, she needed to put aside her worries about her own physical well-being, now and for the future. "Women in particular must bear most of the burden from reproductive technologies" (Imeson, 1996, p. 1019). Following Christine's question, there were some reports published in the 1990s showing a "significant risk of infertility therapy for ovarian carcinoma development, although subsequent studies reported only slightly increased or no significant risk….Therefore the association between ovarian stimulation and ovarian carcinoma remains controversial" (Konish, 2006, p. 1).

Social Impact of Infertility

As discussed earlier, Christine felt "out of the loop" when others would talk about pregnancies, labor and delivery, and their daily experiences with their children. She felt drawn to women who were also unhappy about being childless and could identify with her feelings and "stories" about being infertile. She found it increasingly difficult to attend "milestone" events in the lives of her family and friends that involved their children, and eventually she would "pass" on attending events such as baby showers or children's birthday parties. At one point, she found it very distressing when she felt unable to travel to visit her sister who was close to giving birth to her second child. Christine wanted to celebrate with her but she could not stop crying each time she thought about holding her sister's new baby. She *was* able to visit her sister after she had an honest conversation with her, but Christine realized again the toll that her infertility experiences were having on her. Much as she wanted to be connected to close friends and family who were parents, the times were increasing when she felt unable to control her grief reactions and she became more likely to isolate herself. "Couples were in desperate need of support, but did not feel that others could understand the extent of their pain" (Cudmore, 2005, p. 304).

Psychological and Emotional Impact

One of the unique aspects of infertility is the strong fluctuation in moods that occur throughout the course of a month. Hope and anxiety during the ovulation phase give way to intense grief when menstruation begins, signaling another failed attempt to conceive a child. For many couples, there is a tiresome repetition of this hope/loss cycle month after month. For the female partner, the addition of strong fertility drugs often affects her mood as well, amplifying feelings of anxiety, anger, exhaustion, sadness, and depression. During one month in particular, Christine realized that the word that best described her feelings during the loss phase of the cycle was "barren," an older term that captured both her emotional and physical experience. One recent study finds that "37% of women experiencing infertility reported depression scores in the clinically significant range" (Peterson, Newton, Rosen, & Shulman, 2006, p. 229). The list of other emotions that individuals might experience is "quite lengthy and may be the source of considerable pain: guilt, shame, inadequacy, stigmatization, anxiety, stress, fear of spousal rejection, devastation, rage, anger, isolation, helplessness, powerlessness, loss of control, doom, despair, mourning, depression, frustration, feeling cheated, fatigue, moodiness, tension, disappointment and loneliness" (Watkins & Baldo, 2004, p. 397).

There were many situations faced by Christine and her husband that would trigger some of the emotions just described. The couple felt embarrassed by the intrusion of the medical profession into the most private aspect of their relationship, their sexual life together. In one procedure, they were required to schedule intercourse at home prior to a "postcoital" test performed on Christine in her physician's office to determine how many sperm were produced. There were other times when her husband was required to drop off semen samples on his way to work for the sample to be prepared and then inseminated into Christine later the same day. The most intimate act between the couple now included additional steps, and several other people, on a regular basis.

In addition to embarrassment, the couple often encountered situations that made them angry. For example, they sometimes felt an existential anger similar to other people experiencing a loss, wondering "why" they are the ones to have to suffer. At times, Christine felt enraged that people who did not want children were able to have them, while other people would abuse the children they had. She also became angry when others offered simplistic and insensitive advice about why she was not getting pregnant. She resented how easy it was for many others to achieve, in her words, the "miracle" of conception. Sadly, "80% of infertile couples reported being subject to negative comments from others regarding their infertility status" (Watkins & Baldo, 2004, p. 394). She dreaded the occasional thoughtless remark made by others, "You won't understand until you have kids of your own." At times, her husband was at the receiving end of a different type of insensitivity, such as the time when his male work colleague made a joke about how he must be "shooting blanks."

In addition to the ongoing anxiety about whether their efforts would lead them to a successful pregnancy, they were worried about the impact of infertility on their lives in other ways. For example, Christine was scared that her frequent and necessary trips to the doctor for tests and procedures would continue causing her supervisor to question her commitment to her job. She worried that she and her husband would never be able to enjoy an unpressured sexual relationship again. Couples "may lose a positive sense of their sexuality and feel like sexual inter-course has become a chore" (Watkins & Baldo, 2004, p. 398). Christine and her husband worried about the drain on their financial resources because of poor insurance coverage for fertility treatments. They felt anxious about whether they could afford either the continued treatments or an adoption if they chose that route to parenting.

Feelings of grief were often present throughout the years of trying unsuccessfully to have a child, particularly as they faced the time when they were deciding when to end medical treatments. "For couples who decide that enough is enough, finishing treatment may be the time for the mourning process to begin" (Cudmore, 2005, p. 305). Certain experiences became almost unbearable for Christine, such as visiting friends who had just given birth or saying good-bye to beloved nieces and nephews who lived far away. There were times when Christine would cry unexpectedly and uncontrollably when the reality of the losses associated with infertility would hit her. Particularly after the early miscarriage, Christine became acutely aware of the absence of religious rituals or social customs available to mark the loss of a pregnancy or to acknowledge the ongoing suffering she and her husband experienced. "Our Western culture offers no recognized mourning ritu-als for such reproductive losses, and clients may feel it is inappropriate to express their grief when others have lost 'real babies' " (Pike & Grieve, 2006, p. 5). Both the miscarriage and the monthly experiences of loss often felt like "little deaths," and she anticipated that letting go of the hope of getting pregnant would feel like a different type of death. "There are particular complexities mourning an intangible loss....There are no memories to recall....This is the loss of a person to be, rather than a consciously known person who was. It is the loss of a future as opposed to the loss of a past" (Cudmore, 2005, p. 306).

Social Work Interventions

Ultimately, the worker assisted Christine in deciding when to give up the medical pursuit of a pregnancy. "For 95% of the couples, treatment was terminated by the patient rather than the physician. Emotional exhaustion was cited as the most common reason for moving on (50%)" (Daniluk & Tench, 2007, p. 91). An earlier social work intervention that helped the couple decide to discontinue treatment at this point was a well-timed question asked by their worker regarding how much time they thought they wanted to devote to pursuing medical treatments. Given this couple's ages, health concerns, the strength of their desire to be parents, growing comfort with the idea of parenting a nonbiological child, and financial constraints, Christine and her husband settled on a 3-year limit to their medical pursuit of a pregnancy. Other factors that couples must consider are research regarding the success rates of different methods, family support, comfort level regarding permanent childlessness, religious and cultural influences, emotional well-being, and more. In the face of these factors and others, couples make very different decisions regarding the best option for them. However, having the worker raise the often painful question about how long they want to continue trying can begin a difficult but important dialogue between the couple. As in all other social work interventions, the worker must not impose his or her own beliefs regarding the best option, and must be ready to witness considerable grief as the couple struggles to think about this question.

When Christina and her husband arrived at the point where they were ending their treatments, the social worker encouraged them to consider meaningful rituals that symbolized their loss of hope for a biological child. "Creating a ritual to let go of the hope of having a biological child…may be helpful" (Watkins & Baldo, 2004, p. 401). The worker provided the idea, but the couple decided on the rituals that felt right for them.

> After 4¹/₂ years of trying to become pregnant, Christine and her husband decided to end their medical treatments and to take some time to recover and to grieve the loss of their "hoped for" child and to consider adoption. Their last trip to the infertility specialist proved to be especially difficult since there was a new treatment available and it was hard to let go of the hope that this time a treatment might work. In part, Christine wanted to regain a sense of control and to be the one to end the period of treatments and constant uncertainty. To mark this ending, Christine and her husband created several small rituals to help them express what they were feeling and to create a bridge to the next chapter of their lives. They each wrote letters to the biological child they would probably never have. They made a large donation to UNICEF for children who had been born but needed help to survive. They gathered together all of the equipment used during their infertility treatments and threw it all away. Finally, they gave away two items of clothing that they had bought for the biological child they had hoped to have.

This final section describes a number of additional social work interventions that assisted Christine and her husband to cope effectively with their infertility. These interventions are recommended for any social worker who is providing counseling to an individual or a couple going through this particular developmental crisis.

■ The worker provided information about "Resolve," the support group for infertile individuals. Resolve's website (www.resolve.org), local chapter meetings, and valuable conferences provide up-to-date medical information and research, emotional support, access to a phone hotline, and advocacy for infertility treatments to be covered by more insurance companies. (This website is equally informative for professional social workers.)

■ Christine found it very helpful to have all of her feelings validated, and to have her worker convey solid understanding of the multiple losses she endured because of her infertility. "Primarily the counselor needs to bear witness to the pain and normalize the experiences" (Watkins & Baldo, 2004, p. 399) of the infertile client. As Christine could express fully all of her feelings, she was able to cope more effectively.

■ Christine was also encouraged to write about all aspects of her infertility experience. She found this intervention to be particularly helpful, and she eventually sent a small essay to an author who was writing a book about infertility and had asked for contributions.

■ Christine's worker learned the medical terminology associated with infertility and also kept informed regarding the latest treatment options for infertile couples. Having the appropriate knowledge is an important piece of homework when working with any client struggling with a medical condition.

■ Christine's worker provided periodic marital therapy to help the couple to cope with the impact of this experience on their relationship. "Based on family systems theory, a partner's adjustment to infertility is likely impacted by the systemic nature of the couple's relationship" (Peterson et al., 2006, p. 228). The worker helped them to talk openly about what each one was experiencing and to accept the reality that they would not necessarily be having the same reactions at the same time. A very important intervention was to encourage the couple to "take breaks" from the medical treatments, and to enjoy an occasional month free of the pressures associated with the medical intrusions into their lives. Like most infertile couples, Christine and her husband initially resisted this idea but were ultimately very grateful for the suggestion to take the breaks.

■ The worker encouraged Christine to be assertive with medical personnel regarding her physical and emotional needs.

■ It was important to explore with Christine and her husband their ideas about the meaning of "family" to them, and to understand how those ideas were informed by their cultural backgrounds and other experiences in their families of origin.

■ The worker asked Christine at points to reflect on the life lessons she had learned as a result of her infertility experiences. Questions such as "Where did you find surprise sources of support?" and "What untapped strengths have you discovered?" helped Christine to find meaning in her experience (Bridges, 2005, p.11).

■ It was important for Christine to find ways to speak to others in her life about the painful aspects of her experience of infertility, and to ask for appropriate understanding and support at times. For example, Christine was able to have the difficult conversation with her pregnant sister that was mentioned earlier, and to arrive at a plan that considered *both* of their needs.

■ At other difficult times, it was important to support her right to take care of herself by not attending child-centered functions such as baby showers.

■ The worker emphasized to the couple that their loss of a biological child needed to be mourned, even if they proceeded to adoption as their route to parenthood. It is necessary for the couple to understand the reality that "adoption does not cure infertility" (source unknown), and that some losses related to infertility would continue to arise throughout the life cycle even if the couple adopted a child. In fact, Christine and her husband did adopt a child 2 years after ending their treatments, and eventually encountered the moment when her 4-year-old son put his hand on her stomach and asked if he had grown inside her tummy. She was very grateful to her worker for preparing her earlier for moments such as those. "If a couple has been able to…digest the pain of their infertility…[and] can talk about their experience, they will be in a better position to…welcome a child into their family" (Cudmore, 2005, p. 307).

■ Other couples will require help in adjusting to their choice to remain childless and to construct meaningful and satisfying lives that do not include parenthood.

Summary

Christine's experience illustrates many of the issues facing infertile individuals and couples. Many of the losses that are "part and parcel" of the experience of infertility were described. In one study, 39.2% of couples going through infertility indicated that they would find it useful to have help/guidance from someone other than a medical specialist (Watkins & Baldo, 2004, p. 394). It is important for social workers to understand the relevant developmental issues, the wide range of emotions experienced by clients, the physical and biological losses, the multiple stresses on a couple's relationship, the impact on their social relationships such as isolation, and the challenges of finding meaningful ways to express their grief about the loss of a hoped-for biological child. Finally, recommendations were provided that should enable social workers to counsel people who encounter painful obstacles on their journey to parenthood in later adulthood.

CASE OF A YOUNG ADULT STRUGGLING WITH ADDICTIONS

Theresa M. Agostinelli, MSW

Theresa M. Agostinelli is a licensed social worker in private practice. She is the owner of Glen Mills Counseling Center, which specializes in counseling women struggling with grief and loss issues. She has also counseled clients with a dual diagnosis. She has designed, facilitated, and led groups for women who were struggling with abuse, grief and loss, and addictions. A graduate of Widener University, Theresa has both an undergraduate and a master's degree in social work. She is affiliated with the Pennsylvania Society for Clinical Social Workers. Theresa currently runs educational/support groups at her counseling center for women with issues of stress, anxiety, and relationships. Her grief groups are for those who are grieving the loss of a child as well for those who want to help someone who has lost a child. Other groups are designed for those who are grieving the loss of a life partner/spouse as well as for those who are supporting someone who has lost a partner or spouse.

Case Presentation

"Ricky" is a 40-year-old African American male who identifies himself as gay. He states that he knew as early as age 8 that he was "different" from other boys his age. Ricky liked to wear his mother's dresses and would sometimes put on makeup when his parents were not home. Eventually his parents noticed traces of lipstick and eye makeup and, although his mother was very supportive and nurturing, his father constantly told him that he needed to "snap out of it" and told him repeatedly that he was "abnormal." Ricky's father took him to the doctor on several occasions to see what was "wrong with him." Even when the family doctor told Ricky's father that Ricky was not sick, but that he was "only gay," Ricky's father still did not accept it. Many times Ricky cried at being labeled abnormal at home and in school. Ricky was always closer to his mother and always felt safe with her. Ricky never really felt safe with his father and never felt accepted or loved by him. Ricky's parents had a volatile relationship and when Ricky was 12 years old his father murdered his mother in a jealous rage. Ricky witnessed the shooting. According to Erikson (1978), the developmental theme of adolescence is identity versus identity confusion. Because Ricky witnessed his mother's shooting and because of the trauma he experienced during puberty, his identity formation was hindered. Depression and acting-out issues were evident, along with struggles with gender and sexuality, alcohol and drug use, and delinquency in school. Ricky has often exhibited and discussed symptoms of PTSD. Ricky states that he was hospitalized a year after his mother's death because of what he describes as a nervous breakdown. On release from the hospital, Ricky was sent to live with his maternal aunt, where his younger brother and sister had been living since the death of their mother.

The loss of his mother led Ricky to experience deep emotions that he could not handle because of his grief and so he turned to drugs. He was also struggling with his sexual identity and lack of acceptance by friends and family members. According to Ricky, "using drugs seemed to deaden the pain." He also comments on many flashbacks to the witnessing of his mother's death, nightmares, and cold sweats. He can become aggressive when feeling threatened and has had some confrontational outbursts during group. When Ricky began to use drugs heavily, he also began having sexual encounters with men. For all of his young adulthood Ricky states that he has been prostituting for drugs while using crack cocaine. Since age 30, Ricky has had a partner, but his partner recently ended the relationship because of Ricky's drug dependency. This loss is particularly difficult for a young adult who is struggling to master the developmental task of intimacy with others. Ricky was arrested for prostitution and possession of crack cocaine and was sentenced to 3 months in jail and 90 days house arrest. Ricky was sent to a drug-and-alcohol treatment program for help.

Losses Incurred by a Young Adult With Addictions

Dealing with grief and loss is a very important part of recovery. Many of our clients have had significant losses as a result of their addictions. Others have become chemically dependent because of their inability to handle the grief associated with significant loss. It is true that many of our clients are suffering from losses that society does not recognize, as in the case of Ricky. He identifies as gay and is somewhat reticent about sharing his homosexuality. The loss of Ricky's relationship with his partner was a part of life that he lost as a result of drugs. Because society does not recognize or validate these types of losses it can be more difficult to work through this type of grief. These losses that are not given public validation are experienced as disenfranchised by the client (Doka, 1989, 2002).

Ricky did not want to be in treatment because of his fear that he would be treated unfairly because of his homosexual lifestyle. He stated that he has tried to get help many times yet he could not find a local drug-and-alcohol treatment center for gay men with chemical dependency, so he tried to stay clean and sober on his own. Many drug-and-alcohol counselors are very unfamiliar with the grieving process, especially in the lives of gay and lesbian addicts. Some counselors do not work under the premise that grief and loss are associated with addictions. It is even more evident that most therapists are not trained to work with gays and lesbians who are also addicts. "Negative bias among counselors and other treatment providers are the most common reason cited among gays and lesbians for not seeking help" (Cochran, 2003, p. 5776).

Many clients are also grieving the loss of their addiction. Several instances show that clients' lives may be getting better and better all the time, yet for some reason they miss their addiction because it represents the way things "used to be." Many adults have trouble accepting new ways of life. One task that is important for both clients and clinicians is to help resolve these losses at the client's pace. Ricky stated that he grieves over time lost in his life because of years of addiction. Ricky has had many losses in his life that may have contributed to chemical dependency as a way of coping with feelings of grief and loss by self-medication. Ricky states that he still grieves the loss of his mother, even after 28 years.

Ricky is suffering other losses not related to a death. For instance, Ricky has stated that he grieves over the loss of the last 15 years of his life as a result of being addicted all of his young adulthood. Ricky grieves over the loss of his adolescence because of the trauma he experienced early in his teen years. However, he has expressed hope and is slowly relieving the pain of the past by looking to the future. "To be able to think in terms of past, present and future, to love and to grieve is part of the human existential plight and dignity" (Lindstrom, 2002, p. 20).

Ricky could be considered one of many clients in the recovery program who is dealing with disenfranchised losses. When society does not validate their losses, clients may believe they are not worthy of grieving those losses. Ricky turned to drugs, alcohol, and prostitution as a way to cope with the alienation and stigmatization of being an African American homosexual male, while grieving many losses in his life. For some clients the need to grieve for time lost and the years they have spent in their addiction is very important in recovery. Some losses that have gone underground and have been self-medicated rather than experienced, understood, or integrated may resurface at a later time. This often leads to relapse.

Interventions

Some distortions of addicted clients are evident in statements such as: (a) "I am a horrible person," (b) "My drug use is not that bad," or (c) "I am an addict and therefore will never be able to stop using." Cognitive behavioral therapists believe that thoughts, beliefs, and feelings shape human behavior. Many times these cognitive processes may be irrational, causing unhealthy behaviors. Cognitive behavior therapy is a treatment that has a problem-oriented focus and is beneficial in helping clients change thinking and behavior with regard to substance abuse (Corsini & Wedding, 2000).

A number of other interventions were also used to help Ricky. Role training was used as an opportunity to apply cognitive principles between sessions by learning new behaviors such as skill building and advocacy for self. We discussed the importance of boundary setting as well as the self-esteem issues Ricky suffered in his life resulting from his addictive, self-destructive behaviors, and his issues around his sexuality. I also used drug-and-alcohol treatment principles such as the Twelve Step Models (Finley, 2004) and Relapse Prevention Models (Marlatt & Gordon, 1985). A strengths-based perspective and empowerment techniques (Poulin, 2000) were incorporated over time. Ricky has become empowered by my allowing him to feel "normalized" in a treatment group that gives him a strong sense of acceptance, support, and safety in sharing some of these highly emotional experiences that he has faced.

I have also been able to use spirituality in our group and individual sessions as I believe that spirituality is an important aspect in healing and recovery. In the United States, several studies have indicated that "Americans are much more likely to pray, read scripture, or talk to a religious healer than to seek help from a mental health professional" (Ashford, Lecroy, & Lortie, 2001, p. 10). Spirituality works in conjunction with cognitive behavioral interventions because our beliefs about ourselves can inform our feelings and actions and become our reality. According to Granvold (1995), "when spirituality is part of therapy, it provides the shared awareness and meaning base from which the client and social worker collaboratively proceed" (p. 526). Spirituality is central to the empowerment model because it allows the client to embrace his or her own spiritual beliefs and the significance of each spiritual experience during recovery. If Ricky had not been able to embrace his spiritual beliefs, then it may have added to the oppression he experienced.

Ricky was very receptive to each intervention and learned to apply principles outlined in each. It is not clear yet whether this will have an effect on the longer term issues for this client but, for now, I believe he is getting stronger. Ricky tells me that he has finally been able to forgive his father who has since passed away. He has also been able to forgive many people who have hurt him the past, and he has been finally able to forgive himself for not being able to help his mother.

Ricky has survived the trauma he experienced in childhood and as a young adult, during which time he experienced discrimination as an African American homosexual male who has a substance-abuse history. Ricky is a survivor who is beginning to thrive by not using drugs and applying the principles that he learned in treatment. My time with Ricky has been invaluable and we have both learned many lessons about life and death, grief and loss, and how they interact with addictions. Making meaning out of grief and loss has been part of the treatment goal for Ricky in our therapeutic relationship. It has been my aim to allow Ricky to embrace his grief and not to fear it. Ricky has told me on several occasions that he is slowly learning to accept his losses and move on in his recovery. He still grieves but his grief is no longer paralyzing him.

SUMMARY

The main theme that emerges from the literature and the case studies about losses encountered by young adults is that they are "off time."

Young adults do not expect to suffer losses of health, such as breast cancer, or losses of spouses, partners, and parents. Their first real loss is a maturational one when they separate both physically and emotionally from their parents, which often goes unrecognized as a loss by the young adult as well as by others in his/her life. Young adults do not receive adequate support from their peers who have not experienced such losses and often look to others in the same situation, as in the case study of Christine who suffered the loss of infertility. In addition, young adults assume that they will be able to procreate, so that a discovery that they are infertile is shocking to them. Because childbearing is a "normative transition," infertility thwarts a step in adult development. Christine found it very difficult to attend "milestone" events of the young adults among her friends and family. However, Christine and her husband, with the help of a social worker who validated their loss, were able to mourn the loss of having a biological child and to make meaning of their experience by recognizing life lessons that they had learned as a result of their infertility experiences.

Despite the fact that these losses are off time, most young adults are resilient, as in the case study of Andrea, whose mother died from breast cancer. Although Andrea struggled to cope with the demands of a new marriage and those of caring for her mother, once her mother died, Andrea was able to shift her priorities and reframe her loss so that she could begin to embrace the idea of becoming a parent, one of the important milestones of young adulthood. Andrea continues to have a bond with her deceased mother by taking on some of her mother's roles in the family, which provides comfort to her and allows her to move forward in her life. In the case of Ricky, his entire young adulthood was deeply affected by his strong addictions, which prevented him from leading a life in which he could make good decisions regarding work and partnership. For example, his addiction cost him a 10-year love relationship. The losses inherent in addiction as well as the need of an addict to become self-absorbed during recovery have intersected to inhibit the primary need of a young adult like Ricky to invest in meaningful relationships with intimate partners, friends, and co-workers. However, with appropriate intervention with an addictions counselor, using a cognitive behavioral/spiritual approach, Ricky is learning how to live his life without drugs. He is slowly learning to accept his losses and move forward in his recovery.

7 Middle Adulthood

David was 59 when his 62-year-old brother, Jim, died in a car accident. David is the principal of a high school and his brother was a physician. At the time of Jim's death, David was living by himself, having gone through a nasty divorce 5 years earlier. His brother had never married and he and David had always had a very close relationship. In fact, Jim was very supportive of David through the time of his marital struggles, separation, and divorce. Although David has two adult children, they live some distance away from David and are married and very busy with young children of their own. Jim and David spent more and more time together following David's divorce so that when Jim was suddenly killed in a car accident on an icy stretch of roadway, David felt extremely alone. At first, David was devastated and could not go to work or be with anyone except his adult children, who surrounded him for several days. When his children left 1 week after the funeral, David realized how few other relationships he had developed other than collegial relationships with several other administrators at his high school and other local high schools. He also realized how isolated he felt in his grief because none of the friends or colleagues that he knew had lost a sibling. For the first time in his life, David realized that he needed to seek out a therapeutic relationship. He found a clinical social worker through a colleague and began weekly sessions in which the social worker helped David to understand the meaning of the death of his brother for him. David also began to realize that he needed to expand his social network now that his brother was gone. During the therapeutic sessions, the social worker helped David to realize that he would always keep Jim's memory close to him and began to discover ways that he might continue his bond with his brother. The week following Jim's death, David had removed all of the pictures of Jim from the walls of his condo as it was too painful for David to see images of his brother. About 3 months following Jim's death, David searched through his closet for his favorite photos of Jim—ones that captured Jim fly fishing as well as those of Jim with David at a family reunion. After 1 year of therapy, David began to date a woman he met at a dining club for singles and began to expand his social network by joining a hiking club and a local Rotary organization. David was beginning to integrate the loss of his brother into his daily functioning by finding ways to develop continuing bonds through photos and by beginning to reconstruct a new social network.

DEVELOPMENTAL CRISIS: GENERATIVITY VERSUS STAGNATION

Psychological Aspects of Development

Within this text, midlife adults are defined as those adults between the ages of 40 and 65. However, with increased longevity for both men and women middle adulthood may extend into the early 70s; chapter 8 describes adults who are redefining their identities through their 60s and 70s. Midlife adults want to experience a personal sense of effectiveness and "a sense that one is making a difference in the lives of others" (Newman & Newman, 2006, p. 457). Midlife adults want to leave something behind for the next generation. The psychosocial crisis for this developmental phase of life can be understood as a pressure on the adult to be committed to making life better for future generations. The term *generativity* includes the processes of creativity, productivity, and procreativity. *Procreativity* refers to a type of self-generation that is concerned with further identity development. Adults at midlife may change the world by introducing new ideas, things, or bonds of relationships. Generativity involves making contributions to society on both personal and public levels that stand some chance of continuing after one's death. The opposite end of the spectrum of generativity is represented by the concept of stagnation, which refers to a lack of psychological movement or growth. Adults who experience stagnation become self-absorbed and often unable to take up the challenge to mentor new employees or invent new approaches to work. Instead they become resentful, avoidant, and withdrawn. These adults are unable to invest in the needs of others.

Findings from a survey of 1,200 midlife adults who reported that they perceived middle age as a time to invest in acts of caring and of deepening relationships (Coleman, 1992) support Erik Erikson's assumption that a sense of generativity is the pivotal point of personal growth in midlife for both men and women (Erikson, 1959/1980). Levinson and colleagues (1978) and Levinson and Levinson (1996) defined tasks within midlife for both men and women even more clearly. Levinson and Levinson (1996) found that women and men go through a similar sequence at similar ages. Just as with men, even the most traditional women struggled with questions about family, work, independence, and marriage. Qualitative research (Arnold, 2005) exploring the developmental journey of women who are moving into their 50s supports this idea of deepening relationships for adult women during this life phase. The results of this study suggest that women in midlife believe that having strong relationships with others remained an important focus for them, but they also expressed a need to redefine and "to reconnect with significant people and spirituality in deeper, authentic and proactive ways" (Arnold, 2005, p. 642).

During the midlife phase, many adults reassess and reorder their goals or priorities. Midlife is a time of "stock-taking," when adults attempt to assess how their lives are going to turn out (Gould, 1978; Neugarten, 1979). Midlife adults consider external achievements but also focus on inner satisfaction with the hope of achieving a sense of fulfillment. Some midlife adults continue to work on "their dream" created during early adulthood. They may also be formulating a new dream, either because their earlier dreams did not work out or because they are trying to "be more true" to who they really are. In a reading at the end of this chapter, "Loss of a Vision: Professional Identity and Career Aspirations," Ben uses the process of stock-taking to examine his career options.

Midlife adults are also confronting their own mortality for the first time. Death becomes more relevant as the midlife adult faces the fact that s/he has probably lived more years in the past than s/he will in the future. The press of time is heavy and there is a heightened sense that whatever s/he is going to do, s/he must do now. One study reports that all 23 of the women who participated in the study and who were moving into their 50s viewed time as a very precious commodity as they became aware of the "finiteness of life and the need to live it wisely and meaningfully while one still has her health" (Arnold, 2005, p. 645).

Biological Aspects of Development

Another issue faced by midlife adults is the biological aging process, including hormonal changes for both men and women (menopause), graying hair, weight changes, and beginning declines in energy, hearing, and memory. This is a time of life when body image comes into focus as the midlife adult must adapt to many changes and losses in his/her "youthful" body. It is both the midlife adult's own recognition of these changes that is significant, as well as the observations of others. For women, this is particularly poignant because our American society has even less social acceptability of the physical aging process in women than in men (Oktay & Walter, 1991). Some adults view these changes as "narcissistic injuries," whereas others seem able to adapt to these losses with more resilience. New research on the female brain provides evidence that the hormone estrogen has a protective effect on many aspects of brain functioning. A decrease in estrogen during midlife "creates a constancy in the flow of impulses through her brain circuits," which replaces the "plunges of estrogen and progesterone caused by the menstrual cycle" (Brizendine, 2006, p. 136). A woman's brain in midlife operates more steadily. These brain changes seem to provide the motivation for women to be less interested in nesting and more interested in exploring the world around them.

Social Aspects of Development

The midlife adult also faces many emotional losses as adult children move out of the family home, creating a change in the family system so that the couple must "relearn" their relationship after years of devoting time and energy to rearing their children. Many marriages undergo transformation and the couple moves forward with a renewed sense of their relationship. Other marriages suffer and may end in separation and divorce. Another area of transition involves the relationship with parents. At midlife, adults often face the loss of the parent they once knew as a result of serious illness and/or actual loss from parental death.

Many midlife adults are caregivers to their aging parents, which can place a strain on their marriage and on relationships with their own children. Although role reversal has been documented as an issue faced by the midlife adult, when the midlife adult becomes more like a parent to his or her parent, other research (C. Walter, 1991) indicates that parents really want to remain in their role as parents, while adult daughters prefer to remain in their role as daughters.

LOSS EXPERIENCED BY MIDLIFE ADULTS

Transformation of Identity and "Letting Go of Past Dreams"

This concept of transformation of identity is further developed in the early part of the next chapter of this text, which focuses on retirement and reinvention. The idea that the midlife adult is letting go of previous meanings, understandings, and dreams is well documented in the literature (Arnold, 2005; Gould, 1975, 1978; Levinson et al., 1978; Levinson & Levinson, 1996). Although letting go of previous beliefs and aspirations can allow room for new meaning and dreams to be embraced during this phase of life, there may be a sense of loss as the adult observes him or herself moving from one dream to another. Levinson et al. (1978) speaks of the "dream" both in early adulthood and in midlife as being associated with "the experience that I exist, that self and world are properly matched" (Levinson et al., 1978, p. 246) and contains a variety of aspirations, goals, and values. In addition, the adult has to find some way to live out this dream. In midlife, adult men are reappraising the life they created during early adulthood and are trying to "understand and evaluate the place of the dream in it" (Levinson et al., 1978, p. 245). Often a man has to cope with an earlier dream that no longer fits who he is. Further, he may have to cope with the consequences of failure to fulfill his life in the way he wanted. Found at the end of this chapter, the case of Ben is an example of a midlife man who practiced law for nearly 30 years, but who is frustrated between what he expected to accomplish at the beginning of his career and what he has actually been able to accomplish. The loss that Ben experiences is related to the loss both of a goal and of a vision of himself. As this case study illustrates, Ben is able to cope with his thwarted expectations and to modify his vision for professional and personal success only after he grieves the loss of what he hoped to create in his early adulthood.

Immigration as an Example of Transformation of Identity

With regard to loss and the transformation of identity, immigration is an issue important to understand as our nation continues to face ways to help those children and adults who immigrate to the United States. Imberti (2008) (who emigrated from Argentina) acknowledges how difficult it can be to strike a balance between acknowledging and accepting the very real losses that immigrants often deny. Similarly, it is difficult for immigrants to embrace their accomplishments and victories (Imberti, 2008). The concept of ambiguous loss (Boss, 1999) may characterize the experience of the immigrant who feels that "You are no longer who you were or who you wanted to be, but somebody else" (Imberti, 2008, p. 37). Although this new person may feel that s/he is better off than s/he might have been had s/he not immigrated to a foreign land, s/he will, in all probability, still experience a sense of loss. Many immigrants, but particularly those whose status may be undocumented or ambiguous, experience a "chronically hypervigilant state" because of the danger and possible catastrophe that they may experience (Imberti, 2008, p. 39) if they are deported.

Research by Hani, Stiles, and Biran (2005) documents the deep sense of loss of self-identity that may result among immigrants who have experienced the "loss of the mother language" (Hani et al., 2005, p. 110). Immigrants may feel that they do not measure up to mainstream cultural language standards, which causes a more silent, persistent grief for them within a culture that devalues others who are different (Imberti, 2008). For immigrants, loss of mastery of surroundings creates an internal shame "which often silences the real self and renders the person essentially powerless and voiceless" (p. 38). Furthermore, immigrants suffer a concrete loss of family networks and an erosive loss of everyday life, which can all contribute to a loss of identity. In the case of Kudu (at the end of this chapter), her loss of connection with her tribe in Africa following her migration to the United States made it difficult for her to adjust to life in this society because within Africa, specifically Zambia, "It is to the tribe that one attaches self and finds identity."

As Kudu's ties with her tribe began to weaken over time, it became increasingly difficult for Kudu to form an identity or to connect with her new world. Kudu found herself quite isolated and alienated, but was able to use her tribal connections in a new way to overcome self-esteem and identity issues. Kudu realized that she could no longer cling to her Zambian identity but used her tribal connection to enable her to bond with her new church family in the United States. Kudu's response is an example of using the continuing bonds of mourning to heal from a traumatic experience. The continuing bonds model of mourning (Klass et al., 1996), discussed in our Introduction and referred to throughout this text, suggests that instead of letting go of internal representations of lost loved ones or valued events, the bereaved continues to identify with, integrate, and create a bond with the lost object. In Kudu's case, she transformed her connection with her Zambian identity to enhance her day-to-day functioning in her new home.

Researchers have added to this groundbreaking idea by discussing how an individual reaches a new understanding of the world so that it matches reality in which "mourning optimizes function and potential by mixing previous experience with the present reality of loss" (Hani et al., 2005, p. 111). Research on the immigrants' experience suggests that they can be empowered by helping them to assimilate resources represented by their culture of birth. Immigrants can learn to "preserve the inner representation of their lost countries and use them as a source of solace that may help them face their new realities" (Hani et al., 2005, p. 112). In their research with Arab immigrants, Hani et al. (2005) used the Assimilation Model (Stiles et al., 1990; Stiles, 2002) to elaborate the continuing bonds of mourning to describe how elements of the lost culture were assimilated into immigrants' new life patterns. Their research demonstrated how Arab immigrants were able to build "a meaning bridge" between their native culture and their new host culture (Hani et al., 2005, p.117). This process is similarly described by Imberti (2008) when she speaks of how "we immigrants need help in creating a space within ourselves for incorporating the transforming experiences we undergo, for understanding and accepting our losses and for acknowledging our achievements" (p. 37).

Facing a Chronic or Life-Threatening Illness

"We are a society that is preoccupied with maintaining health, believing that health is a normal state and illness is abnormal. We appear to have lost sight of the fact that except for the possibility of sudden death, everyone with a disability will age, and everyone who is aging will acquire one or more disabilities" (Zola, 1991, p. 293). Facing chronic illness at midlife can be especially difficult because midlife adults are focused on the biological changes of aging and their body image. Kralik (2002) reports that midlife women facing chronic illness had "four constructs emerge[d] from the women's narratives: (a) how quickly life changes, (b) extraordinariness, (c) confronting life with illness, [and] (d) reconstructing life with illness" (p. 146). The construct of transition emerged as salient to women with chronic illness as they discovered that they moved from one of the preceding constructs to another in a cyclical rather than linear fashion. Oktay and Walter (1993) found that midlife women dealing with breast cancer faced vulnerability in the areas of body image, marriage, relationships with adolescent children, confronting death, reassessing one's life, and generativity. However, their research also revealed that midlife women with breast cancer used this opportunity to learn how to take better care of themselves as individuals and found a new purpose in life as they reassessed their lives and dreams. Most of the midlife women who were interviewed felt increased self-confidence as a result of confronting their illness. They learned to become more self-reliant and to say "no" to activities that were not meaningful to them.

With regard to body image, Jessica was 45 when she was diagnosed with breast cancer and faced a mastectomy. Three years after her surgery she was still adjusting to an altered body image:

> I've slowed down since the mastectomy, I've put on some weight. I'm not as physically active as I used to be. I don't do aerobics anymore…I have an ugly keloid scar from my surgery….You really can't tell (when in a bathing suit) unless you knew and would look. I'm my own worst critic. (Oktay & Walter, 1991, p. 111)

This research study also revealed how sensitive women were to the loss of their hair from chemotherapy. In some cases, they were more concerned about the loss of their hair than their breasts. Although most breast cancer patients no longer have radical mastectomies, many undergo chemotherapy treatment, which makes this finding still significant. Gwen was 59 at her diagnosis of breast cancer. She believes that having to actually confront death at this stage of life has helped her on a new trajectory for living:

The issue of my life has always been one of control—wanting to be in control. Cancer really throws you out of control, for sure. But then you realize that there are things you can control, your energy, for example. I'm learning to think that when something doesn't work out as I wanted it to, that's not necessarily bad. It just wasn't right for me....Cancer really hits you with "What's this all about? I was struggling with this issue when I got the diagnosis. What am I supposed to be doing with my life? The cancer helped me in terms of some of these questions....I'm also trying to find value in just being, rather than always doing. (Oktay & Walter, 1993, pp. 146, 147)

Research on breast cancer also validates Kralik's (2002) findings about the construct of transition. Midlife women move through transitions when confronting a chronic illness, as they initially feel as though life has changed too quickly, move to a place where they can view their illness as transformative, and finally reconstruct a life learning to live with their illness. Gordon and Feldman's (1998) research with younger and older women diagnosed with multiple sclerosis, systemic lupus, rheumatoid arthritis, osteoporosis, or a combination of these disorders documents a similar transition, with emphasis on the point that the "ability to see illness in the larger context of life events seemed a resulting strength of age" (Gordon & Feldman, 1998, p. 9). Research on fibromyalgia indicates that women have learned and can learn to live with chronic illness and find new ways to restore balance to their lives (Friedberg, 2006; Sandstrom & Keefe, 1998). Many researchers agree that adaptation to chronic illness or disability involves a "spiritual reexamination and a search for purpose as one learns to accept the circumstances of one's chronic condition" (Gordon & Feldman, 1998, p.1). This search for meaning interfaces positively with the midlife woman's developmental work of stock-taking and reassessment of her life. In chapter 9 we shall focus on the losses faced by a patient and an adult caregiver who cope with Alzheimer's disease and dementia. The story of Rachael and Hal demonstrates these losses.

Death of Parents

The loss of one's parents during this phase is considered normative but is a major life transition and involves much despair as the midlife adult comes face-to-face with the eventuality of his or her own aging and death. The loss of one's parents heightens the midlife adult's developmental task of coming face-to-face with his or her own mortality. When parents die, the barrier between a midlife adult and death is removed as one has moved up the generational ladder (Peterson & Rafuls, 1998). The loss of one's parents in midlife increases the adult child's awareness of time left to live (Lutovich, 2002) and can provide a turning point "that can foster a new sense of responsibility for oneself and others" (Umberson, 2003, p. 195).

The relationship with one's parents is "usually the longest of life's relationships which [typically] involve a deep sense of mutual commitment and responsibility" (Fennell, 2004, p. 314). When one grieves the death of one's parents, one also grieves for himself or herself, as one's self-image and how one evaluates his/her self-worth is primarily influenced by one's parents. Most adults recognize characteristics in themselves that remind them of their parents. For many adults, parents were the most influential and powerful figures throughout childhood and have provided a "haven of security for us" (Hooyman & Kramer, p. 268). However, this may not be true for adults who were neglected, abused or abandoned in childhood and "may feel little connection to their parents" (p. 268).

The death of one's parents, even if it occurs long after parents have ceased being the provider, protector, and caregiver, often brings up feelings of intense vulnerability, isolation, and loneliness (Rando, 1986a). Seventy-five percent of adults are likely to have lost both parents by age 62 (Hooyman & Kramer, 2006). For those adults who have lost both parents, the idea of becoming an orphan in the sense of no longer being a daughter or a son comes into play. In a sense, the midlife adult loses a direct link to his or her past and with important traditions. Parents may be the only people who knew the adult as a child. No matter how powerful one may feel as an adult, one is always a child alongside one's parents. Childlike feelings may get resurrected, which many adults tend to deny because of the many responsibilities and activities that preoccupy a midlife adult (Rando, 1986a).

Because society does not define a parental death in midlife as a major disruptive loss, the midlife adult may underestimate the impact of the grief that she or he is experiencing (Bevcar, 2001; Harvey, 2000; Umberson, 2003). The death of a parent in midlife may be minimized by our society because one's parents are expected to die before the adult child (Umberson, 2003). However, this loss can be intense and profound. The loss of one's parents is often experienced as a disenfranchised one because our society doesn't recognize the depth and meaning of such a loss as it is an expected loss and therefore may be trivialized.

Often there is sadness and frustration over not being able to "make it all better" for one's parents as they so often did for the child. Conversely, if the relationship has been extremely conflicted or there has been caregiving around a long illness, the midlife adult may experience a sense of relief. If the relationship has been a conflicted one, the memories and messages from one's parent may be indelible in one's mind and the adult child may feel angry at the loss of an opportunity for further growth in that relationship (Rando, 1986a). On the other hand, loss of one's parents can often propel the midlife adult into redefining him/herself so that s/he makes new meaning out of his/her life. As the midlife adult moves up the generational ladder s/he can take a more mature stance. The midlife adult can also begin to see him/herself as the keeper of traditions, which will be passed down through other generations.

This can also be a time for spiritual awakening for many midlife adults. Spirituality can be an antidote to the abandonment the midlife adult may experience when his parents die. "Healthy spirituality is inviting, meeting us where we are, as we are, not where others are" (Gilbert, 2006, p. 10) and can help heal wounds from the past regarding unresolved issues with one's parents. Furthermore, as with any transition, as one door closes another may open, and the adult may deepen his or her relationship with other family members or with a partner (Fennell, 2004, p. 314).

Death of a Sibling in Adulthood

Little attention has been paid to the loss of an adult sibling, yet this is a loss that most adults face, which for some (as in the vignette of David presented at the beginning of this chapter) can be devastating. It is not uncommon to be one of several siblings within a family, thereby exposing adults to the death of a sibling more than to other losses (Rando, 1986b). Furthermore, as they continue to live, one's siblings are a part of an adult's life longer than anyone else, making their eventual loss all the more significant.

Despite common beliefs, the sibling relationship "does not dissipate when people leave their parental home" (Godfrey, 2006, p. 6). Once parents are gone, siblings provide an important tie to an adult's past, so that sibling ties often strengthen following the death of both parents. Sibling relationships are important in adulthood and can provide companionship and support (Connidis, 2001) and contribute to a "significant part of one's sense of self and family" (Godfrey, 2006, p. 6). When an adult loses a sibling s/he often misses the understanding, support, and companionship of the sibling relationship, but on a deeper level s/he may be grieving for a part of the self that is missing (Godfrey, 2006).

Nevertheless, sibling relationships are often fraught with rivalry and ambivalence so that the meaning of such a loss can differ depending on the nature of the relationship. One must remember that "sibling relationships are often marked by attachment as well as antagonism" (Rando, 1986b, p. 154). Depending on the nature of the relationship, the bereaved sibling may experience guilt, which can emanate from the ambivalence of the relationship. Sadness and guilt can develop when the bereaved adult remembers being closer as a child but feels more distant as an adult. Additionally, a bereaved adult can also experience regret, sadness, and guilt because the relationship was never quite what one expected that it might be. Robinson and Mahon (1997) suggest that relationships with siblings change over time as siblings approach adulthood, "with a decrease in reciprocity and, for many, an increase in complementarity" (p. 495). The relationships of siblings seem to exist on a continuum; some can go years without seeing siblings, whereas others, who have a close relationship, talk to or see one another frequently (Robinson & Mahon, 1997). Thus, when understanding the meaning of the death of a sibling in adulthood, one must understand the nature and intensity of the relationship (Eaves, McQuiston, & Miles, 2005). For many adults, sibling loss is experienced as a disenfranchised loss because the surviving sibling is often overlooked as a griever, with the majority of support and attention going to the immediate family (Hooyman & Kramer, 2006). Sibling loss in midlife is somewhat off time as most adults "will not lose a sibling to death until they are past seventy years of age" (p. 313).

THE LOSS OF THE MIDLIFE ADULT AS EXPERIENCED BY OTHERS

Death of a Spouse

For midlife adults, loss of a spouse or partner is not normative or expected, but by later midlife is certainly a possibility. For this reason, bereaved spouses in midlife can be isolated with their grief as few friends in their cohort have experienced this loss. In fact, friends may sometimes distance themselves from a bereaved midlife spouse because of fear of contagion—that this might happen to them. Issues such as how the bereaved spouse grieves for the part of the self that was a part of the relationship were discussed in chapter 6. The issue that is heightened for midlife adults who lose a spouse is confronting his or her own mortality, as s/he sees the spouse or partner's death as a harbinger of his or her own death. Because one of the developmental tasks of midlife is to begin to confront the reality that one will die, this loss may catapult the midlife adult into a perspective adopted by those in later adulthood, for whom this issue is more of a concern. The other midlife issue that is heightened by loss of a spouse is reassessing one's life. The identity shift that occurs from "we" to "I" following the loss of a spouse forces the midlife adult to discover who s/he is without the spouse. Frank lost his wife when he was 42 and was left caring for their 4-year-old daughter. In one case study from Walter's work (2003), Frank believes that he has changed dramatically since the loss of his wife:

> I do think it has affected my personality. I don't think I'm as goofy as I was before. I'm not as lighthearted as before. I'm more vocal. There's a weightiness that I feel…it's just an excellent way for me to grow up….I have to deal with the tough stuff sometimes and unpleasant stuff, and that's what the real world is about. Maybe I wouldn't be doing that if Sarah were around. I had a buffer there. (C. Walter, 2003, p. 68)

Although there may be increased fears about physical safety and health and/or being alone, many bereaved spouses use this increased awareness of their own mortality in a positive way (C. Walter, 2003). The loss of a spouse/partner propels the midlife adult to accept the fact that only s/he has ultimate responsibility for his or her life and happiness.

Death of a Nonmarried Opposite-Sex Partner

Just as with gay and lesbian partners, when the partner dies in an unmarried relationship there is no transitional role assigned by our culture following the death, such as there is with widows and widowers. This role of spouse carries with it a certain status that is recognized by the larger community (Doka, 1987, 2002). There is often little sympathy for the emotional reactions of unmarried opposite-sex partners and their grief goes unrecognized. Walter's research (2003) provides documentation of this experience. Consider the example of Laura, who was 40 when her partner, Jake, died of cancer at 46:

> I was just constantly reminded that I had no worldly tie to this person other than the fact that I had lived with him and taken care of him and loved him. It seemed as if nobody recognized this....We partners live in a very small segment of society that sanctions a lot of things, but this isn't the rest of the world. What I was doing was crossing a boundary. As long as I was within that little circle I was fine, but every time I had to cross that boundary it was one of the great difficulties. Losing a partner is an experience that brings home in a very fundamental way how different our lives are. I have friends who are gay and have lost partners. They have a community that supports them and gives them sustenance....I think they had more in the sense of an understanding community than I did. (C. Walter, 2003, pp. 120–121)

Laura experienced feelings of abandonment following Jake's death as she had no support for her feelings within the larger society. Furthermore, Jake's children, who had become like her own, distanced themselves from her once their dad was gone. This experience increased Laura's struggles with the developmental task of generativity as she had no children of her own. Laura believed that her changed relationship with Jake's children following his death prolonged the healing process for her (C. Walter, 2003).

Death of a Lesbian Partner

Although there is a dearth of research about bereaved lesbian partners, the available literature (Deevey, 1997; C. Walter, 2003) reports that lesbian partners in our society face discrimination at the time of the death of their partner. Lesbian women also face bigotry and discrimination by society during the illness preceding death. This is illustrated by the case "Illness Doesn't Discriminate: One Story From the Gay and Lesbian Community" presented at the end of this chapter, in which Arden's partner describes the discrimination that she experienced as she sat in the chapel of a hospital where Arden was having surgery for breast cancer.

"Families can prevent lesbian partners from participating in hospital visits, caregiving responsibilities, and funeral services by leaving them out of arrangements" (Mirkin, 1994, p. 100). In the case of Lea, who was 46 when her partner, Corky, died from cancer at 43, Corky's family was particularly brutal toward Lea in the final days of Corky's life. Although Lea remained the primary caregiver for Corky throughout her illness, "When the family gathered with the family physician they took the case away from me" (C. Walter, 2003, p. 187). Neither Corky's mother nor her sister would speak with Lea because they felt she had taken Corky away from her husband (who was abusive). Lea believes that the idea of a married woman moving out into a gay community was not accepted and led to the increased difficulty Lea experienced in receiving needed support when she was grieving. Similar to the aforementioned case study, Lea and Corky's legal documents of power of attorney were not recognized by the hospital. This same case study will further illustrate this discrimination and with it the disenfranchised grief faced by the bereaved partner.

The midlife task of stock-taking and reassessment is clearly demonstrated in Lea's belief that she has changed dramatically since Corky's death:

> I've become a softer, kinder, more introspective person than I was. I think I was a real hard core business woman, who was much more aggressive in my quest for fixing things and improving the quality of life for the people I love. What I learned from my experience is that there are things you can't fix and I didn't know that at the tender age of forty-six. I had previously been called the fixer and that label is gone forever. (C. Walter, 2003, p. 190)

Lea has found a way of staying connected to and honoring the memory of Corky by creating a pet-loss bereavement foundation, as Corky "loved all animals." Lea also talks to all of her new friends about Corky and finds they are receptive to hearing this because "that's a way of getting to know me." This ongoing bond with the deceased partner is an example of the continuing bonds theory, which posits that connection to the deceased is one of the core facets of the grieving and healing process.

Death of a Gay Partner

In chapter 6 some issues faced by young bereaved gay men were addressed. One issue not addressed was the complication that gay men face from the medical profession when a partner dies. Tom was 42 when his life partner, Rob, died from an AIDS-related illness. Tom has vivid memories of the way he was treated by doctors at the hospital when Rob was dying:

> I went to enter his room and the nurse said, "He does not want you in here." There was a new doctor and this was her first residency assignment. She was clearly not happy having a dying AIDS patient on her hands. …She [nurse] looked up at me, as if to tell me that my table was ready at a restaurant, and said, "You know he's probably going to die tonight." I said, "Well I didn't know that but thank you for telling me." I couldn't get into his room, so I went into the waiting room and made a bed for myself. Then this nurse came out and told me that Rob was gone. I never saw the doctor. (C. Walter, 2003, p. 146)

It is so difficult for any spouse or partner to be denied access to witness the death of her or his loved one. The healing process for this midlife gay man was complicated by this denial of an important ritual. For gay men in midlife who face the death of their partners from AIDS, mourning is particularly complicated because in addition to the loss of their partner they are confronted with the possibility of their own mortality. Richmond and Ross (1995) report that the bereaved partner of an AIDS patient faces the fact that he may be infected himself and may face the demands of coping with his own illness and possible death. These partners have a "sense of watching what they will be going through or a rehearsal of their own death" (p. 162).

MATURATIONAL LOSSES OF MIDLIFE ADULTS

Loss/Transition of Employment

During midlife, the family and the workplace are the arenas in which most adults exercise their developmental tasks. In fact one of the major tasks of midlife is to balance work and family life. The experience of work has special meaning during this phase of life when adults are exploring their own sense of creativity and how this intersects with the workplace. Many midlife adults are meeting new skill demands and/or achieving new levels of competence in the world of work, such as leadership, mentorship, and expanding personal relationships at the workplace. This achievement can lead to a new sense of generativity. During midlife some adults recognize that the kind of contributions they thought they could make are simply not possible within their chosen work structure. Others may recognize that they have succeeded as much as possible in a given career and may decide to retrain for new kinds of work. The case study of Linda in chapter 8 provides an illustration of this type of change. Both of these transitions involve some loss, but the midlife adult is more in charge of some of this transition. However, there is always some fear and apprehension attached to finding a new career or place of work.

Because of the restructuring of the labor market, "plant closings, downturns in the economy, and workforce reorganizations, many midlife adults who had a history of steady employment, including increased responsibility and advancement, have recently faced job loss" (Newman & Newman, 2006, p. 441). Many adults do not have control over this transition and are laid off from their jobs and cannot be rehired in the same field. This type of work transition can be viewed as a severe loss, as these adults find themselves out of work at a time in their lives when many adults are reaching the peak of their careers as well as matching their own style and creativity with the workplace. Unemployment can be a devastating loss that interferes with a basic developmental task of middle adulthood. Furthermore, because of the American cultural emphasis on work for both men and women, chronically unemployed adults in midlife may experience guilt, shame, and anger (Newman & Newman, 2006). These adults may not be able to direct their energy toward creative solutions to life's problems. Joblessness often has a major impact on a midlife adult's sense of self-worth and hope for the future, which can lead to depression, passivity, and social withdrawal (Neimeyer, 1998). What makes job loss even more difficult to endure is that although, like other losses, it requires mourning and time to cope with confusing feelings, there is no ritual that recognizes this loss or "provides a socially sanctioned period of grieving and recovery" (p. 34). In this sense, job loss is a disenfranchised loss. Complicating this further are social expectations that unemployed adults be continually self-motivated and effective in seeking new work at the same time that they are depressed, self-doubting, and confused about how to move forward (Neimeyer, 1998).

In addition to the primary loss of one's job, there are many secondary losses that occur following job loss. At this time in life, job loss can be associated with disruption in family life, financial deprivation, and increases in marital conflict. Because the United States is a society that prides itself on working hard and providing income for one's family, both the unemployed midlife adult and the entire family can experience feelings of alienation from the society and its institutions as a result of joblessness. Spouses and children clearly experience the effects of a spouse or parent who loses a job. Family members and close associates often bear the brunt of anger experienced by the adult who has lost his/her job because it is more difficult for the unemployed adult to ventilate anger toward the employer (Neimeyer, 1998). Children may have difficulty in school or act out their anger and depression within their peer groups. On the flip side, "social support—especially family strengths and marital satisfaction—are important buffers for the negative effects of unemployment" (Newman & Newman, 2006, p. 44). Social support plays an important role in providing hopeful encouragement and helping the unemployed midlife adult believe that his or her job search is worthwhile. This can result in encouraging the jobless adult to engage in actively pursuing new work. Furthermore, when the job search is unsuccessful, one's social network and/or family can provide a deep sense of caring about the unemployed adult, which is critical to his/her functioning.

The other resilience factors that emerge from unemployment occur when the midlife adult uses this time to rediscover his or her other talents, which may have been dormant throughout adulthood thus far. This process involves a redefinition of self and an opportunity to find work that is more meaningful to the adult and helps to reestablish an improved fit between the self and the environment, often leading to a more positive sense of self-worth for the adult.

Loss Experienced by Parents When Adult Children Are Leaving Home

During midlife many adults are experiencing the phenomenon of the "empty nest." When the last child leaves the parental home, there are often remarkable changes in the marital structure, particularly when the home has been "child centered," with parental activities, behaviors, thought, and feelings having been focused on the children. Many couples experience conflict at this point because they realize that they have not had much "couple communication" during the years they have focused on being parents. The loss of adult children when leaving home is a maturational loss that for some can be experienced as a disenfranchised loss because family and friends may only view the change as a positive one, as the couple gains freedom from demands of family.

Some couples are able to manage this time by reworking their own marital relationship so as to increase and enjoy activities with each other and friends. Other couples cannot manage this transition and move toward separation and/or divorce. If the latter occurs, more loss ensues as the spouses must face life without their partner. On the other hand, some couples feel "freed up" by the empty nest and use this opportunity for their own personal growth and for their growth as a couple. There are also many families in today's society who experience adult children returning home because of financial issues, the child's own marital conflicts, and/or problems with their own children. This "return to the nest" requires restructuring family life again, as the couple may be enjoying their newfound freedom and resent giving it up. Couples who are able to restructure their marital or partnered relationship can explore new interests (both together and separately) and establish new couple friendships and/or enhance longer term relationships.

The Loss of the Family Home

Midlife is a time to take stock and to assess how one's life is going to turn out, given the realization that there is a heightened feeling that whatever one is going to do s/he must do now. There may be further recognition that the family home where children were reared is no longer the right fit with the midlife adult's wish to balance work, leisure time, and family life. One of the major motivating factors for a downsizing of one's home and/or relocation of home comes when young adult children move out of the home, either to college or later on when they establish their own families. Other factors that promote a move from the family home may include the death of a spouse or partner, which catapults the midlife adult into seeking new paths or direction in his/her life, and a decline in energy—a noticeable change in midlife (Hooyman & Kramer, 2006).

Some adults become less active and less mobile, whereas others develop a chronic illness that makes if difficult to remain in a home that has been established for the rearing of children. Functional disability may make physical space and the need for climbing steps impediments for the midlife adult who is then unable to remain in the home established in early adulthood (Oswald & Wahl, 2005). Retirement from the workplace or relocation/redefinition of one's job are other contributing factors to moving from the family home; these will be discussed in more detail in chapter 8.

There is a dearth of literature about the loss of the family home in midlife, but the authors concur that home loss is a dominant theme in the lives of midlife adults. Although many adults are seeking a new home because they wish to establish a new, more satisfying lifestyle for this phase of life, there is still a huge loss involved, which often goes unrecognized, given the energy that is required to reestablish the nest. Home is a place that helps to define our sense of place, contributes to our identity, and adds predictability to life (Hooyman & Kramer, 2006). Once the move has occurred, memories of activities and milestones of life that occurred in the family home can disrupt establishing one's new lifestyle.

The other big secondary loss that occurs is the physical availability of lifetime friendships. For both sexes, but primarily for women in this cohort, friendships have been made as children are born, grow, and develop. Although good friendships can be maintained at a distance, it is different when one cannot have more spontaneous contact with good friends. It is the authors' opinion that this loss must be grieved in some way for the adult to move forward. Recognition of this loss by the midlife adult and his or her spouse/partner/significant other can be helpful by encouraging the adult to cope with his/her feelings of loss. However, just as a new lifestyle presents the midlife adult with new opportunities for challenge and growth and a renewed sense of community, new friendships can also encourage growth in one's relational life.

Off-Time Issues of Parenthood— Fertility Issues Arise Again

Midlife women must grapple, once again, with the issue of infertility as they are faced with the transition of menopause and the end of possible childbearing, if it has not occurred earlier in their lives. Levinson and Levinson (1996) found that many women at age 40 who had never had children suffered a mild depression regarding a growing realization that they never would bear children. This realization was true for women who chose not to bear children as well as those who wanted to bear children but could not. This loss may go unrecognized in a culture that is now more supportive of women who choose not to have children as well as those who have chosen careers instead of childbearing.

Women who have waited to bear children until their late 30s and early 40s are a growing group in our society. In Walter's (1986) *The Timing of Motherhood*, which provides descriptions of women who have waited until later to have children, late-timing mothers are found to be enjoying their young children, but worry that they may not live to see their children marry and have children of their own. Many of these women experience some loneliness in their role, as it is not "in sync" with their cohort. However, because of increasing numbers of women choosing the option to wait, this experience of isolation may be reduced.

READINGS

ILLNESS DOESN'T DISCRIMINATE: ONE STORY FROM THE GAY AND LESBIAN COMMUNITY

Rev. Susan Vollmer

The Rev. Susan Vollmer is an ordained minister endorsed by the Unitarian Universalist Church of the Lehigh Valley in Bethlehem, Pennsylvania. She currently works as a Chaplain for the Hospice of the Visiting Nurse Association of St. Luke's in Bethlehem and serves as their Bereavement Coordinator. Sue has a Master's of Divinity from Moravian Theological Seminary in Bethlehem and a Master's in Pastoral Ministry from Boston College. Sue has many years of ministry experience in family-life education, marriage preparation, marriage enrichment, parenting training, and in teaching communication skills. As a counselor, Sue has worked with at-risk youth and their families, and with children with special needs. She has training in addiction, co-dependency, trauma, and crisis intervention. A published author, Sue has spoken nationally on topics related to relationships, family, communication, trauma, and end-of-life issues. Sue has two amazing college-age sons whom she enjoys spending time with, is a beach-lover, gardener, runner, and caregiver to two fun-loving little fuzzy dogs.

Before Their Time*

She sat on the edge of our bed in the home that we had created… a warm, nurturing, and safe place. The fall afternoon sun bathed the room in a golden glow of light and warmth through the windows and skylight. It was a classic fall day with blue skies, puffy white clouds, and a nip in the air.

The rays of sunlight touched her curly brownish hair catching her highlights in a glisten like the sparkle that I had so often seen in her eyes.

But this scene was different from any that we had shared before. It felt as if we stood on holy ground immersed in an awareness of awe, tenderness, and gentleness, unlike any we had ever known.

The body of this strong woman was wrapped in white bandages and her once broad back made strong by years of competitive swimming was feebly bent over in pain and fatigue. It now carried the unfathomable, the unimaginable weight of her recent diagnosis of breast cancer.

We sat on the bed together gazing with dazed and disbelieving eyes at what had become of her body, of the lymphoedema that was disfiguring her arm, of the bandages across where her right breast had been and of the raw sites where tubes had been protruding from her chest. What had just happened…to her? To us? To what we had envisioned our lives to be?

How did we get from there to here? What were we to do now?

Helplessly I watched as she unwrapped her fragile arm, her swollen hand and fingers, her eyes pleading with me to somehow make this

---

*From S. Vollmer (in press). *Journal of Pastoral Care and Counseling*.

all OK, to spread my love around her protecting us from what may lie ahead.

There were no words here, nothing that made any sense. Only love as infinite as the stars and as deep as the ocean floor. But, there were eyes and hearts here, holding on as if tomorrow could steal this moment away like a thief in the night. Holding on as if this moment was all that there was.

Two lovers thrown into the fragility of life before their time.

So we wrapped and unwrapped her being, the delicate work of love for years beyond that moment. Held tighter and then more loose, each finger a gift of life in the moment, a reminder of the separateness of intimate love and the unity of the effort to maintain it.

We cherished that sacred sunlight warming us in our afternoon task, holding fast to the love and cloaking ourselves in it for many times yet to come.

It was all that we had standing naked in the grip of the disease.

Case Discussion

Sometimes stories end in ways that we never anticipate, turning from life-giving gifts, to pleas for hope, to endings where beginnings had hardly had a chance to find root. For $2^1/2$ years my partner, my two sons, our dog, and I fought breast cancer. Compared to some, it was a relatively short fight. But in our lives, it was a hard fight, a draining fight, and a fight for life. Now it's not that our story is an unusual one, or a particularly valiant one, or that we didn't share the same journey as any family faced with cancer. What is unusual about our story, is that it has become a story about loss and a story about grief in a family that was made up of two women, two boys, and a fuzzy dog. We know that illness, death, grief, and loss happen in all families, no matter the shape, size, or genders. It does not discriminate. And so this is the story of illness, loss, and grief for one family and one couple who happened to be two women.

In August 2000, Arden and I were married in the presence of our family and friends within the church community that knew us, supported us, and accepted us. My sons read readings, lit candles, and played violins, and two of our best friends co-officiated the service. We celebrated together and anticipated a full life ahead of us. There was nothing to suggest otherwise. But exactly 2 months later we were thrust into a whirlwind. Arden was diagnosed with stage-4 breast cancer and 3 weeks later, on my eldest son's 11th birthday, she had a mastectomy. In that moment, the image of the life that we knew quickly faded into the cancer that would consume it. Two months later, barely recovered from the first, Arden had her second surgery, a major abdominal surgery for what we had been warned would probably be ovarian cancer. Gratefully, it was not cancer, but rather an ovarian cyst about the size of grapefruit.

While Arden was in surgery I paced the hallways, not knowing if she would survive and if she did, what life would hold. So I wandered down the hallway into the chapel, hoping for some quiet and privacy for my prayer. Across from the chapel was the office of Pastoral Care, the place where the chaplains worked and spent time listening. I was grateful at first that I had found their office in case I would need their help if Arden's surgery went wrong or the news was as bad as I had expected it to be. It was a comfort to know that I was not alone if I needed help. But my sense of safety and comfort didn't last long. As I sat in the chapel I heard the clear sound of three voices, all talking about patients with whom they had visited, who they were certain and were quite pleased it seemed, would go to hell. "They deserve it," said one. "Disgusting perverts," said another. And then I heard one voice say what whipped away the safety net in an instant…"Those damn gays should all be dead." There I sat, my partner in surgery, feeling afraid and unsure of the outcome, and the chaplains of the hospital, the people who were supposed to be the comforters and the godly ones, were damning Arden, me, and our amazing circle of friends to be dead, banishing us to their "hell." For what seemed like a lifetime, I don't think I even breathed. I was terrified, panic-stricken, furious, and devastated all in the same moment. But what I knew most is that we were not safe here and that most certainly I was alone if anything went wrong.

So I left the chapel dazed and fumbled my way down the hallway to friends who had arrived to wait with me. And as I told them tearfully what had happened I searched my pockets for the Power of Attorney, Medical Power of Attorney, and Living Will documents that I had brought along. I knew beyond a doubt that for me to see Arden or to have her wishes followed if need be, I needed these documents on my person at all times. In this facility I did not have the rights that a husband would have with his wife or a wife would have with her husband. Instead, as the rotations of ICU nurses stated hours later, I was her "sister," "such a good friend," or her "mother" (she was actually a few months older than me). I was not seen as her partner or her spouse but rather as just some nice woman who came to visit this unfortunate soul. Luckily for us, Arden's surgeon was not only a skilled physician but a welcoming and warm man. To the surprise of the nurses, he allowed me access to Arden's side in ICU at any time. "You know how to do this," he told me and left me to finally be Arden's partner in a room full of nurses who just stared at the two of us, not sure who either of us was.

The proper legal paperwork is lifeblood in the gay and lesbian community. It is the best chance we have for "rights" in our relationships, "rights" that mixed-sex couples assume in their wedding vows and marriage licenses, "rights" that same-sex couples are denied. I learned to keep the paperwork close by for every appointment, every surgery, and every treatment. Because sometimes well-meaning people make decisions that are not in our best interests.

While Arden was in a medical facility, the medical records person who took her initial information and emergency contact information thought it better to list "next of kin" as one of Arden's relatives who the records person knew, rather than listing my name as Arden had requested. I accidentally bumped into her decision one day while in Arden's room when I was reading her chart, which was hanging at the end of her bed. There I saw this relative's name listed. As I struggled to keep my composure, I casually said that I needed to step out of the room for a moment but would be right back. Here was Arden, lying in a bed stapled from her groin to her mid-chest, a gastrointestinal tube protruding from her nose and struggling with her pain. I didn't think that she needed to know all this just now. I succeeded in finding the medical-records person, straightened out what she thought was in Arden's best interest, and stated that I intended to report her to the hospital administrator. I never did. I think she got my point. I never had the time. And the amazing thing was that the change in paperwork showed up on Arden's chart in record time.

A new life resumed after this surgery and Arden went home to heal and to get ready for chemo and radiation. She started chemo in January

2001 and ended in November of 2002. During this time, as she started to lose her hair, I shaved her head and my sons and I all cut our hair very short so that she wouldn't have to bear it all alone. She worked, and taught, took classes, and continued toward her dream of ministry. She tried to do everything that she had done before. But she only let me and a few trusted friends know that it wasn't working. I used to pack her bags, edit her papers, drive her to meetings, and sit up at night and hold her as she cried in pain or fear or frustration. Life was starting to slip away. She was only 42. She started radiation in July 2001 and could be heard down the hospital corridors flip-flopping in her colorful summer sandals. But by the end of radiation, she started to slow down and needed to rest more.

Sierra

In the spring of 2001 Arden wasn't able to keep up with her regular schedule. Chemo had really exhausted her so she was home alone a lot while the kids were at school and I was at work. She talked about "maybe getting another dog someday that [she] could have as company." Bailey, our basset hound, was too big and too smelly, not to mention an "oaf" to have around. Plus he loved to chew on the wooden furniture. Anyway one evening Arden suggested going to the pet store to "look" at the puppies. I let her out at the front door since her joints were inflamed and painful because of the medications she was being given. She went in while I parked the car.

When I finally got inside, at first glance she was nowhere to be seen. However, after walking to the back of the pet store, I spotted a shiny bald head in one of the play areas where prospective buyers could play with the animals for sale. I quietly moved closer to the area not wanting to upset the dog or startle Arden. When I got close enough to see over the little walls, the picture was awesome. There sat Arden, bald, with a steroid-induced moonface holding a tiny buff-colored cock-apoo. The puppy was snuggled into the crook of her neck and both R and the pup had their eyes closed. It was a sight that brought tears to my eyes. I stood there for a while just watching until Arden opened her eyes and smiled, a smile that I hadn't seen on her face for a very long time. We talked about the puppy and how cute she was but R kept saying that she wasn't sure if we should get another dog, that it would make life "more chaotic." But looking at her face, I couldn't see how we could not. Well, she put the puppy back into her cage and walked out of the store into the center area of the mall where she sat down on a bench. When I caught up to her I found her with her face in her hands sobbing. It was if the weight of everything that she had been dealing with had fallen on her all at once. I sat down next to her and put my arm around her pulling her close. Who cared what passers-by thought!

"She's too expensive. We don't have the money," she repeated over and over again. She was right both times…but sometimes money isn't the biggest concern. After she calmed, she told me that that was the kind of puppy she had always wanted. She rested while I went in to talk to the manager. Meanwhile the manager had been observing what had happened and had seen Arden upset. Within moments, she had the puppy in her hand and had started the paperwork for a puppy that just happened to come with a discount! I carried little "Sierra" out into the mall area where Arden was still sitting and pressed her paw against Arden's ear. Arden turned and I handed "Sierra" to her. We both cried, not for the puppy but for what the puppy symbolized in our lives… loss of life as we knew it, loss of health, fear, anxiety, and the unknown. Sierra was a gift of legacy for Arden and it turned out, for me as well.

Arden carried Sierra back into the pet store while I finished the paperwork. When I turned to leave, I saw Arden standing next to a pen where there was another puppy. It was a larger dog, maybe a golden retriever or a lab. (Sorry, I'm not a dog person.) Anyway standing next to Arden was a little girl, maybe 5 or 6 years old. Standing and looking at them, I felt like an intruder on a very private moment. They were kindred spirits as they stood together, both bald, puffy faced, with a yellowish pallor. It was obvious that they were sharing the same journey, each fighting for their future. Alongside and at a distance I saw a young couple watching too. They were her parents. I could tell because they too had that long-faced, weary, scared look that I saw in my mirror. No one spoke. There weren't any words.

Finally the little girl said to Arden that this was her puppy and that she was going to take it home. I couldn't hear Arden's response, but the little girl smiled at her. Eventually, we walked out toward the car, Arden with her Sierra and her little friend with her new puppy too. They looked at each other and waved as they got into their cars and drove away.

In October 2001 we received the news that Arden's cancer was now also liver cancer. It took the wind out of our sails and stated clearly to all of us that we wouldn't have much time left as a family of four. Arden sat one night in the rocking chair in our family room and talked with the boys about hoping to take a trip together across the country next summer. There were more places that she wanted to show them, more adventures that she wanted to share with them. She asked them if they would take care of her beloved Sierra if she wasn't here to do it. She asked us three to take care of each other. For the remaining months we rallied our amazing supportive friends and church community and surrounded Arden with people who knew and loved her.

At Christmas we drove through a blizzard to her brother's home so that she could be with her family. The next day we ventured to New England to spend time with my family and then drove to our favorite beach on Cape Cod for the days between Christmas and New Year's. She was dying and I knew it. Potentially I was the only one who knew it because before we started our holiday traveling I called an oncology nurse who had befriended us during chemo and asked the dreaded prognosis question. How much time did we have left? You see, Arden never was able to ask that question, never wanted to hear the results of tests and clearly told her physicians "tell Sue, she'll tell me what I can handle." So I asked. And I traveled with the directions to the closest cancer center right next to the legal documents in my pocket. I was warned that I might need them. We drove home on January 2, 2003, and Arden died in my arms 19 days later. I had promised her years before that if and when the time came, that I would hold her and talk her through it until she was at peace. I was graced with keeping that promise.

The Face of Death*

I held you as you faded in and out
Between this world and the next.
No words were exchanged.
You were already too far there.
Just touch and gentle caressing.

---

*From S. Vollmer (in press). *Journal of Pastoral Care and Counseling.*

I watched your face as it changed with each fleeting breath.
I watched you go farther and farther away.
Our dreams and hopes, our future drew beyond us
No arm could stretch to touch them anymore.
They had once been ours, but no longer ours to share.

I held my breath as your breath would slow
Hoping that mine would help yours go on.
But moments frozen in time watched mine go on
While yours retreated to silence.

I watched your face, willing it
To breathe, to move, to blush
And saw instead the face of death looking back at me
An unwelcomed visitor and a forever loss.

The silence deafened my heart and blinded my soul.

Grief and Discrimination

Grief is increased when discrimination becomes a part of it, when there is a double standard, when there is judgment, when the grieving people are silenced or treated as if they are invisible, when their loss is not recognized. I could not cover Arden under my health insurance. Instead we paid thousands of dollars for insurance on top of the thousands we paid for treatment and medications. After her death, I paid taxes for the home that we owned together. I was denied her Social Security, which would have helped me with the medical bills, lawyer fees, and estate settlement. A friend once told me of a couple whom she knew. They were two men with quite a large age gap between them. The elder man was dying and so to protect himself and his partner, he legally adopted his partner as his son so that this man would then have legal rights.

Her obituary listed me as her "companion." I had been her companion. But I had also been her partner, roommate, friend, caregiver, confidante, lover, cook, housecleaner, bather, wound dresser, medication provider, launderer, social planner, medical appointment planner, chauffeur, full-time employee, work bag packer, editor, organizer, and the list goes on. I was not only her companion...I was her partner. I did what partners and spouses do for one another. I lived out my part of "for better or worse, in sickness and in health, until death do us part." But around me, our relationship was not identified, validated, or honored. We as a couple were invisible. I as her partner was invisible. I could not claim to be a widow. And both my sons and I were silenced in most of the areas of our lives as she declined and as we grieved afterward. The boys could not talk about this at school freely. They could not say that their stepmother had died without receiving lots of stares, ignorant comments, or consequences. We were denied the status of a grieving family.

Grief is hard enough. But being denied opportunities to grieve and be comforted makes it unbearable and disorienting. It was as if our pain and our loss needed to be negated and didn't exist. Gratefully we did not have to be silenced at church but rather had the embracing arms of the members of our church around us. And, we were surrounded by loving and supportive friends. It is what helped us through. But not every same-sex couple or family shares the same experience. In fact, most do not.

The day after Arden's death a neighbor showed up at my doorstep with dark glasses on and a casserole dish in her hand. When I answered the door, she said how sorry she was and offered to help with my sons. I thanked her for her generosity and thoughtfulness and she turned to leave. As I watched her she abruptly stopped, turned toward me and fell into my arms sobbing. She had struggled mightily when we had moved into the neighborhood and had at times turned her head and looked away. It's not clear why. And really it doesn't matter. But her grief was as real as mine. We had learned together that day that sometimes the events of life are just outside our control, whether it was having us as neighbors, realizing that we were just like everyone else, or that death takes the young as much as the old. Whatever it was, we have been different neighbors since that day on my front porch.

Grief in the gay and lesbian communities goes underground. Grieving partners stay quiet. They are not offered the same opportunity or status as a mixed-sex partner whose loved one has died. It is often not safe to talk about the loss because people's responses are unpredictable and there may be consequences for disclosing sexual orientation. Grief is hard enough to live with when it is not silenced. But being made to feel invisible and that your loss wasn't a "real" loss, that your relationship wasn't a "real" relationship is devastating. Arden was a real person. We were a real couple and a real family. Our grief just like the grief of every family who has lost a loved one, it hurt and still hurts sometimes.

Months after Arden's death I returned to school and now serve as an ordained minister and work as a hospice chaplain. The hospice team that I am part of works hard not to let anyone be invisible and we welcome partners and family. Illness and grief don't discriminate. What right do we have to?

Plastic*

Only you would know how I feel here without you.
Only you would know the emptiness in my heart.
Only you would know the questions without answers,
the thoughts left unspoken,
the dreams left unshared.

Only you would know the feel of a cold bed.
Only you would know of making one cup of coffee
or peppermint tea instead of two.
Only you would know three places at the table
and an empty chair.

Only you would know
how to program the front lights
reset the computer
change the numbers on the TV
where the paperwork is for the stereo
how to teach the dog new tricks.

Only you would know how to be the other half
of this half empty life.

Is the glass half empty or half full?

I use plastic.
Glass can shatter too.

*From S. Vollmer (in press). *Journal of Pastoral Care and Counseling.*

LOSSES OF PROFESSIONAL IDENTITY AND CAREER ASPIRATIONS

Corey S. Shdaimah, LLM, PhD

Corey S. Shdaimah is an Assistant Professor at the School of Social Work, University of Maryland at Baltimore. Dr. Shdaimah studies the way in which professionals and clients work with, around, and in opposition to what they conceive of as hostile social policies. The following case study draws on data collected from 2002 to 2004 in intensive interviews with lawyers serving indigent clients at a large, urban legal services practice (Shdaimah, 2004, 2009). It focuses on Ben,* a lawyer in the consumer division, who at that time worked primarily with clients on predatory lending.

Case Presentation

Ben became a lawyer in the early 1970s. His career choice came to him as a result of experiences he had teaching in a maximum security prison while attending an elite college. He felt that his work in the prison was grounded in a reality that transformed his worldview and gave him a sense of purpose. From the outset Ben knew he wanted to be a legal services lawyer to use the law to bring about social change. By 2003, Ben had been practicing law for nearly 30 years. Still at the same legal services program, Ben reflects on how his aspirations changed, not only as his career developed, but as the social climate changed. He is disappointed because at the outset of his career, he viewed "becoming a lawyer as being somehow at the cutting edge of social change, which I think in a lot of ways made sense given the early 1970s, '60s." But this is no longer the case. He views that time as "this little blip in legal history where the courts were actually a vehicle of social change as opposed to their historic role, which has now been reestablished as keeping order on the plantation."

Ben is not the only lawyer at the legal services program where he works who is frustrated by the gap between what he had expected to accomplish at the outset of his career and what he has actually accomplished. Some of his colleagues express disgust or disappointment, many ultimately leaving their practices. One colleague, Pete, is frustrated with accomplishments he considers paltry in the sense that they are a drop in the proverbial bucket, although he concedes that what is viewed as paltry over a trajectory of a career makes a difference to the individuals who he has helped. "If I do a great job on trying to get somebody who's being kicked off of welfare I've gotten them, let's say a single mother and 2 kids, $403 a month to live on. That's abhorrent. It's a joke, it's a farce...It's hard to figure out, well, what

---

*All names used here are pseudonyms to protect the confidentiality of the study participants.

am I doing, in terms of the broader vision?" Pete is thinking of leaving his law career for something that would allow him to have the impact he imagines might be possible and that he feels compelled to work toward.

Description of Loss

Ben wanted to create a more socially just world. Often people come into their careers with personal and professional aspirations. These can include goals for themselves and/or for others they may serve, or for certain outcomes or products that they envision creating or helping others create.

Various triggers may precipitate professional stocktaking, which involves a sense of loss. Sometimes the precipitating event is itself a loss, as in the case when one loses a job. Other times a disability may prevent one from being able to practice a chosen profession. Stocktaking may occur unexpectedly—when one is promoted, or when a colleague is promoted and one is overlooked. Even when a child asks for career advice one may reflect on the goals one started with and what has been accomplished.

Either way, goals that may have been set that are not accomplished and are viewed as now unattainable involve a loss. The loss is connected to loss of the goal; it is also connected to loss of a vision of self. It is possible to articulate three distinct losses connected to this type of stocktaking: (a) loss of idealism, (b) loss of potency to effect desired goals or outcomes, and (c) loss of sense of self. These losses may occur individually or in combination. Losses seem to be experienced most severely when they are experienced on all three of these levels simultaneously.

Assessment and Interventions

It is important to assess the impact of this loss on the individual, which will help to inform assessment and intervention strategies. Sometimes such losses impede workplace functioning and may make some options, such as waiting it out or searching for another job immediately, less feasible. It is also important to assess whether the impact carries over to other aspects of the individual's life; work disappointments are often taken home and can affect the individual's mental health and/or his or her relationships with family members. A number of Ben's colleagues spoke of lawyers who were unable to build personal barriers to separate themselves from workplace disappointments, despite a sense that this was necessary for their emotional well-being.

Working within the individual circumstances assessed, discussions with professionals in situations similar to this case led to the recommendation of a number of interventions that might prove fruitful. Helpful to Ben and a number of his colleagues is the ability to view positive accomplishment alongside his personal loss. In any stocktaking process, it can be easy to see deficiencies, particularly in comparing intended and actual outcomes and goals. However, just as some goals might have not been achieved, most people, over the trajectory of their careers, may have achieved personal and professional goals that they did not anticipate and thus are not on the "ledger" in the stocktaking process. For example, Ben ended up using his skills to make local change and to work with advocacy groups on lobbying. These are not the traditional (or even legal) skills that he was trained for or imagined, but they resulted in tangible results that were meaningful to him and to his clients. Therapists can assist clients to enumerate what their accomplishments have been, and can help them to place these on the ledger to provide a more balanced stocktaking process.

Further, identifying strengths and weaknesses can assist clients to view the stocktaking as a learning process. What is he or she good at? What are his or her weaknesses? A number of Ben's colleagues left legal services law and/or left the practice of law altogether. To the extent that they may have seen this as a compromise or abdication of their commitment to social justice or a particular cause or group of clients, many of them have found ways to make a contribution that helps to assuage these concerns. These have taken the form of offers of financial and public relations resources and services in kind. Although we may have dreams for ourselves, until these are tested in the reality of our own temperaments and personal lives within actual social, economic, and political contexts we really do not know if our dreams are a good fit for our personal and societal realities. Thinking about stocktaking as an adjustment of these, rather than a measuring up of worth, can help to reenvision the process. This should be coupled with a realistic assessment of what the options are for clients, and may also involve career counseling. Some of the options recommended here may not be affordable luxuries for individuals constrained by health, family, or financial concerns.

Lastly, allowing Ben and others to grieve over the loss of a vision also seems crucial. Other interventions should not belittle the sense of loss. Doing so will often prevent a reframing of that loss or reintegration of it because it truncates the process of examination. It also discounts the grief that many do feel over career losses that have an impact on our sense of who we are, particularly those with highly socialized work-related identities that can be professionally based (e.g., lawyer, social worker), group-membership based (e.g., union member), or identity based (e.g., career woman, third-generation carpenter). These career losses need to be recognized to be mourned. One must recognize that failure to attain career trajectory goals is different from a sense of losing one's youthful ideals and both require recognition and mourning.

Supports and Resources

It appears that for those who have been able to "hang in there" and have the resiliency to reimagine themselves without an overwhelming sense of loss, certain supports are central. One is the support of colleagues who have had similar experiences. This can help the client to think not only about the individual characteristics that led to the gap, but also to recognize other forces that might be at work. Differentiating the contributions of oneself as an individual, oneself as a professional, from the social and structural milieu is part of processing these losses. To the extent that there are shared concerns, coping with others through sharing stories, allowing one another to express anger and sorrow, and/ or engaging in gallows humor are all useful coping mechanisms. Relying on insiders for this, when possible, can help to legitimate the shared concerns and also allow individuals to address any political and societal concerns as such, which can be helpful in coping with the losses described here. In the words of Steve: "I mean, am I changing the world? No. But the revolution still isn't happening and at some basic level this office, legal aid programs, and myself personally make a difference in people's lives on basic bread-and-butter issues."

These strategies also apply to losses affected by economic upheaval such as company layoffs or underemployment. These may be amenable to reframing, at least in part, as being caused by factors beyond individual control. This can pave the way for mutual assistance and coping mechanisms that are not only individual, but also political or societal. This can involve working together to advocate for broader changes at the workplace or in the political arena that address shared concerns rather than ask for individual redress or career trajectory changes.

Other social supports can come from the workplace itself or from family members or friends. This can be in the form of allowing the individual coping with a loss of professional vision of self to explore an alternative vision of self that is useful. Creative alternatives can include taking on new social roles and responsibilities in a family, or finding a new way of practicing the profession inside or outside of an existing workplace framework. Ben's organization provides its professional workers with tremendous leeway to experiment with forms of legal practice and advocacy. Many of his colleagues have taken advantage of this to reframe a professional practice that is personally and professionally fulfilling as well as validated by the organization. Marjorie, another lawyer who works with Ben, finds collaborating with others gives her a sense of working on something larger, and helps her to cope with the diminished sense of what is possible.

Prognosis

It appears that Ben has found ways to cope with thwarted expectations. He has been able to modify a vision for personal and professional success without feeling disillusionment or the sense that his modification is mere rationalization for failure or cooptation into a system he opposes. His experiences would suggest that a number of alternatives are available. In assisting people to cope with loss of professional vision of self, social workers may use the intervention tools mentioned here to help clients identify the causes of the gap between vision of self and actualization. What are the options available? How do the client's strengths and weaknesses match up with what is available to her or him? These assessments cannot take place in a vacuum, but must consider available social supports, including workplace, financial, and family resources. Further, they must account for the larger structural forces in place, such as the political climate and the economic climate in which the professional practice options are reviewed.

KUDU'S STORY: CHANGING LIVES

Chawezi Mwantembe

Chawezi Mwantembe was born in Zambia. She now lives with her husband and two sons in Philadelphia.

Loss of Tribal Connection

Kudu is an administrator working for a health system based in Pennsylvania. She is African born and migrated to the United States in the mid-90s after living and studying in England for a number of years. In this case study she talks about how migrating into the Western culture has affected her life. Kudu thinks that breaking away from a culture or a tribe that one belongs to is not so much the problem in itself as what it leads to.

Case Presentation

I left my country of origin, Zambia, Africa, soon after high school to pursue further studies in England in 1986. It was customary in those days to see young people leave Zambia and go to various parts of the world in pursuit of their dreams. Prospects of studying abroad promised economic prosperity, which most of us found attractive given that Zambia is a developing nation. Other than economic benefits not much was shared in terms of social and emotional challenges that could be faced while living in a country that is culturally different from mine. Zambia, by and large, practices extended family values. This means that families are comprised of many generations: grandparents, parents, siblings, uncles, aunts, and cousins are looked at as one family. They share food, money, gifts, costs, and other necessities of life. Apart from being a family in themselves, they also belong to a larger group called a tribe. This group is comprised of many different families bound together by a common language. As in many southern and central African countries, Zambia has many tribes. These tribes share a similar vocabulary but the languages are not mutually comprehensible (a speaker of one may not understand another). It is to the tribe that one attaches self and finds identity.

My new life in England and later in the United States definitely improved my standard of living and increased the number of choices I had as an individual. For example, once I qualified for permanent residence, I was eligible for employment with benefits, I could purchase a home through a mortgage, and I was eligible for student loans. These and many other benefits were the driving force behind my desire to go abroad. What I didn't know was that leaving my home (Zambia) meant unintentionally breaking social bonds that tied me to my tribal group. As a student, even if I wanted to communicate with my extended family, the cost of calling Zambia regularly was prohibitive. Thus, most of my communication was via snail mail. I was able to visit only after being away for years. With long breaks in communication I started feeling disconnected from my tribe. As ties continued to weaken over time it became increasingly difficult to form an identity or connect with my new society. Part of that feeling came from the racism and discrimination I experienced.

Description of Loss

Tribal identity defines and places an individual within the self and within the larger context of the world. One's tribe defines identity, social bonds, relationships and commitments, and gives a sense of security, continuance, and well-being. Loss of tribal identity means loss of custom and loss of a consistent value system, which one depends on for stability and sense of security. The loss of identifying with a tribe fragments the conceptual framework used by one to make sense of the world and give life meaning. When this loss happens, a sense of purpose is hard to perceive, as is an understanding of what it means to be a member of the society.

Coming from a culture where Bantu encompasses the value of human beings as themselves and the roles they play in society, Western culture identities are often based on employment roles such as doctor, engineer, architect, trainer, and so on; these do little to define us as people or our value as human beings. The roles, socioeconomic status, and prestige people use to define themselves can all be threatened. Divorce, death of a spouse or child, job loss, economic setbacks, or many other losses can be devastating to a person's self-esteem, sense of identity, sense of worth, well-being, and even existence. Defining ourselves by the roles we play or the place we occupy in the social structure or organization does not provide the stability or constancy that a definition of self defined by a tribal identity provides. Such sense of identity is very fragile. It could lead to uncertainty and loss of relevance, which in turn could lead to other emotional problems.

In my culture, all terms that tribal people use refer to us as human beings—*bamuntu*—and the same is used to define what it means to be part of a tribe or group. In my new society I could not find nor feel that sense of connectedness because Western culture is no more inclusive than it is exclusive; becoming a naturalized citizen lacked the sense of belonging found in a tribe. Progressive understanding of self only in terms of one's own self or the individual and not in the context of the importance and connection to a larger group or tribe leads to increasingly exploitative "self-centered" lifestyles, which further exacerbate the sense of isolation and alienation. Cultural identity based on self-centeredness, exploitation, and dominance can't enhance self-esteem or sense of belonging or worth.

Assessment and Interventions

Loss is inevitable; at some point in life we all experience it. For some of us the experience comes through losing our tribal connection, others experience it by losing a loved one, a pet, or property, and so forth. Loss may also be experienced more than once in a lifetime. Disturbing and painful as it is, in its own way, it forces us to learn new ways of relating to our world after the loss. In his theory about grief, Worden (2002) has proposed that the final stage of grief involves "emotionally relocating" what has been lost rather than ridding oneself of the loss or finding a replacement for the loss. It is worth mentioning that although I do not feel a tight connection with my tribal society and the relationship between us has changed, it is nonetheless still a relationship.

Supports and Resources

Generally, holding on to the lost culture leads to isolation and alienation. A healthier response is to let go and move on. In my case, accepting the fact that I may never go back to my country was very painful because I did not see myself in any other way than as a Zambian. I tried to cling to that identity for as long as I could. The longer I clung to it, the more disturbed I became. Through my church and its programs, I was able to let go of my struggle and have now found what I call my extended family. I once again feel connected to something larger than myself. In this extended family our identity is in Christ. Although I was afraid of losing my tribal ties, finding a sense of security and belonging in my church family has allowed me to incorporate elements from my tribal society such as identity, language, values, and traditions into my new life.

Instead of abandoning emotional attachments, immigrants can use their tribal connections to overcome self-esteem and identity issues. In the United States it is common to find groups of immigrants living in one area as this gives them a sense of connectedness, purpose, and shared values. By and large, the sustaining element for me is hope in my family's future.

SUMMARY

Middle adulthood is a stage in one's life when much energy goes into transformation of the self as the adult becomes aware of the time limits of his/her life. For the first time the adult is aware that he or she has probably lived more years in the past than s/he will in the future. Losses in middle adulthood are characterized by this realization that one is mortal. There is a press to contribute in a meaningful way to society so that one can leave a legacy to mark the adult's experience in life. Losses are colored by this need for making a meaningful contribution as well as the energy spent in transforming one's identity. The case studies of Ben and Kudu specifically examine two different types of self-transformations that result from different types of losses. Ben's career crisis was driven by his disappointment and frustration between what he had expected to accomplish at the outset of his career and what he had actually accomplished by midlife. The goals he set for himself as a young adult had not been attained—his dream had not been realized—and this loss had to be grieved before Ben could decide what career path he should take at this juncture. Ben was able to find ways to cope with thwarted expectations by modifying a vision for personal and professional success.

Social workers and counselors can work with adults like Ben by helping them to identify strengths and weaknesses that are realistic and helping them to realize what they have accomplished, which is often denied during this process of change. Kudu's self-transformation was triggered by her migration to a culture that was foreign to her. She experienced a loss of self-esteem and identity, but was able to use her bond with her tribal society to help her navigate within the American society by identifying with a church family, which had some similar characteristics to her tribal connection and provided her with a sense of extended family.

Adults in middle adulthood face many losses such as that of an adult parent, sibling, spouse, or partner, as in the case of Arden's partner in "Illness Doesn't Discriminate: One Story From the Gay and Lesbian Community." During the grieving process, Arden's partner was able to make meaning of her tragic loss of her lesbian partner through her writing and her poetry, which describes their relationship with one another and their journey with cancer. Arden's partner also used continuing bonds with Arden through her relationship with the couple's dog, which Arden had chosen during her cancer treatment. Meaning-making and the use of continuing bonds with the lost person, tribe, or aspiration seem to be ways that midlife adults can weather the storm of loss, disappointment, and chronic illness. Social workers and grief counselors can encourage bereaved midlife clients to work through their losses by validating losses that may be disenfranchised (such as in the case of Arden's lesbian partner), help any bereaved midlife adult express his/her feelings, and help the adult find meaning in the loss. Finally, a practitioner can help his/her client to emotionally relocate the deceased by internalizing the relationship so that s/he can continue to feel connected to the deceased while also having meaningful ties with the living.

8 Retirement and Reinvention

Helen was 66 when she retired from her full-time position as a high school history teacher. Helen had worked in this same high school for 22 years; prior to leaving she experienced much ambivalence about whether or not she was doing the right thing. She kept wondering, "What will I do with my time?" and "How will I structure my days?" Yet, she was discouraged with her job and found the students increasingly difficult to reach and to engage in the work of learning. The last year of teaching convinced Helen that she had made the right decision and she began to put the retirement process into motion. This was no small feat; it required hours of time on the telephone and in person with the human resources department to finalize retirement income and benefits she had accrued as a long-time employee. The summer following her retirement, Helen was elated about her decision and totally enjoyed the freedom of sleeping-in when she wanted and spending more time with her adult children, grandchildren, and friends. She and her husband planned a trip to Europe, which they had been putting on the back burner for several years. They also spent several long weekends traveling to visit family and friends who lived at some distance from their home.

During the fall season after her retirement Helen was on a "high" and began training as a docent for a local art museum where she began to make new friends who had similar interests. Helen relished having free time during the day when she could read several books that she had put on hold and clean out closets that she had not visited in years. She felt that her new life was moving along quite nicely when an old friend asked her "How is it going now that you are retired?" Helen also engaged more frequently in her hobby of jewelry making and began substituting for a teacher at the same school where she had worked. This began to feel like a poor fit for her during this time as she was exposed to the politics all over again from which she was trying to remove herself by retiring. As the spring approached, Helen found herself "at odds" with herself, her husband who was still working full time, her adult children, and her friends. She began to see traits in some of her friends that she did not admire, having more time to spend with them now that she was retired.

Helen began to realize, with the help of her family, that she needed to speak to someone about this time of transition and reinvention. One of her college friends suggested that Helen see a coach who specializes in helping adults who are trying to reestablish their lives after retirement. Helen was reluctant at first because she had never been to a counselor or therapist and viewed herself as someone who could figure it out on her own. After several sessions with her coach Helen began to realize that she needed to make new connections, both in terms of her network of friends, but also with herself in terms of discovering her passion for this stage of her life. She had been filling her time with lunches with friends, cleaning out closets, preparing special dinners for her family, attending daytime theatre productions and training to become a docent at a local museum. These activities seemed to lack the feeling of satisfaction that she once had had in her career. She realized that she still needed to feel worthwhile and that she was giving back to society in some way. Helen's coach worked with her over a period of 7 months to help Helen define those activities that brought her the highest levels of satisfaction. Following her coaching sessions, Helen was able to recognize her need to invest more time in her passion of studying art history and registered for a course at a local university. She also decided to inquire at other art museums in the area about programs they might have in which she could volunteer as an educator. Helen realized that she truly missed her role as a teacher and needed to discover other ways she might satisfy this passion.

THE TRANSITION TO THE THIRD QUARTER OF LIFE: RETIREMENT OR REINVENTION?

The very title of this chapter suggests the difficulty inherent in defining this life stage. This chapter will be organized somewhat differently than the others as no other text in human behavior currently acknowledges this newer life phase, which can span the years between 50 and 80 (Trafford, 2004). We, as authors of this text, believe this phase to be so critically important for those working with the current cohort of baby boomers that we have devoted an entire chapter to this phase of adult development. During this period, the adult is renegotiating one's relationship with time and with the loss of the conception that there is much time left to do what one wants to do. The transition to this phase is marked by the importance of setting priorities and deciding what is most important in the "third quarter" of one's life.

Trafford (2004) speaks of the "low-grade drumbeat of anxiety spreading across the land...of restlessness that affects people of a certain age" (p. 4). This is a social symptom of longevity. One has to confront the fact that at age 50, 60, or even 70 one may have to gear up instead of winding down. Many authors have termed this phase one of reinvention (Freedman, 1999; Levine, 2005; Stone & Stone, 2004; Trafford, 2004), whereas another has spoken of "pruning oneself in portfolio" (Corbett, 2007, p. 7). Corbett (2007) speaks of a "revolt against the prospect of coasting through retirement" (p. 6). Corbett's emphasis on making a difference at this phase of life is similar to Erikson's sense of generativity, which marks the transition into middle adulthood, as discussed in chapter 7.

In 1900, the "life expectancy in the United States was forty-seven" (Trafford, 2004, p. xx). Statistics from 2004 indicate that the average life expectancy for White females is 80.4 and for White males, 75.2 (U. S. Census Bureau, 2008 Statistical Abstract). However, as Trafford (2004) points out, the "quantity of years is only part of the longevity revolution. The real transformation is in the quality of later years" (p. 9). The "retirement/reinvention" revolution is more about planning ahead to increase the quality of life in one's later years. As scientists discover how to prolong the life of an aging adult, adults come face-to-face with the task of making those extra years as meaningful as possible.

The emergence of a generation of adults who are living longer with more quality in their lives, compared to their parents and other generations whose average life expectancy was much briefer, poses some anxiety for adults in the third quarter of life. There are many possibilities, yet no clear-cut paths to take on this journey. "There are few clear expectations...of what one does between the ages of fifty and eighty, how one does it, and how to tell if one has succeeded at doing it. This lack of concrete measures can be unsettling. For many, prior expectations they have had have been upended" (Corbett, 2007, p. 14). When adults in the retirement/reinvention phase were younger, turning 60 was viewed as a signal to prepare to step down within the next 5 years to become a retiree. Today as adults become 60, this signal is not working because of the prospect of prolonged good health for many years ahead. "Most people no longer retire for good at age sixty-five. Two out of three Americans work for pay, full-time or part-time, after reaching that age. In survey after survey, four of five people indicate that they intend to work" (Corbett, 2007, p. 14).

Corbett believes that adults are "choosing to weave work into their life portfolio because of a basic psychological change in how we see later life" (Corbett, 2007, p. 15). Although once a passage of time characterized by living through memories, now later adulthood has become a time of new beginnings. This new passage is similar to the historical norm, in which people worked and remained active in society as long as they could. In American agrarian society, retirement was basically unknown (Corbett, 2007). This was true for various classes of society—from farmers and merchants to older adults with financial means who wanted to feel productive and stay connected to society. Retirement was actually an invention of the industrial era; with the passage of the Social Security Act in 1935, the retirement age of 65 was institutionalized (Corbett, 2007). Now the tide is turning, because of economic factors and adult desires to remain employed. To cope with socioeconomic changes and with the wave of baby boomers approaching 65, the age one is eligible for social security has slowly risen to the late 60s, depending on one's age. The dream of the adult is changing from "freedom from work" to "freedom to work in rewarding jobs in new fields" (Corbett, 2007, p. 18). Many adults are now retiring so they can do something meaningful rather than retiring from a job, career, or company. Among the clients with whom Corbett (2007) works, he sees men and women who have a genuine desire to find work that enriches them beyond meeting financial demands. Americans have come to realize that this third quarter of life does not mean that one is finished with work but that now one has the time to contribute and serve, as well as a time to learn and experiment. This stage in life has become an adventure for many adults, rather than an ending or an experience to be feared.

LOSSES EXPERIENCED BY ADULTS DURING RETIREMENT AND REINVENTION

Loss and Transformation of Identity

Just as in any transition that one traverses, the issue of identity is critical. Retirement is a "qualitatively different condition from our previous life" (Schlossberg, 2004, p. 28). Leaving a job or career signifies a big change partly because of the complexity of this transition and the many ways that it changes an adult's life. One reason it can be so difficult for many is that it involves not one transition, but many. Leaving a job or a career involves much more than ceasing to work. Work often provides an identity, a lifestyle, and maps out interpersonal relationships. One important way an adult can prepare for this transition prior to retirement is to think of the degree to which s/he expects life to change (Schlossberg, 2004). This transition forces adults to reexamine their roles, relationships, routines, and assumptions both before and after retirement (Schlossberg, 2004). Frequently, the adult cannot look to his or her parents as models because they probably did not see themselves as having these choices. Similar to an adolescent, an adult in this transition period has to "break away from traditional adulthood the way teenagers break away from childhood" (Trafford, 2004, p. xxi). Some experts believe that an important driver in this process is to listen to oneself and to others and to use instinct and intuition to identify what feeds the "core self" (Corbett, 2007, p. 8). In reclaiming oneself, the adult in this phase of life is "rediscovering and reclaiming our unique spark as individuals" (p. 10). When one gives up a job or career, one learns how to stop identifying oneself through his or her company, title, or industry. To engage in this rediscovery, one must be able to tolerate some discomfort and anxiety. As the adult begins to recognize the "light" within herself/himself and to actualize the gifts that s/he has been given, s/he can begin to follow a new or deeper path. Corbett (2007) gives an example of a professor who delayed retirement because he felt that it would signify that he was no longer a scholar or the person he was and continued to be. This professor had to surrender full-time status at age 70, but he did not identify himself as a retired person because that still made him feel uncomfortable. Perhaps the role or status of Professor Emeritus reflects this wish to keep a role that is comfortable for an academic who is retired from active life at the university. Many retirees are concerned that they will be dismissed or not sought out for suggestions and advice. However, just "being busy" may mean that a retiree is too busy with activities that do not represent or connect with his or her soul or being.

Ibarra (2003) challenges some of the conventional wisdom with regard to how work identity shifts are made. The usual method of career planning, in which one does not make a move until one knows where one is going, is not helpful during the reinvention phase. According to Ibarra "we learn who we have become—in practice not in theory—by testing fantasy and reality, not by looking inside" (p. 43). Ibarra (2003) believes this is so because, for him, identity does not represent so much an inner core or true self as it does the existence of many selves, which are defined partly by our histories, but just as powerfully by our present and our hopes and fears for the future. By the time an adult reaches the phase of reinvention/retirement, s/he has had much more time than the young adult in developing a working history of who s/he is. Ibarra believes that our "possible selves" (all we hope to or fear to become) lie at the heart of the career-change process. An adult in this phase can change only when s/he has enticing alternatives that s/he can touch, taste, and feel. "Working identity, as a practice, is necessarily a process of experimenting, testing, and learning about ourselves" (Ibarra, 2003, p. 43). Although knowing oneself is important, it may be the outcome of, not the input into, the search for a new working self. In this approach, action becomes critical, as the adult needs to get out of his or her head and act so as to reinvent. In trying out new activities and professional roles on a small scale prior to taking a completely new path, the adult is allowing herself/himself to explore a variety of "selves" in action. This is so because during a major transition the adult's possible selves are making major shifts. The importance of "crafting experiments, shifting connections, and making sense of the changes we are going through" (Ibarra, 2003, p. 45) is the most appropriate way to redefine oneself in work. Experimenting with new options such as a course in photography, a different house in a new location, a new lifestyle, a new job, and/or volunteer work is a way of figuring out what one wants to do at this phase of life.

Although Schlossberg (2004) agrees with Ibarra that for many adults in this phase the "path is marked by trial and error" during which time "it is not unusual for a retiree to start on one path, find that it is not satisfying, and to resume searching" (p. 95), she believes that for many adults this phase of life might contain a combination of the two approaches. Many adults may start out in a very planned, logical fashion by making one move prior to making another. These same adults may then discover that they need to discard the method of planning and move to a more experimental, searching experience in which there may be many fits and starts. Although exploring lifestyles and experimenting with new interests may lead to frustration in realizing that this is not the right fit, this path can lead to gains in self-awareness as to who one is and what is most gratifying and/or meaningful.

This transition, although reminiscent of adolescence with its need to create a new identity, can be frustrating because adults in this phase of life expect that they should know who they are (Schlossberg, 2004). It may also be a difficult process because the adult facing reinvention often has young adult children who are trying to match their skills and sense of self with the environment. For young adults, the world is their oyster in terms of time available for identity work, whereas for older adults the press of time is heavy. For adults whose work was central to their identity, retirement may trigger depression. The greater commitment one has had to one's work, the greater the loss when that role disappears. For many adults this transition may be experienced as a maturational loss and in some sense a disenfranchised loss, as others may not validate the intensity of the loss because of the personal growth that is observed following this transition.

Some retirees do not experience an identity crisis because they are pleased with their new status. Schlossberg (2004) discusses the case of a couple who were skilled professionals and had devoted decades to their work. They became retirees who wanted to make the most of the time after they retired at ages 55 and 56. They adapted to their new status quickly and easily by deciding not to work in their professional fields, either as volunteers or professionals. They moved to a different part of the country and began traveling to spend more time with their children and many grandchildren, to engage in sports as well as a fulfilling social life. They appeared to be content with their retirement, neither retreating nor searching. To this couple, work was not part of their new equation for fulfillment. There is no right or wrong path through retirement or activities undertaken. Whether it is working, knitting, singing in a chorus, studying, volunteering, traveling, or all of the above, whatever engages the adult and makes her/him feel satisfied, needed, appreciated, and pleased is what is important during this phase (Schlossberg, 2004).

Loss of Routine: Search for Balance

The loss of reassuring routines and sense of structured time that comes with full-time work can lead an adult to feel somewhat disoriented. The routine of getting up every morning and "working on a schedule provides a pace and structure to the week, the month, the year" (Schlossberg, 2004, p. 40). Some individuals are more comfortable with less structure, whereas others feel adrift, not knowing how to spend their time. One retiree reported, "I miss Saturdays...every day is similar and I miss the break from weekday to weekend" (p. 41). As the commitment to work loses its intensity, the structure of the workday is gone, and ties with children loosen, the adult has more time to indulge in his/ her passions (Levine, 2005). Many people in the phase between enmeshment in a career and entering total retirement want to discover or rediscover their passions. This discovery of his/her passion can be a return to an interest of adolescence or early adulthood (or even childhood) that has been dormant for years or a deepening of a passion that has guided one's life all along the journey. Passion involves making "contact with that unique inner drive that fuels our most important decisions" (Levine, 2005, p 106). Passion is a "vitality, a life force, an energy, a quickening that is translated into action...the expression is unique" (Levine, 2005, p. 106). When one is involved in a passionate endeavor one is lost in time; examples include artists when they are creating, writers when they are writing, musicians when they are playing an instrument or conducting, and tennis players on the court. In Corbett's (2007) "portfolio" perspective, it is the adult who defines the job that s/he does rather than the job defining the adult. Although Corbett (2007) does not believe there is a right way to create a "fulfilling alternative to retirement," among those who manage to find fulfillment and meaning are those who slow down and take the time to "assess their lives and their goals" (p. 7).

Loss of routine and a structured sense of time can also lead to new focus on creating more balance in one's life. The process of reinvention or "pruning one's life portfolio" (Corbett, 2007, p. 7) is based on the concept of balance. This sense of balance relates to energy for work, for leisure-time activities, for relationships, and for time with self. Time with self is what many adults fear most. Prior to or during the retirement transition, most individuals search for new ways to organize their time. As retirees move out of, through, or into new roles, they face different issues. For some adults, this process leads to excitement with new activities, whereas for others "there is sadness for what one left" (Schlossberg, 2004, p. 23).

The other concept that is critical to reinvention or designing a life portfolio is that of meaning-making or actualizing one's life. This brings the concept of generativity to the foreground because adults need to think about the purpose and meaning of what they are doing and have done with their lives from early adulthood through later adulthood. The concept of growth and transition throughout the life cycle—even through years that may be laden with chronic illness and pain—is critical to sustaining one's life. Caregivers, counselors, social workers, and educators need to heed this message and encourage adults struggling with this passage to embrace this premise of growth, rather than acceptance, which has been more of the norm.

Loss of or Change in Relationships

Most workplaces provide the adult with an opportunity to interact with many other adults who may be diverse or similar in style. The emotional energy provided by workplace relationships cannot be underestimated in terms of the degree to which some of these relationships must be grieved. "Work furnishes a sense of place and belonging in a valued community. This sense of place and belonging in turn provides individuals with feelings of worth" (Schlossberg, 2004, p. 39). It is important for the adult who is either contemplating or facing retirement to examine the degree to which her/his relationship needs will, or have, already changed. Schlossberg (2004) addresses different qualities that relationships provide. The first is the need for attachment, which is served through marriage, partnerships, or close friends. The second is the need for social integration, which is satisfied when adults work together toward a common goal in a workplace or volunteer setting. The third is the opportunity for nurturance, which occurs in relationships in which we care for family, children, and friends. These relationships make adults feel as though they matter because the adult feels needed. The fourth is reassurance of worth, which is validated when "our competence is affirmed by the relationships in our family, community or work" (p. 57). Those adults for whom work provided a great amount of self-worth can look to other experiences for recognition, such as part-time paid work or volunteer work in the community. The fifth quality is a sense of alliance with or sense of continuity in relationships with family. Many retirees enjoy spending increased time with adult children and grandchildren at a more relaxed, easy pace. The authors of this text would add another value, which is the relationship with oneself and how that shifts during and after this stage of transition. Adults are urged to consider how these relationship needs were met prior to the phase of retirement versus once the adult began to change his/her lifestyle so that the adult can assess his/her support system and the need for changes within it.

Changes Within the Marital/Partner Relationship

For most couples, the transition to the retirement years marks a time of major adjustment. For some marriages/partnerships, the retirement experience affects the relationship in a positive way and for others it has a negative influence. J. Kim and Moen (2001) report, as one might expect, differences in reactions to retirement along gender lines because of different work histories. For the majority of men, work has been more continuous, but for many women work has been discontinuous, because they have moved in and out of the workforce more frequently than men. It is the authors' belief that during the time that women have not been in the workforce, they have been more able to assess their level of gratification with regard to leisure-time activities and may also have built more lifelong friendships as a result of rearing children and having the opportunity to build relationships with other mothers. In some ways, this could give women an advantage in the reinvention process, as they may feel more comfortable coping with the time at home as well as involvement with the community and/or religious activities.

Conflicts can emerge around turf issues if both partners or spouses are at home at the same time. Matusow (2004) reported that many women secretly objected to having someone around the house all day, sharing space that they considered to be more theirs. Other woman felt irritated by having to be asked where they were going whenever they went out of the home. Negotiation between spouses and partners is a critical task of marriage when these types of scenarios develop. Sometimes this negotiation might result in each partner discovering a part-time job or a volunteer experience that will remove him or her from the home part of the week. For others, simply carving out individual physical space that belongs to each partner provides a solution. For others, relationships bloomed amidst retirement changes. For couples who have worked different shifts most of their married life, new excitement about being together more frequently can result in a positive adjustment to retirement. For most couples, however, a combination of both positive and negative experiences comprise this transition. Schlossberg (2004) reports that one couple, although looking forward to spending time together after retirement, missed the former routine of each having his or her own space. This couple had to "work out a new rhythm of being together" (p. 62).

Another issue that emerges for couples during this phase is being out of sync with regard to the retirement cycle. Conflict may arise when a women is sometimes ramping up her career at a time when her spouse wants more time for travel and leisure-time activities. Other conflicts arise when one partner is busy with participation on boards and committees and is irritated by the other partner who stays at home and is content to watch TV. The increasing number of women involved in the workplace over a longer period of time may affect this circumstance. Increasingly, a partner or spouse may wish to retire early, but has a partner or spouse of a similar age, who (for varying reasons, such as owning a business, or following a new interest) may want to continue to build and nurture his/her career well into the 60s and 70s. This phenomenon may increase marital conflicts over work/retirement issues.

Even so, there are indications that some couples find this period of being out of step with one another to be more gratifying. Schlossberg (2004) reports on a couple in which the man is retired but whose wife is still working in a very responsible position. The husband of this couple encourages his wife to continue working as he enjoys his space and privacy at home. With regard to negotiating, Vinick and Ekerdt (1991) found that in a study of 60 couples, during the year after retirement, nearly all of the couples were looking for ways to negotiate household tasks. It is significant that those couples "who perceived that there was equity in the arrangement of household tasks rated high on the researchers' Satisfaction Index" (Vinick & Ekerdt, 1991, as reported in Schlossberg, 2004, p. 66).

Changes in Relationships With Friends

Friends are important throughout life but become especially precious in the third quarter of life (Trafford, 2004). During middle adulthood, adults are usually too preoccupied with raising children, working on or out of a marriage or partnership, and finding one's place in the workplace and the community to pursue friendships. During this phase, "Relationships tended to flow from family and work" (Trafford, 2004, p. 165). Although most adults, particularly women, made friends wherever they were living, time was scarce for intimate friendships. Friends who lived at a distance or who were from an earlier stage in life tended to drift. During the third quarter of life, the adult has more leisure time available to spend with friends—either with or without a spouse or partner. Research has documented the importance of friendship to health, mental health, and longevity (Levine, 2005; Taylor et al., 2000; Trafford, 2004). During the third quarter of life, when the adult becomes more vulnerable to loss from death of one's spouse/partner and parents, and/or development of a chronic or life-threatening illness, close friendships can provide the buffer to stress and pain. During this stage of life, friends can become a substitute for family, which may be slowly disappearing.

For those adults for whom the workplace provided their extensive friendship network, there must be a critical readjustment. Although an adult can stay socially involved with some friends from work, it is not so easy to stay connected with friends at one's former workplace for whom work is still their major focus. Deepening friendships or developing new friendships outside the workplace becomes increasingly important, as these friends can often substitute for colleagues (Schlossberg, 2004). There are many ways that adults can expand their friendship network—through travel groups, educational groups, retirement communities, leisure-time pursuits, and volunteer activities.

At this phase of life, when friendships are so important but do not go well, the adult can experience emotional pain that can be reminiscent of adolescence (Schlossberg, 2004). Some adults find that they are not in the part of a social group to which they aspire and suffer feelings of loss and even shame. On the flip side, because of the adult's greater self-awareness, s/he can recognize her or his own needs and move on to other activities that can offer new friendship possibilities. Levine (2005) speaks of the need to "recalibrate friendships....In the same way that women who are starting a business quickly form a network, we need to find advisors that can help us figure out what's next. Not all your current friends may be good at it" (Levine, 2005, p. 146).

Reinvention can be a rocky road that can disrupt relationships with family and friends. It is significant that when it comes to reinvention, "the people that know us best are the ones most likely to hinder rather than help us. They may wish to be supportive but they tend to reinforce or...try to preserve the old identities we are trying to shed" (Ibarra, 2003, p. 44). In trying to brainstorm with close friends and/or family about what an adult in this transition wants to do, the family member or friend may worry that the adult is taking too many chances and should consider doing things in slower motion. Sometimes colleagues and mentors can also hinder the adult in his or her transition process by "mirroring his normal doubts about moving outside his comfort zone" (p. 44). To make a break with the past an adult may need to move into networks unknown to him/her. It is often strangers who are best able to help the adult who is in the stage of reinvention (Ibarra, 2003). The adult needs to grieve the loss of friendships that no longer meet certain needs and welcome new relationships that can foster new emotional growth.

Loss of Financial Resources

For some adults, retirement can bring about a time when they have the opportunity to use the financial resources that they have saved over the course of their adulthood. However, for others it is a time during which money becomes very tight, as income from a job is no longer available and in many cases the adult's workplace does not provide a retirement plan, nor did the adult plan for the need for resources beyond income from Social Security. With the current economic crisis in the United States, this issue is especially relevant as many private and public workplaces are reducing retirement plan benefits and in some cases terminating retirement plans.

During this phase, adults often examine their perspective on money. Adults may begin to accept the fact that "money is part of life, neither the most important part nor something we can avoid" (Stone & Stone, 2004, p. 28). This may be a time for adults to examine their emotional issues with respect to money and to create a financial plan that will allow for balance and more simplicity in one's life.

Loss of or Change in One's Belief System: The Importance of Spiritual Growth

During this phase of life, when grappling with the significance of one's own life as well as of life in general, the adult may move toward deepening his/her sense of spirituality. For some adults, formalized religion becomes important in this search for a new belief system, whereas for others solitude and/or therapy is crucial for deepening one's sense of self. For many, a turn inward involves increased solitude, which can be difficult when emerging from a busy life with family and work. Although silence can be frightening, it can also provide an environment in which the adult is able to confront issues that s/he may have avoided for years (Trafford, 2004). It is also true that psychospiritual growth often emanates from discomfort and loss, when one feels frightened and needy. Because at this phase of life the future beckons but is unknown, "being optimistic, even partly optimistic is crucial...is linked to survival and satisfaction" (p. 237). Although adults cannot avoid sorrow in their lives, their hope that they will find a meaningful path helps to keep them centered and satisfied. Part of the spiritual agenda for this phase of life is finding the hope that one needs to live fully in the next decade(s) and the hope to find one's way through a new path. Just as with other losses and transitions presented in this text, the opportunity for meaning-making can lead to new growth and development.

Changes in Relationship to One's Community

During this reinvention stage of life, many adults explore more fully opportunities presented by the community. The face of community volunteerism is changing, with the baby boomer generation wishing to continue to contribute to society in meaningful ways, whether through a part-time job or through volunteering. Community organizations are faced with the task of designing volunteer positions that resonate more with the needs of this generation, which seeks to make a difference in the world around them. Some authors believe that "What we are witnessing is the reemergence of the 'we generation.' People who were once inspired by JFK to ask what they could do for their country appear ready to embrace their idealism once again" (Stone & Stone, 2004, p. 55).

In identifying possible pursuits and activities that one can build into his or her portfolio, Corbett (2007) refers to: (a) employment-related options such as consulting, entrepreneurship, and board directorships; (b) community service and giving back options such as civic and nonprofit organizations, philanthropy, and the international arena; (c) passing on your knowledge through coaching, mentoring or advising, teaching, writing, speaking, and continuing education; (d) other pursuits such as involvement in hobbies and avocations, fine arts and performing arts, fitness and sports, real estate, and travel. It seems as though the possibilities are endless for a match between an adult and community work that is generative in nature. One of the gifts of maturity is an awakened sense of responsibility, which is symbolic of the midlife task of generativity, as defined by Erikson (1978).

The Process of Change: Coping With the Transition Process

Schlossberg (2004) describes three important phases of the retirement process that she encourages adults to pursue. The first phase is "moving out," which involves the task of "letting go of your work role." The way to move through this phase is to grieve. Some adults choose to deny this grief process as exemplified by a newly retired director of an organization who decided to stay on at her organization as a volunteer. This client could not let go and tried to "micromanage the activities of her replacement" (Schlossberg, 2004, p. 23). To "move on," it may have been helpful for this client to acknowledge any regrets about leaving her position and to grieve for the position she relinquished (Schlossberg, 2004). Just as with the loss of a partner, as discussed in chapters 6, 7, and 9 of this book, the adult in this phase of life needs to recognize the loss and express emotions and thoughts about it prior to taking on a new task.

It is significant that the yearning and searching phase of the grief process described by Bowlby (1980/1998) in his study of widows is documented by Schlossberg (2004) in her work with clients who are working through the second phase of the retirement process, which she terms "moving through." This transitional phase occurs after adults have left their major activity and before they have found something new that absorbs them. It is in this phase that adults are searching for a new way to organize their lives and are often engaged in "searching behavior, trying this, then that" (Schlossberg, 2004, p. 24). This can be an uncomfortable phase because adults are unsure of their path, but Schlossberg advises adults to label this period as "your retirement moratorium" so that one can suspend "making any lasting decisions, giving oneself permission to explore" (Schlossberg, 2004, p. 24). Transitions involve time during which one's emotions and reactions shift from days of feeling elated to days of depression. These shifts may be more intense for those for whom more of their roles, relationships, routines, and assumptions are altered. The vignette of Helen, summarized at the beginning of this chapter, is illustrative of this searching behavior during which time Helen has times of elation and other times of sadness and confusion.

The third and final stage is called "moving in" and occurs when the adult begins to create a new life by "investing in new activities, establishing new roles, routines, relationships and assumptions about the new world" (Schlossberg, 2004, p. 24). It is during this time that an adult may begin to realize that s/he has established or created a new path for himself or herself.

LOSS OF ADULT AS EXPERIENCED BY OTHERS

Adult Children

Most adult children have some expectations of how their parents should live. When adults divorce, remarry, or repartner, adult children have a wide range of reactions, depending on their own expectations and the reality of the lifestyle chosen by the adult parent. When expectations and reality do not mesh, conflict can occur. Some adult children whose parents have been widowed for a short or long period of time have difficulty accepting the status of a newly married parent or one who chooses to cohabitate (Schlossberg, 2004). Other losses for the adult child occur when the parent moves to another part of the country to live a new lifestyle that feels comfortable for the parent. Many adult children do not expect their parents to move far away from them and react with surprise or negativity when this occurs. Conflict can also emerge when parents who are retired move closer to their adult children and disrupt routines that have been established by the adult child, who has developed a life that centers on his or her friends and own children.

In her interviews with adult children, Schlossberg (2004) found that "many children expressed concern that their parents would have time on their hands or perhaps become depressed" (p. 67) following retirement or loss of a spouse or partner. Other adult children expressed worry about the cost of health care consuming their parents' income and savings. Others felt rejected by their parents' involvement with retirement activities, because parents were not as available on a regular basis to provide nurturing needs to the adult children. In addition, adults who are in the process of reinvention and very busy with their lives may not be as available to baby-sit for their grandchildren. Unresolved issues that were in the background when parents were working may come to the foreground when parents retire (Schlossberg, 2004). It may be important for adult children and their parents to have open discussions about mutual expectations during and following this transition period.

Parents

During this phase adult children may also be less available to their aging parents, for whom life has probably drastically changed in terms of their medical conditions. Parents can experience a sense of rejection at this phase as they lived in an era when they, as adult children, probably cared for their aging and/or ill parents. These parents may not understand this new age of reinvention in which the child[en] is engrossed in a major transition, often involving new activities, pursuing his or her passion and/or new work. Because parents have not provided a model for adults in this reinvention phase, there may be a sense of disconnection between the generations. Parents of adults in this phase were among the cohort for whom retirement meant just that—leaving more time and energy for family.

READINGS

CASE STUDY ON MIDLIFE CAREER/LIFE TRANSITION

Susan M. Larson, MEd, NCC

Susan M. Larson is currently in private practice in Rochester, New York, specializing in reinvention and transition. A trained career coach and nationally certified career counselor, Susan uses her expertise to coach and counsel individuals wishing to focus on achievement as well as transitioning adults making lifestyle changes. Susan is currently a consultant to Rochester Career Development Services, having previously worked with the Career Development Services staff for 18 years, most recently as Director of Individual Services. In her 25 years of experience, Susan has worked in industry, educational/academic settings, and the nonprofit arena, providing coaching, training, and transitional services to a broad cross-section of individuals and groups. She has been a presenter and facilitator at the National Career Development Association, the Mid-Atlantic Career Counseling Association, and the Chautauqua Institution. In the Rochester area, Susan facilitated programs for Preferred Care, The St. Ann's Community area school districts, and has also consulted for the William E. Simon School of Business.

Case Discussion

This case highlights a midlife woman who is struggling to cope with many transitions and losses in her life, past, present, and future. Linda Blair is 53 years old and has identified that she needs to replace a loss of purpose and daily parenting role with a new set of challenges and roles. Her two daughters are both in college, living on their own, and Linda's husband is working long hours with frequent travel. Linda has been "filling her time" with volunteer work at church and working 2 days a week at a friend's retail gift store as a sales associate. Linda has found herself missing her past career success and recognition when she previously worked in corporate sales and training, and is asking herself, "Are my best years behind me?"

Physical/Biological Loss

Physically, Linda is a well-proportioned and attractive woman with silver-gray hair cut in a classic blunt style. Linda expressed concern that the color and style of her hair may date her. She hired a personal trainer to help improve her stamina and regain her figure and build up her self-esteem. She also shared that her doctor was treating her for mild depression, triggered in part by her struggles with loss of youth.

Psychological Loss

Linda participated in a three-part "Reinvent Your Life" Workshop, offered by a local career agency. During the workshop discussions, she shared that she was missing her earlier career where she could measure her value to others as they learned new job skills in her training classes. She also missed her job title, paycheck, and the status that her earlier corporate career had afforded. At this time in her life, Linda was grieving the loss of her past identity and work/parenting roles and is asking these questions:

"Can I still add value?"

"Where can I add value and make a difference?"

She was buoyed by her free time to reconnect with family, friends, and old colleagues and occasional travel with her spouse.

Interventions

As mentioned earlier, Linda began to assess and explore her assets and options in a three-part "Reinvent Your Life" Workshop, using the Reinventing Process, which involves a six-step process including: (a) learning about yourself, (b) questioning the givens, (c) discovering options, (d) evaluating "fit," (e) planning action, and (f) moving forward (S. Davis & Handschin, 1998).

Linda inventoried her current values, motivational skills, and interests and explored the topics of call and legacy. She constructed a potential list of options using this information and resurfaced her long-held interest in hospitality and food service, in addition to her continued interest in sales and training. After completing the workshop, Linda stayed in touch with the transition coach who facilitated the workshop and asked to follow up as a private client. The coach and client agreed to meet a minimum of six times in a 3-month period. Linda came to the first coaching session with her most recent résumé, a list of peak work experience, and potential employers.

The first coaching session began with the question: What are you clear about and what do you come in knowing? Linda spoke quickly and freely, listing her desire to learn something new and be challenged, use her training skills, do something to improve the lives of others and establish new work affiliations. As the conversation progressed, she expressed her concern that she had been away from the workplace for many years and she had tears in her eyes when she expressed how terrified she was of rejection and appearing stupid. She then shared that she had tried to settle for her current life but her dissatisfaction and restlessness was interrupting her sleep and propelled her to seek the help of her doctor and transition coach. The coach suggested the resource, *My Time: Making the Most of the Rest of Your Life* (Trafford, 2004) as timely reading for Linda's transition process. She also agreed to formulate a mission statement and set future goals, based on the mission statement. Referring back to the Reinventing Process (S. Davis & Handschin, 1998), step two, Question the Givens, Linda expressed a desire to retain some of her newfound flexibility and expressed a desire for a part-time or contract work arrangement, versus full-time work.

During the next few coaching sessions, Linda clarified her mission to:

> Design and deliver quality training programs in a customer service driven organization.

Linda rejoined her national professional organization, American Society for Training and Development (ASTD), and began attending meetings. She edited her revised résumé and learned about the process of informational interviewing to aid in increasing her network and knowledge of opportunities. She also realized the importance of making room for new activities, and ended two volunteer commitments that were no longer satisfying. The coach noticed that Linda was coming to their sessions with renewed energy and enthusiasm for following through the reinventing process. Linda often interjected humor in their discussions, sometimes poking fun at herself and not taking herself quite so seriously. Linda now began her coaching sessions proactively, sharing her progress since the last session and setting the agenda topics she thought were most useful to cover.

To support her transition, Linda set up a Personal Board of Advisors, comprised of a friend, former colleagues, and her spouse to support, advise, stimulate, and celebrate Linda periodically during the reinventing process. Linda had 10 affirmations that she meditated on each morning and coined her own motto: "Do It Scared!" In the remaining coaching sessions, she wrote and practiced her elevator speech, a 60-second marketing pitch tailored to highlight Linda's unique qualifications and to spark interest in follow-up with other persons or her "audience." In addition Linda crystallized her key employer targets. The transition coach provided a Human Resource contact at a large food retailer, nationally known for outstanding customer service. Linda was enthusiastic and feeling more confident now, enabling her to pursue this contact, providing her résumé and cover letter for consideration. She was called in to interview after a lengthy phone-screening process and subsequently hired on a 3-day-a-week contract basis to deliver customer service training and eventually work on program design.

In addition to her new work assignment and role, Linda has chosen to take a computer class and join a book group where she can be challenged and learn. In her successful reinvention, Linda has gone through the process of discarding, reducing, keeping, and adding activities, roles, and relationships. She has replaced some of her former life and laid claim to new horizons and challenges, learning to "Do It Scared."

During follow-up phone calls with her coach, Linda has shared that reentering the professional training arena has been an adjustment, including earlier hours, more formal dress, and structured time. But she also commented that the steep learning curve has provided the challenge that she was looking for and has stretched her in ways she had not imagined.

EARLY RETIREMENT AMONG BABY BOOM WOMEN: SOME LOSSES AND SOME GAINS

Fontaine H. Fulghum, MSW, ABD

Fontaine H. Fulghum, MSW, held senior-level management and public policy positions in both government and the private sector for over 20 years. She has taught social policy and human behavior at the graduate and undergraduate levels in several schools of social work, including Bryn Mawr College and Tulane University, but most recently at Rutgers University. She is currently a doctoral candidate at Bryn Mawr College Graduate School of Social Work and Social Research, where she is completing her dissertation research on women's retirement.

As the "leading edge" of the baby boom generation nears retirement, research on the issue of retirement appears to be moving beyond an earlier preoccupation with the workforce exit, retirement transition, and adjustment of White males. The paucity of research on later life employment and retirement of women (Calasanti, 1993; Dailey, 1998; Slavin & Wingrove, 1995) and of racial and ethnic minorities (Honig, 1996; Quinn & Kozy, 1996) is now being increasingly redressed. Although the retirement of women in this country born prior to World War II might not have been deemed particularly significant because of their limited workforce participation, we might certainly expect something different with respect to "leading edge" baby boom women, those born between 1946 and 1954. This cohort of women has moved into the workforce in significant numbers over the last several decades, finding employment not only in those occupations long open to women, but also in occupations traditionally reserved for males, such as the law, medicine, and finance. Boomer women's reshaping of the workforce has led to some changes in the domestic sphere as well, as men increasingly take on, at least anecdotally, some aspects of housework and child care.

Thus, changing workforce participation has served to broaden retirement research to include women and minorities. Another shift in retirement research comes from gerontologists, who now suggest redirecting some of the focus from the timing of the workforce exit to the values, attitudes, and preferences of older persons regarding retirement or the years traditionally set aside for retirement. Further, a new prospective focus is emerging that assumes that the way we anticipate the retirement years, and the meaning we assign to them, or prepare for them, will significantly shape that period of life (Myers, 1996). The author here, Fontaine Fulghum, has been exploring some of these issues in her qualitative research on "leading edge" baby boom women who have recently retired at a relatively early age, in their 50s or early 60s.

Case Presentation

Carla* was born in 1948; she is part of the leading edge of the massive cohort born in the years after World War II. She grew up in a small town in a working-class family. Carla's father, a factory foreman, left high school in his senior year to support his mother after his father's sudden death. Carla's mother did not attend college and was a housewife. Carla's family held traditional values, with the father as household head. Their social life centered around their church and its activities. Carla had two brothers who were expected to go to college. She had a close relationship with her mother, who she remembers as a strong, independent woman. Her father, too, was a major influence on her, encouraging her, as well as her brothers, to go to college.

From the time she was in high school, Carla worked outside her home in part-time jobs. A strong student, her family could not afford the tuition at the private university where she hoped to study languages, so she continued her part-time jobs to pay for her education at the state university. She and her brothers became the first of their extended family to go to college.

While at college, Carla met Tom, a classmate whom she married right after graduation. With her new degree, she secured a position at the county welfare department. She enjoyed her work as a caseworker, and except for a brief time off for maternity leave, remained at her job for 30 years. Carla moved through the ranks of her department, from line supervisor, to unit supervisor, and finally to departmental administrator. She was able to obtain a master's degree on weekends while working when her employer offered her tuition reimbursement.

Carla was a successful and competent administrator, running a department that served thousands of clients a year. Her husband, whose degree was in accounting, worked in the for-profit sector as an auditor. Even though Carla held a position with enormous responsibility, she never thought of her work as a career. She believed that she worked to help support her family and to provide opportunities, such as private schooling, for her son. According to Carla, it was her husband who had a career; she did not.

After 30 years at the welfare department, Carla looked forward to retirement. She had begun to have stress-related health problems that were beginning to interfere with her job. Her husband had retired, and he had begun

---

*This case is derived from the experiences of 20 women interviewed; it is not characteristic of any particular interviewee.

to urge Carla to do the same. She would receive a good pension, as did her husband, so finances were not an issue. Carla put in her retirement papers, was given a nice farewell party, and was anticipating some time for herself after years of heavy responsibility and a pressing schedule. After a month or 2 at home, Carla realized that she felt lost, without purpose, and rather bored. By contrast, her husband seemed to relish his retirement and didn't understand her dissatisfaction. About 6 weeks after her retirement party, Carla was invited back for the department's annual Christmas party.

"I looked forward to seeing all of my colleagues at the party, but when I got there, people barely spoke to me. I felt like a ghost! It was as though I were not there. I was no longer important. I went home early and was extremely depressed."

Discussion of the Experience of Loss

In considering Carla's mid- to late-life dilemma, we might look within the field of gerontology to the life-course perspective, which frames much of aging discourse today. The life-course approach to aging as forged by Elder (1992) and others focuses on the dynamic interplay of historical events and patterns with the particular life experiences and opportunities of individuals. For Carla, who came to young adulthood with her peers in the late 1960s and early 1970s, her generation was shaped by, and often participated actively in, the Vietnam War, the Peace Movement, the Civil Rights Movement, and the Women's Movement. Given the small-town atmosphere and traditional family in which she grew up, Carla was aware of these movements but, unlike her college roommate who was arrested in several antiwar demonstrations, was not a participant. Because of a serious sports injury, her husband was exempted from the draft and did not serve in the war. After an era heavy with change, Carla's cohort saw the country move away from the activism of the 1970s to conservatism in the 1980s, with economic and political shifts continuing well into the 1990s. Although neither Carla nor her husband were particularly political, both were concerned about cuts in government social services and in corporate middle-management positions, which many of their friends held.

Aside from the interplay of historical forces and individual lives, the life-course perspective focuses on the concepts of social position, social role, role transition, and a series of role transitions termed "trajectories," as these are experienced over the life course (Quadagno, 2002). Social position, according to Atchley (1980), may be viewed as slots in the organization of society that are based on common attributes. For example, the position of a retired person is (usually) based on the common attribute of age. Social roles are attached to positions, with social role denoting that which is expected of a person in a given position (Atchley, 1980). Thus, we see Carla struggling to determine which roles she might now assume that seem to coincide with her newly acquired social position of retiree.

Atchley further indicates that social structure is age-differentiated; the concept of the life course is thus an idealized and age-related progression or sequence of roles and group memberships that individuals are expected to follow as they move through life. Infancy, childhood, adolescence, young adulthood, middle age, later maturity, and old age are stations on the life course that can be correlated with chronological age, occupational cycle, family cycle, and economic cycle. Thus, in the early to middle 20s one is in young adulthood, moving from job experimentation to occupational choice; one has left the family home prior to marriage and parenthood, and is moving from dependency to economic power and major purchases. At age 65, one has entered the period of later maturity, with retirement the marker on the occupational cycle, an "empty nest" and the prospect of widowhood looming on the family cycle. On the economic cycle, as dependence nears, the adult may become involved in health care purchases and asset management (Atchley, 1980).

In the case of Carla, the life marker of retirement brought with it the loss of social position, interaction with colleagues, and a sense of being a contributing member of society. The social impact of her retirement meant that she no longer had power and influence in the world; she no longer supervised others; she no longer had colleagues to lunch with and shop with. Yet, even with these losses, there were gains. Her husband and her son said they liked having her at home—she was now more accessible, better able to focus on them and their problems in a helpful way, and less likely to overreact to them after a busy stressful day.

The psychological impact of Carla's retirement included having to cope with the loss of her identity as worker. She had worked since the time she was a teenager; work structured her day, gave it purpose. Now retired, she could discern no structure in her world. Time seemed endless and without purpose. She said to herself, "Okay, I've retired.

What's next?" But most troubling for Carla was the realization that her very identity was bound up with her role as worker, supervisor, colleague, client problem-solver. Carla no longer knew who she was. She now had to grapple with creating some new vision of herself and her future.

In addition, she was dealing with health issues that had begun to affect her mobility. Her high blood pressure made exercise difficult, but necessary. She found that she had to spend more time at the doctor's office, scheduling appointments for tests and treatment. She began to mourn the loss of her ability to function physically as she had before. As Carla likes to read, she had looked forward to long days with a good book, but this too became a disappointment. Although she has more time to read now, it has also become more difficult as her eyesight has deteriorated.

Intervention and Resources

As Bronfenbrenner (1979) suggests, human development continues across the life course. Pivotal life transitions, such as retirement, provide at the macro level, a significant opportunity for the ongoing study of human development and, at the micro level, the opportunity for individual reinvention of self. Carla, now facing such a transition, needs help in reframing her life at this developmental stage, specifically help in finding meaning, and in again finding herself, in a new life, postretirement. Throughout her long work life, whether seen by Carla as career or family necessity, Carla has exhibited both resiliency and strength and developed specific skills, all of which she might draw on now.

Recently, a close friend and former colleague who is also an MSW suggested that Carla seek short-term, problem-focused treatment. However, the work she began with a therapist has proven more extensive. With the therapist, she has begun to examine those aspects of her work life that were productive and meaningful to her, and to grieve their loss. She has identified some aspects of that loss, such as the loss of work to structure her days, which might be replaced or mitigated in her new life. She has come to recognize that much of her anxiety stems from her current situation without an obvious "role," and that this has contributed to her loss of sense of self, and can also be mitigated as new, valued roles emerge. She has reviewed some of her life choices, including the nature of her work and how she viewed it, the timing of marriage and family, even retirement, and how these were affected by societal values and expectations. She is looking at the impact of the retirement of her spouse, and her own retirement, on her marriage and at what changes retirement has made in the quality of their relationship. Further, Carla is considering how retirement has affected her ability to have time for herself. Although Carla's husband, Tom, is happy with his retirement, he seems to want Carla's constant companionship, something not characteristic of their earlier married life and not comfortable for Carla.

In therapy Carla is confronting the notion of what it means to be an older woman in today's society. Although many vigorous baby boomer women entering the retirement years may see "sixty as the new forty," this view is not embraced by Carla, who speaks of walking in her neighborhood among "all those other faceless old folks."

After working with the therapist, Carla has begun taking stock of her personal strengths and internal resources, as well as those she can draw on from her family, friends and acquaintances, her neighborhood, and her community. Carla recently joined a gym, where she met Simone, also a female baby boom retiree, who after leaving her position as human resources manager for a large corporation has begun a new career as a life coach. Simone, whose particular interest is in helping both younger and midlife women with career-and-family issues, wants to work with Carla to help her find a new vocation, a new life plan. Already they have begun discussing Carla's interest in serving on the boards of some nonprofit organizations serving women.

Future Plans

Carla has begun to find a new sense of direction but recognizes there is still much to do. In the midst of interesting new activities she still feels the familiar pain of loss. However, she is now more positive, hopeful, and future oriented. Recently, after spending time with her son and his fiancée, an architect, she spoke of the "brave new world" being entered by today's young women, a world where all avenues of vocation appear open to them, but where most will continue to carry primary responsibility for home and family, despite their career paths. "There are now so many choices for these young women, perhaps too many, for them! And 'having it all'—career, husband, family—hasn't gotten much easier." Carla also worries that both her son and his fiancée "don't seem to be planning for their retirement, but then I didn't either, at that age." Carla seems to hope that better preparation will make things less difficult for them, when it comes their time to ask, "What's next?"

SUMMARY

One of the themes of this life phase seems to be "letting go of what doesn't really matter, experimenting with what seems to work, and getting on with whatever is next" (Levine, 2005, p. 150). Another theme that emerges during this life phase is that of rebalancing work, family, and time for self. This phase is also marked by a search for discovering what is most meaningful for the adult as s/he explores and experiments with new activities. During this phase of retirement/reinvention, adults face the task of making their remaining years of life more meaningful. We see this illustrated in the case of Linda who hired a life-transitions coach to help her with her concerns about adding value to life and making a difference, as she moved from her role as homemaker (once her children were college students) to working part-time as a customer service trainer. This allowed Linda to retain some of her time that she enjoyed with friends and family, while reentering the world of work. On the other hand, Carla, for whom retirement brought with it the loss of social position, interaction with colleagues, and a sense of contributing to society, sought therapy to help her discover how she might appreciate her new status as a retiree and find fulfillment in the volunteer, nonprofit sector of society. Prior to reinventing her life, Carla had to grieve the loss of the aspects of her work life that were meaningful to her.

Both of these women were trying to discover what really mattered to them and were seeking a meaningful role for themselves in a revised life structure, while facing the losses they had endured and recognizing the gains they had achieved. Practitioners who are working with adults in this phase of life need to understand and recognize the importance of helping clients recognize their strengths and "let go" of some aspects of their lives as they struggle to build a bridge to a new life structure in which they can make new meaning in their lives.

9 Older Adults

Helen was 79 and a widow when her 52-year-old daughter, Leslie, developed ovarian cancer. Helen was devastated when Leslie called to break the news to her mom; she sobbed while telling Helen about the results of her recent biopsy, which revealed the severity of her diagnosis with ovarian cancer. As Leslie talked with her, Helen tried to remain hopeful by telling her that she had discussed Leslie's illness with her own doctor, who had said, "there are many new treatments out there which can save your daughter's life." Leslie didn't want to listen to her mother's responses because she believed that she was going to die, despite her friends and family members who encouraged much hope. Leslie had been married for 24 years and had two grown children on whom Helen doted—loving the role of grandmother from the day the children were born. Helen's initial reaction to Leslie's bad news was to think to herself and to say to her friends, "Why my daughter who has so many years left to live and not me?" Helen turned to her faith, began attending Bible classes at her local church where the members of the Bible group and the minister were praying for Leslie every day. Helen's friends tried to be supportive but none of them had experienced the loss of their child; so she felt very alone with her worries.

Helen took Leslie for her chemotherapy treatments every week and then to radiation. During this time Helen continued to keep a stiff upper lip and remain optimistic. Yet, when the treatments ended and 1 year had gone by, the doctor told Leslie that the cancer had returned and there was not much they could do for her. Helen cried every morning and called her daughter every day and took her to lunch once a week. Helen had become much closer to Leslie following the death of Helen's husband, 4 years prior to Leslie's diagnosis. Leslie and her family had become her closest support network, although she still had lunch with some of her friends every week. Helen was now feeling very depressed and was unable to get up in the morning and often stayed in her bathrobe all day. Leslie began to worry about her mother more than herself. Leslie even suggested to her mother that she consider seeing a therapist, but Helen did not want to talk to a complete stranger. Leslie had made peace with the fact that she was probably going to die but her mother could not do that.

When Leslie died 2 years following her diagnosis, Helen and Leslie's family did not agree on how to deal with the funeral. Helen thought Leslie should be buried with Leslie's father in their family grave plot, but Leslie's family wanted to cremate Leslie, as they believed that was what Leslie wanted. Helen had to go along with what her son-in-law and grandchildren wanted.

About 3 months following the funeral, Helen was still having trouble with daily functioning and had become a hermit in her apartment. Her friends began to worry about her—her son-in-law and grandchildren were caught up in their own grief and did not even call Helen to see how she was doing. Finally, one of her friends suggested that Helen see a grief counselor. The counselor helped Helen to recognize that her own grief about the loss of Leslie had not been supported or recognized by Leslie's family. In addition, she helped Helen to understand that her grief for Leslie was bringing forth some of the sadness and grief she was still processing from the loss of her husband. During the course of counseling, the counselor suggested that Helen bring in a favorite photo of her daughter, which they placed on a table in the counselor's office so that Helen could feel the presence of her daughter as she spoke with her and about her. After about 1 year of counseling Helen began to feel "lighter" and returned to those activities and relationships that she had enjoyed prior to the loss of her daughter.

DEVELOPMENTAL CRISIS: INTEGRITY VERSUS DESPAIR

Within this text older adults are described as those living beyond age 65. Some texts (Newman & Newman, 2006) have divided older adults into two groups, the first age 60 to 75 years (later adulthood) and the second consisting of the very old, age 75 until death. In describing losses for the purposes of this text, we have decided that one life phase of older adults is most appropriate.

Just as with individuals from other life phases, older adults are confronted with opportunities for growth and development as well as many stressors, risks, and forces (biological, psychological, and social) that can disrupt growth. It is fair to say that the average older adult probably has more confrontation with physical losses (health) and social stressors (environmental conditions, losses of friends, homes, family members, etc.) than adults or children in other life phases. The view that it is not what you experience that determines your state of well-being, but rather how you perceive and respond to what you have experienced, is quite appropriate for those adults coping with losses in later adulthood.

Social Changes

For older adults it is most essential to consider individual differences in both physical and mental health when considering growth patterns in later adulthood (Hooyman & Kramer, 2006; Hooyman & Kiyak, 2008; Newman & Newman, 2006). There is also great variability among older adults in their productive activities, their family situations, and status of their health (Hooyman & Kiyak, 2008). Research on various aspects of aging continues to clarify greater appreciation "for the fact that patterns of aging are neither universal nor irreversible" (Newman & Newman, 2006, p. 470). Many older adults lose aerobic capacity and become more sedentary, whereas others continue to remain free of major health problems and perform quite arduous labor. Many older adults continue to work in the labor force both part and full time. Life situations such as limited health care, poverty, and malnutrition can accelerate the aging process, whereas having access to a stimulating social environment, a well-balanced diet, and participation in a program of physical activity can enhance both the intellectual and physical functioning of older adults (Rowe & Kahn, 1998). Understanding the person–environment perspective with regard to a discussion of the elderly and loss is particularly significant, because how the older person is able to respond, adapt, and change to the demands made by the social and physical environment may affect his/her response to loss.

For older adults, the final 30 years of life can be a time of reinvention, as this phase of life does often bring a gradual release from the daily demands of work and family and an opportunity to create a new life structure, depending on the health and resources of the older adult. Older adults also provide role models for adult children and grandchildren who can be inspired by the vitality and sheer courage demonstrated by their elders. This inspiration can enable younger adults and children to continue to face the challenges of their daily lives with optimism. Because older adults do have more life experience and have often faced challenges and opportunities that younger adults have not yet faced, they possess wisdom that they can pass along if the younger generation is willing to accept it.

Psychological Changes

The major developmental task of later adulthood is accepting one's life so that the older adult can achieve a sense of integrity or wholeness about oneself rather than face despair (Erikson, 1959/1980; Hooyman & Kramer, 2006; Newman & Newman, 2006). This acceptance comes from introspection and life review in which the older adult examines both positive accomplishments and negative experiences to arrive at a sense of satisfaction about one's life. Older adults must be able to take pride in various achievements at the same time that they may be examining personal goals and expectations that may not have been met. They must be able to incorporate disappointments and areas of personal failure without being overwhelmed by a sense of inadequacy.

This developmental task can also be described as one of maintaining self-esteem in the "wake of biological, psychological and social stressors" (Cooper & Lesser, 2008, p.110). Disorders of the self can be manifested in some of the following ways: wide vacillations in self-esteem; overdependency on others for approval; extreme sensitivity to perceived slights and insults; and an overemphasis on possessions, physical attractiveness, and past accomplishments to cope with feelings of diminished self-esteem. The restoration of the self is one of the major goals of therapy with the elderly. The therapist can aid the older adult by engaging with her/him in reminiscing about past accomplishments, listening to or bearing witness to past emotional insults suffered by the client, and mourning various losses experienced by the client.

Biological Changes

Among older adults there are many obvious physical changes that bring sensory losses in hearing, eyesight, and sense of smell and taste, as well as joint degeneration (Hooyman & Kramer, 2006; Newman & Newman, 2006). Chronic diseases, such as heart disease, cancer, osteoarthritis, strokes, and diabetes, are all physical threats to many older adults. Later in this chapter we discuss life-threatening disease in more depth.

Cognitive changes are often prominent among the elderly. Reaction time, memory, and "visual-motor flexibility (translating visual information into new motor responses) show evidence of decline with age" (Newman & Newman, 2006, p. 476). With regard to memory, researchers have identified a decline over time in the ability to "recall" information but few differences in "recognition" (Hooyman & Kiyak, 2008; Newman & Newman, 2006). Furthermore, the context in which older adults are likely to learn affects their ability to achieve cognitive tasks. "Positive feedback appears to be a valuable tool for eliciting responses from older adults in both learning and test situations" (Hooyman & Kiyak, 2008, p. 190). The pacing of the delivery of information as well as the presentation of relevant and familiar material also supports the ability to learn in the older adult (Hooyman & Kiyak, 2008). Despite cognitive losses among older adults, neurobiology and brain-imaging techniques have demonstrated, however, that "brain development can also occur in later adulthood through new experiences and relationships, including…the therapeutic relationship" (Brandell & Ringel, 2004, p. 553).

LOSSES EXPERIENCED BY OLDER ADULTS

Resilience

Resilience is a concept based on "social work's historical emphasis on a strengths perspective" (Hooyman & Kramer, 2006, p. 65) and on the belief that those who have suffered loss and are able to discover ways to integrate loss into their lives are resilient to some degree. Bonanno (2004) defines resilience as the ability of an adult to maintain a stable equilibrium with "healthy levels of psychological and physical functioning" (p. 21) following a highly disruptive event such as the loss of a close relative or a violent/life-threatening situation. Bonanno (2004) reports that the difference between resilient adults and others is that for resilient adults, these disruptive experiences "were transient rather than enduring and did not interfere with their ability to continue to function in other areas of their lives, including positive affect" (p. 24). Hooyman and Kramer (2006) report that although older adults may experience multiple losses during their lifetime, they may demonstrate much resilience, "especially if their community, family and cultural capacities are strong" (Hooyman & Kramer, 2006, p. 306). Lund, Caserta, and Dimond (1993) report that, among older bereaved adults, resiliency is a common pattern of adjustment, as the elderly find effective ways of coping with their grief and developing satisfying adjustments.

Many of the elderly bring strong personal capacities to coping with loss. Some are able to reevaluate negative events to find something positive in the experience, whereas others lower their standards and goals to handle adversity (Cartensen, Gross, & Fung, 1997; Lawton, Windley, & Byers, 1982). Moss, Moss, and Hansson (2001) report that older adults may be more effective in finding meaning in their losses and confiding in others (through reminiscence) than are younger adults. If an older adult has found comfort and peace with the concept of his or her own death, losses may be less devastating than for younger adults who perceive death as far in the future (Hooyman & Kramer, 2006). However, an older adult's declining health, degree of religiosity/spirituality, socioeconomic class, concurrent stressors, personal capacities, relationship with the deceased, and degree of familial and social support systems tend to affect how they experience loss (Carr, Nesse, & Wortman, 2006; Hooyman & Kramer, 2006). What seems essential to resilience is the ability of the bereaved to rely on helpful networks, refuse those who are no longer useful, and create new meaningful networks for themselves (Hooyman & Kramer, 2006).

Research on the resilience of the elderly in the face of spousal loss indicates that although there is diversity in response to spousal loss, "common grief was relatively infrequent and the resilient pattern was most frequent" (Bonanno et al., 2002). Furthermore, Bonanno et al. (2002) found that in their prospective study of older widows and widowers, among the five core bereavement patterns identified ("common grief, chronic grief, chronic depression, improvement during bereavement and depression" [p. 1150]), 45.6% of the respondents fell into the resilient category. These findings (Bonanno et al., 2002) indicate that the resilient older adults are "more accepting of death and believe more clearly that the world is just" (p. 1161). Bonanno, Nesse, and Randolph (2004) suggest that the findings from Bonanno et al.'s prospective study are consistent with a "growing body of empirical evidence suggesting that bereaved individuals who experience little or no overt disruptions in functioning and who evidence the capacity for positive emotional experiences are exhibiting a healthy resilience to loss" (p. 261).

However, it is not uncommon for an older bereaved spouse to develop a serious illness or to die within 1 year of the death of his or her spouse (Hooyman & Kramer, 2006). Social support can help to mitigate the stress surrounding an older adult's loss of a spouse. Whether or not social support is perceived by the grieving spouse to be meaningful and helpful is a critical aspect of the benefit of social support to resilience or positive aging (Hill, 2005). Furthermore, "what people actually do or the behaviors they engage in to assist the older grieving spouse is perhaps more important than just being available to help him or her" (p. 197).

Developing a Point of View About Death

During this life phase older adults are also developing a viewpoint about death, as they experience the loss of their peers, siblings, spouses, and their own health. Older adults have to grieve these losses and try to make some meaning of them to be able to formulate a viewpoint about death, including their own mortality.

It is difficult to anticipate how dying may affect an adult in later adulthood. However, because dying in Western society is primarily associated with old age, death is more predictable as a function of age. "Death in old age has thus come to be viewed as a timely event, the completion of the life cycle" (Hooyman & Kiyak, 2008, p. 540). Most deaths in old age occur as a result of chronic disease because of improved medical technology, early detection, and diagnosis. Among the elderly, those with chronic illnesses are cared for longer than what may be natural, so that many older adults are not "achieving a peaceful death" because of the professional and societal "ambivalence about whether to fight or accept death" (Hooyman & Kiyak, 2008, p. 540).

There is general agreement in most literature (Cicirelli, 2002; Corr, Nabe, & Corr, 2006) that "the elderly are significantly less fearful of death than younger persons" (Corr, Nabe, & Corr, 2006, p. 422). However, the fear of death is a complicated notion, with social and physical variables creating differences among the elderly. What people seem to fear most about death is their inability to predict the future and the process of dying—most are particularly concerned about dying a painful death (Hooyman & Kiyak, 2008).

In their end-of-life decision making, older adults seem to prefer choosing quality of life, although this may vary depending on the type of illness they have. Many older adults are choosing to complete advanced directives and living wills prior to death (Y. M. Johnson, in press; Johnson & Stadel, 2007). However, it is significant that older African Americans "are more likely to want lifesaving technology and to resist advanced directives, even though their belief in the afterlife may reduce their fear of death" (Hooyman & Kiyak, 2008, p. 541). Because of cultural differences regarding end-of-life issues, health care providers need to allow older patients to educate them about such differences so as to promote a good death. There are multiple factors that influence attitudes and fears about death and dying, such as age, gender, and previous experiences with the death of loved ones. For example, older women are more likely to report fear and anxiety about dying, but are less fearful of the unknown than older men. However, as Hooyman and Kiyak (2008) report, this difference may emanate from gender differences in socialization and in women's greater ability to express emotions. There are mixed findings comparing the fear of death among younger persons compared to older adults (Lynn, Lynch-Schuster, Wilkinson, & Noyes-Simon, 2007). The oldest older adults seem to talk and think more about death and appear less afraid of their own death as compared to young-old and midlife adults (Hooyman & Kiyak, 2008). However, Cicirelli (2002, 2006) reports that those adults over 75 who are aware of their limited survival seem to desire more time beyond what is expected. A nearly universal fear, despite age, is the pain of dying, and concern about an afterlife, such as a threatening type of afterlife or the possibility of no afterlife (Cicirelli, 2006; Fortner, Neimeyer, & Rybarczyk, 2000).

Some research (Oktay & Walter, 1991) indicates that older adults who have coped with previous loss are prepared in some ways for coping with death. Dying may be more devastating to an older adult who has not experienced previous loss or to one who has experienced a series of losses without a strong support system. Over and over again, research points to the importance of social supports in mitigating the dying experience for the older adult (Carr, Nesse, & Wortman, 2006;

Hill, 2005; Hooyman & Kiyak, 2008; Newman & Newman, 2006; Oktay & Walter, 1991).

Coping With Chronic/Life-Threatening Illness

Living with a chronic/life-threatening illness or disability is a very common occurrence among older adults. Living with chronic pain or with disability incurred from a chronic illness makes it difficult for many older adults to return to normal functioning (Hooyman & Kramer, 2005). However, some older adults can reconstruct their identity to include living with an illness or a disability and "are able to discover new strengths, capacities and positive meaning" (Hooyman & Kramer, 2005, p. 320). These older adults can move beyond the loss and create new realities for themselves.

Because loss is a theme in the lives of most elderly, breast cancer (as an example of a chronic/life-threatening illness) brings new losses to the life of the elderly adult. Breast cancer is a serious issue for older women, as one in eight women will develop breast cancer during her lifetime (American Cancer Society, 2008, retrieved on July 24, 2008). The good news for older women is that if they develop breast cancer, it is usually at a stage that can easily be controlled with chemotherapy and/or radiation. Breast cancer can represent a loss of beauty, a loss of sexual attractiveness, and a loss of health. "This can have both advantages and disadvantages for the elderly woman. If she has coped successfully with other losses, she may be better prepared to deal with the breast cancer" (Oktay & Walter, 1991). In Oktay and Walter's study some of the women found that the cancer was easier to deal with than other losses that they had incurred. For example, Jeanne, who was 73 years old when she was diagnosed with breast cancer, used skills that she had learned from earlier crises to help her cope with breast cancer. Jeanne had a terminal illness of the liver that was diagnosed when she was 62 years old. At that time she was told that she only had 5 years to live. Jeanne said:

> I was devastated that I even had such an illness and the doctor said to me, "I don't know how many years you have—make the most of it." I'm a very strong person. I had a lot of adversity in my youth, but I was a survivor. I never went down. I never let anything get me down. I always had a philosophy—there's always tomorrow. (Oktay & Walter, 1991, p. 178)

Jeanne is an example of an older adult who has a resilient personality and sees herself as a survivor. Some older adults bring strong personal capacities to their confrontation with loss. They have learned how to reappraise negative events to find something positive in them. Some have been able to lower their expectations and goals as a way of coping with adversity (Hooyman & Kramer, 2005).

On the other hand, breast cancer can represent another in a long serious of losses that can lead to a serious depression. Judith is an example of an older woman who experienced severe anxiety and depression following her diagnosis and treatment of breast cancer. Judith has been single all of her life and following the loss of her father, Judith's mother came to live with her. Ten years later her mother developed cancer and Judith cared for her mother until her death when Judith was 54. Although Judith's work was helpful to her during the time of mourning following her mother's death, Judith decided to take early retirement after working at one place for her entire work life. At first, Judith did well with her retirement but then she began to cope with a series of health problems—arthritis, eye surgery, skin rashes—and when diagnosed with breast cancer at age 62 she decompensated emotionally. Judith was angry at her doctor for the way he handled the diagnosis, and had severe panic attacks during her chemotherapy for breast cancer. Although she found some solace from religion shortly before her mastectomy and sought support from her cousin who had also had a mastectomy, Judith was never able to rebound. Judith saw a psychiatrist for the panic attacks and used relaxation exercises but resisted medication for her anxiety. Judith reported that:

> Ever since I had cancer a lot of things have changed. I used to like going to the theatre...but even that's losing interest for me now. I'm withdrawing almost all of the time. I don't go out too much anymore. I used to have friends too, but I have gradually left those friends behind. I'm not interested. I've withdrawn. And I don't seem to want to do anything about it. I fight it. I really do. (Oktay & Walter, 1991, p. 171)

Judith is an example of an older adult who does not have a strong social network and has had a series of losses that have been overwhelming for her. Unfortunately for the elderly and for someone like Judith, many life events are stressful and involve a loss of social support. Judith is single and her parents have both died. Retirement seems to have removed her from a network of some support and her experience with breast cancer has removed her from her friends. Judith, herself, may be less resilient than Jeanne, described earlier. Oktay and Walter (1991) reported that most of the older women (including Judith) with breast cancer they interviewed engaged in personal religious activities such as prayer to help them cope with breast cancer.

Other chronic illnesses, such as Alzheimer's disease, may have a different impact on both the patient and the caregiver. At the end of this chapter the case of "Rachael and Hal," reported by Hal's wife and caregiver, Rachael, reveals that one of the most difficult issues for her as a caregiver is the unending multiple losses involved for both herself and for Hal (when he was in the earlier stages and aware). Additionally, a disease like Alzheimer's represents an ambiguous loss (Boss, 1995), in that there is confusion because it is unclear how one is to adjust to the loss. Hal is physically present but psychologically absent so it may seem premature for Rachael to grieve in socially sanctioned ways because this would remove the hope of the return of Hal to Rachael's life; yet on one level she knows he will never return. Long-term ambiguity, which Rachael endured, can create a sense of loss of identity and mastery, leading to helplessness and hopelessness in the family system and within the primary caregiver's life. The loss of recognition by the patient and the loss of intimacy can be especially painful for the Alzheimer's caregiver compared to other caregivers; those involved with care of Alzheimer's patients are at greater risk of strain, depression, and physical problems and have less time for leisure and for other family members (George & Gwyther, 1986; Hooyman & Kramer, 2005; Ory, Hoffman, Yee, Tennestedt, & Schultz, 1999; Schultz et al., 2003). The caregiver of an Alzheimer's patient continually redefines and reinterprets the relationship with his/her loved one. This in itself is stressful. In the case of "Rachael and Hal," Rachael stresses the importance of caregiver support groups, which decrease the isolation experienced by the caregiver and validates his/her concerns. Respite care is another support that can be offered to caregivers who one hopes will seek it out and take advantage of those programs available within the community.

Death of a Spouse

One of the most common losses experienced by individuals in later adulthood is the death of a spouse. Of the nearly one million individuals who are widowed each year in the United States, "nearly three-quarters of them are over the age of sixty-five" (Carr, Nesse, & Wortman, 2006, p. 82). Compared to young or middle-aged adults, older adults are more likely to experience this type of loss. Because spousal loss is so common among older adults, various studies seem to indicate that an important feature of the aging process is successful mastery of the transition from being a couple to functioning on one's own (Carr, Nesse, & Wortman, 2006).

Although most older adults (especially women) expect to lose their spouse during this phase of life, some research (Arbuckle & deVries, 1995) has found that a partner's death in late adulthood is most devastating. Hooyman and Kramer (2006) indicate that "little difference in grief responses has been found in older adults losing an adult child compared with losing a partner" (p. 307). Some reasons for why the elderly find it particularly difficult to cope with spousal loss are that: (a) the social networks of the elderly are frequently narrowed because of death and deteriorating health among their peers; (b) spousal relationships among the elderly assume increasing importance for the older adult because, in a highly mobile society, fewer relatives are available to provide support; and (c) many older couples have formed deep and strong attachments over the course of their lifetime so that they are highly dependent on one another for companionship and are highly interdependent because of roles, commitments, and traditions (Moss, Moss, & Hansson, 2001). The case presentation of Ms. Ramsey at the end of this chapter describes the difficulty an older widow has with her day-to-day functioning following the death of her husband on whom she was very dependent for companionship. Finally, the older adult is more likely to experience loss of a spouse or partner at the same time that s/he is facing chronic illness, disability, diminished physical stamina, and/or negative cognitive changes. Older adults face the real possibility of bereavement overload. At a time when financial, social, and adaptive resources are declining, the loss of a spouse or partner in later adulthood requires greater coping efforts than may be needed for those in middle or early adulthood (Carr, Nesse, & Wortman, 2006). The vignette of Helen, presented at the beginning of this chapter, demonstrates the multiple losses of a widow who has also lost a daughter with whom she is very connected; this has all occurred at a time when cognition is slowing, which makes coping more challenging.

Other research examines forces that may make this loss less difficult for older adults. For example, Neimeyer (1998) and Calhoun and Tedeschi (2001) have found that widowed persons who find purpose in their suffering and can make meaning of the death of their loved one adjust better than those who are unable to do so. Meaning-making involves reconstructing new worldviews and understanding the loss. People find meaning in various ways. Some widowed adults find comfort from helping other recently bereaved persons, whereas others feel gratified by assisting survivors with more instrumental challenges, involving home repairs, car maintenance, or paying bills. Still others focus on finding "benefit" instead of finding meaning, especially if their loved ones experienced a death that was violent, untimely, or random (C. G. Davis & Nolen-Hoeksema, 2001). Finding benefit involves focusing on personal value or significance of the event, including developing new strengths as a result of the experience (C. G. Davis & Nolen-Hoeksema, 2001). Those who find benefit often grow stronger, more self-confident, and feel more compassion for others than they did before the loss. Meaning-making processes resemble the conceptualizations that Hogan and Schmidt propose in The Grief to Personal Growth Model (2002). These scholars asserted that when people grieve they seek to "avoid" their painful feelings by sharing their feelings with confidants. Hogan and Schmidt (2002) argue that by talking to other people, bereaved persons find relief from their emotional pain, which helps them process their feelings and make sense of their loss.

People become transformed by their losses, and over time survivors develop more optimism, feel less emotional pain, and reconstruct more meaningful identities and purposeful lives. They also become more compassionate and tolerant of others' emotional struggles. Similar to Stroebe and Schut (1999), Hogan and Schmidt (2002) believe that bereaved persons oscillate between yearning for the lost person and dealing with the inevitable intrusive thoughts that emerge about the deceased and avoiding reminders about the deceased by seeking comfort from other people.

Continuing bonds theory (Klass, Silverman, & Nickman, 1996) also suggests a higher level of adjustment and functioning as the bereaved spouse finds ways to stay connected to the deceased spouse through creative memory-making and the use of photographs. In relationship to the continuing bonds theory, which involves an attachment to the deceased spouse, other researchers (Hansson & Stroebe, 2007;

Stroebe, Stroebe, & Schut, 2005a, 2005b) have integrated ideas from attachment theory, initially proposed by Bowlby (1980/1998) and subsequently tested with bereaved persons by Parkes (2001) and Schaver and Tancredy (2001). In these recent conceptualizations it has been suggested that people will grieve differently depending on whether their attachment styles are secure or insecure; presumably, complicated grief reactions arise more often among those who experienced insecure attachments.

Lund and colleagues (1993) report that there is considerable diversity throughout the course of bereavement among older bereaved spouses. Some older bereaved spouses had great difficulty managing their personal lives for several years, whereas others remained socially active, independent, and motivated to make the best of the situation. However, within individual older adults there is diversity in emotional reactions to grief. "It was not unusual for the bereaved to feel angry, guilty, and lonely, yet at the same time feel personal strength and pride in how he or she was coping" (Lund et al., 1993, p. 245).

C. Walter (2003) describes the reactions of two older bereaved spouses who demonstrate this diversity in bereavement reaction. Flora was 89 when Jim, her spouse of 60 years, died of massive heart failure at age 87. Additionally, 1 month following the loss of Jim, Flora suffered the loss of her adult son, who was 39 when he died. Although the interview was focused on the loss of her spouse, it is interesting that Flora did not speak in any detail about the loss of her adult son. Perhaps this reflects the research about older adults and the severe impact of the loss of a spouse. Although Flora missed her husband's presence in her life, she was quite vocal about her angry reactions toward Jim after he died when problems arose with a furnace that she had to replace because he had insisted on "nursing the old furnace along." Flora also felt left out of an important part of Jim's life because "he often shut me out about some of the things that he talked to his friends, but he didn't talk to me. He was a very into-himself person. He was not a sharing person at all" (C. Walter, 2003, p. 74). Flora believes that her ability to be angry at Jim after his death has contributed to her well-being as a widow. However, Flora is now able to balance both the positive and negative aspects of her relationship with Jim as she works on transforming her ongoing relationship with her deceased spouse. Although she can still feel angry about being shut out of some of Jim's life, she can express pleasure over the pride that Jim took in Flora's professional accomplishments. Flora is redefining her continuing relationship with her deceased spouse through these reactions. Although Flora believes that she has lost a part of herself and some of the social relationships she shared with her spouse, she spoke about finding a new part of herself and building on that. Flora is reworking her definition of herself to include an understanding of that part of herself that is not as outgoing as she once thought. She is becoming more content with being by herself and enjoying the new part of herself that is emerging. Flora's story demonstrates the developmental task of this phase of life regarding the issue of developing a sense of integrity and wholeness.

George's reaction at 78 to the loss of his spouse just following the couple's 52nd anniversary is quite different from that of Flora's. George spoke of feeling devastated for months following Barbara's death. Even 4 years following her death he reports that "I'm gradually getting over the trauma...but I still find myself weeping a lot...I still find myself very lonely" (C. Walter, 2003, pp. 78, 79). George is just beginning to socialize with a few women friends but says he will never remarry. Although he reports feeling better each year he does not like to discuss Barbara's death and cries only with his adult children. These differences in reaction could be attributed to gender (C. Walter, 2003) or to the different reactions among the elderly to spousal loss. In the case study of Ms. Ramsey at the end of this chapter, the reader can see how differently this widow responds to the loss of her spouse than does Flora, who was more independent in her functioning prior to the loss of Jim than Ms. Ramsey, who depended on her spouse for most of her companionship. Ms. Ramsey had more difficulty in daily functioning following her loss and was quite withdrawn for the 2 years following her husband's death. Research findings (Bonnano et al., 2002) underscore the variability in the ways that older bereaved spouses respond to the loss of a spouse.

Death of a Nonmarried Opposite-Sex Partner

One of the largest growing groups of nonmarried couples in our society is the elderly (C. Walter, 2003). In her text Walter (2003) describes such a bereaved partner from the older adult population. Barry was 76 years old and a retired real estate salesman when his partner, Julie, died of cancer at age 57. Barry and Julie had both been widowed for about 3 years when they met at a dance for widowers and widows. Although there was a large discrepancy in age (which concerned their adult children) both Barry and Julie enjoyed living together and sharing many of their similar interests. Following Julie's death, Barry was devastated but was grateful "that I was the one that was with her when she died" (C. Walter, 2003, p. 99). Despite Julie's daughter's attempts to make all of the funeral arrangements, Barry was able to plan most of the funeral because he felt strongly that he knew what Julie would have wanted. Barry's involvement in organizing Julie's funeral is an example of "loss-oriented coping" as described by Stroebe and Schut (1999) in their Dual Process Model of bereavement. Other activities include dealing with medical costs from treatment of the deceased as well as organizing clothing and other belongings of the deceased partner. Loss-oriented coping represents one of the two phases of oscillation experienced by bereaved persons following the loss of a loved one. During this first phase the bereaved is deeply involved in the grief work, experiencing the sadness and other emotions involved in coping with the loss. The second phase around which the bereaved adult oscillates is called "restoration-oriented coping" and represents the bereaved partner's attempts to cope with ongoing life activities and commitments following the loss. Literature from ongoing research about the Dual Process Model of coping with loss suggests that, during both early and late phases in the bereavement process, restoration-oriented coping is more helpful to both widows and widowers (Caserta & Lund, 2007). This type of coping can range from socializing with friends to distracting oneself with home repairs or hobbies. When surviving partners learn new tasks that their deceased partners previously performed, the surviving partner can feel more empowered and independent.

Following Julie's death, Barry took a computer course as a new venture, but also chose a sewing class as well because of his relationship with Julie. Barry reports, "Julie was a great sewer. She made all the costumes for her grandchildren...she used to do a lot of work for me, too...cuffs, my trousers, my sport shirts. And there's a couple that she started and didn't finish. I figured...it's a beautiful sewing machine, and it's sitting here, and somebody's got to learn to use it....I'm the only male who shows up for the course" (C. Walter, 2003, p. 101). Barry's comments reflect not only his experience with "restoration-oriented coping," but also his attempts to rework his ongoing relationship and to maintain his continuing bond with Julie, a task that the postmodern grief theorists believe is so important in coping with the loss of a loved one. Barry also stays connected with his memory of Julie by talking with her and by staying in touch with her son and her brother, with whom he can share memories. Because Barry is an older adult he has had an opportunity to enjoy one marriage prior to his relationship with Julie. Barry keeps photographs of both Marie (his deceased wife) and Julie in his bedroom and hallway entrance to his home. Soon after Julie's death, when his grandson applied for a big promotion, Barry "said prayers to Julie and Marie every night, and I asked them both, especially Julie, to help him get his promotion" (C. Walter, pp. 100, 101).

Barry's comments reflect his ability to work on one of the developmental tasks of older adulthood, achieving a sense of integrity and moving toward an increasing sense of self-actualization. Barry's ability to engage in new tasks, such as computer programming, sewing, and traveling to Europe with his sister, illustrate this point, as do his attempts to try "to figure out how to begin his life again" (C. Walter, 2003, p. 101). Barry believes that meeting new people in the courses he is taking, as well as engaging in activities that he loves, such as gardening and dancing, are helping him with his grief and his ability to move forward in his life. Richardson (2007) would note that Barry's experiences with restoration coping and his ability to learn new tasks that Julie, his deceased partner, performed (i.e., sewing) help him to experience more positive affect and to feel more empowered and independent.

Death of an Adult Child

As longevity continues to increase, many older adults in our society will experience the loss of an adult child. Although there is a growing wealth of literature (Applebaum & Burns, 1991; Clements, DeRanieri, Vigil, & Benasutti, 2004; Robinson & Marwit, 2006) about the loss of a young child or teen when a couple is in early or middle adulthood, there is very little research about the loss of a child in older adulthood. Rando (1986c) speaks about the unique features of bereavement for parents of an adult child. As a child grows older, a parental relationship with that adult child changes to one of sharing mutual interests and companionship rather than one of protection and physical caretaking. Adult-to-adult connections in a more peer-like, egalitarian relationship are characteristic markers of the adult child–parent relationship. Parents of an adult child have enjoyed the life of their child over a long period of time and may not feel as protective as do parents of a younger child. It may seem almost incredulous that an adult child who has survived all of the possible tragedies that can befall a younger child should die before his or her life expectancy is reached (Rando, 1986c).

Older adults also wonder "Why her and not me," as the vignette of Helen at the beginning of this chapter suggests. Many older adults are at an age when their own deaths would seem more likely than that of their adult child, regardless of his/her age (Corr et al., 2006). Similar to parents who lose a young child, survivor's guilt is still quite high among older adults who experience the loss of an adult child (Corr et al., 2006; Rando, 1986c).

Older adults facing the death of an adult child do so at a time in their lives when they are facing many other losses such as their health, their friends, and spouses. Their shrinking social network can make it very difficult for the older adult to have a diversion from the deep sense of loss they are experiencing as a result of the death of their child.

The older adult is also at high risk for complicated mourning and disenfranchised grief because society seems to expect that older individuals are more prepared for the death of a loved one, because they have experienced other losses and because their older age means that they are more comfortable with death, being closer to it themselves (Rando, 1986c).

Death of Friends

Because of increases in average life expectancies and the life stage of older adults, they are at highest risk of all age groups for the loss of friends and colleagues (Corr et al., 2006). This is especially true for those adults whose social networks are comprised primarily of peers of similar age, rather than a mix of younger and older persons. Yet, "The death of a friend is also often overlooked or minimized" (Hooyman & Kiyak, 2008, p. 579). Lifelong friends share a history of experiences and memories that no one else can fully understand (Hooyman & Kiyak, 2008). There is little known about the "cumulative effects of numerous friends' deaths in old age" (Hooyman & Kramer, 2005, p. 314). Because the older adult is facing so many types of losses, s/he may not have as much energy to invest in new relationships. When friendships end through death, making new friends may be more difficult. The importance of senior centers and other programs for the elderly that provide opportunities for socialization cannot be overemphasized.

MATURATIONAL LOSSES

Loss of Home/Relocation

As adults age, the immediate home environment becomes more important because (a) generally, older adults have less mobility and spend more time at home than other age groups; (b) "home acquires new meaning in old age because it serves to compensate for the reduced functional capacity of the aging individual, especially in very old age" (Oswald & Wahl, 2005, p. 25); and (c) the home and surrounding neighborhood may represent a lifetime of continuity for older adults. Moving from one home to another for any age group is difficult, but for the older adult who has probably lived in his/her home for many years, a move to a new location can be much more traumatic, despite the fact that the move may be viewed as an improvement to a more comfortable, safer home (Hooyman & Kiyak, 2008). A survey by the American Association of Retired Persons in 2005 found that "among all respondents 50 and older, 89 percent" wanted to stay in their home and never move, with this preference increasing with age so that "95% among those 75+" preferred to stay in their homes (Hooyman & Kiyak, 2008, p. 435). The elderly elect to stay in their homes "where the environment is familiar, neighbors can be relied on for assistance and socializing, and the aging person has control" (Hooyman & Kiyak, 2008, p. 436).

The support network of the older adult may find it strange that an older adult does not want to leave a large home that is too difficult to navigate or for whom repairs are too numerous to be accomplished. Families and caregivers need to recognize "the meaning of home to the older person as a symbol of self-identity, control, autonomy, and emotional and cognitive bonding with their social and physical environment" (Hooyman & Kiyak, 2008, p. 434). If an older person needs to move to a retirement facility or assisted living arrangement because of a chronic illness that limits his or her abilities to perform activities of daily living, the adjustment can be even more difficult because there is little time for preparation. Finally, when severe or sudden disability requires a move to a nursing home, the older person may feel even more distraught. The importance of examining the close relationship between self-identity and home is especially relevant "in the context of older adults moving from their homes into long-term care facilities. The move is a threat to personhood and it is critical that care settings provide a responsive context for the preservation and continuity of selfhood" (Rubinstein & Medeiros, 2005, p. 59).

Regardless of the nature of the move, many older adults experience feelings of loss associated with giving up a familiar setting as well as their possessions. This is an example of a maturational loss that can be experienced as disenfranchised by the older adult when family and friends do not understand their feelings of sadness and loss. Whether the older adult is moving to an apartment, assisted living arrangement, or a nursing home, s/he is faced with disposing of a lifetime of possessions. Memories are attached to favorite possessions, which can result in difficult decisions, increasing the feelings of loss the elderly experience associated with a move (Hooyman & Kiyak, 2008). When moving an older adult to a nursing home, it might be wise for family members and/or caregivers to help the adult select a few special possessions that can function much like that of a "transitional object" for a young child. The older adult can feel more soothed by having specific pieces of furniture or smaller objects that hold special meaning for the adult.

Positive outcomes of moving from one location to another may include: (a) the older adult finding him/herself in a situation that provides much needed stimulation from others and (b) involvement in daily activities that may be interesting to the older adult who had been unable to drive to locations that provided outlets for hobbies and other recreational interests.

Grandparent Caregivers

Grandparent-headed households are one of the fastest-growing family units in the United States (Hayslip & Kaminski, 2008; Hooyman & Kiyak, 2008). These are households in which "grandparents are providing the sole primary care of their grandchildren" (Hayslip & Kaminski, p. 3). The concept of ambivalence emerges as a major theme when considering relations between the generations. Many grandparents feel caught between the wish to help meet the needs of their adult children and grandchildren but are "reluctant to take on the parent role while giving up plans for retirement" (Hayslip & Kaminski, 2008, pp. 3, 4). Hayslip and Kaminski's (2008) loss/gain analysis is an intriguing one as it helps to understand the losses incurred by grandparent caregivers, while at the same time examining some of the gains and rewards experienced by this cohort of older adults.

Custodial grandparents frequently experience a sense of loss connected with their inability to be traditional grandparents who can enjoy their grandchildren without the responsibility of disciplining them (Hayslip & Kaminski, 2008; Kolomer & McCallion, 2005; Strom & Strom, 2000; Weber & Waldrop, 2000). Other losses that custodial grandparents experience are related to their attempts to make meaning of the family crises that led to them becoming custodial grandparents. Grandparent caregivers often face harsh realities related to their own adult children, who are mentally or physically ill or have suffered with addictions (Hayslip & Kaminski, 2008). "Economic costs of custodial grandparenting are significant. Compared to noncustodial grandmothers, they are more likely to live in poverty" (Hooyman & Kiyak, 2008, p. 358).

Because custodial grandparenting is "nonnormative" in nature, the grandparent can experience loneliness and loss, as the majority of his or her peer group does not share similar responsibilities (Hooyman & Kiyak, 2008).

However, some custodial grandparents see dramatic improvement in their grandchildren's development and realize how their involvement in the role of parents has contributed to the grandchildren's growth. Other research documents the gains in self-worth, self-esteem, achievement, and competence that custodial grandparents experience as a result of raising their grandchildren (Delman-Jenkins, Blankemeyer, & Olesh, 2002; Essex, Newsome, & Moses, 2004; Weber & Waldrop, 2000). The opportunity that custodial grandparents have to instill a sense of culture and family history in their grandchildren, as well as an opportunity to use the wisdom and knowledge that they have acquired, can strengthen the grandparents' own identity (Hayslip & Kaminski, 2008). Similar to assumptions about themselves, custodial grandparents can perceive their care for their grandchildren as a meaningful contribution to his/her family and to the world (Hayslip & Kaminski, 2008).

Hospice as a Resource for Patients and Their Families

Hill (2005) describes hospice care as an example of positive aging in dying. "Hospice care is the idea of dying in place or dying in a way that is consistent with the expressed wishes of the patient" (Hill, 2005, p. 216). The hospice service derives directly from the hospice philosophy of holistic care, "which requires it to address the needs of both the dying person and his/her family member" (Corr et al., 2006). Even when the patient is in an institutional setting or hospital, hospice tries to create a homelike environment for the patient and attempts to support the patient's family. Decisions about end-of-life care "are reevaluated from the viewpoint of preserving the quality of life and the dignity of the individual in his or her final stage of life" (Hill, 2005, p. 216).

One of the goals of hospice care is to focus on the quality of life so that positive reassurance and comfort can be provided through a "family-centered approach to care that involves an ongoing dialogue with the dying patient, the family and the health-care provider" (Hill, p. 217). In her research with hospice caregivers (including family) and dying patients, Clukey (2007) found that through exploration of the anticipatory grief experience, the major theme that emerged was the importance of being present. Both dying patients and caregivers (when asked what they would do for a friend in a similar situation) reported that what was most helpful was "being available just to listen" (Clukey, p. 152). The experience of anticipatory grief and "knowing that death was imminent, while still having each other's presence, gave people the opportunity to resolve issues that may have been left unresolved with a sudden death" (p. 154).

In the case of Olivia, which follows later in this chapter, the reader will find a lovely demonstration of how hospice care provided a high quality of care so that Olivia could die with dignity and independence. As the author of this case study states: "Living through dying is the ultimate goal of hospice care."

READINGS

THE STORY OF RACHAEL AND HAL

Carol Lovett, LCSW-G, CADC

Carol is a graduate of the Center for Social Work Education at Widener University. She worked for 30 years as a clinician and supervisor. During her career she developed and facilitated psychoeducational programs for clients with the co-occurring disorders of severe and persistent mental illness and substance abuse. Concurrently she coordinates trainings for the staff working with this population. Since her retirement Carol has volunteered in the training office of the Division of Substance Abuse and Mental Health (DSAMH) in Delaware, where she facilitates caregiver trainings for organizations that provide care to people suffering with dementia. Carol has also served on the Board of Directors of the Limen House, a halfway house for men and women recovering from addictions. Currently she is their clinical supervisor. Carol serves as a volunteer at the Delaware Valley Chapter of the Alzheimer's Association. In 1997 the DSAMH awarded Carol the Patrick Kelly Memorial Scholarship Award. The Alzheimer's Association honored her with the volunteer-of-the-year award in 2005. Carol was a caregiver for her husband throughout his illness and death.

Case Presentation

Today is Hal's 83rd birthday. He has not understood birthdays, anniversaries, or the significance of any holidays for a long time. Now he is physically gone; he died 5 months ago. Hal suffered with dementia.

Hal was an emergency room physician and psychiatrist. When he retired he had transitioned smoothly into spending his time with his many hobbies: fishing, photographing nature, and fixing up the home he loved. Shortly before he retired he taught himself how to carve decoys, stencil, and make things out of leather and soap stone. A proud father and husband, he was thrilled to give his creations to family and friends. People described Hal as a great talker who loved to teach, tell stories, and laugh.

It is difficult to pinpoint when the illness began. Not too many years after he retired, Hal's family noticed changes in his behavior, speech, and problem-solving skills. He had trouble finding words. He became angry and irrational for no apparent reason. A very private and fiscally conservative person, Hal began sharing personal business publicly. Suddenly he began obsessing over the Power Ball and the lottery. Although Hal never said anything to his family, they suspect he knew that something was happening to him. In 2003, Hal entered the final stage of the illness and life became a nightmare for himself and his wife, Rachael. Gradually his memory failed. He became increasingly anxious and frightened.

He awoke each morning at 3:00 a.m., compelled to shower, shave, and dress. He wore two watches and asked the same question again and again, writing the answer on small scraps of paper that he placed in his wallet. It was difficult to interest him in anything for very long because his attention span was short and he was easily distracted.

Hal walked all the time, following Rachael everywhere. He picked up anything he saw and moved it. All surfaces were cleared and all doors were bolted closed. Hal approached strangers and got in their space. On occasion he tried to eat things that were not food. Someone had to be with him all the time; he could not safely be left alone.

In the early stage of the disease, Hal could do most of his own grooming. But by the end he required total care. Sometimes he talked nonstop, often in his own private language. Finally communication was reduced to simple sounds then ultimately silence. Frequently he would awaken during the night and walk throughout the dark house. Rachael decided to lock them in the bedroom they shared together and watched him throughout the night. About 9 months before Hal died he began falling and he did not know how to get up. Two months before he died the twinkle left his eyes and he was gone. This is how Hal's wife describes her husband and his descent into dementia: "By its very nature dementia denies the sufferer the opportunity to assess his successes and disappointments. 'Such tasks are left to the spouse.' "

Dementia is defined as the loss of cognitive ability, when actually it is the gradual death of one's self (Doka, 2004). The person may look the same during most of the illness, but he does not act the same (Saunders & Corley, 2003). Dementia is a fatal illness for which there is no treatment and no cure. It leaves the sufferer unable to care for or protect him or herself. In the end s/he is totally dependent on others.

The disease affects the life of the caregiver as much as the person suffering with the condition. When one is watching a loved one die of dementia, one is simultaneously adjusting one's life to compensate for the losses caused by the illness. For example, the female spouse who becomes the caregiver often relinquishes her role and her identity to care for her partner. Soon her life is controlled by the effects of the illness (Loos & Bowd, 2007; Meuser, Marwat, & Saunders, 2004; Svanstrom & Dahlberg, 2004).

According to the Alzheimer's Association there are 70 different forms of dementia. Symptoms can appear anywhere from age 35 for early-onset Alzheimer's disease (AD) to midlife for such dementia as frontal temporal dementia to between 65 and end of life for adult AD.

Currently AD is the most commonly diagnosed form of dementia. Age is said to be the biggest risk factor for AD and by the time one reaches age 85 the risk of developing the disease is 50%. Presently it has the potential to reach epidemic proportions (*Alzheimer's Disease Facts and Figures,* 2007).

Dementias are brain diseases in which brain cells, called neurons, gradually die. The portion of the brain in which the cell death occurs and the type of protein abnormality that leads to the cell death usually helps physicians and researchers distinguish one dementia from another. Unfortunately, despite a number of laboratory advances and clinical tests, a definitive diagnosis can only be obtained through autopsy.

The Course and Symptoms of Dementia

The course and symptoms of AD and the other dementias vary. For some, the course may be slow and insidious, with the person surviving perhaps 10 to 20 years. For others, it may be rapid and the sufferer may die within a few years of diagnosis. Although memory loss is the symptom most commonly associated with AD, in actuality people suffering with the disease also lose the ability to plan, reason, concentrate, communicate their thoughts and feelings, regulate their emotions, and understand their environment and negotiate in it.

Symptoms of AD and other dementias are broken down into what are know as the 4 As: agnosia, amnesia, aphasia, and apraxia. Agnosia is also described as mind blindness, which means that the person can see or touch an object or hear a sound, but he does not recognize it. It impairs the sufferer's ability to recognize objects, name them, or know their use. Amnesia is the loss of memory. People with memory loss do not store new information, and gradually lose touch with stored information as well. They forget how to do routine things such as pay bills, take medication, or prepare a meal.

Aphasia is the loss of ability to use and understand language. People have trouble finding the word to express a thought or a need. Often they end by talking in their own language or they become mute. They also lose the ability to understand what is said to them and what they read. At this point, it is essential to remember that their behavior becomes their way of communicating.

Apraxia is the loss of the ability to perform skilled movements. People will have trouble writing, dressing, and feeding themselves. Eventually the patient who is suffering can develop difficulty walking, chewing, and swallowing.

There may be similarities among symptoms for each subtype of dementia, yet each person's decline is unique. No two people experience the illness in exactly the same way.

As the illness progresses the sufferer is less able to care for himself. The caregiver becomes increasingly responsible for providing care and safety. Witnessing the psychosocial death of a mate is not the only loss experienced by the caregiving spouse. In fact, the journey of the caregiver is in many ways similar to that of the sufferer, but for different reasons (Doka, 2000b). As the person with dementia is less and less able to care for him/herself, and as those responsibilities fall increasingly to the caregiver, both the caregiver and sufferer alike lose control over their lives (Meuser et al., 2004).

The Caregiver's Grief

While Rachael was losing her husband, and the intimacy they had once shared, she was simultaneously sacrificing those things that defined her. She freely admits she had no experience with dementia and was unprepared for the effects the illness would have on both their lives. Rachael gave up her career. Next she gave up her hobbies; her cherished perennial garden became a mere memory. At the same time, she lost the freedom to come and go as she chose even within her own house. Hal was so anxious and fearful that he would follow her outside and insist that she come back into the house. Rachael also curtailed visits to family and friends; Hal needed them both to be at home. Household chores were frequently postponed until Hal was asleep. Recreational activities and vacations were out of the question and dreams of the future died. While focusing totally on Hal she neglected herself and ultimately compromised her own health. She recalls that following her daughter's wedding and just before her son's she was so tired she could not even muster the energy to change a light bulb. Well-meaning family and friends told her to "place" Hal and get on with her life.

Hal's illness spanned more than a decade. During that time he and Rachael became increasingly isolated. Friends stopped calling and family was swallowed up in turmoil with each loss. Like most dementia sufferers Hal lived at home and for respite care Rachael turned to dementia-specific community programs.

During his illness Hal attended several different day-treatment programs, he was hospitalized once and he spent anywhere from a weekend to a few months in three different nursing facilities. The combination of Hal's behavior and the staff's limited knowledge of dementia compounded the couple's stress rather than providing relief. Sadly Rachael recalls several occasions on which Hal was restrained either chemically or mechanically because he wanted to enter the nurses' station.

As one might expect, there is a panorama of grieving that goes on around this cacophony of losses. Often because the spouse is so consumed coping with the next loss, she fails to recognize that she is in fact grieving.

There are several names for the type of grief experienced by the spouse who is caring for a loved one suffering with dementia. Doka (2004) describes one state of grief as chronic sorrow. He explains that the psychosocial loss of the loved one, the secondary losses of role and sociability, and the increased demands of caring for someone with a debilitating illness may lead to an unceasing state of grief known as chronic sorrow.

In an article by Walker and Pomeroy (1996) the caregivers' grief is distinguished from clinical depression. The author describes the spouse's experience as one of anticipatory mourning and explains that "family members don't just mourn losses that they expect to occur, they grieve those that have already occurred and those that are occurring daily while the person remains physically present" (p. 249).

In *Grief and Dementia*, Doka (2004) describes the experience as disenfranchised grief because family and friends are unfamiliar with a psychic loss. They see the person as still physically present and they do not acknowledge the loss or provide the support the spouse needs (Doka, 2000b; Saunders & Corley, 2003). Yet dealing with psychic loss is more difficult than dealing with physical loss (Loos & Bowd, 2007). Walker, Pomeroy, McNeil, and Franklin (1994) add that disenfranchised grief also occurs because the person with AD is undervalued.

Our society values youth, cognitive ability, and self-reliance. Elders have little value and, of course, elders who have lost their cognitive ability and are now dependent have even less. Doka (2004) notes that the experience of grief is complicated by feelings of ambivalence on the part of the healthy spouse who has given up her or his life to care for a person s/he hardly knows anymore. The healthy spouse reports feelings of anger, guilt, hopelessness, and despair as, like Rachael, s/he strives to keep his/her loved one safe and comfortable while wishing the whole ordeal were over (Saunders & Corley, 2003).

Interventions and Caregiver Support Groups

Studies have shown that interventions that break the isolation and provide education improved the quality of life for the caregiver. Such things as home visits, regularly scheduled telephone contacts, individual and family counseling, and participation in support groups have all proven helpful. Two valuable resources are: (a) Reach II, Resources for Enhancing Alzheimer's Caregiver Health, a project funded by the National Institute on Aging and (b) NYU Counseling and Support Intervention: Evidence Based Intervention for Caregivers of People with Dementia, a project also funded by the National Institute on Aging.

From a counseling perspective, Doka (2004) stresses that it is important to validate the unique losses experienced by the caregiver—past, present and future—while providing a safe environment in which the full range of feelings that accompany these losses can be expressed. It is equally essential to help caregivers explore ways in which they can care for themselves and regain some control over their own lives.

Caregiver support groups are key to decreasing isolation. Here the caregiver finds a safe place to ask questions and share his or her story, to laugh, and to be hugged. For Rachael the support group was a godsend. Initially she attended several different meetings, but the stories she heard were not hers. Finally, under the auspices of the Alzheimer's Association, she and a fellow caregiver established a frontal temporal dementia (FTD) support group. She continues to facilitate that group today. She describes the members of that group as cornerstones in her life.

Unfortunately the death of the ill spouse is not always synonymous with the end of pain and grieving. When death occurs, the need for caregiving abruptly ends and the healthy spouse is again without a role or an identity. "The physical and emotional effects of the caregiving experience last well beyond the death of the spouse and are attenuated in direct proportion to the length of care and the severity of the spouse's symptoms" (Loos & Bowd, 2007, p. 503). Rachael recalled that even though on some level she knew Hal was dying, on another level she was not ready for it and when he died she hit a wall. For years Hal's care had defined her life and filled her thoughts and suddenly he was gone.

Today, 13 months after Hal's death, Rachael says she is beginning to come out of the fog. Hal was not easy to care for but she misses him every day. She still suffers bouts of exhaustion and episodes of profound sadness, but they are shorter and less frequent. Her new friends are a great comfort to her. She confesses, however, that since Hal's death she has struggled with survivor guilt and becomes very sad when she thinks of others going through this same journey.

These days Rachael is passionate about changing the world for other dementia sufferers and their caregivers. To that end she freely gives of her time to talk with caregivers and to offer and prompt dementia training to staff in any facility providing care to dementia sufferers. She knows this experience has changed her forever and she is fine with that.

Losing a spouse to AD involves the loss of a mate, the loss of self, and often the loss of social support systems. Frequently caregivers are not in a position to find new support systems and their grief goes unrecognized and untreated.

As the disease relentlessly progresses toward the final dimming of the sufferer, it forces us to experience death in a way it is rarely otherwise experienced. What is usually a quick flicker we see in super slow motion over years. It is more painful than many people can even imagine, but it is also perhaps the most poignant of all reminders of why and how human life is so extraordinary. It is our best lens on the meaning of loss. (Schenk, 2003, pp. 225–226)

MARITAL BEREAVEMENT IN LATER ADULTHOOD

Virginia Richardson, PhD

Virginia Richardson received her PhD from the University of Michigan in 1980 and has served on the faculty of The Ohio State University College of Social Work for 28 years. She also has a courtesy appointment with the Department of African American and African Studies and served as the Director of Aging Research for The Ohio State University's Transdisciplinary Program in Aging from 2000 to 2003. Between 1997 and 2000, she was President of the Association for Gerontological Education in Social Work (AGE-SW). She received the College of Social Work's Tony Tripod Distinguished Researcher Award in 2004 and Outstanding Gerontology Educator in Ohio award in 2001. She has published several book chapters and articles in peer-reviewed journals in gerontology and currently serves as the editor of the Columbia University Press Series on End-of-Life Care. She recently co-authored and published a book, *Gerontological Practice for the Twenty-First Century*, with Columbia University Press.

Case Presentation

Ms. Ramsey, a 75-year-old woman, has adjusted poorly to the death of her husband, with whom she lived for almost 50 years. Although he died 2 years ago, Ms. Ramsey still yearns for her husband and the lifestyle they shared. Before he was diagnosed with lung cancer, the Ramseys traveled frequently, visiting friends and family members around the country. They enjoyed concerts and eating out at restaurants. Although initially chemotherapy treatments kept the cancer abeyant, Mr. Ramsey eventually succumbed to the cancer and died in the hospital after several complications from the treatment. Ms. Ramsey described her marriage as "almost perfect," stating "We did everything together." Since her husband's death, Ms. Ramsey rarely goes out and spends most days watching television and talking on the telephone.

Although Ms. Ramsey resembles many widows from her cohort, she experienced a more complicated grief reaction than her peers because individual and circumstantial factors exacerbated her situation. The protracted caregiving that Ms. Ramsey experienced, the suffering that her husband endured, along with the closeness and dependency that characterized the Ramsey's relationship all contributed to the intense and chronic grief reactions that Ms. Ramsey confronted.

Various factors, ranging from health status to social supports, affect how people experience bereavement, and I will discuss relevant factors underlying a biopsychosocial approach to understanding bereavement. First, I define important concepts, and then I briefly present contemporary models of bereavement that experts recently have proposed. Finally,

I apply these ideas to Ms. Ramsey's case. Although older adults experience many losses, which sometimes accumulate and can lead to depression, we focus on spousal bereavement, given its significance. According to Holmes and Rahe (1967), the death of one's spouse is the most significant life crisis that anyone can experience, although future cohorts of older adults most likely will experience bereavement differently, as more people remain single, marry later, and divorce than in previous decades.

Biopsychosocial Perspectives on Bereavement

A biopsychosocial perspective incorporates interactions between individuals and their environments, psychological and social-structural factors, and micro and macro influences. Gerontologists and especially gerontological practitioners, must consider these individual and personality factors, social support networks, financial resources, and ecological and environmental influences when studying or assessing older adults if they expect to effectively address their concerns. Bereavement does not occur within a vacuum; this event occurs within the context of multiple factors that usually interact with each other. People enter late life with different biological and social resources, worldviews, and life experiences, which gerontologists must consider.

The health status of bereaved persons will affect how mobile they can be during widowhood, whether they can live alone and care for themselves, and how they will spend their time, that is, in what recreational activities they will participate. Hansson and Stroebe (2007) conclude that a widowed person's predeath health status predicts his or her physical well-being more than any other influence during bereavement. Caregivers typically are the most vulnerable bereaved persons, especially if they neglected their own health while caring for their ill spouses; often they enter widowhood with impaired immune systems.

Bereaved persons' psychological resources also affect their adjustment, and those with well-developed coping skills and cognitive capacities will adjust better to their losses than bereaved adults without these resources. In addition, relationship characteristics, such as how close and dependent a couple was, affect how well a widowed person will adjust to bereavement (Carr et al., 2000).

Environmental influences, and especially social supports, also influence how easily people adjust to bereavement (Dimond, Lund, & Caserta, 1987). Hansson and Stroebe (2007) attribute the greater depression among older bereaved men relative to older bereaved women to the more restricted social networks that widowers usually maintain. Compared to older widows, older men's social networks typically are smaller and less intimate, which might explain why widowers tend to remarry more often than widows (Lee, DeMaris, Bavin, & Sullivan, 2001). Death circumstances also influence how people respond during bereavement. For example, Richardson and Balaswamy (2001) and Carr, House, Wortman, Nesse, and Kessler (2001) found that survivors feel less distress when their spouses die at home, when they are with them at the moment of death, and when they have opportunities to talk about death and the dying process with their spouses than when widowed persons lack these opportunities. When spouses die violently, such as from an accident, suicide, or homicide, bereaved persons have an increased risk of developing traumatic grief reactions (Zisook, Chentsova-Dutton, & Shuchter, 1998).

Interventions

Most widowed persons adjust well to the loss of their spouse without formal counseling, and if clinicians offer counseling prematurely, they risk alienating bereaved persons' friends and family members. The people who benefit most from bereavement counseling are those who seek out these services, but researchers who have evaluated the efficacy of clinical interventions for bereaved persons have found only moderate benefits from these treatments (Jordan & Neimeyer, 2003). New models of grief counseling have emerged over the last few years and preliminary evaluations of these contemporary models are positive. Caserta and Lund (2007) currently are testing out the Dual Process Model of bereavement (DPM), which Stroebe and Schut proposed in 1999. Hansson and Stroebe (2007) continue to refine the DPM and integrate theories about stress and coping, attachment styles, and meaning-making into their model.

The Dual Process Model of bereavement, which Stroebe and Schut (1999) developed from the work of Lazarus and Folkman's (1984) cognitive stress theory, is organized around three concepts: loss-oriented coping, restoration-oriented coping, and oscillation. (This model of bereavement was described in the Introduction to this text and summarized briefly in the present chapter with regard to the older bereaved partner, Barry, but is herewith more completely described as an evidence-based practice treatment strategy.) Loss-oriented coping is comprised of activities associated with the death, such as organizing burials, funerals, and memorial services; dealing with finances and medical costs from treatment of the deceased; and organizing clothes and other items belonging to the lost spouse. This coping approach focuses on the deceased and resembles what many experts previously have referred to as "grief work." Restoration-oriented coping involves what needs to be dealt with following the loss and varies from socializing with friends to distracting oneself with hobbies or home repairs. When widowed persons learn new tasks that their deceased spouses previously performed, survivors feel empowered and more independent. Although loss-oriented coping evokes negative feelings, restoration-oriented coping usually leads to more positive affect (Richardson, 2007). Although most bereaved persons engage in more loss-oriented than restoration-oriented coping early in bereavement and more restoration-oriented than loss-oriented activities later, most bereaved persons shift back and forth between these two types of coping throughout bereavement. Stroebe and Schut refer to this as "oscillation," which is the third major concept in the DPM. According to Hansson and Stroebe (2007), oscillation involves the process of alternating from attending to and focusing on feelings and events associated with the loss to avoiding those feelings and experiences related to the loss. For example, most bereaved persons take respites from grieving by visiting with friends, watching a movie, taking a walk, or eating at a restaurant. Over time people develop new routines, friends, and activities, yet they maintain their bonds with their deceased spouses and still think about them.

Few researchers have tested out the DPM, but findings from recent studies are encouraging. Caserta and Lund (2007) developed the Inventory of Daily Widowed Life (IDWL) to measure loss-oriented and restoration-oriented coping and are evaluating a 14-week intervention for widows and widowers based on the DPM. The findings from this ongoing research will shed light on how well the DPM improves bereavement outcomes for widows and widowers and on which components of the model work best under which conditions. One surprising finding is that restoration-oriented coping seems more efficacious than loss-oriented coping, both early and later during bereavement (Caserta & Lund, 2007). Richardson and Balaswamy (2001) found support for the DPM using a cross-sectional analysis of older widowed men, and, in a later replication of this study using a longitudinal research design, Richardson (2007) found similar results: specifically, that bereaved persons engage in both loss-oriented and restoration-oriented coping throughout bereavement. Bisconti, Bergeman, and Boker (2004) found support for the oscillation process that Stroebe and Schut (1999) proposed in their study of newly bereaved widows.

Lund, Caserta, deVries, and Wright (2004) explain that the DPM represents a "paradigm shift away from the long-standing and pervasive approach of using an almost exclusive emphasis on psychoemotional aspects surrounding loss orientation issues" (p. 13). Hansson and Stroebe (2007) already have expanded the DPM and incorporated new developments into an integrated framework of bereavement. As experts revise and test out these models, we will better understand the relevant predictors, circumstances, and resources that lead to favorable bereavement outcomes that practitioners can apply with those who need counseling.

Implications and Interventions for Ms. Ramsey

In the case of Ms. Ramsey, a practitioner using a biopsychosocial approach first would consider Ms. Ramsey's health, given the prolonged caregiving she experienced. Many caregivers become depressed, stressed, and exhausted after caring for someone with a protracted illness. The practitioner also would need to address Ms. Ramsey's dependency on her husband and explore how she might learn new skills, strengthen her resources, and, in general, become more independent. In addition, the practitioner needs to consider the social context surrounding the death of Ms. Ramsey's husband. This would involve exploring the circumstances of the death, location of death (i.e., whether her husband died at home or in a hospital), family supports, and access to formal and informal assistance. Finally, the practitioner should consider Ms. Ramsey's cultural background and evaluate how this might affect how she copes with her feelings.

A comprehensive assessment of Ms. Ramsey would reveal that she overemphasizes loss-oriented coping at the expense of restoration-oriented coping, and requires help developing a more balanced coping strategy. The practitioner ideally would work with Ms. Ramsey to engage in more restoration-oriented activities that would boost Ms. Ramsey's confidence, pleasurable experiences, and positive affect. For example, the practitioner and Ms. Ramsey might identify a homework assignment for her to visit a neighbor or drive to a mall to shop. She also needs to experiment with activities to identify new pleasurable activities in which she might participate. By encouraging Ms. Ramsey to talk about her feelings with others, the practitioner will help Ms. Ramsey make more sense of her experience and find meaning from her loss. To the extent that she learns new tasks she previously avoided, Ms. Ramsey will develop more resources and become more independent. The practitioner also might link Ms. Ramsey to community services, such as a widow support group, if she is interested. By using a biopsychosocial approach and applying ideas from the contemporary models of bereavement, the practitioner inevitably intervenes with Ms. Ramsey on many levels, taking into account her unique background and individual characteristics, including her dependency and relationship styles, as well as social influences, including the gender roles she experienced throughout her life. This integrated approach will encourage Ms. Ramsey to engage in more restoration-oriented coping that will improve her well-being, broaden her worldview, and help her become more independent. The practitioner will empower Ms. Ramsey by encouraging her to develop new skills and resources. The prognosis for Ms. Ramsey is excellent. Most women who have lost their husbands adjust well to widowhood. Widows and widowers typically learn new tasks and adapt new routines, hobbies, and relationships, but practitioners can facilitate bereaved persons' personal growth by keeping abreast of new developments that emerge with respect to bereavement in late life and by applying intervention models that are well grounded conceptually and empirically.

OLIVIA'S JOURNEY

Michelle Brooks, MSS, LCSW

Michelle Brooks is the Director of Social Services at Keystone Hospice in Philadelphia, Pennsylvania. Michelle's social work career has been dedicated to end-of-life care both in bereavement counseling and hospice social work. The work of Robert Neimeyer has heavily influenced her practice in end-of-life care. Metaphor is used extensively in hospice work, both by the patient and by the worker. "Olivia's Journey" is an example of using metaphor and meaning-making.

Relevant History

Born in Romania in 1935, the eldest child of working-class parents, Olivia spent most of her childhood escaping Nazi occupation. Primarily traveling by foot, the family was on the move until arriving in America in 1951. Olivia was 6 years old when this journey began.

A year after arriving in the United States at age 17, Olivia accepted a position as a nanny. Unable to speak English, but motivated to learn, Olivia spent her free time at the movies learning the language of her new home. Many years later, at age 62, Olivia earned a G.E.D. (General Educational Development) degree.

Olivia married, had one biological daughter, and was mother to countless foster children. Olivia's home was a designated safe house for abused children—some would stay a few days, others stayed through adulthood. Olivia raised four foster children as her own. In 1975 Olivia was suddenly widowed. With five children at home, she reentered the workforce, retiring only a few months prior to the hospice referral for terminal cancer.

Meeting Olivia

The work with Olivia spanned a period of 7 months. I first met 71-year-old Olivia when she and her daughters arrived at Keystone House for a tour. Immediately I was attracted to this bright and humorous woman. A fiercely independent woman, Olivia wanted a plan of care that would allow her to maintain her independence, which for Olivia meant remaining at home. Anna, Olivia's biological daughter, was most concerned for her mother's safety and felt strongly that inpatient care would be a better option. Keystone Hospice is unique in that it offers both levels of care. The daughters were split on what type of care Olivia needed, but ultimately deferred to Olivia to make the decision. Hospice would begin at home, with the option of moving to Keystone House if she required additional support.

During the next 7 months there were to be two inpatient stays: the first shortly after being admitted to home hospice and the second for the last 5 weeks of Olivia's life. The disease progression was a course of slow debilitation. The effect of overall weakness and compromised motor skills (specifically walking) were the most challenging biological changes for Olivia.

Discussion of End-of-Life and Terminal Illness

End-of-life losses are numerous, complicated, and interdependent. The losses begin with the diagnosis. Instantly Olivia's identity was transformed from Olivia the healthy vibrant independent person into Olivia the sick cancer patient. Chemotherapy altered her physical appearance. Her hair was now replaced by wigs and scarves, her ruddy complexion now gaunt and pasty. Olivia, who would later be eulogized as a person who was always in charge, was now being managed by physicians, tests, scans, and family members. Everyone seemed to have an opinion about what was best for Olivia and the sicker she became, the less they seemed willing to consult with her. The decision to initiate hospice care was decided by someone else; everyone seemed to know what was best for Olivia.

Quality of life is a core tenet of the hospice philosophy. Quality of life can mean many things, but for Olivia it meant getting some semblance of her life back. Remaining at home was essential to Olivia's quality of life. Her home was an anchor to her identity. Supporting Olivia's decision to stay at home was where our work began.

Terminal illness is developmentally challenging. The diagnosis accelerates the process and interferes with the normal progression of aging. Olivia's ego strengths and her capacity to maintain identity coherence throughout her challenging life and childhood were assets. The developmental task of old age is the acceptance of death. Olivia didn't like the idea of dying, but from the moment I met her it was clear that she accepted the idea of death. The theoretical acceptance of death is only the beginning of the process. Olivia really was dying. To support Olivia's integrity through this process, the work focused on acknowledging, witnessing, and validating her losses.

The first admission to the inpatient facility was during a respiratory crisis. Modifications to symptom management had Olivia feeling better in a few weeks and she was ready to return home. The family, fearful of Olivia living independently, insisted she remain at Keystone House. Olivia was heartbroken. She pined to return home. The losses were stacking up. The tangible loss of her home was also attached to the loss of her social role as the head of the family and it severed her ties to her community. The woman who once made the decisions now had no voice in the process. Olivia's earlier losses of having been driven from her homeland and ultimately settling in a country where people could not understand her native tongue served to compound these new losses. In an effort to reclaim her identity, Olivia did what had worked in the past—she became resilient and persistent in negotiating a way home. After working with Olivia on these issues, I approached the family with a plan to take her home. The plan hinged on two things: a stair glide installation, connecting the main floor to the second floor, and 24-hour home health aide support. Olivia, once staunchly opposed to in-home help, agreed to the plan. Olivia was going home.

My first visit with Olivia after she returned home confirmed that this was absolutely the right decision. Olivia regained a sense of her identity and was once again living her life. Living through one's dying is the ultimate goal of hospice care. In many ways the loss of her identity, which was wound tightly to her home, was a greater loss for Olivia than the physical losses that were simultaneously taking place. The physical losses she could manage, provided she was emotionally connected to her identity.

The next few months were wonderful for Olivia. The holidays filled her home with family and tradition. She finally got around to sharing her cookie recipes with her family, who did all the baking with her instruction. She was getting increasingly weaker, but her spirit was in good shape.

As Olivia's ability to walk became increasingly compromised, she became distressed. This physical loss was particularly difficult. At this point she had undergone so many physical changes (i.e., increased shortness of breath, lapses in memory, vision impairment, hearing impairment, and generalized weakness and fatigue), yet it was the loss of walking that distressed her most. She would often say, "If I could get these legs moving, I will be fine." It was while exploring the meaning attached to walking that Olivia shared the story of her trek across Europe. The story began at age 6. An hour later she was 17 years of age and heading to a strange city for her first job. Her legs had always carried her. No wonder this was such a profound loss. I acknowledged the loss and the importance her legs had played in sparing her life and leading her to freedom. "What a huge loss this must be for you," I said; to which she replied, "It is." The two of us sat quietly for some time, honoring the loss of the legs. Validating and honoring this loss was important for Olivia. She never spoke to me about walking again, and gradually she walked less and less. Reminiscence and life review are commonly used interventions when working with dying patients. This work provided Olivia the opportunity to tell an important defining life story and it allowed the necessary space to mourn the loss of her mobility.

In subsequent visits Olivia began to talk about physically dying. She wondered what it would be like, how it might feel. She wasn't frightened, she was curious. I asked her if she had thought about what a good death would be. She replied, "It should be simple." She defined simple as not a big deal and that she would not feel any pain. Throughout the course of her illness, Olivia did not have significant pain, and there was no reason to believe that her death would be any different. The nurse and I discussed this with her, reassuring her that there were medications that would ease the process. She told us that she didn't know if she wanted to die in her home. She wanted to know if she had the option to return to Keystone House. We assured her that we would support her wherever she wanted to be. At first I was surprised by this inquiry to return to Keystone House but it seemed Olivia was wrapping up her business at home; she was moving on. Her focus had shifted from living to preparing to die. Eventually Olivia did return to Keystone House to die, but this time it was her decision. Olivia was dying, but she was in control.

Olivia was sleeping more and more. She could hardly remember watching an entire TV program, but what Olivia liked about her new sleeping habits was that she was dreaming about her deceased parents. She was enjoying these dreams and, unlike her relationship with them while they were alive, her dream relationship was loving and comforting. Initially the increased fatigue was distressing, but now that she was spending time with her parents, Olivia didn't seem to mind. Olivia's sister Mary found this curious. Olivia had a particularly difficult relationship with her mother; the parents Olivia was describing were not at all like the parents they had known. Olivia was renegotiating her relationship with her mother and beginning her transition.

Endings

As the dying patient gets closer to the time of death, it is not uncommon for the individual to incorporate the use of metaphor. Metaphor provides a safe way for the dying to talk about their death. Hospice workers will join patients in these metaphoric conversations. On one of the last visits to Olivia's home, metaphor was used to talk about Olivia's approaching death. Olivia was getting weaker. She used the wheelchair most of the time and she spent most of her time sleeping. While driving to her home I realized that Olivia and I had now known each other through three seasons. When I arrived Olivia was resting quietly in her recliner. I took her hand and shared with her what I had been thinking about during my drive to her home.

M: The weather is beautiful. While I was driving over here I was thinking about how we have known each other through three seasons.

O: Oh yeah?

M: Well, we met in the fall when you came to Keystone House, we visited together throughout the cold winter months, and now here we are, it's spring.

O: (after a long pause) What's next?

M: (pausing) I don't know.

M: (after a long pause) Would it be enough?

O: (she thought for several minutes) I have always loved spring.

Several weeks later, on a beautiful spring morning, Olivia died.

One of Olivia's goals during her second stay at Keystone House was to live until Mother's Day. She slept most of the time, her language was aphasic, and conversations were always brief. The one thing she always wanted to know was what day it was. Knowing the value of Mother's Day to this woman who had mothered many, I engaged in a daily countdown to Mother's Day. Four days before Mother's Day I told Olivia what day it was and continued the countdown, "Only four days until Mother's Day." Olivia smiled, opened her eyes and said, "Another set of sheets." I was initially confused by this statement, so I repeated it back to her, "Another set of sheets?" She smiled broadly, "Another set of sheets." I then asked, "Do you mean another goal reached?" She shook her head, "Yes, another set of sheets." Olivia had a big rally on Mother's Day. Three of her five children, their families, and her niece helped her to celebrate. She was alert, ate all her favorite foods, and totally enjoyed the day. The following day, she began to decline. She died the following Sunday.

SUMMARY

Later adulthood is filled with a variety of types of losses but provides some opportunity for growth in terms of self-reflection and reinvention.

This phase of life brings a gradual release from many of the daily demands of work and family, depending on one's resources and health, and the chance to invent a new structure of life. There is more individuation at this phase of life than during any other. Thus, although older adults have many issues in common, they also have many differences from one another, having lived long and different lives. Social support emerges as one of the most important factors in mitigating the negative impact of loss. However, it is the older adult's perception of this support, as to its meaningfulness and the actual delivery of the support, that enables the older adult to derive comfort from the social support offered to him/her or sought by him/her. It is important to understand the need for providing meaningful social support for the bereaved elderly and for a counselor to engage the older adult in assessing the appropriate network for her or him to seek so that his or her perception of support will be meaningful.

Resilience is an important issue to consider in understanding and working with the elderly concerning issues of loss. In the case of "Hal," an Alzheimer's patient, his wife and caregiver, Rachael, demonstrated a high degree of resilience, given the high level of stress and loss that she faced each day as she took care of her spouse over the course of 7 years. "Olivia," a hospice patient, demonstrates resilience throughout her life. She spent most of her childhood escaping Nazi occupation, but later raised foster children in her home, which was important to her identity. In her last few months of life Olivia negotiated her right to move back home (with the help of a social worker) for several months to reclaim her identity, before she died in the hospice. In her final days of life she was curious, rather than frightened, about what the process of dying might be like. With Olivia, the social worker used intervention strategies of meaning-making and metaphor. Meaning-making has emerged as an important strategy in working with the older adult on issues of loss, as discussed earlier in this chapter regarding spousal loss.

In the case of Ms. Ramsey we see less inherent resilience as she becomes more mired in the loss-oriented coping strategy of mourning following her husband's death. Her dependence on her husband for both physical and emotional needs may help to explain her difficulties in moving forward in her life and engaging in restoration-oriented, life-affirming activities. In this case the social worker used the Dual Process Model of coping (an evidence-based practice intervention that has been documented in the reading in this chapter, "Marital Bereavement in Later Adulthood") to help Ms. Ramsey develop a more balanced coping strategy with regard to loss-oriented and restoration-oriented coping.

This strategy may help Ms. Ramsey to become more active in identifying new pleasurable activities that she might enjoy, improve her self-confidence, and help her become more independent. Finally, if Ms. Ramsey agreed, the social worker might link Ms. Ramsey to a widow's support group to increase the degree of social support in her life.

10 Conclusions

In the Introduction we began with the premise that loss is at the heart of growth—that the destabilizing force of loss also promotes growth and self-reflection as well as an attempt on the mourner's part to engage in meaning-making, if the mourner's experience is supported and validated. From the prenatal losses such as pregnancy loss, to the teen's experience with the murder of a friend, to the young adult struggling with addictions and the older adult struggling with the pain of the loss of an adult child, the resilience of the individual in his or her response to loss provides hope that human beings can move forward following a maturational change brought on by development or a tragic loss of a loved one. Further, we believe that grief and loss, although uncomfortable, are part of our human existence and that although human beings can process the experience of loss without professional help, most people process losses more readily when they have an opportunity to talk with someone.

Our text has presented teachers and clinicians with an overview of some of the maturational, disenfranchised, and other types of losses that individuals experience across the lifespan. "Sadness is indeed a normal part of human nature" (Horowitz & Wakefield, 2007, p. 27) and a response to certain triggers of loss. Three types of variables that trigger sadness include losses related to attachment, those related to status/resources, and those related to meaning or valued goals (Horowitz & Wakefield, 2007). These types of losses are common across all cultures and are the types of losses that are represented in our text. Any of these losses can threaten long-term well-being and may evoke intense sadness. However, these responses do not necessarily imply depression. Our view on sadness is represented by the thesis of Horowitz and Wakefield (2007), who believe that sadness is a natural response to loss and does not imply that the individual meets a symptomatic criterion for a disorder. "Sadness after loss is found in all societies, among infants, and in our closest primate cousins; it is clearly biologically rooted and not merely a creation of social scripts" (Horowitz & Wakefield, 2007, p. 51). Thus, sadness and grief are adaptive responses to many of the losses experienced by individuals throughout the lifespan and may function to promote growth.

MATURATIONAL LOSSES AS EXAMPLES OF DISENFRANCHISED LOSSES

We have attempted to demonstrate that as children and adults move through the lifespan they will experience various maturational losses that are relatively common in each age group, but which are met with little support by others for the very reason that they are considered "fairly normal" and/or stigmatized. In effect, these losses and the grief that individuals experience are not validated by society in a way that allows the individual to grieve with recognition that this is important work. This makes these losses disenfranchised (Doka, 1989, 2002). One of the first is the loss of the safe uterine environment from which all humans are thrust, surely without their own intent or control. As infants age, they lose the total unconditional caregiving of their parent/s. Most children then move to school environments where they are judged, sometimes for the first time in their lives. None of these are viewed as losses requiring support from others, yet they do seem to entail experiences of loss.

Other maturational losses are more traditionally recognized as losses, but disenfranchised nonetheless. For example, young adults who are making the transition from dependence on family of origin for support to depending on their own resources are often not recognized for the losses they are experiencing as they try to create a new life. In young adulthood, the loss of a romantic relationship is often not validated by friends and family who see the young adult as having many more opportunities to invest in other relationships. The young adult is left having to grieve in silence as those around him or her do not understand the depth of sadness that accompanies such a loss.

Young adults who move from being a couple to becoming parents are often not recognized for the loss their marital relationship endures. A new child demands so much energy and attention, which the young couple once had for one another. Society views the birth of a child as a very positive event so that family, friends, and perhaps the couple themselves are unable to recognize the degree of sadness and grief they are experiencing for a maturational change appropriate for this phase of life. Alternatively, when a young woman suffers a miscarriage, friends and family often say "Don't worry, there probably was something wrong with it" or "You'll have many opportunities to have other children," thereby disenfranchising the loss and indicating that support is not viewed as necessary.

In middle adulthood, many adults are choosing, or perhaps in some cases being forced, to move from the home that they created earlier, often the place where they raised their children. Although for some this move can be a transition that is greeted with joy because they are moving to a place that may represent a more satisfying lifestyle, for many it represents a more severe loss as they are moving because of financial reasons or ill health. For all midlife adults who make a major move at this time, the loss often goes unrecognized given the energy that is required to reestablish the new home. The secondary loss that occurs with the loss of a home is the physical availability of lifetime friendships and familiar surroundings.

The importance of the loss of employment in middle adulthood is also often undervalued by society. It is during this phase of life that adults work on the major task of balancing work and family life. When midlife adults are forced to leave their place of work as a result of downsizing or restructuring of the labor market, this change can be experienced as a severe loss, as unemployment can be devastating in a way that interferes with a basic developmental task. Furthermore, there is no societal ritual that recognizes this loss or provides a socially sanctioned time for grieving and recovery. This is complicated by society's expectations that the unemployed adult be continually motivated and efficient in seeking new employment at a time when s/he feels a sense of shame and self-doubt.

Many midlife adults experience identity crises with the recognition that they need to mourn the loss of the dream of early adulthood and what they had hoped to accomplish. This loss is one that most of society may not recognize because the midlife individual may look like s/he is pleased with his or her new lifestyle, yet underneath s/he may be suffering from a severe change in identity for which s/he may not have been prepared. At the end of chapter 7, the case of Ben illustrates the loss of a goal and a changed vision of himself. However, Ben is able to cope with his thwarted expectations and to modify his vision for professional and personal success only after he grieves the loss of what he hoped for in early adulthood. Also in chapter 7, Kudu's immigration to the United States from Zambia entailed the loss of her tribal identity as well as the loss of an identity that provided and defined social bonds, relationships, and commitments that provided her with stability and a sense of security. To function as an individual in the United States, Kudu had to integrate and use her tribal connections as she redefined who she wanted to be within her church family in her new home.

The older adult is often seen as being able to weather any loss, as s/he has already suffered other losses that should prepare him or her for any that s/he incurs in the later stages of adulthood. In the vignette of Helen, who lost her adult child, we can see what an unjust myth this is. Ms. Ramsey (at the end of chapter 9) demonstrates the struggle she is having with the loss of her spouse, on whom she had depended for many emotional and financial needs. This couple had been married for 50 years and enjoyed doing most of their daily activities together. Clinicians need to be reminded about this cohort of elderly in which the women were much more dependent on their spouses for financial and emotional support than are women in young and middle adulthood. Both Ms. Ramsey and Rachael, a caregiver whose husband suffered from Alzheimer's disease, demonstrate how caregivers are often neglected by health care providers who focus on the patient. Furthermore, because of the continual losses associated with the phases of dementia that she faced with her husband, Rachael was so consumed with each loss that she failed to recognize the fact that she, herself, was grieving. This is disenfranchisement induced by the self to protect the individual from the pain of chronic loss. Disenfranchised losses may present as losses unrecognized and unsupported by others in ways that Doka (1989,

2002) has well described. We suggest that another category of disenfranchised loss may exist in the maturational losses described throughout and summarized previously.

IMPORTANCE OF THE DUAL PROCESS MODEL OF COPING WITH BEREAVEMENT

In our Introduction we spoke of the importance of understanding the Dual Process Model of bereavement presented by Stroebe and Schut (1999) in which the bereaved oscillates between two modes of functioning so as to adapt to his/her loss. One mode describes the bereaved as yearning and searching for the absent person or the lost object, while focusing on the loss (loss orientation), whereas the other mode describes the bereaved as focusing on rebuilding his/her life by engaging in new relationships, activities, and other distractions that move the bereaved away from active grieving (restoration orientation). This cycling allows needed time both for processing the loss and for distraction and restoration, during which the bereaved has a break from experiencing the intensity of his/her emotions of grief. "This back-and-forth process helps people integrate the loss without grieving constantly" (Hooyman & Kramer, 2006, p. 42). Hogan and Schmidt's (2002) research used structural equation modeling to provide more support for the Dual Process Model of coping with bereavement by demonstrating that "intrusion and avoidance are both part of the bereavement process" (p. 631). In the early chapters that describe toddlers and elementary-school-age children, we have seen how children use dual process, moving in and out of loss and restoration modes quickly and with little transition. Although adults are often uncomfortable with children's responses to death, children model well how to move between the two states without judgment, second guessing, and critiquing the very process that will help them heal. Adults often have a much more difficult time permitting this movement between active grieving and distraction or overt focus on moving forward with life. We theorize that this is a place where grief theory has been problematic: as mentioned in the first chapter, many believed the "grief hypothesis" and believed that all therapeutic work after bereavement must stay focused on the active grief work (focus on loss orientation). We see, however, that clients benefit when the grief counselor is able to model dual process and give permission to focus on both the grief and the rest of life, allowing the mourning of tears and the distractions of everyday life.

The examples of the boys' births in readings by Faust Piro (chapters 3 and 4), both of whom were diagnosed with genetic disorders Fragile X and Down syndrome, respectively), show one way that dual process works to enable coping. Had their mother stayed focused on her grief over each diagnosis, she would not have been able to gather information, advocate for her sons' care, or navigate the medical system as well as she did. Taking an active approach to restoration orientation may be seen by some as a way of discharging anger and/or as distracting oneself, yet a good grief therapist understands that the movement between active expression of grief and engagement with the other parts of life allows the griever to find a new balance. Christine (from chapter 6) was struggling with infertility issues and demonstrated her wish to move away from the grief and sadness by not attending events such as baby showers and children's birthday parties so that she could cope with her regular, everyday life. On the other hand, when she and her husband were involved in infertility treatments she found herself dipping into the grief mode (loss orientation) when she felt hopeless each time they were unable to conceive a child.

In chapter 8, during the reinvention process, adults who are moving from one way of being in the world to another demonstrate this same tendency to oscillate between the loss orientation (their former life structure) and the restoration orientation (their newly created/reinvented life structure). In the case of Carla, the life transition of retirement brought with it the loss of social position, interaction with colleagues, and a sense of being a contributing member of society. To adapt to her new life she began to identify some aspects of her loss, such as the loss of work to structure her days, which might be replaced by evolving a new way to build structure into her life. In a sense, Carla had to move between two worlds at the same time to begin to create a new life structure.

In chapter 9, an older bereaved partner dips into an active grieving process (loss-orientation mode) when he experiences sadness and other emotions involved in coping with the loss of his partner. Alternatively, Barry learns new tasks and distracts himself with hobbies and new relationships that illustrate his ability to move between the mode of loss orientation and the mode of restoration orientation. Some literature (Caserta & Lund, 2007) has suggested that restoration-oriented coping is more helpful to both widows and widowers during both the early and later phases of the bereavement process. In chapter 9, an older widow overemphasized loss-oriented coping at the expense of restoration coping, which led to a more complicated grief reaction to the loss of her spouse. Using the Dual Process Model as an intervention strategy, a practitioner might work with this widow by helping her to develop a more balanced way of coping by supporting her to engage in more restoration-oriented activities that might boost her confidence and increase her pleasurable experiences.

IMPORTANCE OF CONTINUING BONDS

A landmark contribution to the world of grief theory occurred with the publication of *Continuing Bonds* by Klass, Silverman, and Nickman (1996). Their new paradigm clearly defined the importance of continuing the relationship with the deceased as the more heavily weighted work in grief and challenged the concept that disengaging from the deceased or lost loved one was the function of grief and mourning, "thereby freeing the survivor to invest in new relationships in the present" (C. Walter, 2003, p. 5). In fact, Klass et al. (1996) view these continuing bonds as a resource for enriching functioning in the present. Within this paradigm there is no zero-sum game with regard to the emotional energy involved in the grief process, so that the bereaved can invest in new relationships while still grieving the loss of their loved one (C. Walter, 2003). In this way the relationship with the deceased can, in fact, help the bereaved to prepare for or enrich any new relationships in which the survivor becomes involved. One of the most helpful concepts related to this new paradigm is that although one has lost a person or an ideal, one has not lost the relationship with that person or ideal. Instead the relationship with the deceased or the ideal changes and evolves over time. This new paradigm has been comforting to many bereaved adults who previously thought they had to "let go" of one relationship prior to forming a new one. Furthermore, the new paradigm questions the idea of closure in the experience of grief.

One area where this is particularly challenging is in the aftermath of perinatal death. Unlike death losses in which the continuing bond can be enhanced with linking objects (Volkan, 1985) and other memories, parents who lose a potential baby prior to birth are stymied in maintaining and continuing their relationship. They fear the idea that others will not recognize their loss of one relationship when another (a new pregnancy and healthy baby) comes along (McCoyd, 2007). They often need help affirming the ongoing relationship to the baby they dreamed of having (and lost) and differentiating it from a new pregnancy and/ or baby. Here, the work with a bereaved couple is enhanced by acknowledging the continuing bond and differentiating that bond from any new pregnancy to allow the couple to fully embrace the new relationship with the new member of the family. Continuing bonds are also challenging in many of the losses identified in the chapter on tweens and teens. When a love relationship ends, exemplified by the opening vignette about Andrea, whose boyfriend broke up with her, or like Carolyn, whose relationship with an adult of the same gender was deemed inappropriate because of the age difference, the person experiencing the loss often wishes to maintain the relationship with little change. Part of the work of acknowledging a loss is the transition into a new type of relationship that reflects the change in the bond—the continued bond is one of memory rather than ongoing relationship with the ex-lover. This is a difficult transition, but one in which the changed nature of the bond is a major aspect of the way the continuing bond is developed.

The use and transformation of continuing bonds with the deceased are illustrated in the case of Andrea (chapter 6), a young adult who lost her mother to breast cancer. Andrea believes that having her own daughter (becoming a mother herself) would be a way to keep her mother close to her. Andrea derives much comfort in the present by feeling as though her "mother is inside of her." Continuing and transforming bonds with the memory of her mother provides Andrea with comfort and empowers her to enhance her current life functioning.

In chapter 7, Arden's bereaved partner has continued a relationship with Arden by writing three beautiful poems and essays ("Before Our Time," "Sierra," and "Plastic"), included in the chapter, which describe her ongoing relationship with Arden following her death. Arden's partner is also using Arden's dog, Sierra, as a way to comfort herself with a transitional object that belonged to Arden during her life.

In chapter 8 the two cases that are presented at the end of the chapter both illustrate how each woman who was "reinventing" her life continued a relationship with her pre-reinvention world while beginning the process of creating her new world. This does not imply that the women and men who are involved in reinvention are not grieving the loss of their former lifestyle; they are using that lifestyle to inform their new perspectives on themselves and their purpose, goals, or work. In effect, they are shifting the balance so that some parts of their lives receive more energy than others. This shows how the continuing bonds are informative and nurturing of the new involvements in one's life after a loss. Transformation of continuing bonds with the deceased and the capacity to oscillate between the two modes of loss-oriented and restoration-oriented coping help the bereaved to integrate and consolidate the loss, moving the bereaved toward the capacity for meaning-making.

MEANING-MAKING AS A PROCESS OF GROWTH

Social work has always embraced the role of the social context in people's lives. From Mary Richmond and her focus on social diagnosis (1917) to Jane Addams and her assertions that the social environment is critical to any relationships and interventions (Addams, 1910, 1930), social workers have recognized that the person is affected by the environment in which s/he finds him or herself. Also, individuals experience their environments differently based on the ways they make meaning of their social context. Indeed, there is evidence that when people experience tremendous frequency of loss, there is a desensitization that can occur that has the potential for leaving individuals so affected by their environment that they seem not to grieve (Scheper-Hughes, 1993), which shows the way meaning-making actually affects societal norms. Though seldom as dramatic, meaning-making has been shown to be an integral part of the work bereaved persons do as they try to understand the nature of death in general, the impact of the specific death in particular, and the way that any particular loss changes their sense of self and society.

Neimeyer, Prigerson, and Davies (2002) argue that "human beings seek meaning in mourning and do so by struggling to construct a coherent account of their bereavement that preserves a sense of continuity with who they have been while also integrating the reality of the changed world into their conception of who they must be now" (pp. 235–236). Hogan and Schmidt (2002) concur with Neimeyer et al. (2002) in their research study about The Grief to Personal Growth Model tested with bereaved adults. They suggest that the bereaved are transformed by their experience with loss when they are propelled to revise and change their worldview and create a new identity (Hogan & Schmidt, 2002, p. 629). From the experiences of parents who have lost a child, to teens who have lost a friend, to bereaved adults who have lost a life partner, it seems clear that meaning-making is the important process that enables the individual to put the loss together so that s/he can move forward with a revised narrative of how s/he will function in the world.

Going on being—so important to the work of D. W. Winnicott (1953/1965)—propels the bereaved to get more involved in meaningful work. Self-narratives are often profoundly challenged by loss and bereavement; that is, our efforts to preserve a coherent self-narrative are disrupted by the loss of significant others on whom "our life stories depend" (Neimeyer et al., 2002, p. 239). The losses of significant others on whom we have relied to provide a particular "fund of shared memories" (Neimeyer et al., p. 239) as well as to be witnesses to our past may prompt the bereaved to "relearn the self" and "relearn the world" as a result of loss (Attig, 1996, as quoted in Neimeyer, 2002, p. 239). The experience of teens who have lost a friend through murder, presented in chapter 5, and that of bereaved partners and spouses who have lost their significant other, presented in chapters 6, 7, and 9, are similar in their search for meaning and their declaration that they are now living with a new intent—to appreciate life more and to make each day count.

In chapters 2 and 3, we see that making meaning is of critical importance when parents are mourning the death of a child. The sense of needing to find a purpose for a child's shortened life seems to weigh particularly heavy for parents who expected to follow the "normal" societal script and die before their child/ren did. Klass (Klass et al., 1996) ties this need for meaning-making to a form of continuing bond as the parents develop movements and agencies that help to promote societal and children's well-being in the memory of their deceased child. We see this on a national scale as Alex's Lemonade Stands spring up across the United States as a way to raise money to fight childhood cancers. Parents often struggle with the spiritual implications of a God viewed as omnipotent, yet who did not rescue their child from death. Meaning-making is often necessary both on the level of reassessing one's spiritual beliefs and on the level of figuring out how to make meaning of the existence of the child in the parent's life.

Christine (chapter 6) and her husband, with the help of a social worker, decided to end fertility treatments after 4½ years of trying to become pregnant. To help them with the transition of "letting go of treatment," they developed a ritual of writing letters to the biological child they would never have and made a large donation to UNICEF for children who had been born but needed help to survive. Just as the worker did with this couple, practitioners can help bereaved clients to make meaning of their experience with loss by helping them to reflect on the life lessons they have learned from their experiences with loss. Questions such as "Where did you find surprise sources of strength?" and "What untapped strengths have you discovered?" and "How has this loss experience changed your life?" can help clients to make meaning of their experiences. Practitioners can help clients who have suffered disenfranchised losses (such as Ricky in chapter 6) by validating their experiences and helping them to find fulfillment by forgiving those who discriminated against them. Bereaved clients may find that a loss is the impetus that causes them to reassess their spiritual and emotional lives, while also reevaluating their priorities in a way that not only involves meaning-making, but leads to a new self-image.

Resilience through new meaning-making is demonstrated by Arden's partner (chapter 7), who, as a bereaved lesbian partner, experiences incredible discrimination from the medical profession and society at large. Through forgiveness and her own grief work she is able to move forward months after Arden's death to return to school and become a minister and hospice chaplain. This resilience is remarkable in one sense, yet it is present in many of the cases presented throughout our text. Hal's widow (chapter 9) makes meaning of her experience as a caregiver to a spouse with Alzheimer's disease, by becoming invested in training others to work more supportively with patients with this disease through her work with a local Alzheimer's organization.

Among the best predictors for eventual adaptation to a loss is the struggle to make sense of the death or loss by the survivor as well as to discover some "life lesson in the loss" (Neimeyer et al., 2002, p. 240). These survivors tend to experience personal growth through their experience with trauma and loss. Based on their experiential research study, Hogan and Schmidt (2002) urge clinicians to help the bereaved by "rediscovering hope for the future through reconstructing new ways to find meaning and purpose in their permanently altered lives" (Hogan & Schmidt, 2002, pp. 629–630). In addition to being fully present to and accepting of the bereaved adult's story of loss, professionals need to support the survivor to "search for meaning and purpose as they reconstruct their sense of self and worldview following significant loss" (p. 630). In C. Walter's research (2003) with bereaved widows, widowers, and partners, she found that the participants who made meaning of their experiences were able to move forward in their lives. The degree of frustration increases both for individuals and for families who are unable to redefine the loss and tend to focus on the "negatives of the situation and wish that things were different than they are" (Neimeyer et al., 2002, p. 248). In a sense, these individuals and families are unable to grow from their experience with loss.

INTERVENTIONS

The field of grief counseling is undergoing a critical examination, with some researchers questioning the validity of grief counseling (Currier, Holland, & Neimeyer, 2007; Jordan & Neimeyer, 2003), whereas others (Larson & Hoyt, 2007) challenge the pessimism found in the preceding works (Currier et al.; Jordan & Neimeyer). At the 30th Annual Conference of the Association for Death Education and Counseling in April/ May of 2008, during the panel presentation "Research that Matters 2008: Does Grief Counseling Work—Yet?" Currier, Jordan, and Neimeyer argued that there is not much evidence that grief counseling makes a difference in working with a variety of populations. However, in the lively discussion that ensued, it was clear that the variable of the client–worker relationship had not been examined in the research conducted over the past few years. Because this variable has been so critical in understanding positive outcomes in research of other therapeutic methods, it is logical that new research that examines this variable in grief counseling needs to be done.

As should be obvious at this point in the text, all grief is unique to the person, his or her relationship with the lost entity, and his or her specific coping capacities and histories. That said, each grief counseling relationship is thus tailored to the specific individual. Much of the current research is unable to capture the complex, dynamic, and context-specific nature of this kind of grief work and may therefore not adequately reflect the effectiveness and efficacy of grief work overall. Skilled clinicians can tailor the work to the intensity of the mourner's grief, accurately assessing whether it is following a fairly typical grief trajectory or whether there is seemingly prolonged or complicated grief.

In the latter cases, the recognition of this need not move the clinician into viewing the mourner as having some sort of pathology, but rather indicates a likely need for more intensive grief-work services initially. In each case, the full exploration of the unique aspects of the mourner's current loss experience, in conjunction with exploration of his or her loss history, gives an indication of the kind of meaning-making work the individual is likely to use well and benefit from.

The vital importance of the holding environment à la Winnicott (1953/1965), as a facilitating variable in therapeutic work, may be one of the missing links when examining outcomes of grief counseling. For Winnicott, the holding environment consists of fundamental "caregiving activities and processes that facilitate growth and development" (Winnicott, 1953/1965, p. 33). "Furthermore, proper holding facilitates movement toward the achievement of integration" (McCoyd & Walter, 2007, p. 8). The holding environment may provide the bereaved with an opportunity to move back and forth between the two modes of functioning proposed by the Dual Process Model. An individual who is grieving often needs affirmation that his or her movement between these two modes of functioning is normal. The ability of the clinician to bear witness to the pain that the bereaved is experiencing is another part of the important intervention with individuals coping with loss. This witnessing is clearly demonstrated in the case of Christine (chapter 6), when the author discusses how helpful the social worker was for Christine and her husband in struggling with the issue of infertility. If appropriate, it is also comforting and helpful to the survivor if the clinician can help him/her to discover ways that s/he can find (or affirm ways that s/he has found) to continue the relationship with the deceased. In chapter 6 these continuing bonds were clearly helpful to Pauline, who kept her ties with her lesbian partner, Jean, by joining an organ and tissue network, which represented a way for Pauline to stay connected with Jean through one of Jean's volunteer interests.

We believe that loss is at the heart of many problems that are presented to clinicians. Although many individuals and families come to clinicians with various presenting problems that are not current bereavement issues, the source of these problems is often a loss of some kind that has not been resolved. For example, relief from discomfort occurred for a family who was able to grieve the loss of a child who died 10 years prior to their presentation at a local mental health center, although the presenting problem was their 16-year-old son's drug addiction. When practitioners bear witness to a family's tale regarding the loss of a child years ago, they often see family members grow in new ways. Even disenfranchised maturational losses can sometimes spur anxiety and/or depression that brings a client into a clinician's office; in exploring the context for the anxiety or mood disorder, unrecognized but deeply felt losses often emerge as triggers for the current sense of discomfort. We argue that outcome research in the field of grief counseling needs to examine ways to capture and understand how various losses may present in clinical practice and to understand the ways the holding environment and therapeutic relationship promote positive outcomes. Until all clinicians understand the power of the relationship to validate clients' experiences of loss and help them to have a safe environment to actively make meaning while also enhancing continuing bonds, some grief work will be done in ways that have the potential to harm rather than heal.

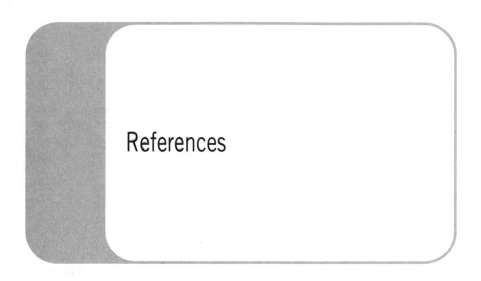

References

Abell, T., & Riely, C. (1992). Hyperemesis gravidarum. *Gastroenterology Clinics of North America, 21*(4), 835–849.

Abrams, L. S., & Curran, L. (2007). Not just a middle-class affliction: Crafting a social work research agenda on postpartum depression. *Health & Social Work, 32*(4), 289–296.

ACOG. (2004). Nausea and vomiting of pregnancy. *American College of Obstetricians and Gynecologists (ACOG) Practice Bulletin* No. 52, *103*(4), 803–815.

Adams, M. M., Harlass, F. E., Sarno, A. P., Read, J. A., & Rawlings, J. S. (1994). Antenatal hospitalization among enlisted service-women, 1987–1990. *Obstetrics & Gynecology, 84*, 35–39.

Addams, J. (1910). *Twenty years at Hull House with autobiographical notes.* New York: Macmillan.

Addams, J. (1930). *The second twenty years at Hull House.* New York: Macmillan.

Ainsworth, M. D. (1969). Object relations, dependency, and attachment: A theoretical review of the infant–mother relationship. *Child Development, 40*, 969–1025.

Ainsworth, M. D. S. (1982). Attachment: Retrospect and prospect. In C. M. Parkes & J. Stevenson-Hinde (Eds.), *The place of attachments in human behavior* (pp. 3–30). New York: Basic Books.

Ainsworth, M. D., Blehar, M. C., Waters, E., & Wall, S. (1978). *Patterns of attachment: Assessed in the strange situation and at home.* Hillsdale, NJ: Erlbaum.

Alzheimer's Disease Facts and Figures. (2007). Alzheimer's Association National Office. Chicago, IL: www.alz.org

American Academy of Pediatrics: Committee on Psychosocial Aspects of Child and Family Health. (2000). The pediatrician and childhood bereavement. *Pediatrics, 105*, 445–447.

American Cancer Society. (2008). *What are the key statistics for breast cancer?* Retrieved July 23, 2008, from http://www.cancer.org/docroot/CRI_2_4_1X

American Psychiatric Association. (2000). *Diagnostic and statistical manual of mental disorders: DSM-IV, text revision.* Washington, DC: American Psychiatric Press.

Anderson, S. (2000). *The journey from abandonment to healing.* New York: Berkley Books.

Applebaum, D., & Burns, G. (1991). Unexpected childhood death: Posttraumatic stress disorder in surviving siblings and parents. *Journal of Clinical Child Psychology, 20*, 114–120.

Applegate, J. S., & Shapiro, J. R. (2005). *Neurobiology for clinical social work: Theory and practice.* New York: W. W. Norton.

Arborelius, E., & Bremberg, S. (1992). What does a human relationship with the doctor mean? *Scandinavian Journal of Primary Health Care, 10*, 163–169.

Arbuckle, N., & deVries, B. (1995). The long-term effects of later life spousal and parental bereavement on personal functioning. *The Gerontologist, 35*, 637–647.

Arnold, E. (2005). A voice of their own: Women moving into their fifties. *Health Care for Women International, 26*, 630–651.

Ashford, B., Lecroy, C., & Lortie, K. (2001). *Human behavior in the social environment* (2nd ed.). Belmont, CA: Wadsworth/Thomson.

Atchley, R. C. (1980). *The social forces in later life.* Belmont, CA: Wadsworth.

Attig, T. (1996). *How we grieve: Relearning the world.* New York: Oxford University Press.

Bachman, D. H., & Lind, R. F. (1997). Perinatal social work and the high risk obstetrics patient. *Social Work in Health Care, 24*(3/4), 3–19.

Bacon, H., & Richardson, S. (2001). Attachment theory and child abuse: An overview of the literature for practitioners. *Child Abuse Review, 10*, 377–397.

Baer, J. (1999). Family relationships, parenting behavior, and adolescent deviance in three ethnic groups. *Families in Society, 3*, 279–285.

Balk, D. E. (1999). Bereavement and spiritual change. *Death Studies, 23*, 485–493.

Balk, D. E., & Corr, C. A. (2009). *Adolescent encounters with death, bereavement, and coping.* New York: Springer Publishing Company.

Ballou, J. W. (1978). *The psychology of pregnancy.* Lexington, MA: Lexington Books.

Bandura, A. (1977). *Social learning theory.* Englewood Cliffs, NJ: Prentice-Hall.

Barrett, R. K. (1996). Adolescents, homicidal violence, and death. In C. A. Corr & D. E. Balk (Eds.), *Handbook of adolescent death and bereavement* (pp. 42–64). New York: Springer Publishing Company.

Barry, H. R. (1980). Attitudes toward the pregnant body. In B. L. Blum (Ed.), *Psychological aspects of pregnancy, birth, and bonding* (pp. 227–231). New York: Human Sciences Press.

Bassin, D., Honey, M., & Kaplan, M. M. (1994). *Representations of motherhood.* New Haven, CT: Yale University Press.

Bassoff, E. S. (1987). *Mothers and daughters: Loving and letting go.* New York: New American Library.

Batten, M., & Oltjenbruns, K. A. (1999). Adolescent sibling bereavement as a catalyst for spiritual development: A model for understanding. *Death Studies, 23*, 529–546.

Bellin, M. H., & Kovacs, P. J. (2006). Fostering resilience in siblings of youth with a chronic health condition: A review of the literature. *Health & Social Work, 31,* 209–216.

Bellin, M. H., Kovacs, P. J., & Sawin, K. J. (2008). Risk and protective influences in the lives of siblings of youth with spina bifida. *Health & Social Work, 33,* 199–209.

Belsky, J., & Kelly, J. (1994). *The transition to parenthood: How a first child changes a marriage, why some couples grow closer and others apart.* New York: Dell.

Belsky, J., & Pensky, E. (1988). Marital changes across the transition to parenthood. *Marriage and Family Review, 12,* 133–156.

Bendor, S. J. (1990). Anxiety and isolation in siblings of pediatric cancer patients: The need for prevention. *Social Work in Health Care, 14*(3), 17–35.

Benedek, T. (1970). The psychobiology of pregnancy. In E. J. Anthony & T. Benedek (Eds.), *Parenthood; Its psychology and pathology* (pp. 137–151). Boston: Little, Brown.

Bevcar, D. (2001). *In the presence of grief. Helping family members resolve death, dying and bereavement issues.* New York: Guilford Press.

Berger, P. L., & Luckmann, T. (1967). *The social construction of reality.* Garden City, NY: Anchor.

Bibring, G. L. (1959). Some considerations of the psychological processes in pregnancy. *Psychoanalytic Study of the Child, 14,* 113–121.

Bibring, G. L., Dwyer, T. F., Huntington, D. S., & Valenstein, A. F. (1959). A study of the psychological processes in pregnancy and of the earliest mother–child relationship. *Psychoanalytic Study of the Child, 16,* 9–24.

Birnholz, J. C. (1981). The development of human fetal eye movement patterns. *Science, 213*(4508), 679–681.

Birnholz, J. C., & Benacerraf, B. R. (1983). The development of human fetal hearing. *Science, 222*(4623), 516–518.

Biro, F. M., Khoury, P., & Morrison, J. A. (2006). Influence of obesity on timing of puberty. *International Journal of Andrology, 29,* 272–277.

Birtchnell, J. (1970). Early parent death and mental illness. *British Journal of Psychiatry, 116,* 281–288.

Birtchnell, J. (1980). Women whose mothers died in childhood: An outcome study. *Psychological Medicine, 10,* 699–713.

Bisconti, T. L., Bergeman, C. S., & Boker, S. M. (2004). Emotional well-being in recently bereaved widows: A dynamical systems approach. *Journal of Gerontology: Psychological Sciences, 59B,* P158–P167.

Black, D. (1998). Coping with loss: Bereavement in childhood. *British Medical Journal, 316,* 931–933.

Blakemore, S.-J. (2008). The social brain in adolescence. *Nature Reviews Neuroscience, 9*(4), 267–277.

Blaxter, M. (1983). The causes of disease: Women talking. *Social Science and Medicine, 17*(2), 59–69.

Bluebond-Langner, M. (1978). *The private worlds of dying children.* Princeton, NJ: Princeton University Press.

Bogen, J. (1994). Neurosis: A MS-diagnosis. *Perspectives in Biology and Medicine, 32*(2), 263–272.

Bonanno, G. A. (2004). Loss, trauma, and human resilience: Have we underestimated the human capacity to thrive after extremely aversive events? *American Psychologist, 59*(1), 20–28.

Bonnano, G. A., Nesse, C. B., & Randolph, M. (2004). Prospective patterns of resilience and maladjustment during widowhood. *Psychology and Aging, 19*(2), 260–271.

Bonanno, G. A., Wortman, C. B., Lehman, D. R., Tweed, R. G., Haring, M., Sonnega, J., Carr, D., & Nesse, R. M. (2002). Resilience to loss and chronic grief: A prospective study from preloss to 18-months postloss. *Journal of Personality and Social Psychology, 83*, 1150–1164.

Bonanno, G. A., Wortman, C. B., & Nesse, R. M. (2004). Prospective patterns of resilience and maladjustment during widowhood. *Psychology & Aging, 19*(2), 260–270.

Booth-Kewley, S., & Friedman, H. S. (1987). Psychological predictors of heart disease: A quantitative review. *Psychological Bulletin, 101*, 343–362.

Borg, S., & Lasker, J. (1981). *When pregnancy fails: Families coping with miscarriage, stillbirth and infant death.* Boston: Beacon Press.

Boss, P. (1999). *Ambiguous loss: Learning to live with unresolved grief.* Cambridge, MA: Harvard University Press.

Bowlby, J. (1977). The making and breaking of affectional bonds. *British Journal of Psychiatry, 130*, 201–210, 421–431.

Bowlby, J. (1979/2000). *The making and breaking of affectional bonds.* New York: Routledge.

Bowlby, J. (1980/1998). *Attachment and loss: Sadness and depression.* New York: Basic Books.

Bowling, A. (1988). Who dies after widow(er)-hood—A discriminant-analysis. *OMEGA—Journal of Death and Dying, 19*(2), 135–153.

Brandell, J., & Ringel, S. (2004). Psychodynamic perspectives on relationship: Implications of new findings from human attachment and the neurosciences for social work education. *Families in Society, 85*(4), 549–556.

Bridges, S. (2005). A constructivist approach to infertility: Loss and meaning reconstruction. *Contemporary Sexuality, 39*(12), 9–13.

Brizendine, L. (2006). *The female brain.* New York: Random House.

Brody, E. (1985). Parent care as a normative stress. *The Gerontologist, 25*, 19–29.

Brody, H. (1992). *The healer's power.* New Haven, CT: Yale University Press.

Bronfenbrenner, U. (1979). *The ecology of human development: Experiments by nature and by design.* Cambridge, MA: Harvard University Press.

Brown, G. W., Harris, T., & Copeland, J. R. (1971). Depression & loss. *British Journal of Psychiatry, 130*, 1–18.

Browne, T. A. (2006). Social work roles and health-care settings. In S. Gehlert & T. A. Browne (Eds.), *Handbook of health social work* (pp. 23–42). Hoboken, NJ: John Wiley.

Bruner, J. (1986). *Actual minds, possible worlds.* Cambridge, MA: Harvard University Press.

Buchsbaum, B. C. (1996). Remembering a parent who has died: A developmental perspective. In D. Klass, P. R. Silverman, & S. L. Nickman (Eds.), *Continuing bonds* (pp. 113–124). Philadelphia: Taylor & Francis.

Cadman, D., Boyle, M., & Offord, D. R. (1988). The Ontario Child Health Study: Social adjustment and mental health of siblings of children with chronic health problems. *Journal of Developmental and Behavioral Pediatrics, 9*(3), 117–121.

Cait, C.-A. (2004). Spiritual and religious transformation in women who were parentally bereaved as adolescents. *Omega, 49,* 163–181.

Calasanti, T. M. (1993). Bringing in diversity: Toward an inclusive theory of retirement. *Journal of Aging Studies, 7*(2), 135–150.

Calhoun, L., & Tedeschi, R. (2001). Posttraumatic growth: The positive lessons of loss. In R. Neimeyer (Ed.), *Meaning reconstruction and the experience of loss* (pp. 157–172). Washington, DC: American Psychological Association.

Campos, P. (2004). *The obesity myth: Why America's obsession with weight is hazardous to your health.* New York: Gotham Books.

Carlson, D. (2008). 2007 AESA presidential address: Conflict of the faculties: Democratic progressivism in the age of "No Child Left Behind. " *Educational Studies, 43,* 94–113.

Carr, D., House, J., Kessler, R., Nesse, R., Sonnega, J., & Wortman, C. (2000). Marital quality and psychological adjustment to widowhood among older adults: A longitudinal analysis. *Journal of Gerontology: Social Sciences, 55B,* S197–S207.

Carr, D., House, J., Wortman, C., Nesse, R., & Kessler, R. (2001). Psychological adjustment to sudden and anticipated spousal loss among older widowed persons. *Journal of Gerontology: Social Sciences, 56B,* S197–S207.

Carr, D., Nesse, R., & Wortman, C. (2006). *Spousal bereavement in late life.* New York: Springer Publishing Company.

Cartensen, L., Gross, J., & Fung, H. (1997). The social context of emotional experience. In K. W. Schaie & M. P. Lawton (Eds.), *Annual review of gerontology and geriatrics* (Vol. 17, pp. 325–352). New York: Springer Publishing Company.

Case, R. (1985). *Intellectual development: Birth to adulthood.* New York: Academic Press.

Caserta, M. S., & Lund, D. A. (2007). Toward the development of an inventory of daily widowed life (IDWL): Guided by the Dual Process Model of coping with bereavement. *Death Studies, 31,* 505–535.

Cate, I. M. P., & Loots, G. M. P. (2000). Experiences of siblings of children with physical disabilities: An empirical investigation. *Disability and Rehabilitation, 22,* 399–408.

Center for Consumer Freedom. (2008). *An epidemic of obesity myths.* Washington, DC: Author. Retrieved February 12, 2008, from www.consumerfreedom.com/news.detail.cfm/headline/2535

Chin, R., Lao, T., & Kong, A. (1987). Hyperemesis gravidarum in Chinese women. *Asia-Oceania Journal of Obstetrics and Gynaecology, 13*(3), 261–264.

Cho, S. A., Freeman, E. M., & Patterson, S. L. (1982). Adolescents' experience with death: Practice implications. *Social Casework* (now *Families in Society*), *63,* 88–94.

Christ, G. H. (2000). Impact of development on children's mourning. *Cancer Practice, 8*(2), 72–81.

Christ, G. H., Siegel, K., & Christ, A. E. (2002). Adolescent grief: "It never really hit me. . . until it actually happened." *Journal of the American Medical Association, 288,* 1269–1279.

Cicirelli, V. (2002). *Older adults' views on death.* New York: Springer Publishing Company.

Cicirelli, V. (2006). Fear of death in mid-old age. *Journals of Gerontology, 61*(B), 75–81.

Cillessen, A., van Ijzendoom, H., van Lieshout, C., & Hartup, W. (1992). Heterogeneity among peer rejected boys: Subtypes and stabilities. *Child Development, 63*, 893–905.

Clarke, J. (2000). The search for legitimacy and the "expertization" of the lay person: The case of chronic fatigue syndrome. *Social Work in Health Care, 30*(3), 73–92.

Clayton, P. J. (1974). Mortality and morbidity in the first year of bereavement. *Archives of General Psychiatry, 30*, 747–750.

Clements, P., DeRanieri, J., Vigil, G., & Benasutti, K. (2004). Life after death: Grief therapy after the sudden traumatic death of a family member. *Perspectives in Psychiatric Care, 40*, 149–155.

Clukey, L. (2007). "Just be there": Hospice caregivers' anticipatory mourning experience. *Journal of Hospice and Palliative Nursing, 9*(3), 150–158.

Cochran, B. (2003). Sexual minorities in substance abuse treatment (Doctoral dissertation, University of Washington, 2004). *Dissertation Abstracts International, 64*, 5776.

Cohen, J. A., Mannarino, A. P., Greenberg, T., Padlo, S., & Shipley, C. (2002). Childhood traumatic grief: Concepts and controversies. *Trauma, Violence, & Abuse, 3*(4), 307–327.

Cohen, M. S. (1999). Families coping with childhood chronic illness: A research review. *Families, Systems & Health, 17*(2), 149–164.

Cohen, S., & Rodriguez, M. S. (1995). Pathways linking affective disturbances and physical disorders. *Health Psychology, 14*, 375–380.

Cole, K. L. (1995). Pregnancy loss through miscarriage or stillbirth. In M. W. O' Hara, R. C. Reiter, S. J. Johnson, A. Milburn, & J. Engeldinger (Eds.), *Psychological aspects of women's reproductive health* (pp. 194–206). New York: Springer Publishing Company.

Coleman, P. (1992). Personal adjustment in later life: Successful aging. *Reviews in Clinical Gerontology, 2*, 67–78.

Coniglio, S. J., & Blackman, J. A. (1995). Developmental outcome of childhood leukemia. *Topics in Early Childhood Special Education, 15*(1), 19–31.

Connidis, I. (2001). *Family ties and aging.* Thousand Oaks, CA: Sage.

Cooper, M., & Lesser, J. (2008). *Clinical social work practice: An integrated approach.* Boston, MA: Pearson Education, Inc.

Corbett, D. (with Higgins, R.). (2007). *Portfolio life: The new path to work, purpose and passion after 50.* San Francisco, CA: Jossey-Bass.

Corr, C. A., & Balk, D. E. (1996). *Handbook of adolescent death and bereavement.* New York: Springer Publishing Company.

Corr, C. A., & McNeil, J. N. (1986). *Adolescence and death.* New York: Springer Publishing Company.

Corr, C., Nabe, C., & Corr, D. (2006). *Death, dying, life & living.* Belmont, CA:Thompson Wadsworth.

Corsini, R., & Wedding, D. (2000). *Current psychotherapies* (6th ed.). Belmont, CA: Brooks/Cole.

Cowan, C., Cowan, P., Heminggertrude, G., Coysh, W., Curtisboles, H., Boles, A., & Coysh, W. (1985). Transitions to parenthood: His, hers and theirs. *Journal of Family Issues, 6*, 451–482.

Cowan, M. (1996). Hyperemesis gravidarum: Implications for home care and infusion therapies. *Journal of Intravenous Nursing, 19*(1), 46-58.

Crenshaw, D. A. (2002). The disenfranchised grief of children. In K. J. Doka (Ed.), *Disenfranchised grief: New directions, challenges and strategies for practice* (pp. 293–306). Champaign, IL: Research Press.

Criss, M., Petti, G., Bates, J., Dodge, K., & Lapp, A. (2002). Family diversity, positive peer relationships and children's externalizing behavior: A longitudinal perspective on risk and resilience. *Child Development, 73*, 1220–1237.

Cudmore, L. (2005). Becoming parents in the context of loss. *Sexual and Relationship Therapy, 20*(3), 299–308.

Currier, J., Holland, J., & Neimeyer, R. (2007). The effectiveness of bereavement interventions with children: A meta-analytic review of controlled outcome research. *Journal of Clinical Child and Adolescent Psychology, 36*(2), 253–259.

Dailey, N. (1998). *When baby boom women retire.* Westport, CT: Praeger.

Dale, P. (1976). *Language development.* New York: Holt, Rinehart & Winston.

Dallaire, D. H., & Weinraub, M. (2007). Infant–mother attachment security and children's anxiety and aggression in first grade. *Journal of Applied Developmental Psychology, 28*, 477–492.

Daniluk, J., & Tench, E. (2007). Long-term adjustment of infertile couples following unsuccessful medical intervention. *Journal of Counseling and Development, 85*, 89–100.

Dautzenberg, M. G. (2000). The competing demands of paid work and parent care. *Research on Aging, 22*(2), 165.

Davar, E. (2001). The loss of the transitional object: Some thoughts about transitional and 'pre-transitional' phenomena. *Psychodynamic Counselling, 7*(1), 5–26.

Davis, C. G., & Nolen-Hoeksema, S. (2001). Loss and meaning: How do people make sense of loss? *American Behavioral Scientist, 44*, 726–741.

Davis, D. L. (1996). *Empty cradle, broken heart.* Golden, CO: Fulcrum Publishing.

Davis, S., & Handschin, B. (1998). *Reinventing yourself: Life planning after 50 using the Strong and MBTI.* Palo Alto, CA: Consulting Psychologists Press.

Davison, K. K., Werder, J. L., Trost, S. G., Baker, B. L., & Birch, L. L. (2007). Why are early maturing girls less active? Links between pubertal development, psychological well-being, and physical activity among girls at ages 11 and 13. *Social Science & Medicine, 64*(12), 2391–2404.

De Bellis, M. D., Keshavan, M. S., Clark, D. B., Casey, B. J., Giedd, J. N., Boring, A. M., Frustaci, K., & Ryan, N. D. (1999). Developmental traumatology Part II: Brain development. *Biological Psychiatry, 45*, 1271–1284.

Deevey, S. (1997). Bereavement experiences in lesbian kinship networks in Ohio (Doctoral dissertation, Ohio State University, 1997). *Dissertation Abstracts International, 58/02*, 630.

Dehaene-Lambertz, G., Hertz-Pannier, L., & Dubois, J. (2006). Nature and nurture in language acquisition: Anatomical and functional brain imaging. *Trends in Neurosciences, 29*, 367–373.

Delman-Jenkins, M., Blankemeyer, M., & Olesh, M. (2002). Adults in expanded grandparent roles: Considerations for practice, policy, and research. *Educational Gerontology, 28*, 219-235.

Den Hond, E., & Schoeters, G. (2006). Endocrine disrupters and human puberty. *International Journal of Andrology, 29*, 264–271.

Diamond, M., Diamond, D. J., & Jaffe, J. (2001, May). *Reproductive trauma: Treatment implications of recent theory and research.* Presented to the National Association of Perinatal Social Workers annual conference, San Diego, CA.

DiGiulio, J. (1992). Early widowhood: An atypical transition. *Journal of Mental Health Counseling, 14*(10), 97–109.

Dillon, C. (2003). *Learning from mistakes in clinical practice.* Pacific Grove, CA: Brooks/Cole.

Dimond, M., Lund, D. A., & Caserta, M. S. (1987). The role of social support in the first two years of bereavement in an elderly sample. *The Gerontologist, 27*, 599–604.

Doka, K. (1987). Silent sorrow: Grief and the loss of significant others. *Death Studies, 11*, 455–469.

Doka, K. (1989). *Disenfranchised grief: Recognizing hidden sorrow.* New York: Lexington Books.

Doka, K. (2000a). *Introduction to disenfranchised grief: New directions, challenges, and strategies for practice.* Champaign, IL: Research Press.

Doka, K. (2000b). Mourning psychosocial loss: Anticipatory mourning in Alzheimer's disease, ASL, and irreversible coma. In T. Rando (Ed.), *Clinical dimensions of anticipatory mourning.* Champaign, IL: Research Press.

Doka, K. J. (Ed.). (2002). *Disenfranchised grief: New directions, challenges and strategies for practice.* Champaign, IL: Research Press.

Doka, K. (2004). *Grief and dementia: Living with grief: Alzheimer's disease.* Washington, DC: Hospice Foundation of America.

Downs, S. W., Moore, E., McFadden, E. J., Michaud, S. M., & Costin, L. B. (2004). *Child welfare and family services: Policies and practice* (7th ed.). Boston: Pearson Education.

Dunning, S. (2006). As a young child's parent dies: Conceptualizing and constructing preventive interventions. *Clinical Social Work Journal, 34*, 499–514.

Eaves, D., McQuiston, C., & Miles, M. (2005). Coming to terms with adult sibling grief. *Journal of Hospice and Palliative Nursing, 7*(3), 139–149.

Eiden, R., Edwards, E. P., & Leonard, K. E. (2007). A conceptual model for the development of externalizing behavior problems among kindergarten children of alcoholic families: Role of parenting and children's self-regulation. *Developmental Psychology, 43*, 1187–1201.

Eisenberg, A., Murkoff, H. E., & Hathaway, S. E. (1991). *What to expect when you're expecting.* New York: Workman Publishing.

Elder, G. H. (1992). Models of the life course. *Contemporary Sociology: A Journal of Reviews, 21*(5), 632–635.

Elkind, D. (1967). Egocentrism in adolescence. *Child Development, 38*, 1025–1034.

Epstein, R., Campbell, T., Cohen-Cole, S., McWhinney, I., & Smilkstein, G. (1993). Perspectives on patient–doctor communication. *Journal of Family Practice, 37*(4), 377–388.

Erikson, E. (1968). *Identity: Youth and crisis.* New York: W. W. Norton.

Erikson, E. (1978). *Adulthood.* New York: W. W. Norton.

Erikson, E. H. (1980). *Identity and the life cycle.* New York: W. W. Norton. (Original work published 1959)

Essex, E., Newsome, W., & Moses, H. (2004). Caring for grandparent-headed families: Challenges and opportunities for school social workers. *School Social Work Journal, 28*(2), 1–19.

Ewalt, P. L., & Perkins, L. (1979). The real experience of death among adolescents: An empirical study. *Social Casework* (now *Families in Society), 60,* 547–551.

Faber, A., & Mazlish, E. (1998). *Siblings without rivalry: How to help your children live together, so you can live too.* New York: HarperCollins. (Original work published 1987)

Farrant, B., & Watson, P. (2003). Health care delivery: Perspectives of young people with chronic illness and their parents. *Journal of Pediatric Child Health, 40,* 175–179.

Farrell, F., & Hutter, J. J. (1980). Living until death: Adolescents with cancer. *Health and Social Work, 5*(4), 35–38.

Fast, J. D. (2003). After Columbine: How people mourn after sudden death. *Social Work, 48,* 484-491.

Felder-Puig, R., Formann, A. K., Mildner, A., Bretschneider, W., Bucher, B., Windhager, R., Zoubek, A., Puig, S., & Topf, R. (1998). Quality of life and psychosocial adjustment of young patients after treatment of bone cancer. *Cancer, 83,* 69–75.

Fennell, G. (2004). Transitions in mid-adult to late life. *Ageing International, 29*(4), 309–316.

Field, T., Diego, M., & Hernandez-Reif, M. (2006). Prenatal depression effects on the fetus and newborn: A review. *Infant Behavior and Development, 29*(3), 445–455.

Filer, R. B. (1992). Endocrinology of the postpartum period. In J. A. Hamilton & P. N. Harberger (Eds.), *Postpartum psychiatric illness: A picture puzzle.* Philadelphia: University of Pennsylvania Press.

Finkbeiner, A. K. (1996). *After the death of a child: Living with loss through the years.* New York: Free Press.

Finkelhor, D. (1984). Sexual abuse in the National Incidence Study of Child Abuse and Neglect: An appraisal. *Child Abuse & Neglect, 8*(1), 23–33.

Finley, J. R. (2004). *Integrating the 12 steps into addiction therapy: A resource collection and guide for promoting recovery.* New York: John Wiley.

Firth, R. (1961). *Elements of social organization* (3rd ed.). London: Tavistock.

Fischer, K. (1980). A theory of cognitive development: The control and construction of hierarchies of skills. *Psychological Review, 97,* 477–531.

Fisman, S., Wolf, L., Ellison, D., Gillis, B., Freeman, T., & Szatmari, P. (1996). Risk and protective factors affecting the adjustment of siblings of children with chronic disabilities. *Journal of the American Academy of Child and Adolescent Psychiatry, 35,* 1532–1542.

Fleming, S. J., & Adolph, R. (1986). Helping bereaved adolescents: Needs and responses. In C. A. Corr & J. N. McNeil (Eds.), *Adolescence and death* (pp. 97–118). New York: Springer Publishing Company.

Fleming, S. J., & Belanger, S. K. (2001). Trauma, grief, and surviving child sexual abuse. In R. Neimeyer (Ed.), *Meaning reconstruction & the experience of loss* (pp. 311–332). Washington, DC: American Psychological Association.

Flowers, P., & Buston, K. (2001). "I was terrified of being different": Exploring gay men's accounts of growing up. *Journal of Adolescence, 24,* 56–66.

Foote, C. E., & Frank, A. W. (1999). Foucault and therapy: The disciplining of grief. In A. S. Chambron, A. Irving, & L. Epstein (Eds.), *Reading Foucault for social work* (pp. 157–187). New York: Columbia University Press.

Fortner, B., Neimeyer, R., & Rybarcyk, B. (2000). Correlates of death anxiety in older adults: A comprehensive review. In A. Tomer (Ed.), *Death attitudes and the older adult: Theories, concepts and applications* (pp. 95–108). Philadelphia: Taylor and Francis.

Foucault, M. (1988). Technologies of the self. In L. H. Martin, H. Gutman, & P. H. Hutton (Eds.), *Technologies of the self* (pp. 16–49). Amherst, MA: University of Massachusetts Press.

Fraiberg, S. H. (1959). *The magic years: Understanding and handling the problems of early childhood.* New York: Charles Scribner's Sons.

Frankl, V. E. (1984/1946). *Man's search for meaning: An introduction to logotherapy.* New York: Touchstone Books.

Freedman, M. (1999). *Prime time: How baby boomers will revolutionize retirement and transform America.* Cambridge, MA: Perseus Books Group.

Freud, E. L. (Ed.). (1961). *The letters of Sigmund Freud.* New York: Basic Books.

Freud, S. (1957). Mourning and melancholia. In J. Strachey (Ed. and Trans.), *The standard edition of the complete psychological works of Sigmund Freud* (Vol. 14). London: Hogarth. (Original work published 1917)

Freud, S. (1960). *The ego and the id* (Joan Riviere, Trans.). New York: W. W. Norton. (Original work published 1923)

Friedberg, F. (2006). *Fibromyalgia and chronic fatigue syndrome: 7 proven steps to less pain and more energy.* Oakland, CA: New Harbinger Publications.

Furman, E. (1974). *A child's parent dies: Studies in childhood bereavement.* New Haven, CT: Yale University Press.

Furman, E. (1996). On motherhood. *Journal of the American Psychoanalytic Society, 44,* 429–447.

Furstenberg, F., Kennedy, S., McLoyd, V., Rumbaut, R., & Settersen, A. (2004). Growing up is harder to do. *American Sociological Association, 3*(3), 33–41.

Gadsby, R. (1994). Pregnancy sickness and symptoms: Your questions answered. *Professional Care of Mother and Child, 4,* 16–17.

Gardner, H. (1991). *The unschooled mind: How children think & how schools should teach.* New York: Perseus Books.

Gazmararian, J. A., Petersen, R., Jamieson, D. J., Schild, L., Adams, M. M., & Deshpande, A. D. (2002). Hospitalizations during pregnancy among managed care enrollees. *Obstetrics & Gynecology, 100,* 94–100.

Ge, X., Jin, R., Natsuaki, M. N., Gibbons, F. X., Brody, G. H., Cutrona, C. E., & Simons, R. L. (2006). Pubertal maturation and early substance use risks among African American children. *Psychology of Addictive Behaviors, 20*(4), 404–414.

George, L., & Gwyther, L. (1986). Caregiver well-being: A multidimensional examination of family caregivers of demented patients. *The Gerontologist, 26,* 253–259.

Gerdes, A. C., Hoza, B., Arnold, L. E., Pelham, W. E., Swanson, J. M., Wigal, T., & Jensen, P. S. (2007). Maternal depressive symptomatology and parenting behavior:

Exploration of possible mediators. *Journal of Abnormal Child Psychology, 35,* 705–714.

Germain, C., & Gitterman, A. (1980). *The life model of social work practice.* New York: Columbia University Press.

Getchell, N., & Robertson, M. A. (1989). Whole body stiffness as a function of developmental level of children's hopping. *Developmental Psychology, 25,* 920–928.

Giedd, J. J. (1999). Human brain growth. *American Journal of Psychiatry, 156,* 1.

Gifford-Smith, M. E., & Brownell, C. A. (2003). Childhood peer relationships: Social acceptance, friendships and peer networks. *Journal of School Psychology, 41,* 235–284.

Gilbert, R. (2006). When adult children grieve the death of a parent: Spiritual perspectives. *Forum, 32*(2), 10.

Gilligan, C. (1993). *In a different voice: Psychological theory and women's development.* Cambridge, MA: Harvard University Press. (Original work published 1982)

Ginsburg, F. D., & Rapp, R. (1995). *Conceiving the new world order: The global politics of reproduction.* Berkeley, CA: University of California Press.

Glenn, E. N., Chang, G., & Forcey L. R. (1994). *Mothering: Ideology, experience and agency.* New York: Routledge.

Gluckman, P. D., & Hanson, M. A. (2006). Changing times: The evolution of puberty. *Molecular and Cellular Endocrinology, 254–255,* 26–31.

Godfrey, R. (2006). Losing a sibling in adulthood. *Forum, 32*(1), 6–7.

Goffman, E. (1963). *Stigma: Notes on the management of spoiled identity.* New York: Simon & Schuster.

Goldbach, K. R. C., Dunn, D. S., Toedter, L. J., & Lasker, J. N. (1991). The effects of gestational age and gender on grief after pregnancy loss. *American Journal of Orthopsychiatry, 61,* 461–467.

Goldberg, A., & Sayer, A. (2006). Lesbian couples' relationship quality across the transition to parenthood. *Journal of Marriage and Family, 68,* 87–100.

Golden, J. (2000). A tempest in a cocktail glass: Mothers, alcohol, and television, 1977–1996. *Journal of Health Politics, Policy & Law, 25*(3), 473–498.

Goodwin, T. M. (2004). A practical approach to hyperemesis gravidarum. *Contemporary OB/GYN, 49*(6), 47–62.

Gordon, P., & Feldman, D. (1998). Impact of chronic illness: Differing perspectives of younger and older women. *Journal of Personal & Interpersonal Loss, 3*(3), 239–256.

Gould, R. (1975). Adult life stages: Growth toward self-tolerance. *Psychology Today, 8*(9), 74–78.

Gould, R. (1978). *Transformations: Growth and change in adult life.* New York: Simon and Schuster.

Granic, I., O'Hara, A., Pepler, D., & Lewis, M. (2007). A dynamic systems analysis of parent–child changes associated with successful "real world" interventions for aggressive children. *Journal of Abnormal Child Psychology, 35,* 845–857.

Granvold, D. K. (1995). Cognitive treatment. In L. Beebe, N. A. Winchester, F. Pflieger, & S. Lowman (Eds.), *Encyclopedia of social work* (pp. 525–538). Washington, DC: NASW Press.

Green, B. L., Krupnick, J. L., Stockton, P., Goodman, L., Corcoran, C., & Petty, R. (2001). Psychological outcomes associated with traumatic loss in a sample of young women. *American Behavioral Scientist, 44*(5), 817–837.

Green, S. E. (2007). "We're tired, not sad": Benefits and burdens of mothering a child with a disability. *Social Science & Medicine, 64,* 150–163.

Greenberg, J. R., & Mitchell, S. A. (1983). *Object relations in psychoanalytic theory.* Cambridge, MA: Harvard University Press.

Greenfield, D. A. (1997). Infertility and assisted reproductive technology: The role of the perinatal social worker. *Social Work in Health Care, 24*(3/4), 39–46.

Group for the Advancement of Psychiatry (Committee on Adolescence). (1968). *Normal adolescence.* New York: Charles Scribner's Sons.

Grout, L. A., & Romanoff, B. D. (2000). The myth of the replacement child: Parents' stories after perinatal death. *Death Studies, 24,* 93–113.

Grubb-Phillips, C. A. (1988). Intrauterine fetal death: The maternal bereavement experience. *Journal of Perinatal and Neonatal Nursing, 2*(2), 34–44.

Gundel, H., O'Connor, M.-F., Littrell, F., Fort, C., & Lane, R. (2003). Functional neuroanatomy of grief: An fMRI study. *American Journal of Psychiatry, 160,* 1946–1953.

Haber, J., Hoskins, P. P., Leach, A. M., & Sideleau, B. F. (1987). *Comprehensive psychiatric nursing* (3rd ed.). New York: McGraw-Hill.

Halpern, C. T., Kaestle, C. E., & Hallfors, D. D. (2007). Perceived physical maturity, age of romantic partner, and adolescent risk behavior. *Prevention Science, 8,* 1–10.

Hames, C. C. (2003). Helping infants and toddlers when a family member dies. *Journal of Hospice & Palliative Nursing, 5,* 103–112.

Hani, H., Stiles, W., & Biran, M. (2005). Loss and mourning in immigration: Using the assimilation model to assess continuing bonds with native culture. *Counseling Psychology Quarterly, 18*(2), 109–119.

Hansson, R. O., & Stroebe, M. S. (2007). *Bereavement in late life: Coping, adaptation, and developmental influences.* Washington, DC: American Psychological Association.

Haraway, D. (2000). The virtual speculum in the new world order. In G. Kirkup, L. Janes, K. Woodward, & F. Hovenden (Eds.), *The gendered cyborg: A reader* (pp. 221–246). London: Open University Press.

Hardy, L. (2006). When kids lose parents in our war in Iraq. *Education Digest, 72,* 10–12.

Hart, B., & Grace, V. (2000). Fatigue in chronic fatigue syndrome: A discourse analysis of women's experiential narratives. *Health Care for Women International, 21,* 187–201.

Harvey, J. (2000). *Give sorrow words: Perspectives on loss and trauma.* Philadelphia: Brunner/Mazel.

Hayslip, B., & Kaminski, P. (2008). *Parenting the custodial grandchild: Implications for clinical practice.* New York: Springer Publishing Company.

Helsing, K., Comstock, G., & Szklo, M. (1982). Causes of death in a widowed population. *American Journal of Epidemiology, 116,* 524–532.

Herbert, T. B., & Cohen, S. (1993). Depression and immunity: A meta-analytic review. *Psychological Bulletin, 113,* 472–486.

Hill, R. (2005). *Positive aging.* New York: W. W. Norton.

Hochschild, A. R. (1983). *The managed heart: Commercialization of human feeling.* Berkeley, CA: University of California Press.

Hochschild, A. R. (1979). Emotion work, feeling rules, and social structure. *American Journal of Sociology, 85*(3), 551–575.

Hochschild, A. R. (1998). The sociology of emotion as a way of seeing. In G. Bendelow & S. Williams (Eds.), *Emotions in social life* (pp. 3–15). New York: Routledge.

Hogan, N., & DeSantis, L. (1996). Basic constructs of a theory of adolescent sibling bereavement. In D. Klass, P. R. Silverman, & S. L. Nickman (Eds.), *Continuing bonds: New understandings of grief* (pp. 235–254). Philadelphia: Taylor & Francis.

Hogan, N., & Schmidt, L. (2002). Testing the grief to personal growth model using structural equation modeling. *Death Studies, 26*, 615–634.

Holmes, T. H., & Rahe, R. H. (1967). The social readjustment rating scale. *Journal of Psychosomatic Research, 11*, 213–218.

Honig, M. (1996). Retirement expectations: Differences by race, ethnicity and gender. *The Gerontologist, 36*(3), 373–382.

Hooyman, N., & Kiyak, H. (2008). *Social gerontology*. Boston: Allyn and Bacon.

Hooyman, N., & Kramer, B. (2006). *Living through loss: Interventions across the lifespan.* New York: Columbia University Press.

Hope, R. M., & Hodge, D. M. (2006). Factors affecting children's adjustment to the death of a parent: The social work professional's viewpoint. *Child and Adolescent Social Work Journal, 23*, 107–126.

Horowitz, A. (1985). Family caregiving to the frail elderly. In C. Eisendorfer (Ed.), *Annual review of gerontology and geriatrics* (Vol. 5, pp. 194–236). New York: Springer Publishing Company.

Horowitz, A., & Wakefield, J. (2007). *The loss of sadness: How psychiatry transformed normal sorrow into depressive disorder*. New York: Oxford University Press.

Hughes, P., Turton, P., Hopper, E., & Evans, C. D. H. (2002). Assessment of guidelines for good practice in psychosocial care of mothers after stillbirth: A cohort study. *Lancet, 360*(9327), 114–118.

Ibarra, H. (2003). *Working identity.* Boston: Harvard Business School Press.

Iglesias, E., & Cormier, S. (2002). The transformation of girls to women: Finding voice and developing strategies for liberation. *Journal of Multicultural Counseling and Development, 30*, 259–271.

Ilse, S., & Furrh, C. B. (1988). Development of a comprehensive follow-up care plan after perinatal and neonatal loss. *Journal of Perinatal and Neonatal Nursing, 2*(2), 23–33.

Imberti, P. (2008, May/June). The immigrant's odyssey. *Psychotherapy Networker,* pp. 35–39.

Imeson, M. (1996). Couples' experiences of infertility: A phenomenological study. *Journal of Advanced Nursing, 34*, 1014–1021.

Inside the brains of smart kids. (2006, April 1). *New Scientist, 190*(2545), 21.

Iraq Coalition Casualty Count. (2008). Retrieved November 18, 2008, from http:www. icasualties.org/oif/default.aspx

Jack, D. C. (1991). *Silencing the self: Women and depression*. Cambridge, MA: Harvard University Press.

Janoff-Bulman, R. (1992). *Shattered assumptions: Towards a new psychology of trauma.* New York: Free Press.

Jessner, L., Weigert, E., & Foy, J. L. (1970). The development of parental attitudes during pregnancy. In E. J. Anthony & T. Benedek (Eds.), *Parenthood; Its psychology and pathology* (pp. 209–227). Boston: Little Brown.

Jiang, R., Chou, C., & Tsai, P. (2006). The grief reactions of nursing students related to the sudden death of a classmate. *Journal of Nursing Research, 14*(4), 279–284.

Johnson, B. H. (2000). Family-centered care: Four decades of progress. *Families, Systems, & Health, 18,* 137–156.

Johnson, C. M. (2006). *When friends are murdered: A qualitative study of the experience, meaning, and implications for identity development of older adolescent African American females.* Unpublished doctoral dissertation, Bryn Mawr College, Graduate School of Social Work and Social Research, Bryn Mawr, PA.

Johnson, M. P., & Puddifoot, J. E. (1996). The grief response in partners of women who miscarry. *British Journal of Medical Psychology, 69*(4), 313–327.

Johnson, S. (2004). *Mind wide open: Your brain and the neuroscience of everyday life.* New York: Scribner.

Johnson, Y. M. (in press). The bioethical underpinnings of advance directives. *Ethics and Social Welfare.*

Johnson, Y. M., & Stadel, V. L. (2007). Completion of advance directives: Do social work pre-admission interviews make a difference? *Research on Social Work Practice, 17*(6), 686–696.

Jones, D. R. (1987). Heart disease mortality following widowhood: Some results from the OPCS longitudinal study. *Journal of Psychosomatic Research, 31,* 325–333.

Jordan, J. R., & Neimeyer, R. A. (2003). Does grief counseling work? *Death Studies, 27,* 765–786.

Kaminsky, L., & Dewey, D. (2002). Psychosocial adjustment in siblings of children with autism. *Journal of Child Psychology and Psychiatry, 43,* 225–232.

Kaplan, H. I., & Sadock, B. J. (1998). *Kaplan and Sadock's synopsis of psychiatry: Behavioral sciences/clinical psychiatry* (8th ed.). Baltimore, MD: Williams and Wilkins.

Katz, J. (1984). *The silent world of doctor and patient.* New York: Free Press.

Keefer, B., & Schooler, J. E. (2000). *Telling the truth to your adopted or foster child: Making sense of the past.* Westport, CT: Bergin & Garvely.

Kemp, V., & Hatmaker, D. (1989). Stress and social support in high-risk pregnancy. *Research in Nursing & Health, 12,* 331–336.

Kenny, D. (1995). Determinants of patient satisfaction with the medical consultation. *Psychology and Health, 10*(5), 427–437.

Kent, D., & Hayward, R. (2002). When averages hide individual differences in clinical trials. *American Scientist, 95,* 60–68.

Kiburz, J. A. (1994). Perceptions and concerns of the school-age siblings of children with myelomeningocele. *Issues in Comprehensive Pediatric Nursing, 17,* 223–231.

Kiecolt-Glaser, J. K., & Glaser, R. (1992). Psychoneuroimmunology: Can psychological interventions modulate immunity? *Journal of Consulting and Clinical Psychology, 60,* 569–575.

Kim, J. & Moen, P. (2001). Moving into retirement: Preparation and transitions in late midlife. In M. E. Lachman (Ed.), *Handbook of midlife development* (pp. 487–527). New York: John Wiley.

Kim, K., & Jacobs, S. (1993). Neuroendocrine changes following bereavement. In M. S. Stroebe, W. Stroebe, & R. O. Hansson (Eds.), *Handbook of bereavement: Theory, research, and intervention* (pp. 143–159). New York: Cambridge University Press.

Kitts, R. L. (2005). Gay adolescents and suicide: Understanding the association. *Adolescence, 40,* 163–181.

Klass, D. (1986–1987). Marriage and divorce among bereaved parents in a self-help group. *Omega, 17,* 237–249.

Klass, D. (1996). The deceased child in the psychic and social worlds of bereaved parents during the resolution of grief. In D. Klass, P. R. Silverman, & S. L. Nickman (Eds.), *Continuing bonds: New understandings of grief* (pp. 199–216). Philadelphia: Taylor & Francis.

Klass, D. (2005). The inner representation of the dead child in the psychic and social narratives of bereaved parents. In R. Neimeyer (Ed.), *Meaning reconstruction & the experience of loss* (pp. 77–94). Washington, DC: American Psychological Association.

Klass, D. (2006). Continuing conversation about continuing bonds. *Death Studies, 30,* 843–858.

Klass, D., Silverman, P. R., & Nickman, S. L. (Eds.). (1996). *Continuing bonds: New understandings of grief.* Washington, DC: Taylor & Francis.

Klaus, M. H., & Kennel, J. H. (1976). *Maternal–infant bonding.* Saint Louis: C. V. Mosby.

Kochanska, G., Forman, D. R., & Coy, K. C. (1999). Implications of the mother–child relationship in infancy for socialization in the second year of life. *Infant Behavior & Development, 22,* 249–265.

Kolomer, S., & McCallion, P. (2005). Depression and caregiver mastery in grandfathers caring for their grandchildren. *International Journal of Aging and Human Development, 60*(4), 283–294.

Konish, I. (2006). Gonadotropins and ovarian carcinogenesis: A new era of basic research and its clinical implications. *International Journal of Gynecological Cancer, 16,* 16-22.

Knapp, P. H., Levy, E. M., Giorgi, R. G., Black, P. H. G., Fox, B. H., & Heeren, T. C. (1992) Short-term immunological effects of induced emotions. *Psychosomatic Medicine, 54,* 133–148.

Kralik, D. (2002). The quest for ordinariness: Transition experienced by midlife women living with chronic illness. *Journal of Advanced Nursing, 39*(2), 146–154.

Kroll, B. (2002). Children and divorce. In N. Thompson (Ed.), *Loss and grief: A guide for human services practitioners* (pp. 111–124). New York: Palgrave.

Kübler-Ross, E. (1969). *On death and dying: What the dying have to teach their doctors, nurses, clergy and their own families.* New York: Macmillan.

Lackaye, T., & Margalit, M. (2008). Self-efficacy, loneliness, effort, and hope: Developmental differences in the experiences of students with learning disabilities and their non-learning disabled peers at two age groups. *Learning Disabilities: A Contemporary Journal, 6*(2), 1–20.

Ladd-Taylor, M., & Umansky, L. (Eds.). (1998). *"Bad" mothers: The politics of blame in twentieth century America.* New York: New York University Press.

Lansky, S. B., List, M. A., & Ritter-Sterr, C. (1986). Psychosocial consequences of cure. *Cancer, 58*(2 Suppl.), 529–533.

Larson, D., & Hoyt, W. T. (2007). What has become of grief counseling? An evaluation of the empirical foundations of the new pessimism. *Professional Psychology: Research and Practice, 38*(4), 347–355.

LaSala, M. C. (2007). Parental influence, gay youths, and safer sex. *Health & Social Work, 32*(1), 49–55.

Lasker, J. N., & Toedter, L. J. (1991). Acute vs. chronic grief: The case of pregnancy loss. *American Journal of Orthopsychiatry, 61*(4), 510–522.

Laudenslager, M. L., Boccia, M. A., & Reite, M. L. (1993). Biobehavioral consequences of loss in nonhuman primates: Individual differences. In M. S. Stroebe, W. Stroebe, & R. O. Hansson (Eds.), *Handbook of bereavement: Theory, research, and intervention* (pp. 129–142). New York: Cambridge University Press.

Laurence, L., & Weinhouse, B. (1997). *Outrageous practices: How gender bias threatens women's health.* New Brunswick, NJ: Rutgers University Press.

Lawton, P., Windley, P., & Byers, T. (1982). *Aging and the environment: Theoretical approaches.* New York: Springer Publishing Company.

Layne, C. M., Saltzman, W. S., Savjak, N., & Pynoos, R. S. (1999). *Trauma/grief focused group psychotherapy manual.* Sarajevo, Bosnia: UNICEF Bosnia and Herzegovina.

Layne, L. L. (2003). *Motherhood lost.* New York: Routledge.

Lazarus, R. S., & Folkman, S. (1984). *Stress, appraisal, and coping.* New York: Springer Publishing Company.

Leach, P. (1984). *The child care encyclopedia: A parent's guide to the physical and emotional well-being of children from birth to adolescence.* New York: Knopf.

Leach, P. (1986). *Babyhood: Stage by stage, from birth to age two* (2nd ed.). New York: Knopf.

Lee, G. R., DeMaris, A., Bavin, S., & Sullivan, R. (2001). Gender differences in the depressive effect of widowhood in later life. *Journal of Gerontology: Social Sciences, 56B*, S56–S61.

Lenroot, R. K., & Giedd, J. J. (2006). Brain development in children and adolescents: Insights from anatomical magnetic resonance imaging. *Neuroscience & Biobehavioral Reviews, 30*, 718–729.

Leon, I. (1992). Perinatal loss: Choreographing grief on the obstetrical unit. *American Journal of Orthopsychiatry, 62*(1), 7–8.

Levine, S. (2005). *Inventing the rest of our lives: Women in second adulthood.* New York: Penguin Group.

Levinson, D., Darrow, C., Klein, E., Levinson, M., & McKee, B. (1978). *The seasons of a man's life.* New York: Alfred A. Knopf.

Levinson, D., & Levinson, J. (1996). *The seasons of a woman's life.* New York: Knopf.

Lewis, E. (1976). The management of still birth: Coping with an unreality. *Lancet, 2*, 619–620.

Lind, R. F., Pruitt, R. L., & Greenfield, D. A. (1990). Previously infertile couples and the newborn intensive care unit. *Health & Social Work, 14*, 127–133.

Lindemann, E. (1944). Symptomatology and management of acute grief. *American Journal of Psychiatry, 101*, 141–148.

Lindstrom, T. (2002). "It ain't necessarily so." Challenging mainstream thinking about bereavement. *Community Health, 25*(1), 11–21.

Lloyd, M. (2002). A framework for working with loss. In N. Thompson (Ed.), *Loss and grief: A guide for human services practitioners* (pp. 208–220). London: Palgrave.

Loos, C., & Bowd, A. (2007). Caregivers of persons with Alzheimer's disease: Some neglected implications of the experience of personal loss and grief. *Death Studies, 21*(5), 501–514.

Lund, D., Caserta, M., deVries, B., & Wright, S. (2004). Restoration after bereavement. *Generations Review, 14*, 9–15.

Lund, D., Caserta, M., & Dimond, M. (1993). The course of spousal bereavement in later life. In M. Stroebe & W. Stroebe (Eds.), *Handbook of bereavement: Theory, research, and intervention* (pp. 204–254). New York: Cambridge University Press.

Lutovich, D. (2002). *Nobody's child: How older women say goodbye to their mothers.* Amityville, NY: Baywood.

Lynn, J. L., Lynch-Schuster, J. L., Wilkinson, A. M., & Noyes-Simon, L. (2007). *Improving the care for the end of life: A sourcebook for health care managers and clinicians.* London: Oxford University Press.

Maciejewski, P. K., Zhang, B., Block, S. D., & Prigerson, H. G. (2007). An empirical examination of the stage theory of grief. *Journal of the American Medical Association, 297*, 716–723.

MacMullen, N., Dulski, L., & Pappalardo, B. (1992). Antepartum vulnerability: Stress, coping, and a patient support group. *Journal of Perinatal and Neonatal Nursing, 6*(3), 15–25.

Magnuson, M. (2000). Infants with congenital deafness: On the importance of early sign language acquisition. *American Annals of the Deaf, 145*, 6–14.

Mahan, C. K., & Calica, J. (1997). Perinatal loss: Considerations in social work practice. In R. F. Lind & D. H. Bachman (Eds.), *Fundamentals of perinatal social work: A guide for clinical practice with women, infants and families* (pp. 141–152). New York: Haworth Press.

Mahler, M. (1975). *The psychological birth of the child.* New York: Basic Books.

Mahler, M. S., Pine, F., & Bergman, A. (1985). *The psychological birth of the human infant.* New York: Basic Books.

Manor, I., Vincent, M., & Tyano, S. (2004). The wish to die and the wish to commit suicide in the adolescent: Two different matters? *Adolescence, 39*, 279–293.

Markowitz, M. S. (2007). Allowing adolescents to make life-and-death decisions about themselves; Rights and responsibilities of adolescents, families, and the state. *Dissertation Abstracts International Section A: Humanities and Social Sciences, 67*(9-A), 3433.

Marlatt, G. A., & Gordon, J. R. (Ed.). (1985). *Relapse prevention: Maintenance strategies in the treatment of addictive behaviors.* New York: Guilford Press.

Martin, T. L. (1996). Disenfranchising the brokenhearted. In K. J. Doka (Ed.), *Disenfranchised grief: New directions, challenges and strategies for practice* (pp. 233–250). Champaign, IL: Research Press.

Matthews, L. T., & Marwit, S. J. (2004). Examining the assumptive world views of parents bereaved by accident, murder, and illness. *Omega, 48*, 115–136.

Matusow, B. (2000, November). Retirement blues. *The Washingtonian*, pp. 45-54.

Maughan, A., Cicchetti, D., Toth, S. L., & Rogosch, F. A. (2007). Early-occurring maternal depression and maternal negativity in predicting young children's emotion regulation and socioemotional difficulties. *Journal of Abnormal Child Psychology, 35*, 685–703.

McCoyd, J. L. M. (1987, October). *Supporting families experiencing NICU hospitalization and high-risk pregnancy.* Paper presented at the Parent Care 4th Annual Conference, Philadelphia, PA.

McCoyd, J. L. M. (2003). *Pregnancy interrupted: Non-normative loss of a desired pregnancy after termination for fetal anomaly.* Unpublished doctoral dissertation, Bryn Mawr College, Bryn Mawr, PA. Available: Proquest, Ann Arbor, MI.

McCoyd, J. L. M. (2007). Pregnancy interrupted: Loss of a desired pregnancy after diagnosis of fetal anomaly. *Journal of Psychosomatic Obstetrics and Gynecology, 28*(1), 37–48.

McCoyd, J. L. M. (2008a). Women in no man's land: The U. S. abortion debate and women terminating desired pregnancies due to fetal anomaly. *British Journal of Social Work.* Published online May 28, 2008, pending journal publication: doi:10.1093/bjsw/bcn080

McCoyd, J. L. M. (2008b). I'm not a saint: Burden and capacity assessment as unrecognized factors in prenatal decision making. *Qualitative Health Research, 18,* 1489–1500.

McCoyd, J. L. M. (2009). Discrepant feeling rules and unscripted emotion work: Women terminating desired pregnancies due to fetal anomaly. *American Journal of Orthopsychiatry, 79*(1).

McCoyd, J. L. M., & Kerson, T. S. (2006). Conducting intensive interviews using E-mail: A serendipitous comparative opportunity. *Qualitative Social Work: Research and Practice, 5*(3), 389–406.

McCoyd, J. L. M. & Walter, C. (2007). A different kind of holding environment: A case study of group work with pediatric staff. *Journal of Social Work in End-of-Life & Palliative Care, 3*(3), 5–22.

Melham, N. M., Moritz, G., Walker, M., Shear, M. K., & Brent, D. (2007). Phenomenology and correlates of complicated grief in children and adolescents. *Journal of the American Academy of Child and Adolescent Psychiatry, 46,* 493–499.

Menke, E. M. (1987). The impact of a child's chronic illness on school-aged siblings. *Children's Health Care, 15*(3), 132–140.

Merkatz, R. (1978). Prolonged hospitalization of pregnant women: The effects on the family. *Birth and the Family Journal, 5*(4), 204–206.

Meuser, T. M., Marwit, S. J., & Saunders, S. (2004). Assessing grief in caregivers. In K. Doka (Ed.), *In living with grief: Alzheimer's disease* (pp. 169–195). Washington, DC: Hospice Foundation of America.

Milo, E. M. (2005). The death of a child with a developmental disability. In R. Neimeyer (Ed.), *Meaning reconstruction & the experience of loss* (pp. 113–134). Washington, DC: American Psychological Association.

Mirkin, M. (1994). *Women in context: Toward a feminist reconstruction of psychotherapy.* New York: Guilford Press.

Moore, T. H. M., Zammit, S., Lingford-Hughes, A., Barnes, T. R. E., Jones, P. B., Burke, M., & Lewis, G. (2007). Cannabis use and risk of psychotic or affective mental health outcomes: A systematic review. *Lancet, 370,* 319–327.

Morgan, L. M., & Michaels, M. W. (Eds.). (1999). *Fetal subjects, feminist positions.* Philadelphia: University of Pennsylvania Press.

Morse, J. M., Wilson, S., & Penrod, J. (2000). Mothers and their disabled children: Refining the concept of normalization. *Health Care for Women International, 21,* 659–676.

Moss, M., Moss, S., & Hansson, R. (2001). Bereavement and old age. In M. S. Stroebe & R. O. Hansson (Eds.), *Handbook of bereavement research: Consequences, coping and care* (pp. 241–260). Washington, DC: American Psychological Association.

Munch, S. (2000). A qualitative analysis of physician humanism: Women's experiences with hyperemesis gravidarum. *Journal of Perinatology, 20,* 540–547.

Munch, S. (2002a). Chicken or the egg? The biological-psychological controversy surrounding hyperemesis gravidarum. *Social Science & Medicine, 55,* 1267–1278.

Munch, S. (2002b). Women's experiences with a pregnancy complication: Causal explanations of hyperemesis gravidarum. *Social Work in Health Care, 36*(1), 59–75.

Munch, S. (2004). Gender-biased diagnosing of women's medical complaints: Contributions of feminist thought, 1970–1995. *Women & Health, 40*(1), 101–121.

Munch, S., & Schmitz, M. F. (2006). Hyperemesis and patient satisfaction: A path model of patients' perceptions of the patient–physician relationship. *Journal of Psychosomatic Obstetrics & Gynecology, 27*(1), 49–57.

Murphy, S. A., Johnson, L. C., Wu, L., Fan, J. J., & Lohan, J. (2003). Bereaved parents' outcomes 4 to 60 months after their children's deaths by accident, suicide, or homicide: A comparative study demonstrating differences. *Death Studies, 27,* 39–61.

Myers, G. C. (1996). Aging and the social sciences: Research directions and unresolved issues. In R. H. Binstock & L. K. George (Eds.), *Handbook of aging and the social sciences.* San Diego: Academic Press.

Nader, K. O. (1997). Childhood traumatic loss: The interaction of trauma and grief. In C. R. Figley, B. E. Bride, & N. Mazza (Eds.), *Death and trauma: The traumatology of grieving* (pp. 17–41). Washington, DC: Taylor & Francis.

Naylor, A., & Prescott, P. (2004). Invisible children? The need for support groups for siblings of disabled children. *British Journal of Special Education, 31*(4), 199–206.

Naef, R., Chauhan, S., Roach, H., Roberts, W., Travis, K., & Morrison, J. (1995). Treatment for hyperemesis gravidarum in the home: An alternative to hospitalization. *Journal of Perinatology, 15*(4), 289–291.

Neimeyer, R. (1998). *Lessons of loss: A guide to coping.* New York: McGraw-Hill.

Neimeyer, R. A. (2001). *Meaning reconstruction & the meaning of loss.* Washington, DC: American Psychological Association.

Neimeyer, R., Prigerson, H., & Davies, B. (2002). Mourning and meaning. *American Behavioral Scientist, 46*(2), 235–251.

Newman, B. M., & Newman, P. R. (1987). *Development through life: A psychosocial approach.* Homewood, IL: Dorsey Press.

Newman, B. M., & Newman, P. R. (1995). *Development through life: A psychosocial approach* (2nd ed.). Pacific Grove, CA: Brooks/Cole.

Newman, B., & Newman, P. (2006). *Development through life: A psychosocial experience.* Belmont, CA: Thomson (Wadsworth).

Neugarten, B. (1979). Time, age and the life cycle. *American Journal of Psychiatry, 136,* 887–894.

Niemi, T. (1979). The mortality of male old-age pensioners following spouse's death. *Scandinavian Journal of Social Medicine, 7,* 115–117.

Nolen-Hoeksema, S., & Larson, J. (1999). *Coping with loss.* Mahwah, NJ: Erlbaum.

Noppe, L. D., & Noppe, I. (1996). Ambiguity in adolescent understandings of death. In C. A. Corr & D. E. Balk (Eds.), *Handbook of adolescent death and bereavement* (pp. 25–41). New York: Springer Publishing Company.

Normand, C. L., Silverman, P. R., & Nickman, S. L. (1996). Bereaved children's changing relationships with the deceased. In D. Klass, P. R. Silverman, & S. L. Nickman (Eds.), *Continuing bonds* (pp. 87–111). Philadelphia: Taylor & Francis.

Obeidallah, D. A., Brennan, R. T., Brooks-Gunn, J., Kindlon, D., & Earls, F. (2000). Socioeconomic status, race, and girls' pubertal maturation: Results from the project on human development in Chicago neighborhoods. *Journal of Research on Adolescence, 10,* 443–464.

O'Brien, B., Evans, M., & White-McDonald, E. (2002). Isolation from "being alive": Coping with severe nausea and vomiting of pregnancy. *Nursing Research, 51*(5), 302–308.

O'Brien, B., & Naber, S. (1992). Nausea and vomiting during pregnancy: Effects on the quality of women's lives. *Birth, 19*(3), 138–143.

O'Brien, J. M., Boodenow, C., & Espin, O. (1991). Adolescents' reactions to the death of a peer. *Adolescence, 26*(102), 431–440.

O'Connor, M.-F., Gundel, H., McRae, K., & Lane, R. (2007). Baseline vagal tone predicts BOLD response during elicitation of grief. *Neuropsychopharmacology, 32,* 2184–2189.

Ohannessian, C. M., & Hesselbrock, V. M. (2007). Do personality characteristics and risk-taking mediate the relationship between paternal substance dependence and adolescent substance use? *Addictive Behaviors, 32*(9), 1852–1862.

O'Hara, M. W., Reiter, R. C., Johnson, S. J., Milburn, A., & Engeldinger, J. (Eds.). (1995). *Psychological aspects of women's reproductive health.* New York: Springer Publishing Company.

Oktay, J. S. (2005). *Breast cancer: Daughters tell their stories.* Binghamton, NY: Haworth.

Oktay, J. S., & Walter, C. (1991). *Breast cancer in the life course: Women's experiences.* New York: Springer Publishing Company.

Olshansky, S. (1962). Chronic sorrow: A response to having a mentally defective child. *Social Casework, 43,* 190–193.

Oltjenbruns, K. A. (1996). Death of a friend during adolescence: Issues and impact. In C. A. Corr & D. E. Balk (Eds.), *Handbook of adolescent death and bereavement* (pp. 196–215). New York: Springer Publishing Company.

Ong, K. K., Ahmed, M. L., & Dunger, D. B. (2006). Lessons from large population studies on timing and tempo of puberty (secular trends and relation to body size): The European trend. *Molecular and Cellular Endocrinology, 254–255,* 8–12.

Oswald, F., & Wahl, H. (2005). Dimensions of the meaning of home in later life. In G. Rowles & H. Chaudhury (Eds.), *Home and identity in late life: International perspectives* (pp. 21–45). New York: Springer Publishing Company.

Ottinger, D. R., & Simmons, J. E. (1964). Behavior of human neonates and prenatal maternal anxiety. *Psychological Reports, 14,* 391–394.

Ory, M., Hoffman, Y., Yee, Y., Tennestedt, S., & Schultz, R. (1999). Prevalence and impact of caregiving: A detailed comparison between dementia and non-dementia caregivers. *The Gerontologist, 39,* 177–186.

Panuthos, C., & Romeo, C. (1984). *Ended beginnings: Healing childbearing losses.* Boston: Bergin and Garvey.

Parkes, C. M. (1988). Bereavement as a psychosocial transition: Processes of adaptation to change. *Journal of Social Issues, 44*(3), 53–65.

Parkes, C. M. (2001). A historical overview of the scientific study of bereavement. In M. S. Stroebe, R. O. Hansson, W. Stroebe, & H. Schut (Eds.), *Handbook of bereavement research: Consequences, coping, and care* (pp. 25–45). Washington, DC: American Psychological Association.

Parkes, C. M., Benjamin, B., & Fitzgerald, R. G. (1969). Broken heart: A statistical study of increased mortality among widowers. *British Medical Journal, 1,* 740–743.

Patterson, J. M., & Hovey, D. L. (2000). Family-centered care for children with special health needs: Rhetoric or reality. *Families, Systems & Health, 18*(2), 237–251.

Patton, G. C., & Viner, R. (2007). Pubertal transitions in health. *Lancet, 369*(9567), 1130–1139.

Pauww, J., Bierling, S., Cook, C., & Davis, A. (2003). Hyperemesis gravidarum and fetal outcome. *Journal of Parenteral and Enteral Nutrition, 29*(2), 93–96.

Pavao, M. (1998). *The family of adoption.* Boston: Beacon Press.

Pennebaker, J. W., Kiecolt-Glaser, J., & Glaser, J. (1988). Disclosure of traumas and immune functions: Health implications for psychotherapy. *Journal of Consulting and Clinical Psychology, 56,* 239–245.

Peppers, L. G., & Knapp, R. J. (1980). *Motherhood and mourning: Perinatal death.* New York: Praeger.

Perry-Jenkins, M., Goldberg, A., Pierce, C., & Sayer, A. (2007). Shiftwork, role overload, and the transition to parenthood. *Journal of Marriage and Family, 69,* 123–138.

Petersen, S., & Rafuls, S. E. (1998). Receiving the scepter: The generational transition and impact of parental death on adults. *Death Studies, 22*(6), 493–524.

Peterson, B., Newton, C., Rosen, K., & Shulman, R. (2006). Coping processes of couples experiencing infertility. *Family Relations, 55,* 227–239.

Pfefferbaum, B., Nixon, S. J., Tucker, P. M., Tivis, R. D., Moore, V. L., Brown, J. M., Pynoos, R. S., Foy, D., & Gurwitch, R. H. (1999). Posttraumatic stress responses in bereaved children after the Oklahoma City bombing. *Journal of the American Academy of Child and Adolescent Psychiatry, 38,* 1372–1379.

Philip, B. (2003). Hyperemesis gravidarum: Literature review. *Wisconsin Medical Journal, 102*(3), 46–51.

Phillips, R. S. C. (1999). Intervention with siblings of children with developmental disabilities from economically disadvantaged families. *Families in Society, 80*(6), 569–584.

Piaget, J. (1954). *The construction of reality in the child.* New York: Basic Books.

Piaget, J. (1972). Intellectual evolution from adolescence to adulthood. *Human Development, 15,* 1–12.

Pike, S., & Grieve, K. (2006). Counseling perspectives on the landscape of infertility. *Therapy Today, 17*(8), 28–32.

Pines, D. (1993). *A woman's unconscious use of her body.* London: Yale University Press.

Pipher, M. (1994). *Reviving Ophelia.* New York: Grosset/Putnam.

Podell, C. (1989). Adolescent mourning: The sudden death of a peer. *Clinical Social Work, 17*(1), 64–78.

Pollack, W. (1998). *Real boys: Rescuing our sons from the myths of boyhood.* New York: Henry Holt.

Pollack, W. (1999, October). *Rescuing our boys.* Presented at Amherst Unitarian Church, Amherst, MA.

Pope, D. C. (2001). *Doing school: How we are creating a generation of stressed out, materialistic, and miseducated students*. New Haven, CT: Yale University Press.

Pottick, K. J., Bilder, S., Stoep, A. V., Warner, L. A., & Alvarez, M. F. (2008). U.S. patterns of mental health service utilization for transition-age youth and young adults. *Journal of Behavioral Health Services & Research, 35*(4), 373–389.

Poulin, J. E. (2000). *Collaborative social work: Strengths based generalist practice*. Itasca, IL: F. E. Peacock.

Quadagno, J. (2002). *Aging and the life course: An introduction to social gerontology*. New York: McGraw-Hill.

Quinn, J. F., & Kozy, M. (1996). The role of bridge jobs in the retirement transition: Gender, race, and ethnicity. *The Gerontologist, 36*(3), 363–372.

Rager, D. R., Laudenslager, M. L., Held, P. E., & Boccia, M. L. (1989). Some long-term behavioral and immunological effects of brief, maternal separation in non-human primates: Preliminary observations. *Society for Neuroscience Abstracts, 15*, 297.

Rando, T. (1986a). Adult loss of a parent. In T. Rando (Ed.), *How to go on living when someone you know dies* (pp. 137–151). Champaign, IL: Research Press.

Rando, T. (1986b). Adult loss of a sibling. In T. Rando (Ed.), *How to go on living when someone you know dies* (pp. 154–159). Champaign, IL: Research Press.

Rando, T. A. (1986c). The unique issues and impact of the death of a child. In T. Rando (Ed.), *Parental loss of a child* (pp. 5–43). Champaign, IL: Research Press.

Rando, T. A. (1993). *Treatment of complicated mourning*. Champaign, IL: Research Press.

Rando, T. (1985). Anticipatory grief and the child mourner. In D. Adams & E. Peveau (Eds.), *Beyond the innocence of childhood* (Vol. 3, pp. 5–41). Amityville, NY: Baywood.

Raphel, B. (1983). *The anatomy of bereavement*. New York: Basic Books.

Raphael-Leff, J. (1980). Psychotherapy with pregnant women. In B. L. Blum (Ed.). *Psychological aspects of pregnancy, birth, and bonding* (pp. 174–205). New York: Human Sciences Press.

Rapp, R. (1999). *Testing women, testing the fetus: The social impact of amniocentesis in America*. New York: Routledge.

Rask, K., Kaunonen, M., & Paunon-Ilmonen, M. (2002). Adolescent coping with grief after the death of a loved one. *International Journal of Nursing Practice, 8*, 137–142.

Reilly, J. J. (2007). Childhood obesity: An overview. *Children & Society, 21*, 390–396.

Remschmidt, H. (1994). Psychosocial milestones in normal puberty and adolescence. *Hormone Research, 41*(Suppl. 2), 19–29.

Reyna, V. F., & Farley, F. (2007). Is the teenage brain too rational? *Scientific American* (Special Edition), *17*(2), 60–67.

Rich, L. (1991). *When pregnancy isn't perfect: A layperson's guide to complications in pregnancy*. New York: Dutton Books.

Richardson, V. E. (2007). A dual process model of grief counseling: Findings from the changing lives of older couples (CLOC) Study. *Journal of Gerontological Social Work, 48*, 311–329.

Richardson, V. E., & Balaswamy, S. (2001). Coping with bereavement among elderly widowers. *Omega: Journal of Death and Dying, 43*, 129–144.

Richman, J., Jason, L., Taylor, R., & Jahn, S. (2000). Feminist perspectives on the social construction of chronic fatigue syndrome. *Health Care for Women International, 21,* 173–185.

Richmond, B., & Ross, M. (1995). Death of a partner: Responses to AIDS-related bereavement. In L. Sherr (Ed.), *Grief and AIDS* (pp. 161–179). New York: John Wiley.

Richmond, M. E. (1917). *Social diagnosis.* New York: Russell Sage Foundation.

Robak, R., & Weitzman, S. (1994). Grieving the loss of romantic relationships among young adults: An empirical study of disenfranchised grief. *Omega, 30*(4), 269–281.

Robinson, L., & Mahon, M. (1997). Sibling bereavement: A concept analysis. *Death Studies, 21,* 477–499.

Robinson, T., & Marwit, S. (2006). An investigation of the relationship of personality, coping, and grief intensity among bereaved mothers. *Death Studies, 30,* 677–696.

Roffwarg, H. P., Muzio, J. N., & Dement, W. (1966). Ontogenetic development of the human sleep–dream cycle. *Science, 152,* 604–619.

Rolland, J. S. (1994). *Families, illness and disability: An integrative treatment model.* New York: Basic Books.

Rose, G. L. (1995). Prenatal diagnosis. In M. W. O' Hara, R. C. Reiter, S. J. Johnson, A. Milburn, & J. Engeldinger (Eds.), *Psychological aspects of women's reproductive health* (pp. 161–178). New York: Springer Publishing Company.

Rossi, A. S., & Rossi, P. H. (1990). *Of human bonding: Parent–child relations across the life course.* New York: Aldine de Gruyter.

Rowe, J. W., & Kahn, R. L. (1998). *Successful aging.* New York: Pantheon Books.

Rowling, L. (2002). Youth and disenfranchised grief. In K. J. Doka (Ed.), *Disenfranchised grief: New directions, challenges and strategies for practice* (pp. 275–292). Champaign, IL: Research Press.

Roy-Byrne, P., & Shear, M. K. (2007). Is the stage theory of grief empirically valid? *Journal Watch.* Retrieved April 5, 2007, from http://psychiatry.jwatch.org/cgi/content/full/2007/326/1?q-etoc

Rubin, S. (1999). The two-track model of bereavement: Overview, retrospect, and prospect. *Death Studies, 23,* 681–714.

Rubinstein, R., & Medeiros, K. (2005). Home, self and identity. In G. Rowles & H. Chaudhury (Eds.), *Home and identity in late life: International perspectives* (pp. 47–61). New York: Springer Publishing Company.

Rynearson, E. K., & McCreery, J. M. (1993). Bereavement after homicide: A synergism of trauma and loss. *American Journal of Psychiatry, 150*(2), 258–261.

Safran, J. D., & Muran, J. C. (2000). *Negotiating the therapeutic alliance: A relational treatment guide.* New York: Guilford Press.

Saldinger, A., Cain, A. C., Porterfield, K., & Lohnes, K. (2004). Facilitating attachment between school-aged children and a dying parent. *Death Studies, 28,* 915–940.

Saldinger, A., Porterfield, K., & Cain, A. C. (2004). Meeting the needs of parentally bereaved children: A framework for child-centered parenting. *Psychiatry, 67,* 331–352.

Salovey, P., Rothman, A. J., Detweiler, J. B., & Steward, W. T. (2000). Emotional states and physical health. *American Psychologist, 55*(1), 110–121.

Sanchez, A. (2001). *Rainbow road.* New York: Simon & Schuster.

Sandler, A. (2004). *Living with spina bifida: A guide for families and professionals*. Chapel Hill, NC: University of North Carolina Press.

Sandstrom, M., & Keefe, F. (1998). Self-management of fibromyalgia: The role of formal coping skills training and physical exercise. *Arthritis Care and Research: The Official Journal of the Arthritis Health Professions Association, 11*(6), 432–437.

Sandstrom, M. J., & Coie, J. D. (1999). A developmental perspective on peer rejection: Mechanisms of stability and change. *Child Development, 70*, 955–966.

Saunders, S., & Corley, C. (2003). Are they grieving? A qualitative analysis examining grief in caregivers of individuals with Alzheimer's disease. *Social Work in Health Care, 37*(3), 35–53.

Schaver, P. R., & Tancredy, C. M. (2001). Emotion, attachment, and bereavement: A conceptual commentary. In M. S. Stroebe, R. O. Hansson, W. Stroebe, & H. Schut (Eds.), *Handbook of bereavement research: Consequences, coping, and care* (pp. 63–88). Washington, DC: American Psychological Association.

Schenk, D. (2003). *The forgetting Alzheimer's: Portrait of an epidemic*. New York: Random House.

Scheper-Hughes, N. (1993). *Death without weeping: The violence of everyday life in Brazil*. Berkeley, CA: University of California Press.

Schott, J., & Henley, A. (1996). *Culture, religion and childbearing in a multiracial society*. Oxford: Butterworth/Heinemann.

Schlossberg, N. (2004). *Retire smart, retire happy*. Washington, DC: American Psychological Association.

Schultz, R., Mendelsohn, W., Mahoney, R., Zhang, S., Thompson, L., & Belle, S. (2003). End of life care and the effects of bereavement on family caregivers of persons with dementia. *New England Journal of Medicine, 349*, 1936–1952.

Schwab, R. (1998). A child's death and divorce: Dispelling the myth. *Death Studies, 22*, 445–468.

Schwartz, L., & Drotar, D. (2006). Posttraumatic stress and related impairment in survivors of childhood cancer in early adulthood compared to healthy peers. *Journal of Pediatric Psychology, 31*, 356–366.

Schwartzberg, S. (1996). *A crisis of meaning: How gay men are making sense of AIDS*. Oxford: Oxford University Press.

Seligman, M. P. (with Reivich, K., Jaycox, L., & Gilham, J.) (1995). *The optimistic child: A revolutionary program that safeguards children against depression & builds lifelong resilience*. Boston: Houghton Mifflin.

Shaffer, S. (1993). Young widows: Rebuilding identity and personal growth following spousal loss (Doctoral dissertation, University of San Francisco, 1993). *Dissertation Abstracts International, 54/01*, 94.

Shapiro, A., & Gottman, J. (2005). Effects on marriage of a psycho-communicative-educational intervention with couples undergoing the transition to parenthood, evaluation at 1 year post intervention. *Journal of Family Communication, 5*(1), 1–24.

Shapiro, A., Gottman, J., & Carrere, S. (2000). The baby and the marriage: Identifying factors that buffer against decline in marital satisfaction after the first baby arrives. *Journal of Family Psychology, 14*, 59–70.

Shapiro, V. B., Shapiro, J. R., & Paret, I. H. (2001). *Complex adoption & assisted reproductive technology: A developmental approach to clinical practice*. New York: Guilford Press.

Shdaimah, C. S. (2004). *The practice of public interest law: Power, professionalism and the pursuit of social justice.* Unpublished doctoral dissertation, Bryn Mawr College, Bryn Mawr, PA. Available from: Proquest, Ann Arbor, MI.

Shdaimah, C. S. (2009). *Negotiating justice: Public interest lawyering, low-income clients, and the pursuit of social justice.* New York: New York University Press.

Shernoff, M. (1998). Gay widowers: Grieving in relation to trauma and social supports. *Journal of Gay and Lesbian Medical Association, 2*(1), 27–33.

Silverman, P. R., & Nickman, S. L. (1996). Children's construction of their dead parents. In D. Klass, P. R. Silverman, & S. L. Nickman (Eds.), *Continuing bonds: New understanding of grief* (pp. 73–86). Philadelphia: Taylor & Francis.

Silverman, P. R., & Worden, J. W. (2006). Children's reactions to the death of a parent. In M. S. Stroebe, W. Stroebe, & R. O. Hansson (Eds.), *Handbook of bereavement: Theory, research, and intervention* (pp. 300–316). New York: Cambridge University Press. (Original work published 1993)

Simos, B. G. (1979). *A time to grieve: Loss as a universal human experience.* New York: Family Service Association of America.

Simpson, S. W., Goodwin, T. M., Robins, S. B., Rizzo, A. A., Howes, R. A., Buckwalter, D. K., & Buckwalter, J. G. (2001). Psychological factors and hyperemesis gravidarum. *Journal of Women's Health & Gender-Based Medicine, 10*(5), 471–477.

Sklar, F., & Hartley, S. F. (1990). Close friends as survivors: Bereavement patterns in a "hidden" population. *Omega, 21*(2), 103–112.

Slavin, K. F., & Wingrove, C. R. (1995). Women and retirement: A review and critique of the empirical literature since 1976. *Sociological Inquiry, 65*(1), 1–21.

Sowell, E. R., Thompson, P. M., Leonard, C. M., Welcome, S. E., Kan, E., & Toga, A. W. (2004). Longitudinal mapping of cortical thickness and brain growth in normal children. *Journal of Neuroscience, 24,* 8223–8231.

Spiegel, J. (2003). *SAM: Sexual abuse of males.* New York: Brunner Routledge.

Spock, B. (1976). *Baby and child care.* New York: Dutton.

Sprinkle, R. H. (2001). The missing politics and unsettled science of the trend toward earlier puberty. *Politics and the Life Sciences, 20,* 43–66.

Stellman, R. (1990). Psychological aspects of gynecologic surgery. In J. Sciarra (Ed.), *Gynecology and obstetrics* (pp. 1–5). Philadelphia: J. B. Lippincott.

Stern, D. N., & Bruschweiler-Stern, N. (1998). *The birth of a mother.* New York: Basic Books.

Stiles, W. (2002). Assimilation of problematic experiences. In J. C. Norcross (Ed.), *Psychotherapy relationships that work* (pp. 357–365). Oxford: Oxford University Press.

Stiles, W., Elliott, R., Llewelyn, S., Firth-Cozens, J., Margison, F., Shapiro, D., & Hardy, G. (1990). Assimilation of problematic experiences by clients in psychotherapy. *Psychotherapy, 27,* 411–420.

Stone, M., & Stone, H. (2004). *Too young to retire: 101 ways to start the rest of your life.* New York: Penguin.

Stroebe, M., Gergen, M. M., Gergen, K. J., & Stroebe, W. (1992). Broken hearts or broken bonds: Love and death in historical perspective. *American Psychologist, 47,* 1205–1212.

Stroebe, M., & Schut, H. (1999). The dual process model of coping with bereavement: Rationale and description. *Death Studies, 23*, 197–224.

Stroebe, M., & Schut, H. (2005). Meaning making in the dual process model of coping with bereavement. In R. Neimeyer (Ed.), *Meaning reconstruction & the experience of loss* (pp. 55–73). Washington, DC: American Psychological Association.

Stroebe, M., Schut, H., & Stroebe, W. (1998). Trauma and grief: A comparative analysis. In J. Harvey (Ed.), *Perspectives on loss: A sourcebook* (pp. 81–96). Washington, DC: Taylor and Francis.

Stroebe, M., & Stroebe, W. (1991). Does "grief work" work? *Journal of Consulting and Clinical Psychology, 59*(3), 479–482.

Stroebe, M. S., & Schut, H. (2001). Models of coping with bereavement: A review. In M. Stroebe, R. O. Hansson, W. Stroebe, & H. Schut (Eds.), *Handbook of bereavement research: Consequences, coping and care* (pp. 375–403). Washington, DC: American Psychological Association.

Stroebe, M. S., & Stroebe, W. (1993). The mortality of bereavement: A review. In M. S. Stroebe, W. Stroebe, & R. O. Hansson (Eds.), *Handbook of bereavement: Theory, research, and intervention* (pp. 175–195). New York: Cambridge University Press.

Stroebe, M. S., Stroebe, W., Gergen, K. J., & Gergen, M. (1981). The broken heart: Reality or myth? *Omega, 12*, 87–105.

Stroebe, M. S., Stroebe, W., & Schut, H. (2005a). Who benefits from disclosure? Exploration of attachment style differences in the effects of expressing emotions. *Clinical Psychology Review, 9*, 48–60.

Stroebe, M. S., Stroebe, W., & Schut, H. (2005b). Attachment in coping with bereavement: A theoretical integration. *Review of General Psychology, 9*, 48–66.

Strom, R., & Strom, S. (2000). Meeting the challenge of raising grandchildren. *International Journal of Aging and Human Development, 51*(3), 183–198.

Stuart, H. (2006). Psychosocial risk clustering in high school students. *Social Psychiatry and Psychiatric Epidemiology, 41*, 498–507.

Styles, J. L., Meier, A., Sutherland, L. A., & Campbell, M. K. (2007). Parents' and caregivers' concerns about obesity in young children. *Family & Community Health, 30*, 279–295.

Svanstrom, R., & Dahlberg, K. (2004). Living with dementia yields a heteronomous and lost existence. *Western Journal of Nursing, 26*(6), 671–687.

Swahnberg, K., Suruchi, T. B., & Bertero, C. (2007). Nullified: Women's perceptions of being abused in health care. *Journal of Psychosomatic Obstetrics and Gynecology, 28*(3), 161–167.

Swallow, B. L., Lindow, S. W., Masson, E. A., & Hay, D. M. (2002). Development of an instrument to measure nausea and vomiting in pregnancy. *Journal of Obstetrics and Gynaecology, 22*(5), 481–485.

Taylor, S., Klein, L., Lewis, B., Gruenewald, T., Gurung, R., & Updegraff, J. (2000). Biobehavioral responses to stress in females: Tend and befriend, not fight or flight. *Psychological Review, 107*, 411–429.

Tedschi, R. G., Park, C. L., & Calhoun, L. G. (1998). *Posttraumatic growth: Positive changes in the aftermath of crisis.* Mahwah, NJ: Erlbaum.

Teicher, M. H., Dumont, N. L., Ito, Y., Vaituzis, C., Giedd, J. J., & Andersen, S. L. (2004). Childhood neglect is associated with reduced corpus collosum area. *Biological Psychiatry, 56*, 80-85.

Theut, S. K., Zaslow, M. J., Rabinovich, B. A., Bartko, J. J., & Morihisa, J. M. (1990). Resolution of parental bereavement after a perinatal loss. *Journal of the American Academy of Child and Adolescent Psychiatry, 29*(4), 521–525.

Thomas, A., Chess, S., & Birch, H. G. (1970). The origin of personality. *Scientific American, 223*, 102–109.

Tiwary, C. M. (1994). Premature sexual development in children following the use of placenta and/or estrogen containing hair products. *Pediatric Research, 135*, 108.

Tomlinson-Keasey, C. (1972). Conditioning of infant vocalizations in the home environment. *Journal of Genetic Psychology, 120*, 75–82.

Trafford, A. (2004). *My time: Making the most of the bonus decades after fifty.* New York: Basic Books.

Tritt, S. G., & Esses, L. M. (1988). Psychosocial adaptation of siblings of children with chronic medical illnesses. *American Journal of Orthopsychiatry, 58*(2), 211–220.

Troll, L. (1987). Mother–daughter relationships through the life span. In S. Oskamp (Ed.), *Applied social psychology annual 7* (pp. 284–305). Newbury Park, CA: Sage.

Turrini, P. (1980). Psychological crises in normal pregnancy. In B. L. Blum (Ed.), *Psychological aspects of pregnancy, birth, and bonding* (pp. 135–150). New York: Human Sciences Press.

Umberson, D. (2003). *Death of a parent: Transition to a new adult identity.* New York: Cambridge University Press.

Underwood, N. (2006). The teenage brain [Cover story]. *The Walrus, 3*(9), 48–56.

Uren, T. H., & Wastell, C. A. (2002). Attachment and meaning-making in perinatal bereavement. *Death Studies, 26*, 279–306.

U. S. Census Bureau. (2004). *Statistical abstract of the United States, 2004.* Washington DC: U. S. Government Printing Office.

U. S. Census Bureau. (2008). *The 2008 statistical abstract. Births, deaths, marriages, & divorces: Life expectancy.* Retrieved July 21, 2008, from http://www.census.gov/compendia/statab/cats/births_deaths_marriages_divorces/life_expectancies

Van Der Kolk, B. A. (1998). Trauma and memory. *Psychiatry and Clinical Neurosciences, 52*(Suppl.), S97–S109.

Van Der Kolk, B. A., McFarlane, A. C., & Weisaeth, L. (Eds.). (1996). *Traumatic stress: The effects of overwhelming experience on mind, body, and society.* New York: Guilford Press.

Van Jaarsveld, C. H., Fidler, J. A., Simon, A. E., & Wardle, J. (2007). Persistent impact of pubertal timing on trends in smoking, food choice, activity and stress in adolescence. *Psychosomatic Medicine, 69*, 798–806.

Van Riper, M. (2000). Family variables associated with well-being in siblings of children with Down syndrome. *Journal of Family Nursing, 6*, 267–286.

VanPutte, A. W. (1988). Perinatal bereavement crisis: Coping with negative outcomes from prenatal diagnosis. *Journal of Perinatal and Neonatal Nursing, 2*(2), 12–22.

Videka-Sherman, L., & Lieberman, M. (1985). The effects of self-help and psychotherapy intervention on child loss: The limits of recovery. *American Journal of Orthopsychiatry, 55*, 70–82.

Viorst, J. (1986). *Necessary losses: The loves, illusions, dependencies and impossible expectations that all of us have to give up in order to grow.* New York: Fawcett Gold Medal.

Vitez, M. (2008, January 20). After leap breaks body, a miracle renews spirit. *The Philadelphia Inquirer*, pp. A1, A20, A21, A22.

Vollmer, S. (in press). Before their time. *Journal of Pastoral Care & Counseling.*

Vollmer, S. (in press). Plastic. *Journal of Pastoral Care & Counseling.*

Vollmer, S. (in press). The face of death. *Journal of Pastoral Care & Counseling.*

Volkan, V. (1985). Psychotherapy of complicated mourning. In V. Volkan (Ed.), *Depressive states and their treatment*. Northfield, NJ: Jason Aronson.

Vosler, N., & Mollnow, E. (1996). Predictors of depression among workers at the time of a plant closing. *Journal of Sociology and Social Welfare, 23*, 25–42.

Wachtel, P. L. (1993). *Therapeutic communication: Knowing what to say when*. New York: Guilford Press.

Walker, R., & Pomeroy, E. (1996). Depression or grief? *Health and Social Work, 21*, 247–254.

Walker, R., Pomeroy, E., McNeil, J., & Franklin, C. (1994). Anticipatory grief and Alzheimer's disease: Strategies for intervention. *Journal of Gerontological Social Work, 22*(3/4), 21–39.

Wallander, J. L., & Varni, J. W. (1998). Effects of pediatric chronic physical disorders on child and family adjustment. *Journal of Child Psychology and Psychiatry, 39*, 29–46.

Wallis, C. (2006, March 27). The multi-tasking generation: They're e-mailing, IMing and downloading while writing the history essay. What is all that doing to kids' brains and their family life? *Time*. Retrieved November 29, 2007, from http://www.lexisnexis.com.proxy.libraries.rutgers.edu/us/lnacademic/frame.do?tokenKey

Walsh, F., & McGoldrick, M. (2004). *Living beyond loss* (2nd ed.). New York: W. W. Norton.

Walter, C. (1986). *The timing of motherhood*. Lexington, MA: D. C. Heath.

Walter, C. (1991). Adult daughters and mothers: Stress in the caregiving relationship. *Journal of Women and Aging, 3*(3), 39–58.

Walter, C. (2003). *The loss of a life partner: Narratives of the bereaved*. New York: Columbia University Press.

Walter, T. (1999). *On bereavement: The culture of grief*. Buckingham, UK: Open University Press.

Walter, T. (2000). Grief narratives: The role of medicine in the policing of grief. *Anthropology & Medicine, 7*(1), 97–114.

Watkins, K., & Baldo, T. (2004). The infertility experience: Biopsychosocial effects and suggestions for counselors. *Journal of Counseling and Development, 82*, 394–402.

Weber, J., & Waldrop, D. (2000). Grandparents raising grandchildren: Families in transition. *Journal of Gerontological Social Work, 33*(2), 27–46.

Webster, D. (1993). Interstitial cystitis: Women at risk for psychiatric misdiagnosis. *Clinical Issues in Perinatal Women's Health Nursing, 4*(2), 236–243.

White, M., & Epston, D. (1990). *Narrative means to therapeutic ends*. New York: W. W. Norton.

Wiegernick, R., Harris, C., Simeonson, R., & Pearson, M. E. (1974). Social stimulation of vocalizations in delayed infants. *Child Development, 45*, 866–872.

Willemsen, E. (1979). *Understanding infancy*. San Francisco: W. H. Freeman.

Williams, J. (1923). *Obstetrics* (5th ed.). New York: D. Appleton & Co.

Williams, P. D., Hanson, S., Karlin, R., Ridder, L., Liebergen, A., Olson, J., Barnard, M. U., & Tobin-Rommelhart, S. (1997). Outcomes of a nursing intervention for siblings of chronically ill children: A pilot study. *Journal of the Society of Pediatric Nurses, 2*(3), 127–138.

Williams, P. D., Williams, A. R., Hanson, S., Graff, C., Ridder, L., Curry, H., Liebergen, A., & Karlin-Setter, R. (1999). Maternal mood, family functioning, and perceptions of social support, self-esteem, and mood among siblings of chronically ill children. *Children's Health Care, 28*(4), 297–310.

Willis, C. A. (2002). The grieving process in children: Strategies for understanding, educating, and reconciling children's perceptions of death. *Early Childhood Education Journal, 29*(4), 221–226.

Winnicott, D. W. (1953). Transitional objects and transitional phenomena; a study of the first not-me possession. *International Journal of Psycho-Analysis, 34*, 89–97.

Winnicott, D. W. (1965). *The maturational processes and the facilitating environment: Studies in the theory of emotional development.* Oxford: International Universities Press. (Original work published 1953)

Wohlreich, M. (1986). Psychiatric aspects of high-risk pregnancy. *Consultation-Liaison Psychiatry, 10*(1), 53–68.

Worden, J. W. (2008). *Grief counseling and grief therapy* (4th ed.). New York: Springer Publishing Company.

Wortman, C. B., & Silver, R. C. (1989). The myths of coping with loss. *Journal of Consulting and Clinical Psychology, 57*, 349–357.

Wortman, C. B., & Silver, R. C. (2001). The myths of coping with loss revisited. In M. S. Stroebe, R. O. Hansson, W. Stroebe, & H. Schut (Eds.), *Handbook of bereavement research: Consequences, coping, and care* (pp. 405–430). Washington, DC: American Psychological Association.

Xue, Y. G., Leventhal, T., Brooks-Gunn, J., & Earls, F. J. (2005). Neighborhood residence and mental health problems of 5 to 11-year olds. *Archives of General Psychiatry, 62*(5), 554–563.

Yali, A. M., & Lobel, M. (1999). Coping and distress in pregnancy: An investigation of medically high risk women. *Journal of Psychosomatic Obstetrics and Gynecology, 20*(1), 39–52.

Yancey, A. K., & Kumanyika, S. K. (2007). Bridging the gap: Understanding the structure of social inequities in childhood. *American Journal of Preventive Medicine, 33*, S172–S174.

Young, M., Benjamin, B., & Wallis, C. (1963). Mortality of widowers. *Lancet, 2*, 254–256.

Zilberstein, K. (2006). Clarifying core characteristics of attachment disorders: A review of current research and theory. *American Journal of Orthopsychiatry, 76*, 55–64.

Zisook, S., Chentsova-Dutton, Y., & Shuchter, S. R. (1998). Post-traumatic stress disorder following bereavement. *Annals of Clinical Psychiatry, 10*, 157–163.

Zisook, S., & Shuchter, S. R. (2001). Treatment of the depressions of bereavement. *American Behavioral Scientist, 44*, 782–797.

Zola, I. (1991). Aging and disability: Toward a unified agenda. In R. P. Marinella & A. E. Dell Orto (Eds.), *The psychological and social impact of disability* (3rd ed., pp. 289–293). New York: Springer Publishing Company.

Zoroya, G. (2007, June 19). Troops' 1-month breaks blocked: Psychologists cite mental health risk. *USA Today*, p. A 1.

Index

A

Abandonment, 85, 87, 88
  biological aspects, 86
Abortion
  for fetal anomaly, 39, 47, 48, 58–66
Acceptance, 8, 9, 10
Acute lymphoblastic leukemia (ALL), 80
Addictions and substance abuse
  disenfranchised loss, 205, 206
  drug use in adolescents, 132, 133,
    134
  in early adulthood, 181, 203–208
  interventions, 207–208
  losses incurred, 205–207
  and traumatic loss, 204–205
Adolescents
  bereavement, 139, 155
  biological development, 130–133
  brain structure changes, 131–132
  death awareness phases, 139
  death experiences, 138–142, 153–155
  disenfranchised loss, 141, 146, 155
  "double jeopardy," 141, 146, 169
  gender differences, 132, 136, 140, 145
  grief elements, 132, 156
  homosexuality and, 162–168
  identity development vs. identity diffu-
    sion, 130, 133, 135, 145
  intervention, 160–161, 162
  loss, 133, 135, 137–142
  loss of parental attention, 150
  loss of parental relationship, 164–168
  maturational loss, 143–147
  peers, 136, 139, 151
  religion and spiritual beliefs, 139–140
  sibling chronic illness, 148–152
  sibling death, 140
  suicide, 138, 139, 144, 152
  traumatic grief, 152–162
Adoption, 203
Adulthood
  addictions, 181, 203–208
  biological aspects, 214, 284–285
  chronic illness in, 174–177, 289–291
  death, 213–214, 287–288
  death of an adult child, 297–298
  death of gay/lesbian partner, 185–187,
    224–226, 231–241
  death/loss of parent, 85–86, 174, 177,
    187–194, 219–221
  death of sibling, 221–222
  death of a spouse, 181, 182–184,
    222–223, 286–287, 291–295,
    309–315
  death of unmarried partner, 185, 223–
    224, 295–297
  disenfranchised loss, 180, 185, 221,
    222, 227, 229, 298, 300, 307
  "empty nest," 228–229
  friendships and, 230, 298–299
  gender and, 213, 214, 218–219, 288,
    295, 311–312
  generativity vs. stagnation, 212–215,
    227
  grandparents as caregivers, 300–301
  illness in, 217–219, 315–320
  infertility, 178–179, 194–203,
    230–231

integrity vs. despair, 282–285, 297
intimacy vs. isolation, 172–174, 175
interventions, 193–194, 200–203,
    207–208, 243–245, 249, 308–309,
    312–315
"just world," 175–176
loss of employment, 325–326
loss of home, 229–230, 299–300, 325
loss of identity, 215–217, 223, 241–
    246, 246–250, 304, 306, 326
maturational loss, 178–181, 226–231,
    299–302
normative loss, 173
parenthood, 178, 179–180, 325
psychological aspects, 173–174, 212–
    214, 284
resilience in, 285–287, 289, 321, 333
romantic relationships, 179, 180–181,
    184
social aspects, 172, 214–215, 283–284
Age
    differences in loss perception in chil-
        dren, 110–111
    and the life-course perspective, 277
    neuroimmune functioning and, 22
AIDS
    disenfranchised loss, 19, 185–186
Ainsworth, M. D., 28, 32, 33, 70, 73
Alex's Lemonade Stand, 80
Ambiguous loss, 19–20
    Alzheimer's disease, 20, 291
    immigration, 216
    related to military service, 113
    sibling loss, 222
Animal abuse, 122, 126
Anxiety, 95, 290
    attachment, 75
    and infertility, 198
    and military service, 182
Assumptive world, 16, 17, 46, 137,
    155–156
Attachment theory, 28, 294
    anxiety, 10, 75
    attachment style, 11, 33, 44, 49, 98
    early childhood, 73, 83
    foster care, 97

perinatal loss, 43–46
pregnancy, 28, 31–33, 35
Autism, 119–121
Autonomy vs. shame, 70, 84

B
Bereavement, 9, 10, 11, 139
    biopsychosocial perspectives, 311–
        312, 315
    higher mortality rate and, 21
    neuroimmune functioning, 22
Biological effects of grief, 20–23
Bowlby, J., 10, 11, 16, 28, 32, 33, 35,
    43, 44, 45, 46, 47, 78, 81, 97, 268,
    294
Breast cancer, 187, 188, 191–192, 218–
    219, 233, 289–291

C
Cardiovascular systems, 21, 23
Caregivers
    loss of, 75–78, 82–84, 95
Cathexis, 4, 41, 42, 49, 139
    de-cathexis, 4, 5, 6, 41
Children
    age differences in loss perception,
        110–111
    biological development, 105–107
    death of parent, 115
    deaths of, 5, 116–119
    disenfranchised loss, 19, 108, 114
    gender norms, 105, 109
    industry vs. inferiority, 104
    initiative vs. guilt, 97–98, 104
    interventions, 114–116
    parental divorce, 112–114
    parents in the military, 113–114
    peer relationships, 106, 108, 109
    pet loss, 121–126
    poverty's effects on, 107
    psychological development, 107–108
    sexual abuse, 112
    social development, 108–109
Christ, G. H., 78, 79, 109, 110, 135
Chronic illness, 148–152, 174–177,
    289–291

Compassionate Friends, 80, 117
Continuing bonds, 14, 17–18, 43–44,
      111, 140, 187, 217, 293, 296–297,
      329–331
Control, 100, 198, 219
Culture, 18, 34–35, 47, 48, 216–217,
      246–250, 288

D
Death, 7–10
   of adolescent, 137, 142–143
   of caregiver, 78–80
   of a child, 80–82, 116–119
   issues in adulthood, 213–214,
      287–288
   of a parent, 78–80, 174, 177, 187–
      194, 219–221
   of a partner, 185–187, 223–226, 231–
      241, 295–297
   of a spouse, 181, 182–184, 222–223,
      286–287, 291–295, 309–315
   of a sibling, 140, 221–222
Dementia, 302–309
Denial, 8, 9, 11, 43
Depression, 4, 8, 11, 39, 51, 182, 198,
      204, 227, 259, 290
   biological effects of, 21, 22
   parental, 76–77, 83, 85
Developmental disability, 82
   autism, 119–121
   "chronic sorrow," 117
   parental grief following loss, 117–118
Discrimination, 224–225, 231, 234,
      239–241
Disenfranchised grief, 18–19, 38
   addictions, 205, 206
   in adolescents, 141, 146, 155
   in adulthood, 180, 221, 222, 227,
      229, 298, 300, 307
   in children, 19, 104, 108, 114
   in homosexual partners, 185, 225
   in infants and toddlers, 79
   and maturational loss, 324–327
   and perinatal loss, 45, 47, 48
   in retirement, 259
Disorganization, 11, 16

Divorce, 143
   loss in children, 112–113
Doka, K., 18, 19, 114, 141, 155, 186,
      205, 223, 304, 306, 307, 308, 324,
      326
Down syndrome, 92–94
Dual Process Theory, 16–17, 114, 135,
      183, 296, 312–314, 327–329, 335

E
Emotional ventilation, 7, 24
   inhibiting adolescent mourning, 141
"Empty nest," 228–229, 277
Erikson, E. H., 70, 72, 84, 97, 98, 104,
      108, 133, 134, 155, 173, 204, 213,
      255, 267, 284
Eye movement desensitization reprocess-
      ing (EMDR), 88

F
Five V's, 24
Foster care, 94–100
Fragile-X syndrome, 89–92
Freud, S., 4, 5, 6, 30, 41, 44, 72, 134
Funerals
   cultural differences in, 48–49
   for fetal deaths, 42, 45, 47, 48
   functions of, 47, 79
   for pets, 123, 125

G
Gender
   in adulthood, 213, 214, 288, 295,
      311–312
   bias in diagnosis, 54–55
   differences in adolescence, 136, 140,
      145
   differences during puberty, 132
   differences in retirement, 262–263
   loss of voice in adolescent females,
      136
   neuroimmune functioning, 22
   norms in children, 105
   women and chronic illness, 218
Generativity vs. stagnation, 212–215,
      227, 267

Grief
  biological effects, 20–23
  "chronic sorrow," 117, 307
  defined, 16–17
  disciplining of, 13, 14, 18, 19
  duration, 4, 5, 6, 20
  medicalization, 13
  normative, 18, 19
  parental, 117–118, 142
  as pathology, 8, 13
  pet loss, 121–125
  processes, 12–13
  social construction of, 14, 15, 18
  societal norms and, 13
  traumatic, 152–162, 312
Grief theory, classical
  stage-based, 7–13
  task-based, 4–7
Grief theory, postmodern, 13–14, 184
  ambiguous loss, 19–20
  disenfranchised grief, 18–19
  continuing bonds, 14, 17–18
  Dual Process Theory, 16–17
  meaning-making and, 14–16, 18
Grief work
  effectiveness of, 25–26, 334
  hypothesis, 7, 24
Guilt, 116, 150

H
Hansson, R. O., 286, 292, 293, 311,
    312, 313, 314
Health care professionals
  communication, 196, 197, 203
  gender bias in diagnosis, 54–55
  hospice, 302, 316–320
  ignoring gay/lesbian partners, 225,
    226, 235
  ignoring scientific evidence, 50, 55
  importance of relationship, 57–58
  psychological aspects of, 52–53, 54,
    55–56, 57
Homosexuality
  and addictions, 204–206
  and adults, young, 172
  and adolescents, 137, 146, 162–168

  coming out, 164
  death of gay/lesbian partner, 185–187,
    224–226, 231–241
  discrimination, 224–225, 231, 234,
    239–241
  disenfranchisement, 19, 25
Hope, 8, 20, 206
Hyperemesis gravidarum (HG), 49–58

I
Idealized child
  loss of, 81–82, 89–94
Identity development vs. identity diffu-
    sion, 130, 133, 135, 204
  role in loss, 135, 145
Industry vs. inferiority, 104, 108
Infants
  biological development, 71
  death of, 80–81
  death of caregiver, 78–80
  disenfranchised grief, 79
  loss of caregiving, 75–78, 82–84
  maturational loss, 76, 82–84
  parental depression, 76–77
  psychological development, 72–74
  social development, 74–75
  temperament, 73–74
  trust vs. mistrust, 70, 84
Infertility
  biological and physical loss, 196–197
  defined, 37
  developmental loss, 195–196
  disenfranchised loss, 38
  in early adulthood, 178–179, 194–203
  in middle adulthood, 230–231
  as perinatal loss, 37–38
  psychological and emotional impact
    of, 197–200
Initiative vs. guilt, 97–98, 104, 108
Integrity vs. despair, 282–285, 297
Internalization, 86, 100
Intervention, 23–25, 334–336
  for addictions, 207–208
  for adolescents experiencing traumatic
    grief, 160–161, 162
  for children, 114–116

in foster care, 98–99
for hyperemesis gravidarum (HG),
    56–58
for infertility, 200–203
for loss of identity in middle adult-
    hood, 243–245, 249
in retirement, 271–273, 278–279
termination of pregnancy for fetal
    anomaly, 65–66
for young adults losing a parent,
    193–194
Intimacy vs. isolation, 172–174
Intrauterine fetal death (IUFD), 39–49
In vitro fertilization (IVF), 27–28
Isolation, 8, 19, 183, 198

J
"Just world," 175–176

K
Klass, D., 5, 14, 17, 18, 80, 81, 117,
    142, 143, 184, 217, 293, 329, 332

L
Levinson, D., 173, 176, 184, 213, 215,
    231
Loss
in adolescence, 133, 135, 137–142,
    143–147, 162–168
of adolescent, 142–143
of adults, 222–226
age differences in children's percep-
    tion of, 110–111
ambiguous, 19–20, 113, 216, 222
of child, 80–82, 116–119
divorce, 112–113
in early adulthood, 174, 177, 187–194
of employment, 226–228
by fetus, 36–37
foster care, 98
of health, 80
of identity, 135, 215–217
maturational changes as, 2, 3, 36, 70,
    76, 82–84, 143–147, 178–181,
    226–231
in middle adulthood, 214, 215–222

normative, 1, 2, 3, 70, 83, 219
of parent, 75–80, 174, 177, 187–194,
    219–221
of parental relationship in adoles-
    cence, 164–168
in retirement, 257–262, 265–266,
    270–271
traumatic, 5, 22, 46, 83, 204–205

M
Magical thinking, 41, 79, 125
Maturational loss, 2, 3, 36,
in adolescents, 143–147
in adulthood, 178–181, 208, 226–231,
    299–302
as disenfranchised loss, 324–327
in infants and toddlers, 70, 76, 82–84
in retirement, 259
Meaning-making, 14, 15–16, 18, 22, 23,
    89, 143, 331–334
in adolescence, 141
in adulthood, 177, 179, 286, 293, 315
chronic illness, 219
loss of a child, 117
loss of homosexual partner, 187
loss of parent, 221
pet loss, 122
in retirement, 261, 266
Megan's Law, 80
Military experiences
children with parents in the military,
    113–114
loss related to War in Iraq, 181–182
Miscarriage, 39, 40, 48
Modeling, 33, 34, 87
Mourning, 4, 41, 44, 47

N
Neimeyer, R. A., 5, 14, 15, 46, 89, 180,
    184, 227, 228, 288, 293, 312, 331,
    332, 333, 334
Nickman, S. L., 5, 14, 17, 18, 111, 184,
    217, 293, 329, 332
Neurological systems, 21
Neurotransmitters, 22
Numbness, 10, 45

O
Object constancy, 76, 85
Object relations theory, 28, 31–33, 43–
    46, 72–73, 99
Optimal frustration, 72, 76, 83, 101
Ostracizing, 34–35, 146

P
Parenting, 72, 115
    effects of depression on, 76–77, 83
Parental loss
    of adolescents, 137, 142–143
    of children, 116–119
    in early adulthood, 174, 177, 187–
        194, 204–205
    in middle adulthood, 214, 219–221
    of idealized child, 81–82
    in infants and toddlers, 75–80
    of infants and toddlers, 80–81
Parkes, C. M., 16, 17, 21, 294
Peer relationships, 75, 109, 136
Perinatal loss
    and continuing bonds, 329–330
    delayed grief response, 43, 44
    and depression, 27, 28
    disenfranchised loss, 45, 47
    infertility, 37–38
    intervention, 24
    "replacement pregnancy," 46
    termination for fetal anomaly, 39, 47,
        48, 58–66
Pet loss
    during childhood, 111–112, 121–126
    group support benefits, 123
    resources, 127–128
Post Traumatic Stress Disorder, 98, 106,
    137, 156–158, 182, 204
Poverty, effects on children, 107
Pregnancy
    biological development, 29–30
    complications of, 38–39, 49–58
    emotional bond with fetus, 28, 35
    infertility and, 37–38
    intrauterine fetal death (IUFD), 39–49
    in vitro fertilization (IVF), 27–28
    multifetal pregnancy reduction, 39
    social aspects of, 33–35
    psychological aspects of, 30–33
Prigerson, H. G., 11, 331, 332, 333, 334
Procreativity, 212
Psychoanalytical perspective
    adolescence, 133–134
    pregnancy, 30–31
    pregnancy loss, 41–43
Psychogenic disorder, 50, 51, 55, 78

R
Rage, 87, 88, 198
Rando, T. A., 12, 13, 25, 80, 81, 115,
    116, 118, 142, 220, 221, 222, 297,
    298
Rejection, 86, 109
Religion and spiritual beliefs, 139–140,
    207–208, 221, 266, 286
Reorganization, 11, 16
Retirement
    and biological loss, 270–271
    change in relationship with spouse or
        partner, 262–264
    changes in relationships with friends,
        264–265
    early retirement, 273–280
    gender differences in, 262–263, 274
    interventions, 271–273, 278–279
    life-course perspective, 276–277
    loss and transformation of identity,
        257–260, 277–278
    loss or change in relationships, 261–
        262, 277
    loss experienced by adult children of
        retirees, 268–269
    loss experienced by parents of
        retirees, 269
    loss of financial resources, 265–266
    loss of health, 278, 290
    loss of routine, 260–261
    maturational loss, 259
    meaning-making of, 261, 266
    phases of, 267–268
    "possible selves," 258
    psychological loss and, 271
    rediscovering passion in, 260

as reinvention, 255, 257, 258, 259,
  260–261, 265, 269, 271–273
  religion and spirituality, 266
Rituals, 47–49, 143, 199–201

S
"Sandwich generation," 190–191
Schut, H., 16, 110, 114, 156, 183, 293,
  296, 312, 313, 314, 327
Self-doubt, 52, 227
Self-efficacy, 104, 107, 144
Self-esteem, 52, 284, 301
Separation anxiety, 10, 78
Silverman, P. R., 5, 14, 17, 18, 78, 111,
  184, 217, 293, 329, 332
Six "R" processes, 12
Social construction of grief, 14, 15, 18
Social support, 20, 22, 186
  in adulthood, 245–246, 249–250, 286,
    288, 308, 311–312, 321
  importance of friendships in retire-
    ment, 264–265
  insensitivity, 199
  lack of, 38, 47, 48, 53, 80, 92, 109,
    137, 177, 181, 185, 189, 192, 197,
    223, 290
  optimal support, 99–100
Social workers
  advocating for children in foster care,
    99, 100
  helping children cope with death,
    114–116
  infertility interventions, 200–203
  optimal support, 99–100
  supporting clients, 89, 93, 94, 203
Societal norms, 18, 19, 45, 75
Somatic complaints, 54, 85
Somatization disorder, 54–55
Stigma, 19
  abortion, 48
  disability, 82
  infertility, 198

Stillbirth, 39, 40, 48
Stress, 85
Stroebe, M. S., 7, 14, 16, 21, 23, 25, 26,
  110, 114, 156, 183, 293, 296, 311,
  312, 313, 314, 327
Stroebe, W., 7, 14, 21, 23, 25, 26, 183,
  293
STUG reactions, 24
Suicide, 138, 139, 144

T
Toddlers
  autonomy vs. shame, 70, 84
  biological development, 72
  death of, 80–81
  death of caregiver, 78–80, 85
  disenfranchised grief, 79
  loss of caregiving, 75–78, 82–84
  maturational loss, 70, 76, 82–84
  parental depression, 76–77
  psychological development, 72–74
  social development, 74–75
  temperament, 73–74
Transitional objects, 72–73, 99, 300
Trust vs. mistrust, 70, 84

V
Validation, 15, 19, 24, 25, 38, 52, 114,
  201, 308, 318
Volunteerism, in retirement, 266–267

W
Widows and widowers, 181, 182–184,
  222–223, 286–287, 291–295
Winnicott, D. W., 72, 73, 76, 99, 332,
  335
Worden, J. W., 6, 7, 78, 249
Wortman, C. B., 7, 26, 286, 288, 292,
  295, 311, 312